Before That Generation Passes

A catalogue record for this book is available from the British Library.
ISBN: 0-9539723-0-5

Published by
Escoumains Publications
14 Ashville Park
Greystone Road
Antrim
Co Antrim
N Ireland
BT41 1HH

Acknowledgements

I wish to thank the staffs of the following institutions for their assistance in supplying invaluable information and photographs: -
Mr D A Belson, Crown Copyright Administrator, Ministry of Defence, London;
Mr Phil Boyden BAe Systems, Dunsfold Aerodrome, Surrey;
British Aerospace PLC, Farnborough, (in particular, Mrs Pam Guess, IP Operations
Manager); The Copyright Unit, HM Stationery Office, Norwich (in particular, Margaret
Feere); Greenpark Healthcare Trust (Musgrave Park Hospital) - in particular Mrs Brenda
Mason, Public Relations Department and Mr Kevin Mulhern; The Institute of Marine
Engineers, London; Deputy Keeper of the Records, Public Record Office of Northern
Ireland; National Museums and Galleries of Northern Ireland,
Ulster Folk and Transport Museum; Ulster Museum, Botanic Gardens, Belfast.

I would also wish to record my thanks to the following individuals who were kind enough to take time and enlighten me on many diverse matters:- Mrs Nora Anketell (former Assistant Matron, Musgrave Park Hospital); Mr Andy Barr, Trade Unionist; Jim Bothwell, Master Mariner; Mr Ken Best and Mr Alan McKnight, Public Affairs and Communications Department, Shorts Bombardier, (Shorts Photographs); to Michelle McCabe, Antrim Printers for her enthusiastic manner in helping with the presentation of the book; Mrs Bob Cooper (who also provided her late husband's Merchant Navy Discharge Book); Mr Stephen Creighton and Mr Jack McClay, for advice on publication matters; William Grills, Marine Engineer; Mr Mike Hooks, Croydon, for his permission to use his work "Shorts Aircraft" for reference purposes; the late Mr John Kerr, former Chief Engineer, SS "Fanad Head"; Mr Hamilton Kennedy, for reminiscence of Ministry of Defence days; Dr H McGuigan CBE; Mrs Rosemary McConaghie, Braid Valley Hospital Clerical Staff; Mr Eddy Savage, Estates Services, Musgrave Park Hospital; Mr John Smylie, Estates Services, Downpatrick Hospital; Mr Richard Spencer, Former Test Pilot and Flight Engineer, Messrs Short Bros. & Harland Ltd.; Mr William Smyth, Educational Technology Adviser, Antrim Technology Centre; Mr M I Wild, Former Test Flight Engineer, Messrs Short Bros. & Harland Ltd, and lately Executive Director (Programme Management); Dr Paul Withey, Rolls Royce Plc, Filton, Bristol, for his constructive comments on my account of the Comet 1 disasters, and giving me the benefit of knowledge gained through countless hours of reading and research into these matters.

Acknowledgements are also due to Airlife Publishing Ltd., for extracts from 'Not Much Of An Engineer', by Sir Stanley Hooker; to The Bodley Head Ltd., 1984, for extracts from U333, by Peter Cremer; to Mr Campbell McMurray BA MSc (Econ.), Director, Royal Naval Museum, Portsmouth for extracts from "The Status of Sea-going Engineers"; to the Institute of Marine Engineers, for extracts from 'Victoria Drummond, Marine Engineer', by Cherry Drummond.

I am indebted to a number of kind friends who read various sections of my work, and made helpful suggestions, namely:- Rev Dr J E Chisholm (University College, Dublin); Miss Roberta McCrea; Mr Albert Henry; and Mr Wolf Kay (former Chief Stress Engineer, Messrs. Short Bros. & Harland Ltd.).

Then my thanks to two of my former students - Mr Ian Harvey, for his help in designing a cover for my book, and to Miss Lisa McErlean, for help with graphics.

Finally my grateful thanks to my long suffering sister, Mrs Audrey McClean, MBE, whose home and many weeks of spare time were taken over in typing my scribbles into readable form.

Contents

Front Cover: Shorts SA4 Sperrin Bomber fronting Musgrave Park Hospital.

Author's Note

It is unlikely that I would ever have been motivated to write of myself or my generation, had I not, while standing on a quiet country road in Northern France, one Saturday afternoon, been overwhelmed by a desire to know more of an earlier generation of certain people from this island in general, and from Antrim in particular. That road, on rising ground, lies just in front of Thiepval Wood, falling away steeply to the river Ancre, across which the Ulster Division was astride on the morning of the First of July 1916. Opposite Thiepval Wood is the Ulster Memorial Tower, and not far away at Guillemont is the memorial to the 16th Irish Division.

I had known a number of men from my home town of Antrim who were in this area on the First day of July 1916. I would have liked to have known where Eddie Ashe had won the M.M., or where Dr Norman Graham had been awarded the M.C. and was this road, the "sunken" road where Leslie Bell, late of the 10th Battalion, The Royal Enniskilling Fusiliers (The Derry's) told me he had lain all day, after being wounded by a shell?

Now I would have difficulty in asking them - they were nearly all gone. Antrim town had buried its last Somme veteran a few months previously. He was Jack Allen, late of the 11th Battalion, Royal Irish Rifles. Eventually it was too late.

For another generation I resolved to do better. I would record what I could remember clearly of that generation, my generation, while it was still possible, with clarity, to do so. To do so, in particular I would record something of my fellow apprentices in the firm of Short Bros. & Harland (now Shorts Bombardier) Belfast, and apprentices in the other great engineering firms with whom we came in contact through our studies at that centre of excellence and no nonsense education, the College of Technology, Belfast. That generation grew up under the journeymen who taught us much of our trade - something of them, and what rubbed off them on to us would stand telling. While it would be nice to know what happened to all those one rubbed shoulders with and how they got on along the path of life etc it is not within the capacity of this ramble. So I take my humble self to largely represent the typical travail experienced by the average apprentice. But for me, there was something else I was to encounter, namely the threat to and disruption, of the prospects for my career, in the few shattering seconds in which a horrific accident changes a fit and healthy person into a bedridden shadow.

It follows therefore that illness, convalescence and recovery has become very much a central part of such a story - one of course that can be shared and indeed told by many others - those with whom I shared those hospital wards. Like myself, they would do so in grateful reminiscence of the nursing and surgical care received there. And there were others encountered later along the path of life whose simple deeds and words I consider worth setting down on print.

A unique view from the rear of the Ulster Tower - from a postcard of unknown origin, but probably dating from the 1930's. Someone - a caretaker perhaps, had a garden to the rear. Thiepval Wood is in the background, the River Ancre to the right. Note the white line, centre left. It is probably a trench, filled in, the local chalk showing up. It was up this slope, that the 36th Ulster Division advanced on 1st July 1916.

Chapter 1 - I commence my apprenticeship

I arrive at Shorts

I arrived at the aircraft factory of Short Bros. & Harland Ltd. Belfast at about 7.30 am on Wednesday, 17th September 1952. This was at the end of a journey that had started at Crosskennan, Antrim, at 6.10 am. First there had been travel by bicycle to Dunadry, a distance of four miles; then a bus journey to Waring Street, Belfast. A short walk on foot down Skipper Street, then across "blitzed square" brought me to High Street (or what the Germans had left of it) - this was about eleven years after the Germans had visited the city by plane (or perhaps bomber would be more correctly stated). "Blitzed square" was an area on the left of High Street, extending from Bridge Street towards the Albert Clock. To me it was just part of Belfast that had no buildings on it - I couldn't compare its present state to a former one, because I had not seen it at any time before the German visits. I was well aware that new houses were being built from the bricks belonging to bombed buildings in Belfast - I had actually helped clean such bricks, by knocking off mortar with a trowel. On High Street, one joined a queue alongside blitzed square if wishing to travel to the Aircraft Factory, or the Airport dispersal workshop and hangers. Trams were also travelling in the same direction to "Queens Road" for Harland & Wolff. These trams for me were characterised by a number of features including the peculiar grinding sound they made, the intermittent blue flashes that emanated from some electrical drive contacts or other and a very definite smell which I think in turn emanated from those blue electrical discharges. Driven from either end, I understood that the control was in the form of a "dead man's handle" - a control lever that returned to the "Stop" position if the hand holding it became incapable of doing so for any reason. It was a "Fail safe" device.

Having arrived at the Main Gate and upon producing a letter of introduction, I was directed to the 'balcony' of Centre 30, the main machine shop, to present myself to Mr Ralphson, the Superintendent of the Centre. Eventually he appeared and I was directed to report to Mr W. Clements, detail fitting squad foreman, and there I was introduced to my future as an indentured apprentice fitter and turner. I was assigned to the de-burring bench. Here I wouldn't be building sleek jet aircraft, patting each on the back as I put on the finishing touches, thereof, but I would learn one of the basic hallmarks of a skilled artisan - removing the sharp edges from components before they go into assembly and service. In some manufacturing operations like turning, the operator will be best placed to remove burrs and sharp edges. This would also apply to general fitting. But operations like milling and drilling, require a separate operation to remove surplus burrs - a sort of shave in a manner of speaking.

But there was another reason why a milling machine operator would not be removing burrs - he would probably need to use a file and a file belongs to the kingdom of the fitter. In those days of demarcation disputes, I think I am correct in saying that a machine man doing work that would normally be suitable for giving to a fitter would be enough to cause the fitters in the area to down tools. They could be "up the road" in no time. "Up the road" could mean a walk out and a mass meeting in the centre of Belfast or at some union headquarters or some clubrooms or other. Of course, most disputes didn't reach that level of activity - they would be sorted out at shop steward level, locally.

Time sheets were prepared each day by other workers who were known as the "floor checkers". They took note of the time indicated on each work card - the agreed rate. The total number of hours booked determined whether one got the flat wage for the day or whether some "bonus" would be added. In common banter around the benches, one would hear an inquiry being made, "Are you making it", "it" being the bonus. My chargehand at the de-burring bench was Cecil Collins - a very civil man. Later, a fitter, one Billy Riddles was appointed to supervise our work.

At the detail benches there were about a dozen fitters and perhaps up to six apprentices - the number varied as apprentices moved in and then on to other centres. The apprentices worked on their own - de-burring was a piece work occupation, the more work was sorted out the more one would get paid. As time went on one was given more important jobs - it was possible to damage or destroy components if one was careless or over enthusiastic in using, for example, a large drill to deburr a smaller hole.

My wages, gross, came to two pounds and one shilling*. My first wage packet contained one pound and sixteen shillings. Two bus fares had to be accommodated from that sum.

That morning I started was shared by a colleague from Ballymena Technical College - one Robert Harbinson. I think he came from Cullybackey - I don't recall ever seeing him again after our ways parted in Centre 30.

I should also say that the floor checkers were responsible for lifting our 'cards' from the 'clocking-in' rack. Before leaving my work that day I was given a works number - 1084, and a clocking-in card. To use the card it was taken from the rack upon arriving at the clock and placed in a slot in front of the clock face. A handle was pushed down, thus stamping the time of arrival on the card. A similar operation took place at the end of labour. The number also served when borrowing tools from the tool store, and a number of discs, called 'cheques' were issued with the number stamped upon them - they were exchanged for a tool or tools as required.

Apart from the extreme cold of those years of early morning starts, I have another memory which is worth setting down. Crossing over the Queen's Bridge - the only 'Queen's' Bridge in existence then, I often saw men (and on at least one occasion a young lady) standing on the bridge giving out leaflets. I saw them in all sorts of weather, fervent in their efforts to distribute literature. Since I was always on the bus I didn't meet these people face to face, but I was impressed by such zeal and that they were intent on going on to work was evident in that the men carried their lunch boxes below their arm.

I thought at first they might have something to do with a local mission, trying to spread the Gospel - but I found out how wrong I was in this assumption. They were members or associates of the Communist Party - whether a local Irish branch or an offshoot from Harry Pollit (The Secretary of the Communist Party of England at that time) - I was never sure. But the zeal of such people upon such errands at that time of the morning, cold and wet, has left me marvelling at such endeavours to this day. I noticed that they were received with - I suppose indifference. The people passing on the bridge on foot were those who either lived nearby or had walked from their set down bus stop. Most would work in the shipyard or the Harbour Estate. They would usually take a handout on the bridge and pass on.

Confusion and Travel

The first six or eight months spent de-burring and trying to make bonus was the coldest winter I have spent since leaving school. Riding a bicycle four miles to the bus stop at Dunadry for 6.50 (6.40 at Antrim) is a memory of endless cold and during those hard November mornings I never had a pair of gloves that protected my hands from the painful

(one shilling equals five new pence)*

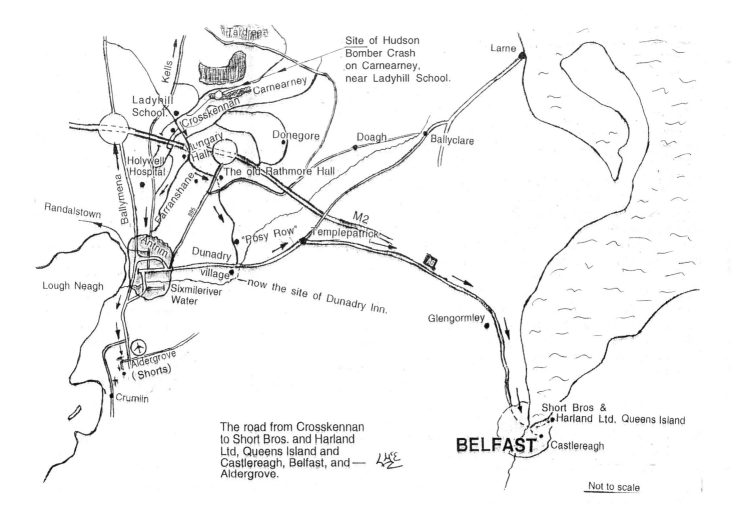

Site of Hudson Bomber Crash on Carnearney, near Ladyhill School.

Tardree

Kells

Ladyhill School.

Crosskennan

Carnearney

Larne

Donegore

Doagh

Ballyclare

Hungary Hall

Holywell Hospital

The old Rathmore Hall

Ballymena

Randalstown

Farranshane

885

M2

"Posy Row"

Templepatrick

A6

Antrim

Dunadry

village — now the site of Dunadry Inn.

Lough Neagh

Sixmileriver Water

Glengormley

Aldergrove (Shorts)

Crumlin

The road from Crosskennan to Short Bros. and Harland Ltd, Queens Island and Castlereagh, Belfast, and Aldergrove.

Short Bros & Harland Ltd, Queens Island

BELFAST

Castlereagh

Not to scale

7

frost. I used to try wool mittens inside leather gauntlets but after a couple of miles - agony in the finger tips. Even in Shorts, the sheer size of the place made it a difficult one to heat (I wonder what their heating bill was?).

Now a brief word about the journey from Crosskennan to Dunadry. The last thing that a first year apprentice (rushing for a bus four miles away) would be thinking about, would relate to the history unfolding as his bicycle careered sometimes on its wheels and at times on its side along that route. A mile from where I lived I passed a drawwell in the townland of Hungary Hall. A few hundred yards and I passed the lane leading to the former home of William Orr, the United Irishman who was hanged at Carrickfergus in 1797. This was the townland of Farranshane and a few hundred yards further I would pass Rathmore, close to the seat of power of the Kings of Dalriada. The old Rathmore Hall was passed close to the home of Sam Orr, a man of advanced years. He played the fiddle*. On an occasion in the nearby hall, Sam was playing his fiddle when the local rustics annoyed him with some interruptions or other. His ultimatum became a much quoted saying afterwards: "Yine mair hough and a'll put the fiddle in the baag".

I never knew if the threat was carried out. Further on, one passed "Posy Row", a row of neat whitewashed cottages and then the Rathmore Road ended at Dunadry village - now the site of Dunadry Inn. However, I want to say a word of my fellow bus travellers who collected at the bus stop at Dunadry. This was where it still is - beside Foxe's Pub (or as it is now known, Ellie Mays). First, Eric Lynn who worked in Shorts, took me under his wing on my first day. He met me after that first long day was over and I had mastered the technique of clocking-out. So, I didn't have to worry about the mystery of how to get to Smithfield that first day. But a couple of nights later, he had to work overtime and I was left to my own devices - and I hadn't a clue as to how to get to Smithfield. Some of the 'inhabitants' of neighbouring benches got their heads together, and one man produced a plan - fail safe which would get me there. "Take a High Street bus tonight. When you get off in High Street, go along High Street, across Royal Avenue (just keep going) along Castle Street, turn right along Chapel Lane and that will bring you to Smithfield". I was glad of this piece of foolproof direction, but although I pride myself in remembering many details of this crisis, I cannot remember who the architect of my salvation was. But it worked and it was a long time before I returned along any other route to Smithfield. One might say - "How on earth was a simple issue like that so life threatening?" Well, for someone like me - a complete stranger to the area, I can assure you it really was a nightmare. I was used with virtually only one street to get lost in, in Antrim, or the well trod paths around Wellington Street or Church Street or Bryan Street in my beloved Ballymena where I had such happy times at the great citadel of learning - Ballymena Technical High School.

Anyway, at Dunadry there was a very civil man called Jimmy Beck. He also worked in Shorts and was in charge of all Shorts transport. He had a number of daughters whom I knew slightly and he also used a bicycle (from Burnside, three miles away). Then there was Willy Patton another stalwart of civility. He had been a footballer of some merit in his young days. He worked in the Belfast Telegraph as a compositor I think. Eventually, he was joined by his sons, Willy and Ronnie, both serving apprenticeships in Belfast - Willy was in Mackies and both were very nice fellows. But Willy senior, one time related a sorrow that he would carry in his heart to the grave. "I had two other sons. I lost both, through illness, when still young men - promising footballers".

Three other early birds joined the ranks. One was a man called Kirkpatrick - from the Corkscrew Road area. He was a painter of advanced years - a painter in the "Yard". I remember him well - for a reason. It was on this wise: Beside a building no longer in existence, there was, right beside the present bus stop, a small lean-to, a kind of building not striking in architectural merit, being mostly composed of roof - but it was very useful to shelter in during the frequent downpours of rain that were part of the scene from time to time. Now bearing in mind that a pub door was but a few

(* - *Some sources attribute this to another local fiddler by the name of Taggart*)

yards away (perhaps it is unconnected) it seemed that our shelter was not only used by us waiting on buses, but by others, who committed unspeakable acts at the weekend.

Now, Mr Kirkpatrick was an early riser and was often first at the bus stop to seek shelter under the "roof". But he often came out quicker than he went in with a torrent of abuse about those who had left their visiting cards. I seemed to hear new adjectives describing them every Monday morning. I remember him making the point, "Women and children have to shelter here!"

Finally, a man called Dick Alley made his way from a house away on the far side of Donegore - by bicycle. Dick was a fitter on Sunderlands - he may have been from Belfast originally and he was usually last to join the group. I think John Kerr* from Dunadry was there also occasionally - he may have been sometimes on the next bus -it was full of characters too, but few joined it at Dunadry. There were conductors on buses in those days - single and double deckers at that time - some colourful characters. I recall one conductor - Mr Carson, I believe, who always wore his war service ribbons on his uniform - and at every stop some familiar face. (Eventually when I had completed my first year in Shorts - a new apprentice joined the Dunadry lot - John Gourley from Cherry Hill - a first year apprentice in Shorts).

It is of considerable interest to me now to recall that from where I sheltered under that 'roof' at the Dunadry bus stop for Belfast I could look over at Dunadry village. When Dunadry Inn was opened, I was asked to pipe in the New Year, which occasion was preceded by an early "Burns Supper". Commodore Shillington who was, I assume, a director of this hotel, stood counting me down in seconds - he certainly had a watch of some sort in his hand - and then gave me the equivalent of the chequered flag and thus I proceeded to sound the arrival of a new year and for which I asked the princely sum of £3. A B.E.A. Pilot, a Scot named Captain McClean had been prevailed upon to address the Haggis. Other performers that night were Wilcil McDowell (accordion) and now with the 'Irish Rovers', Frank Carson (comedian) and Leo McCaffrey (singer). I remember Frank Carson - himself I believe a former paratrooper, recognising the D.F.C. among the ribbons on Captain McClean's chest and having a long chat with him.

Day Release Arrangements

Shorts was in the vanguard of education and training for its apprentices. As a former pupil of Ballymena Technical (High) School, I elected to enrol in the day release classes held there for students in Mechanical Engineering. The day I attended was Friday. I would be in year one of a three year course leading to the Ordinary (or Lower) National Certificate in Mechanical Engineering; two further successful years would be required for the Higher National Certificate in Mechanical Engineering. But it seemed a long way ahead - little did I know or suspect how long ahead that road would be - it's probably a good job that I did not. An evening class had to be attended and in order to be able to get home, have something to eat and then get a bus to Ballymena, I would have to catch an earlier bus from Smithfield - it thus being necessary to get out early on Thursday evening (for the evening class) and catch an earlier bus into town from Shorts. I also had to have special arrangements to collect my pay on Thursday afternoons and a special pass to cover all these arrangements. Mr Ossie Carlisle, the deputy apprentice supervisor, dealt with that and a thousand other matters. The autumn was a busy time for Mr Carlisle. He lived in an office in the Main Office Block at that time not far from where Mr Jimmy Shanks, one of the security officers at the main gate, ruled with iron rod. Jimmy was not a big man by any means but you always knew he was an alert man. Now all the Ballymena first year apprentices, also going to day release on Fridays needed arrangements to collect their pay. So it happened that one day during the first week at work many minds concentrated on sorting out the matter of getting pay on Thursdays instead of Friday - and descended on Mr Carlisle's office, lemming like, asking for passes, etc.

(* - *no relation of John Kerr from Whitehead, the Chief Engineer Officer of SS "Fanad Head"*)

9

Directors :
Sir Edward D. A. Herbert, O.B.E. Chairman.
Rear Admiral M. S. Slattery, C.B., F.R.Ae.S, (Retd.), Managing Director.
J. S. Baillie; Sir Sam H. Brown; F. C. How, C.B.; C. P. T. Lipscomb, Wh. Ex., F.R.Ae.S.
J. L. Parker, O.B.E., F.R.Ae.S.; Sir Frederick E. Rebbeck, D.Sc., D.L., J.P.

SHORT BROTHERS & HARLAND LIMITED

THE FIRST MANUFACTURERS OF AIRCRAFT IN THE WORLD

SEAPLANE WORKS · QUEENS ISLAND · BELFAST

Telephone : Belfast 58444 · Telegrams : Aircraft, Belfast

Ref: FCK/OC/KMcA/App.   9th September, 1952.

Mr. R. Cameron,
Crosscannon,
Antrim.

Dear Sir,

      Further to your interview to-day regarding
an Apprenticeship with this Company, will you please
arrange to report at our Main Gatehouse on Wednesday the
17th September, 1952 at 7.45 a.m. to serve a period of
6 months as a Probationer Apprentice, and if satisfactory
serve a further period of $4\frac{1}{2}$ years as an Indentured
Apprentice Fitter & Turner.

      It will be necessary for you to obtain an
Employment Card and three small photographs approximately
2" square which are necessary for your Works Pass, also
a suit of overalls.

      I am enclosing herewith, Application Form
which is to be completed by you, signed by your parent/or
guardian and returned to this Office as soon as possible.

      On arrival at these works produce this letter
and ask the Patrol Officer to direct you to Mr. Ralphson,
Foreman - Centre 30.

                    Yours faithfully,
          for SHORT BROTHERS & HARLAND LIMITED

                    O. Carlile

                (O. CARLILE)
        Asst. Apprentice Supervisor

LONDON OFFICE : 17 GROSVENOR STREET, W.I · TELEPHONE : MAYFAIR 9541

I can still see a very harassed Mr Carlisle looking up from behind a mass of paper demanding to know (of me in particular, because he knew my surname) what I thought I was doing there - "did my foreman know that I was away from the job and did I not know that he was a very busy man?" I think I probably advanced, like Oliver Twist asking for more porridge - I had no bowl of course. I just stated the facts of life - "that day release fell on pay day - could I get the pay on Thursdays"? I went on, with Mr Carlisle at this stage showing increased impatience, to ask for a pass to enable me to get out early on Thursday as well, to get to evening class etc, etc. Well, such were the trials of life at this stage for me. They were sorted out some way and for the next year, I stopped work around 4.30 and caught a bus outside the Main Factory, at 4.35 pm for town. I can still remember its destination - "Downview Avenue".

So day release and evening classes were attended at Ballymena Technical at Pats Brae (alas, no more). There were other students enrolled there who did not work in Shorts - some Royal Naval Armament Depot apprentices from Antrim, one or two Harland and Wolff apprentices and some from small local firms. We also shared certain classes with students from other disciplines such as the electrical apprentices from various firms.

So as I de-burred and later, worked on the 3A Wards, I absented myself early on Thursday evenings and didn't come back until Monday morning.

As stated, that winter was cold - how Shorts ever managed enough heat to keep us from freezing to the bench I'll never know - the heating bill must have been enormous. Heat was supplied by two (maybe three) Lancashire boilers. These were fire tube boilers where the two or three large combustion tubes were surrounded by water (in a water tube boiler, the water in the tubes is surrounded by the products of combustion, and is capable of generating safely much higher pressures than a fire tube boiler). I imagine the large plate water filled radiators which were placed above head height and angled to radiate heat downwards were of the calorifier types - the "closed" circuit water of this system passing through a heat exchanger, the heat of hot water or steam from the boilers constantly re-heating the water as it returned from the factory heater plates before resuming its journey back to the factory. I was amazed that hot water was pumped over huge distances in the open, between out factories, the pipes being heavily "lagged" to reduce heat loss. Even so, in frosty weather, the heat loss must have been enormous. I was learning at further education that heat travels from a hot area to a cooler area. It's one of the most fundamentally important pieces of knowledge that man, depending upon finite sources of energy on earth, could learn. Studying thermodynamics for a significant portion of my life has raised up an instinct in me to stop that precious heat (so expensive) from precisely going from hot to cold - shut that hot press door, shut all doors, insulate everything that you can afford to - or near enough. Wearing extra clothes, mufflers etc in a workshop can be dangerous. I wore overalls and during the cold weather I certainly hadn't my sleeves rolled up. One day, I was using a bench drilling machine (which had no guard) with a $^7/_8$ diameter inch drill. I had it on very slow speed. When I was offering up some work to it - some hole or other that needed de-burring, the slowing rotating drill took an interest in some threads hanging from the cuff of the overall sleeve. Suddenly the sleeve tightened around my arm and with increasing ferocity - the drill was winding sleeve, arm and all towards itself and before someone could stop the drill, in response to my cries for help, the drill had started cutting into the inside of my arm close to my armpit.

The wound was partly burn and partly cut, and a little shock. I was having my first lesson in the perils of working in industry. Somebody told me not to be such a stupid so and so, and I had a visit to the First Aid and one from the Safety Officer. I remember him telling me that when he was young, cuffs of overalls had buttons to keep them tight against the wrist. (He didn't say if he had scissors to cut fraying threads). I survived.

I should record that I will ever associate two songs - "Innisfree" and "It is no secret" with those early days in Shorts, because everyone (well, near enough) was singing or whistling them. Another shortly to come out was "Streets of Laredo".

I have mentioned Willy Patton Junior, who got the bus with me at Dunadry. We soon were meeting again. We took dancing lessons at Billy Nixen's. Billy and his wife taught dancing, real dancing, in their well-appointed garage which had a nice wooden floor. They lived up the Dublin Road, Antrim and there I learned "The Moonlight Saunter", "The Quick Step" and others. The tunes I remember included "Come This Away Not Thataway", "Pretty Little Black Eyed Susie", "The Shoemaker's Shop", then "To See Someone's Picture Where My Picture Hung", "By The Light Of The Silvery Moon", "Oh, My Papa", "Wish You Were Here" and so on.

Now it is true that some of my friends didn't share my interest in such rhythm, and while mute in condemnation, they didn't partake thereof.

Sadly, with the coming of Rock and Roll and the Beetles, such disciplined forms of dancing disappeared from the average ballroom floor. I remember notices being displayed at one time 'No Jiving or irregular forms of dancing'.

I feel a lot of people including those friends of mine would gladly put the clock back, if possible, "lest a worse thing befall us".

Recollections of those who worked close by

It was understood that an apprentice would serve six months in a centre and after that period (of de-burring in this case) the day when one would leave de-burring couldn't come soon enough. But it must be said that during this period much of the "street wisdom" of industry began to infiltrate apprentice minds. I, in particular, encountered some of the men who had a significant influence on me then, and during my lifetime since.

Two of these stand out. One was a fitter from Lisburn, Len Palmer, whose interest and care for my welfare was absolute - and Len was a soldier of the Great War, 1914-1918.

I remember Len recalling an incident from that war: "One day a shell stuck in the barrel of an artillery piece, a misfire. An officer told me to drive it back out - by hitting it on the nose! I told him it was impossible, the thing might explode. The officer then drew his revolver, pointed it at my head then said "Drive it out or I'll blow your brains out". So I put a length of wooden post down the barrel and struck it - it came out". Len put a wing over me and I rather think he tried to keep me apart from much of the crudeness and rudeness that was part of the local environment. I imagine Len is dead long ago - there are many questions he could have answered that I would like to ask now. I deeply regret that the ensuing struggles in life didn't provide time to look him up.

Another man, another big man like Len in all senses of the word, was Billy Taggart. Tall, moustached and wearing glasses which, I observed, he often looked over as he surveyed some scene or other being enacted around the benches (very often with severity or disapproval). His interest in my welfare was again of a fatherly nature, his questions always serious and sensible, not to say philosophical. Again, as I discovered later he was a much travelled man, a Christian man of quiet witness.

Forty years later I watched a Methodist minister being interviewed on Television, at the end of which the interviewer thanked Dr. Taggart - he looked very like my early benefactor and sure enough when I eventually contacted him I found him to be a son of Billy Taggart whom I had known all those years ago. He also informed me that his father and mother had met while both were working in Montreal, a place I also had a passing acquaintance with by that time.

*   *   *   *   *   *   *   *   *

Some people who passed my bench

The bus which carried me to Belfast left Ballymena at 6.10 am. Alternatively, I could travel in a single decker that originated in Staffordstown at an equally hideous hour, both buses passing Antrim at 6.40 am and Dunadry at 6.50 am. It might interest some to know that Dunadry village still had inhabitants and I distinctly remember one house in particular. Almost opposite that little hut in which we sheltered during inclement weather at the Dunadry bus stop for Belfast, there was a house in the village street with a green panel door and a semi-circular fan light just above, possibly a Georgian style. I can still hear a front door being shut as some unknown left each morning, but that person didn't go to Belfast. I never knew who it was, the mornings being dark at that time of year. That house with the green door, had railings around it, and was the resident of Mr Nat Davidson, who had, in earlier years, a small shop located at the entrance to the village, on the right hand side. There was still an advertising sign, for some commodity or other, outside that premises. I believe that the present entrance to Dunadry Inn, with the circular foyer inside, would be approximately on the site of the door of Mr Davidson's house. Alas, all is now gone, swallowed up by Dunadry Inn.

Now, starting in my year at Shorts were many of my friends of Ballymena Technical High School days, but most elected to travel to Belfast by train, leaving Ballymena Station at 6.30 am arriving at Shorts via York Road station. They had a concession to come in late, they passed my bench every morning at about 8 o'clock, exchanging a variety of greetings with me and other interested comics with whom I worked. There was much banter towards the Ballymena boys, and I was also included in this banter because Belfast people did not differentiate between me (from Antrim) and Ballymena. We were all Ballymena, straight from the plough! The banter was of course good enough humoured although given enough of it, it was tedious at times. These comments through the air could be anything from a reference to "Ballymena Utd beat again" or "pull the straw out of your ears" or "Get awa up to yer work". Among these Ballymena lads were Andy Kirkpatrick from Greenvale Street (who eventually went to South Africa) and Albert Henry, later Head of Technology in Ballee High School, Ballymena. These two had sat beside each other in the old Intermediate School in Ballymena before carrying on the good work together at Ballymena Technical High School. (I used to sit behind this pair). Then my friend, the late Gerald Alexander, (I am still using his Lee Guinness Compass set, still in the original box which I bought from him early in his apprenticeship - he also was to hold managerial positions in post apprenticeship days) and who else, yes, Sandy Spence, he just became Principal of Ballymena College of Further and Higher Education, a position held with distinction for many years. Also there was another life long friend, Ernie Nixen, who since leaving Shorts, has been involved in government training programmes for many years. Three other apprentices I recall were Jim Brown from Kells, who worked close by me and Jimmy Finlay, who was destined to die a young man. James O'Hara, from somewhere near Moorfields, was later to sail as Third Engineer Officer on the SS Carrigan Head, one of the Head Line ships once synonymous with Belfast shipping. Later in my apprenticeship I discovered another, Ivan Hunter from Cullybackey.

Also on the rampage at this time were two persons who represented quite a terror for me, a twin entity, inseparable twins of the workshop floor, further up the factory. The pair, always together, were one Davy Haggan who delighted in calling me "Ballymena" every time he saw me and his "mate" Jim O'Neill. They were both fitters. I can't remember what they did, certainly quite a bit of walking around, always together. Davy Haggan I'm sure, could have been on the stage, as to me he was a perpetual maker of mirth (sometimes at my expense). He also had a kind of face that you might want to laugh at, or cry at, if its mischievous grin was generated by your discomfort. But these things passed of course as I moved about, and eventually depending where I was working, I came to see these terrible twins of yesteryear as today's friends.

*   *   *   *   *   *   *   *   *

Many, many years pass and I am reminded of this pair again. I see Davy Haggan interviewed on television. He is now the Union Convenor in Short Bros. and Harland Ltd. He is expressing concern about proposed redundancies, and he looks much older, he is much older. I resolve to ring him up and arrange to travel to Shorts to meet him, I don't think he can put a face to my name.

But I arrive at the main office block, sign in and wait for someone to take me to Mr Haggan. I find him in his headquarters, a temporary wooden building outside the main hanger. He recognised me immediately and then filled me in about the nature of a convenor's lot. Actually the phone didn't stop ringing - a problem relating to overtime last weekend being worked without medical cover; a problem relating to someone being suspended - "Would you like a cup of tea?" "OK good show". Davy pours me a cuppa, the phone rings again, an overtime ban has been ratified and is official. Davy puts his hand into his pocket and brings out a Breakaway biscuit. I take it but feel guilty (Davy and his wife looked after their incapacitated grandchild and he has been up since 5.30 am). This is a measure of the man. I enquire about Jim O'Neill: "He is a supervisor in Centre 30, let's go and see him before the phone rings". So we go down through the main factory "Through all the changing scenes of life" - actually nothing much has changed, except as we near Centre 30 there is change, I only see strange machines, I have difficulty in seeing the men, well there are not many about in Centre 30, and there he is, Jim O'Neill. Well, well, well this pair again, their close relationship has been maintained over the years. I think they are pleased to see me, but it reminds us all that time is passing, Jim has a few months to go to retirement, Davy the same.

Buster McShane arrives in Centre 30

Shortly after I arrived at the de-burring bench, (I wonder do they still de-burr in engineering) and where I made my initial contribution to Shorts success in those days, I became aware of a fitter who came to work nearby. He was shorter than average, and of an agreeable disposition. Most of my fellow apprentices deemed to know him, they seemed to anyway, often over talking to him etc. Eventually I was told that this was R.B. "Buster" McShane, the well known weight lifter, and presently I too was talking to him. A point of extreme interest to us was his overalls. Brown overalls they were. A boilersuit actually but with a large vee set into the back, probably about six inches across the shoulder and tapering to nothing down the seam at the bottom. I assumed that as a result of weight training, the extra cloth was required for his very wide shoulders. But I had some shocks coming from Buster. First, I understood that he was Secretary of the Young Communist League and some of his views on the performance of the government induced me to feel that it was only a matter of time before he would be carried away in irons, and maybe some of us with him!

Then he proclaimed himself to be an atheist. I certainly made the best protest I could at this state of affairs, but I think he said that my views were totally narrow rubbish. "And do you never go to church?" I cried. "Listen", he said "Do you know what I did to the minister when he came to see my mother?" "No", I said, but hoping he had made the minister a cup of tea perhaps. "I threw him out and that's the way it was," Buster rejoined.

Apart from his political views on the importance of state intervention, a planned economy and his rejection of God, I cannot remember what else he said to me. But years later when I noticed that, as far as I understood, he had become a successful businessman, I wondered if he had ever changed his mind on the two issues, politics and religion. These, he had pronounced upon forcibly. Then I heard he had been killed in a road accident. I never had an opportunity to speak to any of his close friends or relations, in fact I didn't know any of them.

Hard Times

At Shorts there were canteens, in fact at least three in the main factory area, for the works, the staff and an exclusive one for brethren who had ascended the ladder of success into the realms of the senior exclusive executive immortals (well almost).

Who is the successful man? He who inherits a vast wealth? Or he who from nothing builds up an empire from collecting wastepaper or scrap? Or one of the above executives? The question was posed at a certain University lecture on Sociology which I attended later in life. Many answers were confidently proposed, but the lecturer surprised us by suggesting that consensus held that he who was able to resist the stress of life, and cope with it better, was the successful man.

Anyway, the canteen was not for me. I remember the Christmas holidays of my first year in the main factory. Shorts first Canberra had, sometime previous, taken off successfully, to land at Aldergrove where Shorts had a hanger. I understood at that time that the Sydenham runway was not long enough to receive an incoming jet in those days. Anyway, I had stood with others watching it depart and longing to get a posting to Aldergrove with it. Now I stood again looking over the concrete towards the canteen. A special turkey dinner had been on offer at the canteen and I had considered the possibility of indulging thereof. But I turned away and took my lunch out of my coat pocket and sat on the de-burring bench to eat my lowly meal - it was known as one's "piece". The cost of the dinner - two shillings and six pence in old money terms, twelve and a half new pence, was just outside a first year's apprentice's "range".

The "piece", prepared by my mother, had to stretch over the morning, lunch and afternoon breaks. If, during icy and snowy conditions, I happened to fall off my bicycle on the road from Crosskennan to Dunadry, the "piece" would have invariably crashed onto the road, sometimes opening and spilling the contents onto the road. More than once I had the acute dismay of spitting out the gravel which the bread had picked up from the road! I recall my piece invariably contained some of my mother's "currant soda," which Eric Lynn often inquired if I "had an extra bit of it".

But in due course, the piece had to stretch even further. Later in my apprenticeship I changed from Ballymena Technical to that great citadel of learning, the College of Technology, Belfast. The piece had now to last (on one or two days anyway) to provide a meal before I went to Belfast College of Technology during evening classes.

"Happiness lies in the striving and not in the winning".

Captain H.G.G. Stoker, Commander of H.M.A. Submarine AE2, (from "Straws of the Wind")

I remember that first Christmas in Shorts for another reason or reasons. On the Saturday before Christmas, I was returning home in the evening, from some social function in Antrim, as a pillion passenger on a friend's motor cycle. At the top of the then Steeple Hill, the motor cycle skidded gently on black ice and we were deposited, none the worse for wear, on to the road. The next day being Sunday, we were returning home from church on the same motor cycle. In those days there was a left hand bend just before the present Parkhall Road. Growing on the roadside, were a number of large oak trees. On one, was a cross of six inch nails and this cross was a memorial to a motorcyclist who had been killed there some years earlier. Further past Parkhall Road, is a right hand bend and there that Sunday, we again skidded on ice rather heavily, and were taken to the Massereene Hospital, Antrim. I was discharged having only superficial injuries, but my friend was in over Christmas and for some reason, I started getting the bus to work from Market Square, Antrim, from then on. It departed from Antrim at 6.40 am each morning. By the next time I did catch a bus at Dunadry, Dunadry Village was no more, fallen to the bulldozer. Dunadry Inn was to rise from the dust.

Shortly after Christmas, the "Princess Victoria" was lost after leaving Stranraer to sail to Larne. In those days, Shorts had maintained a flying boat base there. One of the returning fitters on board the "Victoria" and rescued from the freezing water, was Jimmy Copely, someone I was to get to know in later years. He now lives at Dundonald.

The Management

As a first year apprentice, I used to regard the passage through the factory of Mr George Gedge, the Works Manager, with awe and wonder. A tall man, always dressed in a dark suit, he was reputed to be earning fifty pounds per week, an enormous income in those days, (whether the truth was more or less, I cannot say). Probably at this time, a garage foreman was earning ten pounds per week, so I imagine Mr Gedge would have "got by". I was earning about two pounds, but if I got a "good" week's bonus, I might earn another one pound.

The Chairman was Sir Edward Herbert, and Mr R. E. Harvey was General Manager. Both Mr Gedge and Mr Harvey had been with the company during the war.

As most staff made their way to the canteen through the main factory, a lowly apprentice would see many of the "prominent citizens" of Shorts from time to time, and get to know them by name only. But time brings chance and change, and I have in the process of this time got to know many of these former important figures, from management and design.

Both George Gedge and Mr Harvey in their time sacked Andy Barr, (Metal Trades Convenor), accusing him of organising union activity in working hours e.g. holding meetings etc. But he was always reinstated, somehow!

During those turbulent years when Andy Barr, Jimmy Grahame and other union leaders held forth, high in the scaffolding, to harangue Shorts management on the everlasting quest for new orders or other perceived threat to workers' welfare, an incident took place which booked a place in my memory, albeit vague. At such a mass meeting, addressed by union officials, such a claim was being made loud and clear, when the scaffolding was mounted by a management figure, it may have been George Gedge. This person proceeded to refute the allegations and I seem to recall that he made the firm's case forcibly because I could hear comments from fitters returning to their benches that "he didn't let Grahame have it all his way". It was the only time I ever knew union and management in public debate there - but it's all water under the bridge.

An interesting story, for which I am indebted to former test pilot Richard Spencer, concerns George Gedge. He, Mr Gedge, recalled the production problems that were associated with the manufacture of the propeller 'spinners' used on all aircraft during the second world war. A 'spinner' is that parabolic like nose 'cone' that fits over the centre of a propeller, the boss, to cover a multitude of sins (i.e. nuts, bolts, etc) and give some streamline effect. These covers were traditionally made by beating them out using traditional sheetmetal craft. It was decided that faster methods would have to be used and experimental work was set in motion to form them by 'spinning' from a flat sheet, in a lathe. Spinning involves rotating a sheet of material held against a suitable former over which profile the rotating sheet is persuaded to follow, being aided by pressure from a lever pressing against the material and forcing it against and over the former. The process initially was going well but friction between the sheet of material, probably duralium, and the lever, caused the material to start disintegrating. All sorts of lubricants were used, to no avail. Mr Gedge was very much interested in getting the 'spinning' to a successful conclusion but the problem of material preservation was apparently insurmountable until Mr Gedge, while witnessing further attempts using new ideas on lubrication had a need to visit the toilet. There he spied a bar of carbolic soap, seized it (presumably as a drowning man would do a straw) and brought it out to where the tests on spinning the spinner were taking place. He suggested using the carbolic soap as a lubricant, and apparently it worked! But in the process of time Mr Gedge disappeared from the scene, and new management figures appeared including a new Chairman and Managing Director, Rear Admiral Sir Matthew Slattery CB, DSc., FRAeS, although Mr R. E. Harvey remained as Director. There were also directors on the board, who were also directors in Harland and Wolff Ltd. But in 1958, someone joined Shorts, who was to make what was probably the longest and most significant contribution to research, development and management than any of his predecessors. His name was Philip Foreman.

That contribution was to extend over thirty years, and he retired as Sir Philip Foreman C.B.E., D.L., Chairman and Managing Director of the company. With vast experience in weapons research - especially associated with naval requirements, Sir Philip was in the vanguard of missile development.

Eventually I had the privilege of meeting Sir Philip. This was the occasion when the Open University conferred an Honorary Doctorship on him on the same day I graduated myself, the former apprentice at the de-burring bench having had the temerity to suggest well beforehand that a photograph wouldn't be out of place, to which suggestion Sir Philip readily agreed.

An early impression! From left, B C, my sister May who is nursing sister Audrey; my brother Bill nursing a neighbour's child.

An early attempt to build a Hydrofoil by a local hospital doctor, Dr. Crawford. I am posing, to give the structure proportion. I commenced my apprenticeship shortly afterwards.

William Orr's house on left.
It is thought to have been a two storey building then.
The building attached on right was added during more recent years.

SOON TO BE NO MORE

Rathmore Memorial Hall which I passed each morning around 6.30 a.m. The road sign read, Dunadry. A school had stood on the site since 1869, run under the National Schools Committee. In its original state, it was a thatched building, the thatch being replaced by slates at a later date. Source: probably from a local newspaper cutting. Shortly after this photograph was taken the old hall was demolished and the B95 now passes over the site en route Antrim from Rathbeg roundabout.

**THE DEMISE OF A LANDMARK -
THE OLD RATHMORE MEMORIAL HALL.**

When a new school was built in 1931 - its situation now the intersection of the Dunadry and Parkgate roads - the former school was renovated by Dr. J. J. Adams and thus became a social centre for the local community. In particular, the Rathmore Young Farmers' Club formed on 20th March 1931, acquired a permanent home, as did a Sunday School, and the Hall also was identified as a place of worship with special services - in particular at the start of each year, and harvest time.

During the Second World War, Young Farmers' Club activities were suspended, the Hall at one time being used to house evacuees from Belfast.

But all is now gone. The Hall was demolished in 1971, victim of the new town of Antrim Development. Rathmore Young Farmers' Club still flourishes in the new Rathmore Hall, built close to the new Rathmore School - now itself closed as a Primary School, and presently used by pupils with special needs from the Local Education Board's area. Thus the irresistible tide of change.

The last meeting of the Rathmore Young Farmers' Club to be held in the Hall took place on 19th May 1971. The next to take place, was at the home of Mr. & Mrs. Joe Campbell, on 8th September 1971 and eventually the new Hall, beside the former Rathmore Primary School, was built.

"Blitzed Square", bounded by High Street and Bridge Street. This has been taken shortly after the bombing. The trams are proceeding towards the Albert Clock. Published with the kind permission of Deputy Keeper of Records, Public Record Office of Northern Ireland.

This photograph has been taken later than the other one of "Blitzed Square". The "square" has been cleared somewhat. In the "square" is shown a Gospel tent and a park for military vehicles. Bottom left is a static water tank - a readily available source of water for fire-fighting and independent of the water mains. Half way up High Street are what appears to be two air raid shelters. Ten years later, I was to walk across "Blitzed Square" each morning to board a bus for the Queen's Island. The bus stop was approximately where the shelters stood. The arrows indicate the path of the falling bombs that did the damage, during the Luftwaffe raid of 4th-5th May 1941. Published with the kind permission of Deputy Keeper of Records, Public Record Office of Northern Ireland.

*Antrim's famous spelling mistake - the Courthouse,
looking towards the church clock.*

*Farranshane - the lane leading
to the former home of William Orr*

*Antrim Castle from the Old Bridge.
Source: National Museums and Galleries of
Northern Ireland, Ulster Folk and Transport Museum.
Original photograph W.A. Green, WAG 972.*

*Sandy Spence, one of those who
"passed my bench" each morning.
Later Principal of Ballymena College
of Further and Higher Education,
M.Sc. (Eng.) C.Eng., M.I. Mech. E.,
M.I. Prod. E., M.I. Mgt.*

B C

Mervyn Kidd

*Albert Henry later
Mr. Albert Henry B.Ed.(Hons.) and
Head of Department of Technology
Ballee High School, Ballymena.*

Dunadry Village - R. Ross

*Dunadry Inn - the entrance is approximately on the site of the former house
with the railings, above.*

Mr. R. E. Harvey, the General Manager of Short Bros. & Harland Ltd., when I went to work there. (Courtesy of Short Bros. & Harland Ltd.)

Mr. George Gedge, Works Manager and Production Superintendent on extreme right - the man "reputed to be earning £50 per week!"
With him on extreme left is Mr. Bert Penny, Chief Production Engineer. The centre two may be Bristol personnel.
Above is a "Proteus" engine - of a Britannia Airliner. (Courtesy of Short Bros. & Harland Ltd.)

Chapter 2 - Escape from the de-burring bench

*H*owever, de-burring days came to a halt and after seven months I was transferred to the machines - Ward 3A's - semi-automatic lathes. At first I was put in a store to assist a man of small stature called Jackie Cunningham. Jackie was known as the Kit Marshal. His job, skilled and responsible, was to select the kit of tools for all jobs being machined. My foremen (there was a nightshift for the turners at the time) were Mr. Tommy Turner and Mr. Tommy McCann, and I might say that there was a senior foreman - Mr. Nelson.

I worked with Jackie for a few days and then I was sent to stand by one of the machines, a 3A Ward Capstan Lathe currently being worked day and night by two very fine men. I was first with James McDowell, then when he went on nightshift I met his 'mate' a man called William Douglas. These men really did show me all they could, and soon I was operating the machine for them and actually producing components on this lathe that passed inspection, and became part of an aircraft.

H McGuigan - a fellow apprentice

At the start of my apprenticeship, I understood that Shorts had about 10,000 people on the payroll. Apart from the Queen's Island complex, comprising of the Main Factory, Extension Factory, and the Airport, there were outlying centres at Altona, Lisburn; Hallmark, Newtownards; Aldergrove, Castlereagh and a flying boat repair facility at Stranraer, Scotland. Apart from aircraft manufacture, developments took place in the construction of aluminium buildings e.g. schools, a small car, general purpose research rockets and some work for, I believe, the Admiralty, in the shape of sonar domes and other devices associated with the underwater detection of "foreign bodies". Such undertakings brought together people of diverse abilities, interests and persuasions in the course of their duties. There were sports facilities, opportunities to learn to fly, using, I believe, Newtownards Airport and if agreed, small deductions were made in one's pay towards the sports fund and also to a small sickness benefit scheme. The company did not operate a sickness scheme as such for shop floor employees.

Here and there in this vast concourse in quiet corners and otherwise would meet men who would spend part of their lunch break in the study of the Scriptures. Shortly after I arrived at the 3A wards, I was kindly invited to such a gathering by Jimmy McDowell. It was held under the balcony at Centre 20, somewhere I was to become well acquainted with, in later years. However, on this day as we made our way over to the venue, I was aware of another apprentice in our group. I must have been introduced to him because I then knew his name and remembered it. He was a big fellow, one you could easily imagine continually growing out of his overalls. His name was McGuigan and although as far as I knew he didn't take up boxing as his name might suggest, nevertheless his enormous contribution to the academic, voluntary and public services of this province and beyond indicates that he took up virtually everything else! However, due to the manner in which apprentices were shifted around, our ways were divergent and I didn't get to know him further. Years passed when much water had flown under the bridge (and with it a lot of my blood as well), and when I was crawling back to normality after the lengthy lay-up described presently, I attended a few extra tutorials in connection with Higher National Certificate studies. I noticed two teachers in the room, one of whom concentrated on marking and correcting homeworks. I immediately recognised him as my erstwhile apprentice companion of the meetings under the toolroom balcony. He didn't seem to recognise me - it was a good job as I was probably making very heavy weather of academic pursuits at the time and as my priority had to do with a lot of catching up, I didn't just then seek to waken his recollection of me. Shortly after, for some reason I was transferred to another class and lost contact with him again.

Years passed and I received an invitation to visit the Annual Prizegiving and Awards Ceremony at Shorts. At the refreshments afterwards, I saw someone I thought I recognised and upon introducing myself, I discovered I was talking to Dr Harry McGuigan!

Some time later I was to discover the remarkable career of this former apprentice in Short Bros. & Harland. Following the successful conclusion of his National Certificate studies and a First Class Honours Degree, he was awarded a PhD by Queen's University in 1965.

He was appointed Assistant Lecturer at Queen's University in 1961, shortly to be followed by a Lecturership in Mechanical Engineering at the University of Aberdeen in 1964. He was then appointed Principal Lecturer in Robert Gordon's Institute of Technology in Aberdeen and later as Head of the Department of Mechanical and Production Engineers in Dundee College of Technology in 1967.

With the establishment of Ulster College (The Northern Ireland Polytechnic), Dr McGuigan was appointed as the founding Dean of its Faculty of Technology in 1971, he became Dean of science and Technology in 1973, and Pro-Rector in 1975. When the University of Ulster was created by the merger of Ulster Polytechnic and the new University of Ulster in 1984, Dr McGuigan was appointed as Pro Vice-Chancellor (Personnel) and became Pro Vice Chancellor (External Affairs) in 1993. He had also been Provost of the Jordanstown Campus since 1988. As well, he has also been extensively involved in various councils in Training, Nursing, Job Creation and Higher Education. He is a past Chairman of the Northern Health and Social Services Board. He was awarded a C.B.E. in a New Year's Honours List.

What can one say of such an achiever?

Those who worked on the Ward 3A Capstans

John Ferguson came from Hillhall near Lisburn and he and I became very close friends, indeed having much in common in nature and outside interests. He like myself was very much interested in what was taking place in the world of motor cycle racing. He was a great Norton supporter and we followed each race with great interest. Now there were a number of men available in our centre to "set up" the Capstan lathes and obtain a "first off" for anyone who didn't set up their own machine. We were not lacking in characters among them. There was "Mandy" - Billy Manderson from Newtownards and quite a lively guy. There was Gus Allen (who later became a ratefixer), Barney Leonard and Willie McKnight. Some time before I arrived at Shorts, Willie had undergone major surgery, a brain related operation - possibly the removal of a growth of some kind. It left him with a tendency to talk with the side of his mouth and one eye slightly shut. Very often a cigarette literally hung from his upper lip while he carried on whatever communication he was engaged in. Often the recipient of such communication was John Ferguson - often on subjects like religion or the Royal Family or such things. Willie shall I say had radical ideas about things. Anyway, as an apprentice I needed a setter and Willie usually, if available latched onto me - a possession in a kind of way - perhaps an apprentice was easier to please in getting the job underway. Sometimes an awkward job would come along and first off after first off would be attempted without making its way to the inspection. It might be a reamer cutting too big, the work would accept the "no go" gauge - scrap again. Perhaps there would be trouble with taps, not cutting properly, too big or too small or perhaps in the area of some peculiar hard material, external threads would cruelly exude "chatter" on the thread flanks which would be the opposite finish to that required, uneven and unacceptable to inspection.

Now of course time waits on no man and after the allowable time for setting up would be expired, additional time in setting up would reduce available time for making bonus. On such occasions I would hang around with impatient interest wishing that things would get sorted out. Meanwhile the bar would be rapidly consumed and suddenly on one such occasion we discovered that there was no more bar left for another attempt. The story got around that I had said in a broad Ballymena accent, "there's nae mair bar". Actually I don't remember making such a comment at all but it pleased my Belfast colleagues no end. It took an honoured place in the almost fetish euphemisms and rallying cries that one would hear as another "Hurrah". Isn't it good that most of us find large pleasure from disproportionate origins while the dark world of the sadist goes, I understand, to extraordinary and complicated lengths to try and achieve the same.

Anyway I often heard "There's nae mair bar", shouted as a kind of rallying call on all sorts of occasions. I wonder how long that clarion call lasted after I passed to another centre and another new circle of colleagues.

John Ferguson introduced me to some other apprentices in Centre 30 who came from the Lisburn area - Fred Lowens and Fred Kennedy, the latter being a member of the Society of Friends and later to emigrate to Canada.

The July holidays drew near - my first summer holidays at work, and a simple but exciting prospect was realised. Every year the C. E. Society organised a day excursion to places like the Isle of Man or Rothesay or on this occasion to Ayr in Scotland. Today, when travel is experienced by many from childhood upwards, it's hard to realise that for the previous generation to my own, travel, holidays etc, simply didn't exist, for a number of reasons. But such a possibility existed on the Wednesday following the Twelfth of July and buses converged on Belfast docks from all over Northern Ireland. I would say that this was just before the boom in overseas holidays affordable through the development of the jet prop and pure jet generations of passenger carrying aircraft, the jet prop Viscount and the pure jet Comet having been test flown in 1949.

So with my father, who, as far as I know had never been out of Northern Ireland before and one of my brothers and his wife we presented ourselves at the bus stop in Market Square in Antrim at 6.30 that morning. There was a lot less tension in this arrival at the bus stop, than the daily nightmare of getting the early bus to work as I normally did - the broad High Street of Antrim never looked more friendly - right there where the Battle of Antrim had taken place one hundred and fifty years before. I have rarely experienced the excitement of that day - so many firsts. I had never really been in the docks before, or on board a ship or sailed away down Belfast Lough to the sea. So we arrived at where it was proclaimed "Isle of Man Steam Packet Company", and boarded the S.S. "Tynwald". The deck of a ship is a good place to see Belfast Docks and there was a lot to see and hear and smell - the latter from the common smell of the dockside warehouse, housing feeding stuff, timber etc. - you name it, it's there. Then there were all the smells of a ship - from the funnel, the galley, paint and oil.

But soon the ship was moving down the "Lough", the open sea, Paddy's Milestone and onto Ayr, I think described by Burns as "that town of honest men and bonny lasses".

So I saw Burn's Cottage and Tam O'Shanter Inn (which was closed), and Auld Brig and all the things that Ayr offered.

My memory of leaving Ayr that day is reinforced by the impression of care bestowed upon leaving: a crowd of considerable size gathered at the pier and gave us such a send off. An elderly clergyman led the singing of hymns and probably psalms as well as waving. There was some nostalgia in the air. This seeing off visitors, who depart by ship is not confined to local occasions, like above. Many years later, I was leaving the Russian port of Yalta and crowds of Russians came down to the barriers that characterised Russian port areas in that era, and - started singing. One of the tunes they struck up was "Tipperary". I often wondered what words were being sung. Then with much waving they too saw us off. Anyway, the content of what we did that day, is not the important thing. What is, concerns how special such an event was. By the way, the bar was closed - and very few people were sick.

Holidays work around and soon one was back to work - back to the 3A Wards. I should say that in the area of the Wards there were people who had distinguished themselves for one reason or another. I remember an Ards Football Team member - always chewing gum but I cannot remember his name - then there was John Kelly - I think at that time the European bantam weight boxing champion.

Another man, who by his bright nature, literally breezed into my life from time to time, was Jimmy Warnock, another well known former boxer. His face showed a lot of scars and I think he was one of three brothers who worked in Shorts. I mustn't forget someone else who worked close by - Charlie Watts whom John Ferguson and I used to banter about his motor cycle idols. Later, Charlie became a very experienced motor cycle racer himself. Finally another man I mustn't forget to mention - a fitter I became friendly with in Centre 30 and who was well know in motor cycle races at the time. He was Norman Crossett who came originally from Magherafelt. Regrettably, after those early days in Shorts, our paths never crossed again.

Nothing happened of an exciting nature until September, and then the "bomb" burst. The Wards and their operators were being uprooted and transferred to Shorts factory at Castlereagh. Things happened quickly. I think advantage was taken of the "long" weekend in September to shift the machines. So we left the Queen's Island one Friday evening and reported to Castlereagh the following Wednesday, to become part of Centre 24.

I would travel to Belfast as before, but now I had to make my way to Cornmarket and Callendar Street. A short distance from Callendar Street, on Chichester Street I would "catch" a trolley bus for the Cregagh Road. Now I would go over the Albert Bridge and learn names like Woodstock, Beersbridge, Bell's Bridge etc. The trolley buses were electrically powered, the 'trolley' being a current carrying component - essentially a long, pivoted pole, spring loaded and mounted on the bus roof. On the other end of the pole there was a pulley wheel or carbon brush skid which was in contact with the underside of the contact wire.

These buses could be "derailed" as for example one trolley might accidentally pass another going in the same direction. When a trolley bus had to stop and park for some reason, the crew member collecting the ticket money - the conductor - would get out and armed with a long pole, would detach the trolley arm from the overhead cables. This would allow other trolleys to pass.

The Blind Men whom I worked alongside

When I joined Jimmy McDowell and all the others mentioned I also had as my fellow workers two blind men. Their names now have escaped me but how remarkable they were. Any kind of lathe enshrines dangers of the first degree - an accident can be caused by carelessness, or through a material failure of the machine's components - although this is unlikely. Years later I was to introduce and teach apprentices and students to use such a machine and foremost in one's mind, would be to highlight the danger of the revolving chuck and other devices which held the work. I was dealing with young people who had perfect eyesight - as far as I knew, in both eyes! Now, the men working the capstan lathes close by, were completely blind - yet were capable of turning out work to the precise dimensions on the drawings. I think the machines were "set up" by some of the setters using collets to grip the work, but the blind men were able to check their own work, using Braille micrometers - and the micrometer is a precision measuring instrument, able to measure to one thousandth part of an inch or metric equivalent. These micrometers had large cylinders with Braille language embossed upon the outside and these blind operators were able to read a dimension just as easy as someone with sight. I believe that one of these men - I think his name was Harry - had lost his sight at Arnhem in World War II. They were just taken for granted - I regret I was so much preoccupied with my own problems that I wasn't in their immediate company too often. But I do remember that both were men of good spirit and humour and appeared to appreciate very much the times when one would stop by their machine and ask "how's it going?" or "are you making it" - (the bonus).

Old Antrim - its characters

At my primary school, the geography books gave Antrim a population of 1300. It also had a 20 m.p.h. speed limit, and its share of characters. It's difficult to know where to start, but Father Davey would be an appropriate person, as few people for one reason or another wouldn't have known him. I always remember him as elderly and bald with a fair amount of colour in his face. Although I think he had a car, I'll always remember him on his bicycle - I can especially see him getting on the bike. Wearing clips as was the custom for all, he was adept at throwing his leg over the saddle. Father Davey was often on that bike, and up Antrim's main street he was quick to speak, if he noticed you - would shout a greeting with a wave, but it was said that he could use his mitts if need arose - so goes the legend. That aside, I think he was a disciplinarian. I believe that during the renovation of the Protestant Hall, he made a very acceptable donation. (His predecessor, Father McCotter - whom I never knew, was apparently very much involved in the community - to the extent that some called him the Protestant Priest. He was on the management committee of the local Technical College etc.) I seldom heard Father Davey speaking publicly, although I had attended funerals at St. Comgall's during his time, I'm sure, but I cannot recall that he officiated. Father Davey is buried in St. Comgall's graveyard, Antrim, close to the chapel entrance. Of the two Presbyterian Ministers, Rev Majury was minister of First Antrim, and Rev William Mitchell, my minister, was minister in High Street Presbyterian Church, beside the Parish Church (it is now a commercial centre - the church having moved to the Steeple). The Rev. J. Hawkins would shortly become Minister of All Saints' Parish Church - Church of Ireland, in the town.

The Rev Mitchell had worked in a company with commercial shipping interests and shipping was always one of his interests, and I believe he was also a philatelist. Anyway he was a most gracious and kindly man. People said they felt better for meeting him in the High Street, during the week. I heard the latter often "come over", as they say.

Kirk's Corner was, in those days, a focal point for many - to talk, leave or recover a bicycle, or simply to observe. Now someone, well known to generations of Antrim's youth, was often seen there, usually dressed in a blue gaberdine raincoat - and a cap. On Sundays he sold newspapers in the area, and would cross High Street just as the High Street Church was ending the morning service. The Rev William Mitchell would then often be seen, in flowing gown and arms uplifted, ushering the newspaper vendor away from the front of the church and shielding his flock from moral reading decline. "Go along, my good man", he would be heard saying, the vendor retreating respectfully away. Antrim man John McCavenagh, who grew up in Castle Street (alas no longer), tells me of interesting meetings that he witnessed between these gladiators of the cloth. It seems that Father Davey was always in attendance at the bank on Mondays - presumably with the takings following Sunday services. His presence coincided occasionally with that of the Rev Mitchell - possibly when the latter was passing - and the Rev Mitchell would then pretend a robbery thereof. Those were the days!

But there were other well known men and women in Antrim of my youth who also merit mention as characters. One was George McAllister who lived down Riverside. He had a donkey and cart and was often seen about the town - sometimes with his mother. To the unfeeling young he was a suitable person upon which to play tricks - like unyoking the donkey or painting his hooves or shouting at him - with him or maybe his mother replying in kind. Then Duncan the painter was a colourful character - as was Mrs Danie who had a word for all. Then there was a man - a milkman and I think his name was Campbell Young, who delivered milk in little tin cans - on a bicycle. I also knew a good many men who had served in the Great War of 1914 - 1918. Among these were veterans of the Somme - who had gone over the top on the First of July 1916. And looking back, my amazement is that with one or two exceptions, these latter were of the most gentle disposition in mind and manner.

Eddie Ashe, who lived at the head of the town and had won the Military Medal at the Somme, was in the first embarkation list of the 11th Battalion (South Antrim), Royal Irish Rifles to leave their base at Borden, in the south of England, for France in 1915. I was friendly with his son. Dr Norman Grahame, the Medical Officer of the 11th Battalion, and the late Clerk of Session in the Old High Street Presbyterian Church, was awarded the Military Cross at the Somme; Jack Allen, wounded at the same battle, carried German shrapnel in his lung and was destined to be Antrim's last Somme survivor. William Scott, Johnny Dobbin and others were of the same temperament. But these were the ones who went "over the top" and survived.

I lived three miles north of the town, and of course like others, I had a bicycle. As we returned from the town, there was a chance of company - you sometimes caught up with someone or they perhaps caught up on you. Now, there lived much further up the road two other Veterans - one may have been in the Second World War as well. This latter was a man by the name of Wright, and for some reason, was known as Whissiker Wright. I suspect the name had some association with the word "whiskey" - "would you have a whissiker?" Local youths, returning home on Saturday night from Antrim stood a good chance of catching up on "Whissiker" as he walked home - probably a distance of five or six miles. As he was usually, as we say, "rightly", there was some mirth in the repartee occasioned by these meetings. Tommy Lowrie, whose family I was friendly with, was another First World War man and had a small farm. Tommy was also like "Whissiker" quite a character, but I never forget that they had answered the call of duty - something I felt was overlooked by some others.

There was another First World War man who appeared in the Antrim area during my youth. He was not exactly local - he had been at school with my father near Kells, but he was now working in a casual manner - sometimes with the local farmers, and was something of a free lance engaged in different little jobs. He was James Swann, a very good singer of local ballads and he had a smattering of the French language, picked up while serving there. I remember one occasion when he was acting as a housekeeper or helper to an old bedridden man who lived with his only son, who was frequently away on business. Now it was not unknown for James to take a drink. Occasionally he went on the "tare", disappeared for days, then turned up, like Toad out of the "Wind in the Willows" and the worse for wear. I often helped, on these occasions, with the old man's son, to put James up to his bed (with a certain amount of youthful glee). He would be dragged up the stairs, by an arm and a leg - kicking and squealing, and of course swearing loudly. The old man, who was bedridden and a devout Presbyterian Elder who loathed such language, couldn't miss but hear this racket from his bed and used to be heard banging his stick and saying "Keep quiet man or I'll put you out!".

A remarkable character indeed was Jack Rainey the barber. His shop is seen in the photograph of the Fair Day, Market Square, Antrim. He was a veteran of the 16th Battalion, Royal Irish Rifles and was wounded in France in 1916. One day, his daughter Molly (Mrs Molly Clark) showed me a badge with "Athenia" on it given to her by a friend Mr William Christie. This made sense to me as I knew Mr William Christie to have been in the army in India and would likely to have travelled on that ill fated vessel. Later the sequel to the "Athenia" linkage will be recalled in the sinking of the S.S. "Bengore Head" in May 1941.

After the Rev Mitchell became too ill to carry on the ministry, the Rev W A Finlay BA was appointed as minister of High Street and was our minister for 17 years. He was to many a modern minister (whatever that is) - at least a young man taking up his first (as I understood it) church. Most things people say to each other are largely forgotten. Some things stand out - I can only remember a few things my father said to me (i) "If a job is worth doing, it's worth doing well", and (ii) "Don't you understand that the animal that takes longest to mature is potentially the most intelligent animal". (I recall a third, later). My mother used to say that "The darkest hour is just before the dawn"; and "every cloud has a silver lining"; she also was fond of saying "It's a long road that hasn't got a turning". Positive thinking for people who left school at 12 or 13 years old.

The Rev William Arthur Finlay, one Sunday morning made profound observation. He stated bluntly that "You cannot scale manure without getting your feet dirty". He was speaking about the people we might keep company with, or do business with etc. I never forgot his observation. He also left me with another line of thought. Two men were in the trenches close to the enemy lines. One turned to the other and said "My, you're shaking - what's wrong with you". The other replied, "If you were half as frightened as I am, you would be a mile away - at the back of the trenches". Every man has his forte. What seems to be the easiest thing in the world to one man, might be a nightmare to another.

It would be amiss not to mention those who repaired bicycles in Antrim. There were at least five that I remember and I probably did a little business with them all. There were the Barr Brothers in High Street - I think Joe Barr, was a director of Belfast Celtic Football team. Then Francey Brothers, in Castle Street. Later Mr Adams carried on a cycle business in Castle Street, probably in the Francey premises. Up Church Street, we had Eddie Byrne and also in Church Street, where the street terminates at the Parish Church wall, there was Sammy Anderson. The Andersons also had a tea-room. But Sammy is remembered for his personality - he was not one to get excited about things. Typical of his manner and approach, is a story alleged to have its origins in that premises, where there is now a barber's shop. A customer arrives at Sammy's shop in some state of distress, having had a bicycle break down of some description. "I haven't got anything to fix that" says Sammy slowly, "but we'll just tie a wee bit of wire round it in the meantime". It was a pragmatism that still holds good to-day. When away from base on long distances, touring etc., it's a precious commodity to have tucked away - when something comes adrift.

It would not be out of place to set down some of the physical features that characterised the Antrim that I grew up in - socially anyway, because I actually lived three miles north east of the town. The town was getting back to normal after the war years, reminders of which were still to the fore. I passed such a reminder every time I visited Antrim - two "barriers", one on either side of the road, about opposite where the Grammar School now stands, on the old part of the Steeple Road. These were pillars of stone, about one metre square and two metres high, designed to impede the progress of German invasion forces, should they arrive. There were other such like obstacles, one notorious as the scene of a horrific accident on the Randalstown Road, Antrim, where four people were killed after their car drove into (or under) a barrier - a steel zig zag type, placed near the Chapel Corner. Everyone still referred to a little triangle of ground at the top of Fountain Street, right hand side going up, as the "Gun". There is now a post box in the wall nearby. I never saw the "Gun", as it, along with another similar weapon positioned near the Courthouse in Market Square, had been taken away as, I believe a contribution to the scrap iron effort set up during the 1939-1945 war. I believe these guns were German Howitzers, and trophies from the First World War. However, one of the guns can be seen in the photograph of the Fair Day in Antrim's Market Square. It was smaller, apparently, than the one in Fountain Street. The plaque, commemorating the handing over of the guns by Col. Packenham to the Antrim Town Commissioners in 1924, I discovered was still in the town - in the possession of Mrs Anna Hunter, to whom I'm deeply grateful for making it available for the photograph.

More Hard Times

The lot of an apprentice was hard financially at least, and more so if one paid out 25% of the wages on travelling. The fare from "blitzed square" into the Queen's Island was two and a half pence (old pence) and I think 3 pence to the airport. Later, when at Castlereagh, a remarkable possibility existed. The fare to Montgomery Road, along the Cregagh, was 3 pence. However, if one choose to get off at Bell's Bridge - 150 yards short of Montgomery Road, one could then run across the former Rugby pitch (on which Castlereagh FE College is now standing) and come out on the Montgomery Road at what was Dobson's Dairy and a little distance from Shorts - Centres 24, 31 etc. The saving was one half pence (old money). I can assure you, reader, that provided we had managed a clear run "out the Cregagh" and there was a good chance of not being in after 7.45 (and being "quartered" i.e. losing 15 minutes pay) we always got off at Bell's Bridge. During my first period at Castlereagh, I was able to run like the rest, but by the time I worked there again a deep gulf separated me from my companions of that era - they were able to run - and I was not. But the deep gulf included years when I was nowhere, except hospital and home, awaiting the slow response of nature, to the healing of a shattered limb.

*   *   *   *   *   *   *   *   *   *   *

When I arrived at Centre 24, Castlereagh, painters were still at work on offices - for foremen, rate fixers, floor checkers - others, and I found my old Ward 3, near the "trimmers shop" where all fabric for aircraft was made up into whatever was required.

I was now working behind a Ward 3 operated by a man called Willie Knowles. Close by was an automatic machine - one that could be set up with tools etc. as the Wards. However, the difference was that through using a system based on cams, the machine could operate continuously - as long as bar was supplied to it. The jobs it manufactured, I would put into the nut and bolt category - although it had a wide capacity. But it was out on its own when huge quantities of some item were required i.e. hundreds. I found this machine a fascinating beast - I was to meet a similar one in the R.N.A.D., Antrim, years later.

Later still when accompanying students from Lisburn Technical College on an industrial visit to James Mackies I discovered they had dozens of automatic machines some large and having four spindles - four bars of material instead of the one I normally "cared" for.

The automatic was operated by Jimmy Gaskins and I built up a fine rapport with him and Willie Knowles - took our tea together. I'm of the opinion that some machines did not come up to Castlereagh - because I don't recall John Ferguson at Castlereagh.

We were next door to a factory that made Foxe's Glazier Mints - we ate their scrap - the girls who made the stuff used to push a handful - a large lump of scrapped mints, through the wire mesh fence that separated the factories.

By this time changes were made in various directions. The first one was concerning one of our chargehands - Billy Carlisle being promoted to foreman and - James McDowell became a rate fixer!

I think there was some mild banter made at the time about "poachers becoming gamekeepers" and I must say James was a very good gamekeeper indeed because he didn't give too much away. He was not an easy touch in his new role (even though there was, as is now said vis a vis UK/USA - a "special relationship" between us). I was now a second year apprentice but still, not a very good badger when it came to "asking for more" from the rate fixer - whoever he was. I must say that Willy Knowles who worked in front of me and who with Jimmy Gaskins shared the tea break with me was a very cheerful man, and was always cracking jokes, but at break times and lunch times he bowed his head to give Thanks. He sometimes told the story of a slightly deaf man being interviewed for a job on the 3A Ward: "Can you read a mike (micrometer)" asked the foreman. "Aye", said the man "I can ride a bike". (Much laughter). A devout Christian man and a Methodist, he also taught me his favourite hymn "Have you any room for Jesus". Before many months had passed I was to hear it again - in a very different setting and not of my choosing. We turners (or strictly machinists - working a semi-skilled machine, as opposed to someone who operated a centre lathe - a turner) invariably had our hands soaked in the oil and water emulsion which was pumped around the machine to cool and lubricate the machining operations. This led to a curious spectacle at the tea breaks. We didn't bother to wash this foul smelling oil off our hands - for a short 10 minute break anyway - perhaps we did at lunch time, and in order to protect our bread or whatever we were eating from such an odour, everyone tore a small corner of ones lunch paper and gripped our "piece" in that, and munched away, nearly everyone kept their lunch in a lunch box and some duly returned their lunch paper to the box upon completion. Most of my former colleagues moved from C30 to Castlereagh - Joe Millar (who was to give a very good piece of advice many years later) - was there as was Norman McGowan, Mandy, Willie McKnight - Gus Allen who had also become a rate fixer, Barney Leonard (the setter) - Billy Hyndman, later to hold responsible training positions with Goodyear and N.I.E.S., Bobby Jelly and Harry Keys - Billy Douglas (my former instructor) - there must have been many others but memory fades. But all the guys mentioned were always willing to help the apprentice when he got a difficult old job - help him on his way.

The New Year followed Christmas and soon the Spring arrived. I was overdue for a change of centre. By this time the new Centre 24 was being added to - many more men becoming employed. The apprentice training school was close to Centre 24 - wire mesh only separated it from main workshops - there was another workshop - C31, which I never had cause to be in - it had to do with guided weapons. The apprentice training school was sandwiched between the two workshops. At that time most apprentices were given a 3 months "off the job" training under Mr Bill Archer. He was assisted by a senior apprentice or two, third year guys. I would think at that time Shorts led the way and helped shape the future - as a role model for the future training of apprentices. But it was not until the White Paper of 1964 - many years later, that a one year "off the job" training was considered an essential, in any apprenticeship.

Anyway, I was now a second year apprentice and of course had missed that initial training. But in this life, nothing of a material nature can be sure and copper bottomed and circumstances can rearrange your life for you. I was destined to pass the portals of that training school in ways not of my choosing. But much muddy water would flow beneath the bridges before that took place.

It was definitely at Castlereagh that push half penny first entered my life and that of other apprentices. Nearby was the trimmers shop - they had nice flat tables and to these tables the apprentices did repair at breaks, lunchtime etc. But of these early pioneers - I cannot remember one name. Time passed and one day I received word that I was to report to C30 (again?) the following Monday morning. I had to leave people who had made me very much at home in their midst - Jimmy McDowell and "Dougie", Mandy, Willie Knowles - all the rest. They probably wished me good luck and no doubt some words of advice. I was leaving the "Wards", but in six months time I would be entering and leaving a different kind of ward (happily I knew nothing of that). I was leaving the Kit Marshal, Tommy McCann the foreman, all the rest - "goodbye to all that" - I was soon away.

The following Monday I arrived at the familiar scene of the main factory. The first thing I noticed was that where I had first been introduced to the "Wards" the whole floor area was taken up by giant planers - long machines that shaped the main wing spans and similar components of an aircraft. The de-burring benches were still there - Billy Riddles welcomed me back and made comments to me about the present herd of apprentice de-burrers. But first I reported again to Mr Ralphson the C30 Superintendent and was sent to the drills - a cluster of very large vertical drills and some radial drills - these were very versatile machines. I wasn't given one, I just stood by one of the operators, most of whom I was acquainted with because at one time the de-burring bench was close by. I think I was there just five days when I got the expected word to move up the main factory and join a centre whose foreman was Mr Jack Spence and chargehand one Mr McFadyean. But more important than this was that the centre was working on the leading "Comet" - the world's first pure jet airliner (designed and developed by the De Havilland Aircraft Company). I was very pleased, now what fitter would I be working with? Soon I knew and if had been able to choose, I would not have chosen otherwise. I was to work with Leslie Webb - an ex-R.A.F. man of the Second World War. I have been blessed in my life through meeting many decent, good sorts of people - mind you I have been aware of the existence of the other lot, but I've always tried to make them the smallest part of my life. Leslie was one of the good, decent and interesting sorts.

The continual fight for work - The Trade Union Leaders in Shorts

One couldn't work in Shorts (when I started as an apprentice) without being aware of the organisation of the trade unions. I believed it was very strong indeed. There were shop stewards in every squad - I imagine that would have been that number of men looked after by one foreman. There were also senior shop stewards. The usual arrangement was that if a worker perceived something wrong with the "ship", a dispute about a rate on the job, maybe a disciplinary matter or something else spoiling his peace of mind, (or body, a dangerous situation, scaffolding at fault, even a slip up by management to arrange first aid cover, especially during unusual working hours) - this could generate a "situation". The worker would report his grievance to the shop steward who would have permission to stop work himself to go into negotiation with the local management i.e. foreman, senior foreman (or senior inspectors, senior rate fixers). If it was something serious - a man being suspended or sacked etc, the shop steward might call a meeting there and then (usually a senior shop steward would be aboard by this time) - then on a show of hands he might declare a strike. Often a strike call would have implications for the whole factory. Notices would go up that a "Mass Meeting would take place" in the 150ft bay or 300ft bay - the "Sunderland bay" and there, the workers would be addressed by the senior stewards or the senior member - known as the factory convenor from a position high on some scaffolding or other.

Now during my sojourn in Shorts, there were four people who dominated the union scene - factory wide. (There were many other shop stewards, in large centres like the machine shop, C30 or other large sections who were also people one could not avoid knowing about). But the four who as I say dominated the mass meetings in the main factory were Jimmy Grahame, the Amalgamated Engineering Union Convenor, Andy Barr, Sheet Metal Trades Convenor (and later a full time Union Official), James McKernan (Electrical Trade Union), and Andy Holmes - Transports and General Workers' Union. I think the usual aid in public address was a hand held megaphone speaker - and Jimmy Grahame didn't spare himself - he really shouted into that speaker - face red from the effort. Andy Barr was likewise a forceful speaker, as was Andy Holmes - natural public speakers. Apart from disputes over wages, there was an ongoing fear of redundancy. I was not then, or now, skilled in the machinery of union power but it must be said that although Shorts management were probably, through new designs and lobbying in appropriate areas, trying desperately to get new work, it seemed that only Jimmy Grahame or other Union officials had visited London to badger Whitehall into awarding contracts. For years, almost without exception, the work in hand was mainly of the war plane variety. It was probably easier to lobby a government for work emphasising the social consequences of unemployment etc. To lobby a private concern - I suppose a low tender would be a chief weapon to use in the search for work. But I now know that the Union's plank here was that the Government (U.K.), that nationalised Shorts in 1943, should be the government to see that it got its share of defence work.

I remember how during a serious crisis - some contract running low with serious risk to jobs etc, Jimmy Grahame co-organised a pipe band to lead a march on Whitehall - I think band members were from throughout the factory and from many different bands.

And then, of course inevitably, there were those days when an "up the road" decision would be made - a strike. It would usually take the form of walking or travelling into some location in Belfast and having a meeting to discuss and further brief the workers.

I remember a time when a number of walk outs had taken place within a short period of time, and to get to the town of course, one had to walk past part of Harland & Wolff - the shipyard (the "yard" to all), and as a group of workers from Shorts walked past, an old yardman shouted at them, "What's up to-day? Did they not leave you any milk this morning" The yard didn't seem to have very many disputes leading to a strike.

Of those men who led the trade unions in Shorts during my time there, James Grahame, the A.E.U. Convenor and James McKernan, the Electrical Convenor, are now dead. Jimmy Grahame was a rather portly figure and I was surprised to learn that he had been a footballer of some standing in earlier days having played for Sligo Rovers and possibly Portadown. He was just sixty-seven, two years retired when he died.

Andy Barr is still going strong, lives in Bangor and maintains his membership of the Communist Party of Ireland. He took part in many of the approaches made to Westminster to win work for the factory and during many visits made to Russia, met most of its leaders including Lionid Brezhnev and M.S. Gorbachev. Andy was born in East Belfast close to the firm in which he served his apprenticeship - Musgraves. Recently he recalled to me how Musgraves sounded three horns at one minute intervals prior to starting time in the morning. Since he lived next door to this work, he would be taking breakfast and counting - "That's the first horn, that's the second" and so forth. Occasionally a miscount would result in a lock out. One of his memories of Musgraves (Albertbridge Road), is of observing the Managing Director, a Mr Shillington, making a daily sort through the factory at about eleven o'clock each day - wearing a white coat - occasionally speaking to a foreman about some job or other. Andy's father and uncles served in the 1914-18 war and he doesn't remember any preferential treatment for them in the matter of work. I asked him what had been the net outcome of Union activity in Shorts and he felt that it had resulted in an appreciation of trade unionism - what trade unions could do, working in unity and or common goals. These goals were of course better conditions. Better conditions meant better wages and the wages were, by and large, very good indeed: the environmental conditions, which would have included workers' safety, were also kept under scrutiny e.g. awareness if workers were working in some area without stand-by medical facilities etc. Unions could represent members who might find themselves in dispute with management (as far as I knew everyone in Shorts belonged to a trade union - on the shop floor anyway). Andy maintains that such conditions set a standard for other workers to aim to achieve. But he also made the point that in some industries where there were many different crafts represented e.g. in the shipyard, unity of purpose was faced with some difficulty.

There were many individuals who were local shop stewards - I remember one called Albert - one of the fitters who worked close to the de-burring benches. Then down in the machining end - Mills, Ward 3A Capstans, Ward 2A Capstans, we had Jimmy McFaul, and Sammy Gardner (Turrets) - a very well known trade union activist, and one Jake at Castlereagh, famous because of a night shift speech when he called the management at Castlereagh "a bunch of Nincompoops". Of course, at Castlereagh I was to get to know Tommy McClean - the Burma Star man, very well. He was the union convenor at Castlereagh. Another convenor there (as mentioned later) was Jimmy Blair, active in trade union matters and late of the M.V. "Inishowen Head".

I can never come to any conclusion as to who kept Shorts going. Was it pressure from the unions on Whitehall that persuaded Governments to award contracts like the Canberra or Seacat, or did Shorts management secure work concurrent with Union exhortation or had Shorts some good things that lots of people wanted? Whatever one concludes, it is a fact that when the great and famous companies that provided the planes to wage war against Hitler went into liquidation, or into the melting pot of British Aerospace, Shorts remained an independent company, and indeed has produced things that people want, especially in the field of guided weapons.

The loss of Comet G-ALYP, Yoke Peter.

As already mentioned I left Centre 24 Castlereagh and returned to Centre 30 - to the drills - but only for a week's observation - and then to the "Comet" production line and on the "leading" aircraft. The Comet was designed by the De-Havilland Aircraft Company, and powered by four De-Havilland Ghost 50 Turbo jet engines, each of 5,000 lbs thrust.

My transfer to the "Comet II" and working as apprentice to Leslie Webb was probably the happiest period during my apprenticeship - and my time with Shorts entirely. This was interesting work in the forefront of technology - the world's first all jet passenger air liner and - most importantly, with a very interesting workmate and companion. Being, as I turned out more interested in people than materials, I don't find it surprising that this was a significant period and Leslie Webb the catalyst which combined work into a pleasurable occupation. He had been a warrant officer in the

R.A.F. in World War II. His conversation was always interesting and I was a good listener. I remember asking him if his life had ever been in danger. He recalled incidents like, one time, flying in a Blenheim in North Africa, the port engine was observed to be spewing oil all over the wing - I can't remember what happened - they got down somehow. With Leslie Webb, were two other men with whom I struck rapport, the late Mr Jack Spence the foreman, and Mr McFadden or McFadyean, the chargehand. It's remarkable that of all the people I have met and worked with - hundreds that I would have known - perhaps by their first name - these three still stand out as people who might have shaped my life in an entirely different direction to that which it subsequently took. Fate however took a hand, when the Comet I, already in service, began dropping out of the skies - one off Elba in the Mediterranean - another in an earlier crash in India - initially to us of no great significance. (Salvage work, by the Royal Navy, was under way by the 25th January 1954 - it would last into August 1954). These aircraft were the first generation of civil airliners where the main fuselage strength lay in the "stressed" skin arrangement - albeit reinforced with frames, stringers - various stiffening components etc. In the case of the comet, the stresses which the fuselage had to withstand included something new - the stress induced by internal pressurisation, something touched on presently. The wings, of course, still relied on various spars, ribs etc. Well, I remember hearing the then Chairman of B.O.A.C. - Sir Miles Thomas - stating on television that if only the skin had been about one thousandth of an inch thicker, it would have had enough strength to have withstood the stress. The aircraft was therefore one of the early pressurised aircraft. Flying in a rarefied atmosphere at say 40,000 feet (about 12,000 metres) and with outside pressure well below normal atmospheric pressure, the pressure inside such aircraft is maintained at that equivalent to atmospheric pressure at 8000 feet - something like 8 lbs/square inch, slightly over half normal atmospheric pressure, i.e. 14.7 lbs/square inch (or one bar). With no pressure worth on the outside of the aircraft "skin", the fuselage is under similar pressure to that of a balloon - and the "skin" would be under great stress from several sources. The Comet I's had square or rectangular windows albeit with a radius at the corners. The Comet which Shorts were building for B.O.A.C. was the Comet Series II version which had, as I remember it, square windows. Looking recently at a photograph (Illustrated History of the R.A.F. (Roy Conyers Nesbit)) of an R.A.F. Comet Series II, I see it had round windows, so a modification must have been made to later series II Comets. These Series II Comets were delivered to the R.A.F. Transport Command in 1956 and were in service for over ten years. I am unaware that any Series II Comets were ever eventually used in a civilian role - I believe that the B.O.A.C. order for Comet Series II's which was placed with Shorts was being shared with de-Havilland.

There are things that I still associate with "my" Comet. My first assignment to an aircraft - the smell of new materials, paint etc. - not to mention the miles of electric cables (the looms). I think it was the first and only time also that I worked overtime in Shorts - one Saturday morning - one only.

Of course, an apprentice had little way of knowing what was going on, and the foregoing knowledge eventually filtered through much later. But what happened off Elba, and later, during the investigation at Farnborough profoundly reverberated across the British Aero industry. I say now (and repeat later), that it was the greatest disappointment I experienced during my entire apprenticeship on the shop floor. The eventual cancellation of all contract work on the Comet - and Shorts was, I suppose, a sub-contractor for De-Havilland, resulted in pay-offs - these things were of more immediate consequence than the technical reasons why. In retrospect, these reasons now provide some interesting grounds for contemplation.

I probably started to work on the Comet I in March 1954. Now, a couple of months earlier, in January 1954, some British Navy personnel had laid a wreath on the waters of the Mediterranean Sea, off the coast of Elba. It was in memory of a Comet I - B.O.A.C.'s "Yoke Peter" Comet G-ALYP, which was incidentally, the first Comet to be delivered to B.O.A.C. - on 2.5.1951. This Comet which had flown 3600 hours, had taken off from Rome on 10.1.1954, bound for London and after clearing cloud at twenty-six thousand feet, had gone silent. In fact, it had gone down into the sea off Calamity Point, Elba, with a loss of 29 passengers and 6 crew. The previous year, and during a tropical storm, a Canadian Pacific Comet, G-ALYV, the "Empress of Hawaii" had crashed on take off at Calcutta, India. (These Comet I's were small compared to the modern jets of to-day - they carried 40 passengers plus a crew of 6). The Comets were grounded, pending investigation. What could be happening?

When the four jet engined Comet flew in 1949, it was on the frontiers of technology, and as a passenger aircraft, it had to be able to carry a payload. Now the jet engines of those days, were thirsty engines, and every effort had to be made to keep the Comet as light as possible, in order to carry a payload and enough fuel, for cross Atlantic flights etc. It was to be the first pure jet propelled passenger aircraft, and the first to have all hydraulic operated controls (previously controls were either operated by cables or push rods, etc). Since jets would operate efficiently at 40,000 feet, some means of supplying air to the passengers would be necessary. Ronald Bishop, De Havillands Chief Designer, decided to pump air into the airtight passenger cabin, so the Comet became the first passenger jet aircraft to be "pressurised". The cabin would be pressurised to a pressure equivalent of the atmosphere of 8,000 feet (about 2500 metres) something below normal atmospheric pressure, at ground level. At 40,000 feet (about 12,000 metres) there would be little pressure on the outside "skin" of the aircraft, but inside, it would be a different story. There would be "X" pounds pressure acting on every square inch of aircraft passenger cabin fuselage. Say it was 8 pounds per square inch, that would indeed be some distributed force, pushing the "skin" outwards (and no pressure outside, to oppose the skin) - tending to "blow up" the fuselage like a balloon. The skin had to be tough enough to stop such a thing happening. I understand that the skin was only 22 gauge thick - 20 gauge in places - aluminium D.T.D. 546 or D.T.D. 746 alloy. The thickness seems incredibly thin (0.028 ins). From memory, the later Britannia aircraft built in Shorts, seems to have had a skin of about 10g (0.128in) or about 3 mm! The Comet 'skin' of course, was the outward covering on a framework of frames, stringers and various reinforcements, some joined not by riveting, but by the use of redux, a bonding of materials, using a form of resin or glue. This was one of the things investigated for possible failure. The stress on a pressurised aircraft fuselage 'skin' is however, dependent on and directly proportional to (1) the diameter of the pressure cabin (2) the pressure of pressurisation. Another first for the Comet, was a high pressure refuelling system. In short, a remarkable aircraft, a real pioneer!

The investigations centred on the possibility of a turbine blade becoming detached, and being flung off into the fuselage (another interesting feature was that the four engines were accommodated inside the wing, thus being remarkably well streamlined, most jets now have podded engines, slung beneath the wings). So some armour was added in case of such a blading mishap. Metal fatigue, was another possibility being looked at. On the 5th March 1954 the Air Registration Board minuted the Ministry of Transport, 'When these modifications are completed, and have been satisfactorily tested, the Board sees no reason why passenger services should not be resumed'. So the Ministry gave permission for flights to be resumed, and the first Comet aircraft to resume passenger service, went back into service on 23rd March 1954.

Shorts were building the Comets presumably under sub-contract. When I joined the Comet production line, Comets had recommenced passenger service after the various modifications had been carried out, e.g. armour around the turbine casings etc, but we were living on borrowed time. After Yoke Yoke was lost of Naples in April 1954, the writing was on the wall, and that production line of Comets in Shorts stopped very quickly indeed.

Later on, in Chapter 10 - an examination of the official accident report into the loss of these Comets, reveals some quite startling information - especially for the "technically minded". But all air travellers of today, have benefited from the lessons learned from that investigation.

*   *   *   *   *   *   *   *   *   *   *

So when that wreath was dropped off Elba it signalled not only the end of an aircraft called Yoke Peter. For me, it was to bring real disappointment - I had been assigned to the leading Comet on the production lines, but was not really conscious of the implications at these frontiers of technology, that this pioneer of British aviation was attempting to cross. I now know what I had missed. It's amazing how I remember some of the simple things associated with the work Leslie Webb and I were doing. I remember, for example, one day Mr. McFadyean, the chargehand, bringing a drawing and a small bag containing one rubber grommet - (a rubber eyelet pressed into a hole in a metal panel to allow the passage of, say, an electric cable without the latter being damaged on the sharp edges of the hole). As well, I was accustomed to the usage of throat microphones, used by people at a distance from each other when fitting electrical connections or such like, and the use of Able, Baker, Charlie, Dog etc, when clarifying words spoken over the air. (The earlier phonetic code).

I also remember clearly that the wing spar terminations were attached to a steel centre piece - I'm sure it was an alloy steel of some sort, and the attachment was by a large number of bolts, $3/_8$ to half inch diameter (about 8mm to 12mm). I recall this, because it was in marked contrast to the Canberra, where each wing was held by a small number of large bolts, I think four per wing, of about 2 inch diameter plus (about 50mm) but sadly, that wreath not only signalled the end of the Comet I, it seems to have signalled the end of large passenger, long haul aircraft, being built by the British Aircraft industry. True, the extended Comet, the Comet 4, was the first jet service on the North Atlantic, on the 4th October 1958, but even the Comet 4, of which one hundred and thirteen were completed by 1962, carried less than one hundred passengers and had a relatively low fuel capacity.

Three weeks after the Comet 4's breakthrough into the lucrative North Atlantic trade, a Boeing 707, which had podded engines - the Comet's engines were enveloped within the wings, also crossed the Atlantic on passenger service, and with a superior fuel capacity/performance became the shape of things to come and the ancestor of later Boeings like the Jumbo 747. The demise of the Comet I was a disappointment for a lot more people than myself. To avoid massive payoffs, about 400 people (including myself) were transferred to the 'Swift' contract, a fighter aircraft being partly built by Shorts on sub-contract. I was directed to the night shift. My life now, was also being directed towards a date with destiny, the consequences of which would remain with me for the rest of my life.

*   *   *   *   *   *   *   *   *   *   *

As I recall presently it was during this period on the night shift work on the 'Swift' that I met one Austin Carson, racing motorcyclist, owner of a new 350cc Gold Star B.S.A. I had met him around Easter time, and I was to know him for about three months. Another chapter will tell about Austin.

Thus, there was a sad price to pay by De Havillands, for being in the forefront of technology at that hour, but undoubtedly these difficulties were overcome and no one could dispute that when the Comet 4 rolled out for its maiden flight in 1958, it was one of the most graceful aircraft the world would ever see. As well, no one looking at the R.A.F. Nimrod aircraft still flying today could mistake their ancestry, in the Comets of the past.

IN MEMORY OF AUSTIN CARSON

After the Comet disaster, I found myself on the 'Swift' fighter plane with 400 fitters who were on suspended notice of redundancy and on the night shift. I was there to meet and alas to know only for a short time, for a few months, a fitter called Austin Carson. I already knew who he was. He was the owner of a new 'Gold Star' BSA motor cycle - was making a considerable name for himself as something of a dashing rider on the race track having already distinguished himself on the grass track.

Currently, however, attention to him was directed by way of a bizarre incident that took place on the day of the 'Cookstown 100' motor cycle race, in May 1954. He was entered for the race and set out towing the 'Gold Star' on a trailer behind a vehicle. For some reason, the 'Gold Star' parted from the trailer and ended up somewhat the worse for wear and Austin was unable to compete.

On the night shift I was to work with him as his apprentice. Austin was always on the 'go', talking about this motor bike, person or thing. He had a mate of like mind who used to dodge around and I seem to remember trying to be around to hear what the latest news was. Eventually as we neared the summer holidays we came to be on the day shift and I was again allocated to Austin, as his apprentice, before working with one Eric Hutley.

The well-known Belfast racing motor cyclist, Austin Carson, who was killed in a motorcycle race in Sweden.

Austin Carson pictured when winning the Carrowdore "100".

Rev William Mitchell, Minister of High Street Presbyterian Church, Antrim. (Source: An Old Church publication).

Rev Father Vincent Davey P.P., St. Comgall's, Antrim. (Courtesy: Seamus Kearney, Antrim)

This most interesting photograph of the fair day in Antrim - a Thursday no doubt, shows the Market Square. The Ulster Bank to the right, is still there. Next to it was Sammy Campbell's pub, then the entrances to the Market Yard (shown closed) and then Jack Rainey's barber's shop - complete with pole. Next to Jack's shop can be seen the gable of Dickie Mullin's pub. If one looks carefully in front of the Courthouse, one of Antrim's two "guns" will be seen. The other was placed at the top of Fountain Street and both went as scrap metal in the war effort. (Source: National Museums and Galleries of Northern Ireland. Ulster Folk and Transport Museum, Original photograph by W.A. Green WAG 1072).

I was delighted when I discovered that the plaque commemorating the handing over of the guns in 1924 to the town Commissioners by Col. Packenham, is still in the town - in the possession of Mrs Anna Hunter, to whom I'm deeply grateful for making it available for the photograph. Photo: Ronald Moffett.

An Antrim that I never knew! Fawcetts Hotel (Antrim Arms Hotel) was burned down before the Second World War. In my youth, a large area of High Street, the site of the former hotel, was a wilderness overgrown with grass, brambles, etc. It extended a fair distance to the rear. Eventually an advertising company enclosed the site with extensive hoarding and advertisements. Then building commenced - possibly in the late fifties and I understand the Northern Bank now stands on the site of Fawcetts Hotel. (© National Museums and Galleries of Northern Ireland, Ulster Folk and Transport Museum. Original photograph by W.A. Green WAG 1075.)

Apart from the destruction of the Antrim Arms Hotel (Fawcetts), this view of High Street in Antrim remained unchanged during my growing up in Antrim. Anderson's premises eventually became that of Mr. Sam Anketell. It was down this wide street that I proceeded every morning to catch the bus at 6.40 am. The bus stop was at Anketell's shop. (© National Museums and Galleries of Northern Ireland, Ulster Folk and Transport Museum. Original photograph by W.A. Green WAG 2843a.)

This most interesting photograph shows the Shorts premises at Castlereagh. Centre was the factory of Centres 24 and 31, with the canteen and security on left. Bottom right is the factory where I had a unique little job making hydraulic seals - in isolation - except for the odd trip in the helicopter simulator! But most interesting of all, is the rugby pitch upon which Castlereagh F.E. College now stands. Note the trodden path between the goal posts - some of us apprentices ran along this path from "Bell's Bridge" trolley bus stop - to save a halfpenny, rather than going on to Montgomery Road which is the white road winding past the factories. Dobson's Dairy is seen approximately in line with the "path". (Courtesy: Short Bros. & Harland Ltd.)

This was my beloved Comet II. Note the time clock in foreground. (Courtesy Short Bros. & Harland Ltd.)

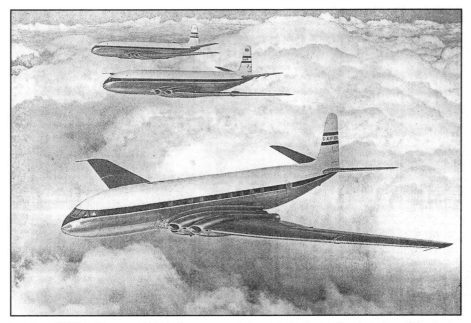

The beautiful Comet I's with G-ALYP in foreground. Note the square windows - in particular, the two on top of the passenger cabin. Eventually trawled up by Italian fishermen after G-ALYP disintegrated off Elba, the panel containing these openings - the A.D.F. windows, showed material failure from lower corner of one to lower corner of the other. (Photograph / Origin: Probably a De Havilland Source.)

This rare photograph shows the Comet bits and pieces shipped to, I believe, Chester in England, where each fuselage was modified to have round or oval windows. This follows the cancellation of the Comet contract held by Shorts. There is a date on the photograph - October 1955 - by then I had passed through Ward 2B, Musgrave Park Hospital, and was on the road to recovery. A side valve Ford Anglia can just be seen at right hand side. Now note the square windows of the Comet and in particular the opening on top of the fuselage in the foreground. This is in line with the second window from front, and is likely to be an A.D.F. window (Automatic Direction Finding). It was in this area that the failure in Comet G-ALYP, "Yoke Peter" was said to have occurred. (Courtesy Short Bros. & Harland Ltd).

Eye-Witness Account Of The Accident At The Pits

Eight, Including Two Riders, Injured

The serious accident occurred after the race was mid-way through. Two riders, J. Allingham, of Cookstown, on a 350 A.J.S. and Thomas Nicholl, 9 Woodcot Avenue, Belfast, on a 500 Norton, collided at the pits only a short distance from the starting point, were thrown off and one of the riderless machines sped on to crash into a group of pit attendants.

Eight in all, including the two riders, were injured and four ambulances and a beach wagon were used to take them to the Waveney hospital. The ambulances belonged to the Larne Division of the St. John Brigade and Mr. John Donaghy, Ballee, owned the beach-wagon.

They were attended at the course by Dr. Robert Simpson, M.P., who had charge of the medical arrangements.

On inquiry at the hospital the day after the race as to the condition of the injured, the only statement available was that George Fee, Tullycrenaught, Randalstown, (arm injury) had been discharged and seven remained, suffering from "compound fractures and head injuries."

The seven others were:—T. H. Nicholl, 9 Woodcot Avenue, Belfast; Jack Allingham, Cookstown, Mrs. Mary A. Browne, 5 New Houses, Craigantlet, Dundonald, who was acting as pit attendant to her husband, R. E. Browne; Robert Morrow, 7 Parkmount Avenue, Shore Road, Belfast; William Edward Cooke, Grand View, Upper Monkstown, Greenisland; Robert Wilson, Tannaghmore East, Randalstown, and Robert Cameron, (18) Crosscannon, Antrim. ——— *

A graphic description of the accident was given by Mr. Stanley Russell, 28 Rosemount Gardens, Belfast, well-known racing motorcyclist. He stated that after his duties of scrutineer were completed it was his job to go to the pits to see that the machines when they stopped there were roadworthy.

Rider Thrown Into Air

He saw the two competitors, Nicholl and Allingham, coming down the road which was straight at that place and downhill at a speed which he estimated to be between 90 and 95 m.p.h. They touched and Allingham was thrown five or six feet up into the air, falling in front of his machine and travelling on his face some twenty yards down the road. "He stopped at my feet," said Mr. Russell, "and was unconscious, so I lifted him gently and placed him on a grass bank." Nicholl was thrown clear of his machine and went sliding down the road in a sitting position. He thought that Allingham's cycle struck Nicholl on the back of the head.

Nicholl's cycle, went on Mr. Russell, shot to the left into the officials at the pits at a speed which he estimated to be between 20 and 30 m.p.h. "I saw three people knocked down by it. The first was Mrs. Browne, (pit attendant to her husband) who received a severe leg injury, the second Bob Morrow, pit attendant, employed by D. G. Andrews, Belfast, and a youth." Morrow seemed to have sustained a broken leg. ——— *

The accident occurred about 200 yards from the starting point and Mr. Russell sprinted that distance to get medical aid to the injured. They were carried by stretcher to a side road adjoining the starting point by members of the Larne Division, St. John Ambulance Brigade and race officials and put into the waiting ambulances.

Nicholl, with his left arm in bandages and after treatment for a head injury was seen for a moment at the hospital by a reporter but was unable to give a clear recollection of what had occurred other than that the two machines had touched.

One pit attendant, it was learned, had had a narrow escape from serious injury. The careering cycle passed him taking part of his clothing with it.

Chapter 3 - Life as I knew it comes to a stop

The annual July Holidays of 1954 in due course came alone. I was working day shift on the Swift fighter aircraft and one of the fitters I was apprenticed to, was Eric Hutley, who, before the 400 pay offs due to the Comet collapse, had been a charge hand, the latter word still outlined in threads where the appropriate 'badge' of office had been removed from his overalls. Later in another employment I was to work with one Frank Hutley, a brother of Eric's. For the first and only period of my apprenticeship I had been a 'tea-boy', bringing hot water in little cans for perhaps half a dozen men at lunch time, I cannot recall such duties at the 'breaks'. One of the above clientele was the foreman, a small bald-headed Englishman. How do I remember? Simple, he didn't make any move to pay me for my services, didn't square up at the holidays ("the bad deeds that men do . . . ").

So came the last Friday, we put away the tool boxes, and I took my leave of the main factory at Shorts. I would be back soon enough - it wasn't an especially happy time for me, I missed the Comet.

However, it would be a long time before I would be in the main factory at Shorts again. I had served one year and nine months of my apprenticeship, but I was about to start serving a different apprenticeship, that of learning to live with trauma, reduced mobility, pain, but live as normal as possible to the outside world. I would shortly join the ranks of those, who, for one reason or another, were unable to walk and earn their living. I would have many painful, depressing and troublesome times in front of me. In a shattering road accident at the Mid Antrim '150' Motor Cycle race, my old life ended and a new one began. Ironically I had been getting a lift to work with my old friend Eric Lynn, by car, and in passing the time in travelling, I had read, most recently, an account of new miracle surgery for those who needed it! It was called bone grafting. As I recall it, the account related how (my memory is somewhat hazy here) bone was available to graft in case of severe damage by using the patient's bone or using bone from young calves, or from a place called the bone bank, whatever it was.

But I was to find out all about it, and in the process, become an old boy of Musgrave Park Hospital, and for ever grateful for a brief period to a surgeon by the name of Mr Baker and similarly for the rest of my life, to another surgeon, a consultant orthopaedic surgeon at Musgrave Park Hospital.

The July holidays came along and I had booked a day excursion to the Isle of Man, on the Wednesday following the Twelfth of July. I had a friend for whom I acted as mechanic at motor cycle races when he was competing in them. I had been at the Cookstown '100' a few weeks earlier (the very day Austin Carson's 'Gold Star' had fallen from its trailer) and my friend was going well, but I had decided that I would be far away, in the Isle of Man on the day of the next race in which he was competing, the Mid Antrim '150' held outside Ballymena. Someone else had agreed to do 'pits' for my friend on this occasion, but a few days before the Mid Antrim, that person found himself unable to go to Mid Antrim. I changed my mind about the excursion and sold my Isle of Man ticket to someone a couple days before the race, and told my friend I would go along and do 'pits' for him. Doing pits usually entailed carrying a bag of tools, some oil and fuel perhaps, and possibly a signalling board. I believe my role that day concerned the fuel etc and the tools. Someone else had the board.

It was a fatal decision.

The day of the race arrived and following the 'scrutiny' of the machines taking part (to ensure that such machines were road and race worthy) it was arranged that I would take my friend's racing bike up to the start, he following in a car. The start was on the Cushendall Road, outside Ballymena.

Around about the Ballygarvey Road, another racing machine pulled up alongside me - it was Austin Carson. I can distinctly remember to this day that, as he pulled away, in front of me, he turned around and waved. It was nearly good-bye. We were both approaching our dates with destiny.

> *Kindness in another's trouble,*
> *Courage in your own.*

What happened that Wednesday after the Twelfth of July opened a chapter in my life that will remain open for the rest of my life. After a few laps my friend retired with engine trouble and I was watching the race with something less than the interest I might have had if he had still been in the running. The 'pits' by the way was simply the roadside somewhere about Kirkinriola, about four miles from Ballymena. There was a somewhat wide bend around which the riders approached the pits. Upon coming out of this bend, two riders collided. One was Harry Nicholl (Norton) and the other Jack Allingham (7R AJS). It appears the Norton stayed upright long enough to career into the 'pits' collecting, I think, seven such pit attendants including myself. In all, or most, severe injuries were to the lower parts of one's body. I incline to the notion that a footrest probably did the damage to most of us. I just remember a moment of awareness that something was upon me - the rest, a memory of being on the ground, trying to stand and collapsing again.

Upon trying to stand I discovered my left leg had ceased to exist as a leg, the lower third and foot were literally held on to the rest of the leg by little more than the Achilles tendon. Blood was everywhere, the pain horrific. I had also an injury to my chest and right leg. Had I been standing half an inch, or even a quarter of an inch further out towards the road, the right leg would have been in serious trouble as well.

The Waveney Hospital, Ballymena

One of the first to be on the scene was David McNie, one of our party from Antrim. I remember asking him for his opinion 'Would they take the leg off?' I also remember this classic reply 'Fifty years ago, sonny, but not today', this in his Scots accent. David, well known in choral circles in Antrim, was a former soldier in the Highland Light Infantry in World War II who, while stationed in Antrim during the war - he had also served in Northern Ireland before the war, met and married Miss Ena McLaughlin, the organist in High Street Presbyterian Church, where I grew up. This church building is, of course, a shop and business centre nowadays, the Church having moved to the Steeple. I was grateful to a number of people that day, not least to the late Dr Robert Simpson from Crebilly, Ballymena. I remember him saying to me that I was lucky, he still had some morphine left when he reached me as he moved through the injured. I was also grateful to the men who managed to find a door and carried me to the home of Mrs Alexander. It is a source of much regret that due to my recovery being lengthy and post recovery being much concerned with catching up on the lost years in hospital etc, I never found my way to that home to say 'thanks'. Anyway, after the race was over, the roads were opened to traffic and ambulances ferried the injured to the Waveney Hospital, Ballymena. As the ambulance threaded its way through the dispersing crowds, braking and accelerating, the almost detached parts of the left leg literally pulled away and then came together in sympathy with this ambulance motion. I did my share of moaning that day. The hospital bed, the operations that evening, the hazy figures of my father, brothers, sister around the bed later were all part of the ghastly shock from which I don't think I ever recovered. The surgeon at the Waveney was Mr W. J. Hanna, an Ex RN Surgeon Commander. His Registrar was a Dr Hannigan. (Some years later, as I re-entered my apprenticeship, I met the latter in Donegall Place, Belfast. I enquired was he now Mr Hannigan and he said he was, thus confirming his membership as a Fellow of the Royal College of Surgeons). This meeting with Mr Hannigan might have been eight years after the accident. I was therefore astonished when he asked me "Were you ever able to pull your foot back towards your body?" That was something I was never able to do again. Too many bits and pieces had been ripped out or disconnected. However, returning to that bed behind the door in Ward 3 Waveney Hospital, Ballymena the immediate problem was the aftermath of shock.

*   *   *   *   *   *   *   *   *   *

Some time later, when I was dozing in and out of consciousness, a period of consciousness revealed Austin Carson standing at the foot of the bed. I believe that he was wearing the typical polo neck I was accustomed to seeing him wear. I don't think I was able to have much chat with him. Sadly, this indeed was to be our last meeting.

Among others from the racing fraternity who visited me were an English couple, a Mid Antrim competitor by the name of Hunt and his wife. They visited me and no doubt the others, on at least two occasions. This kindness and care has remained in my memory as they were complete strangers to me. I'm sure such things mould our characters. Mr Hunt was a relation of the famous Hunt we read about in the pre World War II days. And about Austin, my friend of the 'Swift' days? Later, a few weeks, I was moved from that corner, up to the far corner, next to the Cushendall Road. One Sunday, I was listening to the news in the evening and I got a shock and the pain of bereavement. The announcer simply said that while competing in the Swedish Grand Prix, the Belfast rider Austin Carson was killed, when his motor cycle crashed at a bend during the race. I discovered, many years later, that my understanding of when Austin died now seems not to be according to the facts. According to the paper cuttings which were kindly shown to me recently by Miss Lily Boyle, his mother's cousin, Austin died much later, long after I had left the Waveney Hospital. I can give no explanation why I have the memory of hearing of the death through the radio headphones, and long before his fatal accident. It mystifies me completely.

I seem to recall that Austin came from the Mount area of Belfast and I believe his father had a confectionary and news agency shop in Short Strand. He often spoke of his brother Charles, who also raced motor cycles, I believe, on grass tracks or scrambles. I was deeply saddened, still am, amazingly.

But much of my capacity to grieve was tempered by the predicament I was in myself. Two things stand out as something of concern - one, that of the two injections I got morning and evening, because they caused immense pain. The substance, no doubt to counter infection and promote healing must have been quite thick - took some persuasion to enter my arm. I used to say to a brother, for example, "When will you be in again?" "Oh", he would reply, "Friday Night". Suppose it was Wednesday and I would say "Right, when I see you again I will have got four more below the belt". (I think I found out that I was to be on them for fourteen days). The other thing was, that every so often, a nurse would lift the bed clothes over 'my cage' at the bottom of the bed, and prick my toes with a pin to test my ability to sense touch etc.

Now, Mr Hanna the Surgeon, was a man terse of nature and economic in words. One day he dismissed me during a ward round with "You content yourself - you're going to be here a long time!" I thought that meant six weeks. But I was to be well out in my reckoning.

This was when I was still 'behind the door'. I was initially placed there as a seriously ill patient, in order to be near the Sister's office.

Opposite me was Robert Morrow who had been in the 'pits' for Davy Andrews, the well-known Belfast rider of Excelsiors. We shared many experiences, not all of them pleasant. His leg was fractured something like my own. When a badly smashed leg is encased in plaster the surgeons no doubt try to set it straight, and aligned. I often wonder how they figure out if a guy walks with his feet 'out' or 'in'. Anyway, with the receding of the swollen tissue etc x-rays sometimes shows that there is a 'bend' at the fracture, and it will be necessary to straighten the bend.

Well one day during the 'rounds' I heard a discussion that 'wedging' would be necessary. Robert Morrow heard the same, and on one of the 'operating' days we were duly prepared for the theatre and given the Pre-Med injection. Robert (called thereafter Bob) was taken away first for wedging. I couldn't imagine what this could be, and I eagerly questioned him upon his return. "What was it like?" I enquired of him. "Oh, it wasn't too bad, I didn't have to have an anaesthetic even". I felt reassured. Eventually I was taken to the theatre. Following ancient custom, I was bid "all the best", "good luck" etc as I was wheeled through the ward - by this time I had been moved to the end furthest away from Sister's office.

At the theatre Dr Hannigan and a nurse (whose identity escapes me) awaited me. This is what happened.

I was helped onto my side, duly supported by pillows etc. A small sand bag was placed below the plaster case in the general area of fracture, the lower tibia (shin bone) and foot overhanging the sand bag. Dr Hannigan then approached with what looked like a junior hacksaw and proceeded to cut the plaster on top and front and back, making reassuring comments to me, "I'll not be cutting into the leg, just the plaster, etc". The plaster was thus weakened, except at the bottom where it rested on the sand bag. "Now", said Dr Hannigan, "I'm just going to place a little weight on your foot, to straighten the leg". Well, he started, and the shock of pain that went through the leg made me literally screech with pain. "Go ahead", he said "You're doing well". As one might imagine when this was going on, the cut on top of the plaster opened as the leg was straightened. Into this gap were placed the wedges. I always had the feeling that more wedging would have been required that day but I think Dr Hannigan (I'm probably wrong) took the view that half a loaf was better than no loaf and that they had had enough of yelling for the day. Eventually the wedges in place were plastered over and I was returned to the ward. I looked accusingly over at Bob Morrow. "Aw", he said, "I had to go through it too, I didn't want to upset you before you went, so I didn't tell you how painful it might be".

Anyway, although I didn't know it then, wedging and straightening would hold significance for me that would stay with me for most of my life and it was to be a life indeed, unfortunate in additional leg damage - more wedging on a later occasion might have avoided that.

Nonetheless, as my mother often told me "Every cloud has a silver lining", and while my education was suffering in one way, it was being improved in other ways. I met a great many interesting people, in fact it seems looking back now, I met many interesting people indeed. I even remember some of the names of the staff nurses in the Waveney. Nurse McPartland for example; also Nurse Hunter and Sister Kennan (who had trained in the City Hospital with my eldest sister) and Sister Maud Warwick also known to my family and who had trained in the City Hospital.

Bob Morrow was a Veteran of Dunkirk. Also there was an older man, called Montgomery who was a Veteran of the First World War - he came from the Broughshane direction. I afterwards wondered could he have been in the 36th

Ulster Division, perhaps the 12th Battalion Royal Irish Rifles, in which the men from North Antrim served. In those days the family doctors paid a visit to the local hospital to see their patients - I remember Dr Simpson from Ahoghill and a Dr Bailie (Portglenone) and a Dr Crawford (Kells) and then I got to know many of the Ministers of the district, Dr McCaughey in particular, as he was one of the Chaplains.

I saw very ill people, knew when someone had died in the ward and also saw some patients who had suffered appalling injuries in accidents. I remember a young man called Lamont who had been struck by a falling tree and sadly didn't regain consciousness. Later his brother was admitted for casual surgery some months later.

Well, it is said that the environment shapes us and makes us what we are. I have always been fascinated by the curious circumstances that shape and change our lives. We seem to be forever approaching crossroads. If we arrive sooner we may meet someone who will change our lives for the better. If we arrive later, we miss the first person, but as we proceed to the next crossroads we meet someone who may change our lives for the worse. Those circumstances could be business, social or even marriage possibilities. Anyway, one thing I am certain of: if you lived in a cave and never approached these crossroads you wouldn't meet anyone, therefore you could stay as you were! But then look what you would miss!

I refer again to my injured leg. There was serious damage done, a piece of bone and tissue were missing or had to be removed from the leg and in the case of the tibia (shin bone) there was only a small area in contact, two little points of bone. The muscle and tendon that lifts the foot up were destroyed, no heel action, and the flesh or skin was absent over a large area. I think that the skin was eventually pulled over the bare bone ends and clips were used as well as stitches. There was considerable numbness. I had a cage over the leg to keep the bed clothes off it and as related earlier, each morning the nurses would come and presumably when my attention was diverted, they would test for sensitivity in my foot by pricking the toes for example with a pin etc. They would know by my reaction if something was felt, and eventually they would say "Do you feel anything?" Happily, sensation returned to a good part of the foot although never to the full extent. As already referred to, I was also subject to a ritual which I dreaded, I received that injection morning and evening. It was of an antibiotic nature, Penicillin or Streptomycin - extremely painful. I understand this was because it was very thick. But it did the trick and soon inflammation died away, temperature became normal, and I tried to "settle myself for a long time", as Mr Hanna had directed.

Every so often the leg would be x-rayed. I became familiar with the 'picture' - it was a shattering looking sight, the small bone, the fibula, was intact, apart from being broken, no pieces missing but the ends did not seem to meet head on, they leaned drunkenly against each other. (A long time later I was aware that the fibula didn't take direct weight, it acted as a kind of muscle binder, something to wrap muscles around. But the tibia was another thing, there was not enough of it for the ends to lean against each other - there was just the briefest of contact, very little area touching. As usual the surgeons would hold the x-ray up, comment briefly on it and pass on. An extra surgeon appeared one day, a Dr Wilson. Again, a man economical in words and with a rather brusque manner, Dr Wilson was apparently a Ballymena man, and Ex-army. He joined the entourage one day and each patient's history was explained to him by, I think, Dr Hannigan. As they progressed to my bed they looked at the x-rays and I heard (to my dismay) Dr Wilson say "Have you tried wedging?" Even Mr Hanna, some time later must have had some doubt about the realignment because he mentioned wedging. It made me feel uneasy and I was determined to ask for an anaesthetic if it was attempted again. Dr Hannigan however maintained that it had been wedged and there the matter uneasily rested. The pain of the wedging was to haunt me for a long time, and face me once again, a year later.

The ward rounds in the Waveney Hospital in the fifties had a ritual - probably typical of other hospitals but I reckoned it was something of an uncommon mix. Let me describe the procession, which seemed to arrive at predictable times. I cannot remember the pecking order, but probably Miss Alexander the Matron led off and accompanied by the ward Sister with at least one Staff Nurse. (In those days the SEN was not in evidence, although coming on stream in other hospitals which were graced by my presence in due course). Then came Dr Hannigan - remember he was a young doctor - I think probably the registrar - then Mr Hanna, Dr Orr, the anaesthetist, now Dr Wilson and occasionally I think there were others. Now, I will record for posterity that these were all hard men (and perhaps women). Mr Hanna - an ex RN Surgeon, Mr Orr was ex-RAF and now Dr Wilson who sported a moustache. The ward round had an almost regimental tone - all patients who were able to sit up seem to sit up very erect, while those patients lying flat - well they seemed to be very flat indeed. Sometimes the surgeons ignored me and walked on - although I recall Dr Hannigan as being very courteous and he would acknowledge me as he passed in the train if I caught his attention and I was also graced by the odd word from Dr Orr.

This degree of tension stemmed of course mainly from apprehension as to what would be pronounced - what sentence. Would an operation be advised, or would it be a case of "take him home and be good to him" or as I recall one patient being told "We've opened you up and apart from a few tight leaders(?) we cannot find an explanation for your pain (I especially listened for that dreadful word "wedging"). By maintaining strict discipline of course, people tended to literally do what they were supposed to do. I was left however with an awareness of the awe which attended those rounds because I suppose next to the hangman, no one but a surgeon or medical practitioner has such executive control (and in turn such noblesse oblige) - their decisions, good or less so, might determine whether you lived or not - whether you could be made walk again (without perhaps a shortened leg etc etc). In short, men fear death. Contrast that with the attitude to education for example, vital for a nation to develop.

But the priority of things is well reflected in respective salaries - what the doctors and teachers are paid, and I must conclude that men indeed fear ignorance less than death!

But what people said is the thing that has stuck. For example, I remember an old man - I think his name was Barney Gillen - from Glarryford, outside Ballymena. Barney was one of those who lay flat but listening and joining in the general round of ward chat.

One day an aircraft passed overhead. Most aircraft in those days were military - a small passenger service existed at Nutts Corner - small in comparison with to-day. Well, over came this aircraft drowning conversation and extracting comment. One would say "Boys, it's wonderful where you can go now in an aeroplane". Another said something else about the dangers associated with flying and was replied to by someone saying "Aw, it's not too bad, you can always bail out". Barney was listening to this and probably in keeping with his agricultural knowledge he said in a fearful voice "Ah, but sometimes they don't get much time to get into the bale".

And what was a common tune in those days? Well, I always associate Ward 3 Waveney Hospital, Ballymena with "Three coins in a fountain". When I sailed into Beirut in the old SS "Grecian" almost a decade later - the first song I heard on a jute box was - "Three coins in a fountain".

One of my most faithful visitors was my Aunt Eliza Cameron from Carnaughts. This most friendly lady used to bring me some of her baking every week - always in a small square box - and her chat. My mother used to cycle three miles into Antrim, take the bus to Ballymena - Linenhall Street and walk up to the Waveney - and the same journey upon return. We "sick" people take so much for granted - I probably never thought at all of the tremendous burden that my getting involved in that accident caused to be placed on my parents' shoulders - and other members of my family. On the contrary, I probably saw myself the righteous recipient of people's time, patience, pity (of course) and anything else they had to make a sacrifice for.

Ward 3 was known as male surgical. This was before an extension was built on the Cushendall Road end of the ward - that glass enclosed sun parlour - the first thing you see as you approach the front of the Waveney (well, you will not be approaching it any more - you will most likely be approaching the front door of Antrim Area Hospital). The Waveney is now demolished.

Anyway the surgical ward had patients with a wide range of ailments - most patients knew what was wrong with them, but I remember one man - he was an employee of the Ulster Transport Authority and in spite of undergoing operations of an investigating nature the surgeons could see nothing to cause pain. I remember an English climber falling while walking on the Antrim Plateau and they brought him in unconscious. Happily he recovered. Then how could I forget John Allen, well known in the Kellswater area as a breadman. I remember as a child along with my father on the Moss Road at Ballymacvey and seeing a horse-drawn breadvan - I have often wondered if that breadman could have been the same John Allen who lay beside me in the Waveney with severe arthritis in his knees etc. Then Charlie Graffin - from Randalstown - and others whose names now escape me. But I can never forget George Richmond from Portglenone. George had worked much of his life in England as a lorry driver and was admitted to Ward 3 with a pain in the stomach area. He and I struck up great rapport - I cannot recall what we talked about but he was in hospital some time before a decision was made about his future treatment.

For different reasons, I remember another patient - a boy of fourteen years - Charlie. Tinges of sadness linger around this memory, because this little boy came from an unhappy home background - I seem to recall that his mother had left him and his brothers. Charlie had few visitors. However, some in the ward knew him and occasionally he would be asked to sing - usually a certain hymn. It was "Have you any room for Jesus", taking me back to Shorts at Castlereagh - and Willy Knowles!

At this stage in my career, I can honestly say that my worldly possessions consisted of a few coins that someone had deposited in my hospital locker close to my bed.

*   *   *   *   *   *   *   *   *   *

By this time, Summer had gone and whereas I had earlier sat up in the bed and seen off my visitors each evening, first as they emerged from the hospital front door and then down the avenue or into the car park, I could no longer see their departure, or what went on outside in the dark. The Autumn came, the swallows departed, the leaves fell - occasionally I would think of the de-burring bench, the Kit Marshal, Jackie Cunningham, Jimmy McDowell and the 3 A's - the Comet with Leslie Webb and Mr Spence the foreman. Castlereagh figured of course - running across the rugby pitch (where Cregagh F.E. College now stands) from Bell's Bridge - all to save one half penny. It was looking as if I would never be able to do that again. I also got my study books brought in - but I didn't get much done - I couldn't settle and I needed help - mechanical engineering theory (don't mention the maths) presented problems that needed explanations.

Autumn had just about passed when George Richmond got word that he would have a major operation the next week. As the surgeons delivered this decision to George, I actually remember that he accepted this with reservation - perhaps with some apprehension. After communicating this to George, to my surprise, Mr Hanna - more or less in the same breath turned to me and said "You can make arrangements to go home if you have someone to look after you - nothing much is doing for a while". And that was that. My mother came to see me that afternoon - and got a lift home with me in the ambulance, and as quick as that - it was a Thursday.

There is always something of an anticlimax in coming home after a long spell in hospital. After the accident, I would have given everything I possessed - not much I grant you, but anything, to get home. When I did get home I missed the hospital - the routine, the chat, the never failing unquenchable cup of company. Now things were quiet and I had to change gear again. It was in my own home that I met my own doctor, Dr Weir for the first time. He pondered a question with my father - " Would he (myself) ever get any useful use out of that leg?"

The New Year - I get a Walking Plaster

I knew that I was due to be recalled to Mr Hanna around the new Year and eventually a summons arrived from the External Orthopaedic Clinic at the Waveney Hospital, Ballymena. I believe it was the 4th of January - an ambulance arrived from the Waveney and I was whisked away.

When I arrived at the Waveney a wheel chair was procured and with a blanket wrapped around me I was wheeled into a waiting room. Forty years pass quicker than the awful feeling of total dependence. Only if you have been confined to a wheel chair - even for the odd day, can you know that awful feeling of helplessness. I sat for a long time. My fellow external patients and I were in a Nissen hut which was one of several used for outpatient work. It was cold - I think I had only my pyjamas on - and a full length plaster on my left leg.

Eventually - I was taken to the x-ray department - first an x-ray of the front of the leg below the knee - then one, lying on my side. By the time I had over 20 full length plasters put on, I would become very expert at flicking onto my left side for these x-rays. Then - I think I had waited about two hours, I was ushered into the presence of Mr Hanna. I don't recall the conversation. The x-rays were held up - some discussion took place with the clinic Sister and then he turned to me and said "There has been little or no progress - the bones are not uniting. I'm going to arrange for you to come back here tomorrow and meet Mr Baker of the Musgrave Park Orthopaedic Clinic - here". He probably said "OK?" and that was that. (Years later I was in the Waveney Hospital - I cannot recall what business I was on, but I saw Mr Hanna - in his white coat somewhere on the premises and made myself known to him. I regret to say that, for once, I forget what someone as important to me as Mr Hanna was, said to me or what I said to him.

So back home I went and the next day I returned. This time it was colder, the blanket seemed shorter - I think a button came off my pyjama top - and I felt even more insecure than before.

Eventually after a very long wait again, I was pushed into a side room and there I met someone who for the first time in six months of hospitalisation was to say, "Yes - it could be a leg once again". This man, fairly tall and speaking with an English accent spoke to me - he called me by my surname - this shocked me somewhat - not even during the regimental marches of the ward rounds did anyone address me thus. But come to think of it I cannot remember being called anything then! But, Mr Baker was a pleasant man and I think it was a greeting of the sort, "Now Cameron, old boy, how's it going". I remembered distinctly Dr Weir's query "Will he ever get any useful use out of it - that's the point?", so I asked him if I would ever be able to walk again. "Yes, you should be able to walk sometime" he said, "But we are going to have to give the leg a little help - some encouragement. I am going to put a walking plaster on. I want you to put half your weight on the leg - the idea is to try and stimulate growth at the fracture site".

Mr Baker said he would arrange for an x-ray in a month's time and I would be back in February. I then had a visit to the fitting out bay - not aircraft this time but for a pair of crutches.

*   *   *   *   *   *   *   *   *   *

So off to Ballymena again, there to go through that awful ritual of the plaster being cut down each side, the top lifted off, and trollied off for x-ray. The sister wielding the cutters knew of the agony I faced as the shears sped past the wounds but there was no other option in those days - but just to plough on. So Mr Baker looked at the new x-rays, but was undecided if any improvement had taken place, so on with another plaster and "I'll see you in a month". Back to Antrim! I had regained quite a lot of strength now, and was feeling, I suppose, still optimistic that the leg would start healing and looked eagerly forward to my March appointment.

Well the March appointment was kept, the shears, the x-rays and Mr Baker in judgement. After considering the situation, he turned to me and said "Cameron, old chap, I'm putting your name down for a bed in Musgrave Park Hospital. We will have to give you a bone graft to help this thing along. There is a waiting list but we will put you on the Priority list". And that was that.

*   *   *   *   *   *   *   *   *   *

During late June a horrific accident took place at the Le Manns race in France occasioning tragic loss of life, then it was July. A letter arrived, offering me a bed in Musgrave Park Hospital. I packed my bag.

Some time after I was on the waiting list for Musgrave Park Hospital an event took place that occasioned some unusual activity for me - my eldest brother Bill, got married. Being sort of mobile, I was able to go to the wedding on my crutches. This waiting period had provided some interesting asides. For example, I would some evenings hobble to the end of our lane taking a seat and await whoever would come by. Among these might be some of my contemporaries going by on a social outing - perhaps to see their girl friends. One of the latter had a simple request to make of me - could he borrow my watch, presumably to augment his person in this part of the rutting season. This also shows that not everyone had a watch in those days. I still have that watch - alas it no longer "goes". This is a convenient place to record a joke told against - if that is the word - a Presbyterian Minister who was leaving his congregation in Northern Ireland to take up a position in Canada (I understand this man had been a joiner by trade and he was a brother of a member of the Northern Ireland Education Inspectorate). His congregation presented him with a clock as a parting gift at a suitable social function and he rose to respond. "Dear friends, I'm so pleased that you didn't simply give me money, because as you know, money would go and this clock won't". Well, that's what I was told.

I have sped ahead of certain events. As I have recorded my friend George Richmond, was having an operation and I had told him I would write - when he would be sitting up and taking notice again. (In those days an appendix operation meant a stay in bed of five days and a hernia operation up to three weeks). So, I had written to George after about two weeks. I didn't get a reply for a time. Then his brother Adam wrote to me. George had not recovered from the operation - he died virtually without gaining consciousness - he had been buried before I even started to write! Later Adam came to see me. It was sad news.

But now, I was about to travel to Belfast - to Musgrave Park Hospital and there to become an "old boy' for the rest of my life.

Musgrave Park Hospital

I had been aware of the existence of a hospital called Musgrave Park from an early age, as a fellow pupil from my local primary school had been a patient in a hospital by that name - and it was somewhere in Belfast. During the months I was waiting for admittance, I did nothing to improve my knowledge of the place, I would be happy to be led there and back. But had I done so, there was a great deal I could have learned about the history of Musgrave Park Hospital. In the nineteenth and early twentieth century, one of the most influential and notable families in Belfast was that of Musgrave. They had engineering interests on the Albert Bridge Road, estate in Donegal and the family home was Drumglass House, Marlborough Park South, and built in 1854-56. This house was eventually bought in 1922 by Victoria College School as a hall of residence for boarders, Victoria College itself having been founded in 1859 by one Miss Margaret Byers as The Ladies Collegiate, Belfast. There were several brothers, one of whom was associated with Belfast Harbour, and indeed one of the channels bears that family's name, the Musgrave Channel.

On the 20th February 1920, the late Mr Henry Musgrave presented to the Belfast Corporation 90 acres of land, known as the "Model Farm", to be used as recreational and educational purposes. The Ordnance Survey Map published by the Ministry of Agriculture (1925) shows buildings as "Balmoral Industrial School" completed in 1859. Since then, a spire, apparently of ogee design i.e. an S-shaped curve, has been removed from the Belfry, and a wing to the North has been demolished. Otherwise, much of this impressive and red bricked building remains much as it was then, as does the former Agriculturist's Residence (with its curved gable) standing south of the former 'Balmoral Industrial School', and now an administration building at the hospital.

These buildings, as designed by Frederick Darley of Dublin (during 1852-59) were the nucleus of what became Musgrave Park Hospital, the Park lying on the junction of Stockman's Lane - it takes its name from an old cattle track, and Balmoral. The railway (formerly the G.N.R.) runs close on the Balmoral side.

Henry Musgrave had been elected and admitted an Honorary Burgess of the City in 1917, the highest honour that his fellow citizens could bestow upon him.

* * * * * * * * *

After war began in 1939, the War Office requisitioned part of the park, and the original red brick building - the agricultural school. Prefabricated Nissen huts were built for hospital purposes, and they and the former school, were occupied by American forces. The hospital was eventually taken over by the Ministry of Health in November 1944 as an emergency hospital, much of it being used to treat tuberculosis patients. In 1948 the Hospital Management Committee took over and by the time I got there, it enjoyed the highest reputation as an orthopaedic hospital. There has been continued expansion, with the Nuffield Unit in 1958, McKinny House (Nurses' Home) in 1967, and in 1970, the Withers Orthopaedic

Centre was opened. (I was to become acquainted with it in due course). A most recent development has been the construction of Meadowlands, a Care of the Elderly Unit. Along with all this development was the creation of a five unit Theatre Block.

However 'my' Musgrave, as in 1955, consisted of the large red brick building - used largely over recent years as a rheumatology unit, and the original Nissen Huts. This was the hospital I was waiting to receive a call to, in the Summer of 1955. When it came, it was to open an association with the hospital that goes on and on - either through further bits of 'running repair', fund raising - especially through the Mitre Trust - or even by providing entertainment, at patients' concerts etc (they are not hard to please nowadays!)

No brief history of Musgrave Park Hospital would be complete without mention of the orthopaedic surgeons I was to associate with Musgrave in those days. These were Mr Baker, Mr Martin, Mr Wilson and Mr Withers. There was yet another surgeon - he was the Senior Registrar at the time and younger than the others. He was to play a major part in my rehabiliation at that time, and continued to do so, until his recent retirement as a very prominent orthopaedic consultant in Northern Ireland.

I become a patient in Musgrave Park Hospital

Early in July, therefore, in 1955, an ambulance took me to Musgrave Park Hospital. I had been on the waiting list three months. Mr Baker had given me priority, not top priority, I remember this point being discussed by an orthopaedic Sister and Mr Baker at the Ballymena Clinic. It was considered by most of my family, that I was fortunate in getting in so soon. This was so indeed but I had considerable apprehension as to what lay in front of me. Above all was the fear of more pain. Every time the full length leg plaster was removed the level of pain was something akin to a prolonged session at the dentist. The plaster would be removed when an x-ray was required, for clarity I suppose. As already mentioned, large scissor-like shears cut down each side of the plaster. The passage of the shears past the knee and ankle was uncomfortable, but on approaching the area of the wound, areas where there was barely scar tissue over the ends of the broken bones, let alone muscle and skin, it became a time of extreme pain, literally raw nerves, I suppose, were being trod upon as the wretched shears made their way down past this area. It was at times like these when I recollected how the Nazis did experiments on people, their unfortunate prisoners, without anaesthetic in any form. How indeed could they do it?

Anyway, I was taken to Ward 2B, a place forever sacred in my memory. A red Nissen hut, it was one of many making up most of Musgrave Park in the fifties. It was there that I was eventually told that my leg had responded at long last and the 'little help' that Mr Baker said was necessary was 'doing the trick'.

Now I was allocated a bed on the left hand side of the ward, about four beds from the door. I found myself beside a fellow from Dungannon, I believe, called William Johnston. He had a cage over his legs, the usual indication of one having a leg in plaster. I soon met the Ward Sister, Sister Patterson who was to play a significant part in motivating me on the road to recovery.

My companion, William Johnston and I soon compared notes - I discovered that he had been out shooting the previous Boxing Day and upon going through a hedge had accidentally discharged the shotgun blowing a hole through his leg in much the same position as my own fracture, the lower third. This had necessitated a substantial bone graft and he soon told me (for I was very curious) that bone had been taken from his pelvic girdle, showed me the scar etc. "Was it sore?" "Well, not too bad". Since this was the only concrete evidence as to where bone came from for the graft I accepted that it was likely that this was where a piece would be removed from me.

It was good weather at that time in Musgrave, the doors and windows were kept open to keep the temperature down. This was important, many of the patients were unable to leave their beds - mostly lying in plaster casts of one sort or another. A common illness was that of the T.B. spine - my eldest sister was a Health Visitor working for the Northern Ireland T.B. Authority, at this time. (Eventually they worked themselves out of a job and she returned to general health visiting duties.) Some other patients had broken spines due to e.g. falling off the roofs of buildings, haysheds etc. Both these categories were indeed very long term illnesses. Those confined to a full body plaster lay on their fronts for two or three days, then were turned over to lie on their backs, encased all the while, though the plaster was split in two halves. Some had lain so for several years. What a life! As I took stock of my surroundings, I began to think I was the fittest in the ward.

Soon, I had my first experience of the ward rounds. This was a much less formal affair than the ones in the Waveney. Mr Baker appeared, dressed in a suit and he was not alone, there was another man there, wearing a white coat, with him. Mr Baker, lifting up my most recent x-ray discussed the case in great detail with this man. There was in the 'rounds' procession, apart from the staff nurse and student nurses, probably another doctor. However it was the man wearing the white coat who became centre stage in my subsequent life. He was the Registrar, and with Mr Baker about to go off on holiday, the operation on my leg would be performed by him. He was to do a good job.

In fact, he was to be my mentor, doing various running repairs and operations to my leg for the rest of his working professional life. He was shortly to become well-known as an orthopaedic surgeon and consultant. A day later my plaster was removed, or at least the top portion, and upon examination of the leg, the registrar told me that I was going to be allowed to go outside to let the sun dry the skin, as exposed when the top of the plaster was removed. "Don't give it too much sun, apply gradually, and don't fall with the leg in reduced support - you could put yourself back six months", he said.

So I was allowed out of the Nissen Ward with others and sat in the sun, getting my leg a nice tan. The trains were running by and one day, it just so happened that it was the 12th July, we heard the drums and marching feet. A visitor at this time was a young Presbyterian Chaplain - he may have just been deputising for the Chaplain - anyway, in he came. His name was Martin Smyth, later to become MP for South Belfast at Westminster.

Some of the operations that took place were of great technical interest to me. There was a young man, a long standing patient by the name of West. Earlier he had developed polio which resulted in the shortening of one leg (by 3 inches, as I understood it). The leg was stretched by traction, a painful process but I believe his surgeon, the late Mr Martin, Orthopaedic Consultant, managed to encourage the leg to 'grow' three inches, both legs now being the same length. This was good progress, but he fell one day and broke this leg, resulting in a shortening by one inch. To equalise the legs in length, it was decided to shorten the good leg by one inch. This was accomplished by cutting out one inch of the femur; I saw the x-ray of this leg as it was held up during the 'rounds' and I noticed that it had been cut at about 45 degrees, the piece removed and the ends brought together and held in place by a pin or pins. He came from Tempo, I seem to recall his father was in the police in that area. Eventually he went home, on crutches and I never saw him again. (Roy West eventually came to live near Kells, Co. Antrim. I only discovered this in 1996 and I decided to visit him. When I eventually arrived at his home, it was to discover that he had died quite suddenly, a short time before.)

Another long time man was Fred Johnston from Six Mile Cross, Omagh. He had been lying in plaster for the past eighteen months. I was to get to know him well in the next six weeks. The Ward Sister, daytime, was Sister Patterson, who ruled with a mixture of carrot and stick, kindly enough, firm and I think probably with a sense of humour.

The food in Musgrave was different or at least was presented in a different way - salads with hot, new potatoes, and potted herring, that's what I remember. As well there was a more relaxed atmosphere, which probably included visiting arrangements although it was not open visiting by any means. It was not a ward where people were suffering from life threatening illnesses. The illnesses were related to orthopaedic matters so the atmosphere was not the same as in a ward where people could be suffering from stomach complaints (tubes issuing from noses) or kidney or bladder complaints, with tubes disappearing somewhere below the beds of patients, perhaps terminally ill. Such inputs always call for quiet and measured behaviour, but orthopaedic patients don't usually have such constraints. There would be a coming and going of patients, from Fermanagh and Co Armagh, Down and Antrim and Tyrone. I was to meet a lot of people, patients and nurses. At nights when the ward settled down after the last visitors departed, a trolley would arrive - tea, coffee, hot milk, chocolate, it was good fare. This would coincide with the changeover, the night staff would arrive, and always there would be a slightly mystic figure, Night Sister Frazer, someone loved by the patients. Since it was always night when she appeared, she took on a Florence Nightingale form, gliding quietly through the ward - we never really saw her in daylight. Years later, I met her at Musgrave Park Ex-patients' Association meeting when she gave help to that cause - those were the days when I myself was to be seen rattling a collecting box in Ballymena, for the MPH Ex-Patients' Association.

I am still involved with similar activities at Musgrave Park today. First through the Northern Ireland Cycling Federation's efforts to raise money for the M.I.T.R.E. Trust (Musgrave is the best in rehabilitating everyone) and also as referred to helping to provide entertainment for patients, in particular at the very modern Meadowlands Unit.

After a week or so, a day was set for the operation on which so much depended - Dr Weir's words have never left me as he pondered to my father, "The main thing is will he ever get any useful use out of the leg?"

Anyway, I was prepared for the operation, and here a curiosity unfolded itself, when upon my pyjamas being removed, I was dressed in a large gown, crossed at the back and held by tapes, and another item of attire, this being a strange kind of napkin with four strings attached. It was known, I think, as a modesty cloth or something like that. You can imagine it as a large handkerchief, a handkerchief 'saddle' on which you would set your bottom on, and then secure the thing by tying the tapes in some manner or other. (Some wag in the ward maintained that it had to be worn so that the surgeons wouldn't know whether it was a man or woman they were operating on.) Anyway, on it went, and shortly, drowsy with the Pre-Med injection I was taken to theatre. After all those years I can actually remember waiting in an ante-room and I think it was there I was given the injection to 'put me over', the anaesthetist asking me to start counting. I would soon know where the bone for the graft would come from.

The Operation

The operation was over. I don't recall how I found out where the surgeon got the bone from - I knew that the absence of a wound on the pelvis meant that nothing had been taken there. However on my record I noticed that I had had a sliding bone graft, and eventually I saw in the new x-rays clearly how the fracture was now bridged by what looked like a piece of bone about five inches long by $5/_8$ inch wide, how thick I wouldn't know. It was held in place by two pins $1/_4$ inch diameter (6mm), they are still there. Later, a nurse experienced in orthopaedic theatre work explained that the piece of bone had been removed from sound bone just above the fracture. Then some bone had been removed above and below the fracture, to allow the 'graft' to fit in place.

Those of you who have had anaesthetics will be familiar with the slight discomfort of having to go without food and drink before such operations. I was no exception and after I 'came round' I was greatly desirous of having something to drink. I can actually remember that one thing I drank was appleade - I can distinctly remember that because when I became very sick afterwards I recall someone asking "Were you drinking that?" It was good to have the operation over and although confined to bed, I hoped that eventually, like my companion Johnston from Dungannon, I would be upon crutches again and 'on the mend'.

Sometimes, over the time from the accident, my mind would drift to Shorts. Occasionally I would receive a letter from the Apprentice Supervisor Mr Kirkpatrick or Mr Ossie Carlisle the Deputy Supervisor. Always the letter would begin 'Dear Cameron' and go on to hope I was recovering. At such times there would be memories of Austin Carson, always laughing about something, carefree always, a good fellow for me to be near, then my beloved Comet II - what had they done with all the 'Comet' parts (I imagine they went off to De Havilland's) the de-burring bench; the 3A wards, and all my peers, forging ahead in qualifications and their apprenticeship.

But I had little trouble in returning to reality and Mr Hanna's words 'Content yourself, you are going to be here a long time!'

I cannot remember too much pain and received only a few post operation injections. One day I was x-rayed just before the rounds. Mr Baker had returned from holiday and joined the Senior Registrar in the 'rounds'. I remember he asked me how I was feeling and upon hearing I was well, he looked at the x-ray, then simply said to the Registrar, 'Beautiful'. This sounded good to me. Another x-ray, two weeks now after the operation, produced good news: the Registrar, as he looked at the latest x-ray, said, "Well, calcification is starting to take place. After the stitches are removed and a new plaster put on, you can get up and start moving around". This was wonderful news indeed. Not all plain sailing though. For reasons I can now guess at I was prepared for the stitch removal as if I were to have an anaesthetic. I was taken to the theatre having been given a pre-med injection. The plaster was taken off, and the stitches removed. The leg had been opened from knee to ankle, thereby thirty two stitches had been inserted and these were now removed. However, the Registrar was now looking at the leg, viewing it from the foot towards the body and all was not well. "There is some bowing", he said, "I want to straighten it!" Yes, you've guessed - my befuddled mind went back to that wedging in the Waveney, and already this surgeon was taking the leg carefully in his hands and applying pressure. However at the first yell, he nodded to someone and I remembered no more until I discovered I was back in the ward. The leg was straight again (sadly, as events turned out, it wasn't to remain so, but that's for the future). A couple of days later, with the new plaster dry, I thankfully got my crutches back and was independent, in a sense, once again. I was up.

Some of the men in the ward I never forget. There was a man called Pat Crangle, I think he had a degree and came from Ardglass, but I don't know what the nature of his infirmity was except that his knee was in plaster and that the knee was bent at 90 degrees. He was on crutches, and I recall that Pat was a good singer. Then there was George, from Tassa Viaduct, Armagh. George had a modern record player and some great records of that period. When I say that at this time, Jimmy Shand had made the top ten (maybe top of the pops) with the 'Bluebell Polka', it says a lot for people's tastes, compared to that which obtains now. Some of the other records were of Ruby Murray with 'Softly, Softly' and others, Slim Whitman with 'Rose Marie' and 'China Doll', and James McCleod and his Scottish Dance Band. I was most impressed with this lot and visited George quite a lot - he was getting some discs removed from his back and wasn't moving much. Another great character from No. 2 Coronation Street, Markethill was a Mr White. He was a great companion and contributed much to my 'social life' in the ward, talked a lot to the nurses, he did.

I also remember a man called Alec Jess from, probably Dromore or the Saintfield direction in Co. Down. Another man I think his name was either McNeil or O'Neill. My chief interest here, was that he was a timekeeper for the Northern Ireland Cycling Federation. That year my cousin, Tommy Talbot of the East Tyrone Club, was the time trial champion, so that gave us something in common to take about.

There was a different interest in a man called Murray. He, upon learning that I came from Antrim told me something I found very interesting indeed. "Did I know the Steeple?" Yes, I knew the Steeple well, Sam Fawcett's domain. Now Sam Fawcett would have been described as a leading citizen of Antrim, being heavily involved in local politics. As well, he was associated with the tourist industry, owning a number of hotels, for example, Fawcett's Hotel in Portrush. He had owned a hotel in High Street, Antrim, but this was lost in a fire, before the Second World War. During my early days in Antrim, the site lay abandoned, a large area of grass and bramble chaos where the Northern Bank now stands. "Well", said Mr Murray, "I used to own the Steeple". I think this was just before Sam Fawcett acquired it. Today, it's the home of Antrim Borough Council, but during the 1840's and the time of the famine, it belonged to a Major Clark.

Dr Alexander Irvine recalls in his book "My Lady of the Chimney Corner" that he and his family were often very hungry, to the extent of clandestinely milking the odd cow. He also dug a few potatoes out of a field and took them home to his starving mother, who promptly sent him back with them! Then he went up to a hedge at the Steeple to get some sloes, and Major Clark put the dogs on him. Here he takes a new paragraph: "The sloe bushes are still there!"

Looking again at Shorts, for such a large company, I now had few contacts. Shorts was such a big place, that the only section of workers who knew anything about you were the ones in your centre who worked beside or with you at a particular time. As I had only moved into my new centre, daytime 'Swift', (I think I hated that aircraft, if things had gone OK, I would still have been on my beloved Comet II), nobody really knew me, Austin Carson would have, but sadly, he was no more. The result was that few of my friends in Centre 30, Queen's Island or Centre 24, Castlereagh, or my dispersed friends with whom I had worked on the Comet, or all the Push Halfpenny enthusiasts, knew anything about me and the ghastly accident from which I was endeavouring to recover. It was post Musgrave before I started to get a few visitors, among the first was Albert Henry, Gerald Alexander and Keith Martin, my Ballymena friends, and John Ferguson.

But now I was in Musgrave and I must have had some resignation in 'Whatever will be, will be', a current hit song. Would I ever walk again? Everytime I saw the x-rays of that shattered bone, I really wondered how such a thing would stand up to the wear and tear of life, ever again. But, people said that time was a healer. There the matter rested.

There was a man lying in 2B suffering from a broken back, sustained after he had fallen from a roof. He was turned from his front to his back every three days in his plaster cast. At visiting times, his wife and family, in particular a very bright and beautiful young girl were first to literally rush in to greet him. The memory of that young girl rushing in, arms extended, all smiles, has remained with me through time. He had been there 3 years!

So I was up again, able to visit all those still immobilised. Sadly I don't remember all the names, but I do recall certain beds that I would go up to and pass a word or two, then go to the well known guys, Fred Johnston in the corner by the door, George from Tassa, Mr White (I believe his name was Hugh White), Ivan Turkington from Lurgan, I believe, and so forth. Of great interest to me was a new arrival to a bed in the ward. He was Tommy Gordon who, with his brother Billy, made the famous Gordon racing cycle frame. Both of course were fellow competitors of Tommy Talbot and I had little difficulty in establishing a quick rapport with Tommy Gordon. Actually (haven't I a good memory?) Tommy had cartilage trouble with his knee as a result of a cycling accident and had the cartilage removed while in Musgrave. The Gordons came from Hillsborough where their father had the local smithy. Some years later I had the pleasure of visiting that smithy. There are still Gordon cycles raced all over - wherever men race bicycles.

Apart from the mystery of the loin cloth - there were many other strange things for a young Presbyterian away from home to learn. One evening, just after visiting time, I observed one of the men, bedridden through a back problem, having a visitor in the shape of a nurse. She stayed a fair time with him and then she was off. Now this man had been in the ward for about two years - perhaps more and as I understood it, had been on his back - sometimes encased in plaster - for most of that time. Imagine my surprise when, upon inflicting a visit on him shortly after the nurse left, he, nodding his head towards the door the nurse had left from, told me that "I went with that nurse for about eight months - but we're still friendly". Now "going with someone" to me meant a couple strolling down the Lough Road in Antrim perhaps, or, two people (man and a lass of course) sitting by the local rustic bridge. (Such favourite spots would have had the grass trampled away where countless feet had rested over generations - or standing room below trees was somewhere also that grass didn't get a chance to grow). Eventually, of course, people got cars - they had more comfortable places now to sit than the wall of a bridge over the local stream.

Now, my friend, as he told me this earth shattering piece of news was nothing but sincere in his manner of communication, and didn't elaborate upon the manner of his "going with the nurse", while presumably being strung up like some animal on a spit - turned every third day, as full length plaster cast inhabitants were. I didn't of course ask him. Now, with the hindsight of age perhaps I now understand the man. But then, I went away and pondered these things in my heart. There was obviously more to life than broken legs and backs.

The Nissen huts were big and spacious and not without drama. During heavy rain, it was not unusual to see a nurse or someone bring in a bucket and set it under the local drip. During the hot weather, the doors at each end of the ward - the outside "railway" end door, and the "tunnel door" could be opened as part of the air-conditioning equipment. But we loved our ward 2B - it was a place of surgical excellence, a wonderful relaxed atmosphere and very good food - I always remember those salads and the potted herrings. Recently I made another pilgrimage to that ward (now unused 1996), and found it in beautiful condition and nicely decorated. I know that as time goes on, these Nissen Wards will have to be removed - such are the demands of progress - wouldn't it be nice if Ward 2B could be preserved - as a memorial to the wonderful work pioneered and carried out there?

I was now in my second year in the kingdom of the infirm - I had been in second year of my apprenticeship when the bubble burst for me there. As I glided about the ward on my crutches and wearing my dressing gown, I was constantly advised to be careful - "You could put yourself back six months - if you fall". And Mrs Chivers used to polish the floor every day - she was a lady with plenty of conversation and I was deeply grateful to her for her part in my rehabilitation - she was a very important part of the team. The nursing care was without equal and my rapid recovery I'm sure had something to do with this. In particular there were two student nurses who were especially caring for me in those weeks of hope. One was Nurse Irene Gallagher who came from Omagh and the other, a ginger haired young lady - Nurse McCool from Dungannon (I have a very good memory!). I also remember a Staff Nurse Campbell - in white uniform (student nurses - were they blue or white?) Sister Patterson was firm and just but I imagine she ran a tight ship. I must not forget the administration - the Matron, Miss Chambers, her deputy, Miss Davies, and the Assistant Matron, Miss N McIvor, who came from Cookstown wherein part of my own roots lay. As I was later to discover, these were distinguished ladies indeed. Both Miss Chambers and Miss McIvor were former Alexandra Nurses, Miss McIvor having served in West Africa in that capacity in the Second World War. Our paths were happily to cross again, when she became the wife of a well known Antrim businessman, Mr Sam Anketell. When I entered the teaching profession, years later, Mr Anketell kindly signed the documents then necessary, for people going that way. He was a J.P. and an M.B.E.

Miss Chambers was, sad to relate, killed in a road accident, some years later. Unfortunately, once I left the caring hands of Nurses Gallagher and McCool, I never saw them again to thank them - I had a long path to navigate before I would be independently mobile again, and I was not able to visit Musgrave Park, for a long time.

Post Musgrave Park
The Healing Process

After I returned home from Musgrave, I resumed my roaming commission - where I had left off the previous June. By now, the smell of the new mown hay and the sound of the corncrake had gone. But other things of interest took place - the Ulster T.T. for motor cars over the Dundrod circuit had resulted in a horrific crash - not far from the hairpin. A number of drivers were killed, and the T.T. has not been run since. The monthly visits to the Musgrave Park Hospital clinic at the Waveney continued - Mr Baker becoming more optimistic - half weight one month, full weight the next month - I remember the first two or three steps that I managed without the crutches - a solo effort you might say. I believe it was then that I visited Shorts again - this time to the apprentice Prize Giving - later it became Prize Giving as more adult employees successfully gained qualifications. So I quietly hobbled in with the company I travelled with (including my father). I didn't see one person I recognised - except Mr O Carlisle - and I wasn't speaking to anyone during the whole proceedings. Shortly after, Mr Baker decided to remove the plaster for good (or so he thought). I should record that I also managed a visit - at least once, to see my old friends in Ward 2B, at Musgrave Park Hospital.

So the shears were out for the last time, as it were - just grin and bear the savage thrust over skin and bone - and that's it.

But what a surprise I got when I saw what the leg looked like - thin, misshapen, with all manner of dead skin etc.

However, sister cleaned it up and still using the crutches, I was sent home. It was an important homecoming because in two weeks time my eldest sister May was getting married and I would be able to go to the wedding with both shoes on. By this time I had accumulated a few pounds from Shorts sick fund and this enabled me to visit George Reid, the tailor in High Street - (now Wallaces). As was the custom then, I picked the cloth I wanted the suit made from, and Mr Reid measured me. Mr Reid had a very interesting manner in going about his business - a gentleman with a very gentle and mannerly approach - very professional. (As I recall, he told me that he had served his apprenticeship with the well known firm of Magees). His manners permeated the shop, his staff and probably his customers. I think his right hand man in those days was the late Mr Eamon Kearney (tragically killed in an accident involving a fire service appliance, later). Mr Kearney had mannerisms strikingly similar to Mr Reid - I often thought that their working partnership was very complementary.

So I attended my sister's wedding in a nice blue suit, two shoes on my feet and using a walking stick. The wedding was in the old High Street Church (now a commercial centre) and the reception was in Halls Hotel, that well known Antrim landmark and the site of the present day general stores. Her husband, Mr John Yoxall*, worked for the Hawker Aircraft Company and would eventually become Works Manager with British Aerospace at Dunsfold Aerodrome, Surrey. At that time he was involved in the Hunter project but later was closely involved in the development of the P1127, and thence the Harrier.

The Return to Work
Aldergrove and the S.A.4 Sperrin Bomber

As the months passed following the removal of the nineteenth full length plaster from my leg, my recovery was assisted by various therapies - physio, electro, wax baths, etc and eventually evidence of returning normality appeared - I had tried cycling, and even attempted some tennis. On recent visits to Mr Baker, I got the impression that I was being encouraged to think in terms of a return to "normal" living again - arriving in the Queen's Island for 7.45 am, and back to further education. The long hard slog towards the Higher National Certificate in Mechanical Engineering would have to start virtually at the beginning again - I would have to repeat much of what had already been studied. It was important that I get back to normality as quickly as possible, lest a psychological barrier should arise, and discourage the very thing for which I was striving - getting down to picking up the loose ends. There would be many of these to pick up, in addition to the normal slings and arrows that we all have to learn to step aside and avoid in this life.

So with the Spring of 1956, I was gladdened with the prospect of an imminent return to work and communicated my readiness to do so in a letter to the Apprentice Supervisor at Shorts.

Shorts were very accommodating to my desire to make a return, and accordingly, an appointment was made for me to attend a medical, by the firm's doctor, Dr Smylie, in the firm's medical centre, at Queen's Island. On the morning of the appointment, I was up at shortly after five o'clock - I couldn't sleep longer such was my excitement and anticipation. It was a beautiful morning, and I remember well, hitting a tennis ball against the wall close to the door of my home - the time wouldn't pass quickly enough for me. I had of course been given the all clear by Mr Baker, and Dr Smylie also agreed that a return to work should get underway. I then had an interview with the Apprentice Supervisory Staff - Mr Kirkpatrick, the Supervisor and his deputy, Mr Ossie Carlisle. This was the same Mr Carlisle I had, with some trepidation, asked for that "early" pass - to enable me to get home early for the evening classes in Ballymena Technical College during the first week at work. They made me very welcome, and to feel very much part of the big family of Short Bros. & Harland. During this interview, I took the opportunity to raise an issue, that had been close to my heart, ever since I saw the first Short's built Canberra fly off at Sydenham to Aldergrove - how I would have loved to have been transferred to Aldergrove. But my requests then always met with the same reply: "There are no apprentices at Aldergrove". But now I was back with a begging bowl - what now would be the chances of a "breaking in" period at Aldergrove? - it would avoid all that travelling, for a time. Mr Carlisle and Mr Kirkpatrick agreed to contact Aldergrove, to see if an apprentice could be "carried" and a few days later, I was sent a letter, instructing me to report to Aldergrove, the following Monday. I would arrive there by bicycle - a journey of seven miles.

*   *   *   *   *   *   *   *   *   *

(- Mr John Yoxall died 1997)*

For some time, I had been aware of a slight discomfort in my damaged leg - but accepted, that with increasing effort to be "normal" - trying to play tennis, walking, cycling etc, it would be expected that there might be some reaction. The Saturday night before the great day of my return to work, I was invited to a social evening at the social club of the Royal Naval Armament Depot, Antrim, where I took part in the odd dance - the leg reminding me of what I was standing on - with a mild stab of pain from time to time.

The following Monday, I joined a number of Antrim workers who were riding up to Aldergrove including a former fellow apprentice, Paddy McCormick from Randalstown now "out of his time".

I reported to the Foreman, Mr Nat Gould, and was directed to work with two fitters on a large aircraft in the main hanger. It was the S.A.4 Sperrin bomber. From the first week I worked in Shorts, I had been aware of the existence of this huge four jet bomber. One was parked on the hard standing outside the main workshops near the airport. Two such aircraft had been built by the company. The major components had been built at Queen's Island and transported to the Shorts Hanger at Aldergrove, where assembly took place, and was first flown as VX158, on 10th August 1951.

The Sperrin was Shorts response to a Ministry specification, B.14/46, and related to the need for a multi engine jet bomber, presumably able to deliver a nuclear bomb. Other aircraft manufacturers were promoting their designs - I imagine towards the same end. I have some reason to believe that Shorts, being a partly Government owned company were "allocated" the investigation of the peculiar configuration of the S.A.4 Sperrin, namely one engine on top of the other, on each wing. I think we called it a "figure of eight arrangement".

In the event, the contract for such an aircraft went to the Vickers Valiant, which became the R.A.F.'s first four jet bomber. It entered service in April 1955. Its introduction gave rise to the V-bomber force, Britain's strategic nuclear deterrent, and the Valiant was eventually withdrawn from service in 1965. The Avro Vulcan, first flown in 1952, was the first large strike aircraft in the world with a delta wing, and entered service with Bomber Command squadrons, in 1957, remaining as a first line strike capability, until 1982, having taken part in the Falklands War.

The Vulcan (B2 Version) was able to fly 4600 miles without refuelling. The Handley Page Victor, with a crescent shaped wing, was the last of the trio of V bombers and entered service with the R.A.F. in 1958.

This then, was the generation of aircraft of which the Sperrin was part, and by the time my apprenticeship commenced, the Sperrin was out of the running for the contract relating to a bomber, capable of delivering a nuclear bomb. It was therefore in "wraps" on the hard standing, as related. Of the two originally built, one VX161, was scrapped at Belfast. But now the other was at Aldergrove, to be modified as a test bed for the experimental De-Havilland Gyron turbo jet, a much larger engine and of much greater thrust than the original type of engine, first flown in the S.A.4. The Gyron was first fitted to the lower port position, and eventually, a Gyron was also fitted in the lower starboard position. This latter was the work which was underway when I arrived at Aldergrove in April 1956.

It was an exciting time for me - I had made it, and there was something very unique in that cycle journey, along pleasant roads up to Aldergrove. We rode up past Dungonnell, and at a crossroads close to the entrance to the now International Airport, we turned down a little narrow road, and about one mile along this road, a turn to the left brought us cyclists to the Short's Hanger. A light aircraft company now occupies this site, and hanger.

Normally, I can recall the names of most of the people I worked with in those days, but I forget entirely the names of the two fitters Nat Gould sent me to work with. Later, I was to work close by them again in the main factory. They were both very pleasant lads, and I was more than pleased with the prospects ahead - it was good weather, as well.

Disappointment

But sadly, fate was closing yet again - I was having enough discomfort in my leg to occasion a slight limp. One evening, when returning home, I happened to call at my brother's house. As I got off the bicycle and stepped on to the ground, a searing pain shot into my leg in the area of the original fracture, and I knew immediately that some tragedy or other had occurred. I was taken to the Massereene Hospital where no spare beds were available in the surgical ward, Ward 13. Now something unusual took place. The Massereene Hospital boasted four private wards. These looked out onto the front of the hospital apron, adjacent to Railway Street, and the windows of those wards still do. Now why anyone would have wanted a private ward to be lonely in, is something I have never really mastered. But any port in a storm, and I was duly wheeled into one of the private wards.

In due course, the leg was x-rayed and Mr Coyle, the surgeon at the Massereene, told me that I had a hairline crack in the area of the bone graft. The leg would have to be put in a full length plaster again. A few days later, I was surprised to have a visitor - Mr Baker. Mr Coyle had asked him to see me and there he was. He also verified that the source of the pain was a crack - it should strengthen up in about three months. However, no one noticed that during the cracking process, that the leg had taken a bow. It was to have unfortunate repercussions many years later.

It was a lonely place - that private ward. Soon, of course, I got crutches and was mobile again - I would venture out - occasionally down to the surgical ward, Ward 13. An interesting sequel to such excursions occurred shortly. I had a visit from the Matron - her name I think was Miss Anderson. She explained the state of play. Although I was in a private ward, I was not a private patient - I did not enjoy the rights and privileges of such a person. She also banned excursions from the ward - a private patient could sally forth, but not a common five eight. This was the going rate in those days, and no open visiting of course - my visitors must come at the appointed time.

Eventually after a week or so, this experience came to an end and I found myself at home once more - the castle in the air had tumbled.

It was now approaching Summer time and I would eventually return to work again in the Autumn.

Another return to work - Castlereagh

During my enforced return to crutches after the leg refracture, I was visited by a very old friend of day release days at Ballymena Technical, namely Joe Pollock. Joe was an apprentice at R.N.A.D. Antrim (Royal Naval Armament Depot) and a very clever fellow indeed, as manifested in our studies. He had taken, with some others, to swimming down at the "cut", where the Sixmile River enters Lough Neagh. This was the only place Antrim boys could swim in those days - long before the Antrim Forum pool was available. (Some also swam at "second bay", around the shore of the Lough). Joe had been telling me of swimming across the "cut" under water. I envied him.

One evening I had been expecting him to visit me - but he didn't turn up. Later, the next day, the breadman casually mentioned how sad it was about that fellow Pollock. "What do you mean"? I asked with some concern. "He was swimming at the Lough last night, and after getting into difficulty, was drowned". I was in some state of shock, and unfortunately I didn't get to his funeral. He came from Drumahoe, Londonderry and I have little doubt that academically, he would have gone far.

I believe he was taken from the water by Mr William Magill, a very fit Antrim man and a veteran of World War I and who must have been in his seventies then.

That summer passed slowly - then one day in August, as I progressed along the road on my crutches, a familiar aircraft passed overhead. It was the SA4 Sperrin. She would be leaving Aldergrove for Farnborough, to undergo extensive testing and would not return. By the time I had recovered, Shorts would have left Aldergrove for good, and I would have to pick up the pieces again in the trek back to the Queen's Island or another Short's out factory. During my enforced absence from Aldergrove following the re-fracture of my left leg, the S.A.4 Sperrin was fitted with the second "Gyron". The aircraft had now two of the original engines in the top positions, port and starboard, with the "Gyrons", of much greater thrust, in the bottom positions, port and starboard. As I understand, the test programme was successfully carried out at Farnborough, but the De Havilland "Gyron" project was abandoned, and eventually the surviving "Sperrin" was scrapped in 1958. One might speculate, that had the more advanced technology of the V-bombers experienced difficulties, the Short Sperrin could have had a back up roll.

During the initial design period of the original SA4 - two similar engines on each wing, one above the other, the proposed fin, rudder and tail plane for the new bomber was fitted to a Sunderland flying boat - VPP151, and this aircraft flew with this arrangement as part of the trials for the SA4. But fate decreed that I would play a very small part in the story of the Shorts SA4 - something that disappointed me profoundly.

Autumn arrived, and as I was now putting full weight on the walking plaster, it was decided by Mr Baker to remove the plaster - hopefully for the last time - and so it was. Anxious to get back to climb the ever increasing mountains ahead, and with Mr Baker's consent, I decided on trying work again. So, I contacted Shorts and was invited for an interview with Mr Carlisle - I think I met Mr Kirkpatrick as well. The conversation probably went something like, "Well, Cameron, old chap, the SA4 is now away from Aldergrove - we've pulled out of there. What we have in mind for you is to spend a few months in the Apprentice Training School at Castlereagh as Senior Apprentice. We will arrange for you to go into the classroom and rest any time you feel the leg playing up - we'll break you in gently".

I was returning to the scene of the 3A Wards again - I would be meeting all my old friends as the apprentice training school was right beside them. The wheel had turned another circle.

And so I met two men who were to play another important role in my life - Mr Bill Archer and Mr Wesley Black, the Training Manager and his Deputy, respectively. These two men helped me "back on my feet" and as well have been my well wishers to this day.

I would never run across the rugby pitch again - from Bell's Bridge to Dobson's Dairy. However, it was a triumph being able to be there at all. I had now to take the bus to Montgomery Road and walk carefully down to Shorts, Castlereagh Factory - and the apprentice training centre.

TELEGRAMS:
AIRCRAFT BELFAST

CODES:
BENTLEYS A.B.C. 2ND & 5TH EDN.

TELEPHONE:
BELFAST 58444

SHORT BROTHERS & HARLAND LIMITED
THE FIRST MANUFACTURERS OF AIRCRAFT IN THE WORLD
SEAPLANE WORKS   QUEENS ISLAND   BELFAST

Directors:
Rear Admiral Sir Matthew S. Slattery, C.B., D.Sc., F.R.Ae.S., Chairman and Managing Director
J. S. Baillie ;   Sir James H. Barnes, K.C.B., K.B.E., M.A. ;   Sir Sam H. Brown
H. G. Conway, M.A., M.I.Mech.E., F.R.Ae.S. ;   R. E. Harvey ;   D. Keith-Lucas, B.A., M.I.Mech.E., F.R.Ae.S.
C. P. T. Lipscomb, Wh.Ex., F.R.Ae.S.;   J. L. Parker, O.B.E., F.R.Ae.S.;   Sir Frederick E. Rebbeck, K.B.E., D.Sc., D.L., J.P.
Sir Reginald Verdon Smith, M.A., B.C.L., J.P. ;   C. F. Uwins, O.B.E., A.F.C., F.R.Ae.S.

PLEASE ADDRESS YOUR CORRESPONDENCE
TO THE COMPANY, P.O. BOX No. 241

REF. ....FCK/OC/IAG/App.

14th August 1956.

Mr. Robert Cameron,
Crosscannon,
ANTRIM.

Dear Cameron,

      Further to your medical examination of the 10th inst.
regarding the recommencement of your apprenticeship, I have arranged
for you to be transferred to the Apprentices' Training School,
Castlereagh, as and from Monday next, 20th inst.

      I have discussed your case with the Works Doctor and
Mr. Archer, but due to your leg injury it has been decided that you
should not be employed on work which will involve prolonged standing.
Will you, therefore, please report to Mr. Archer, Supervisor of the
Training School, at 7.45 a.m. on the above date, where you will be
employed in the capacity of Senior Apprentice in the Training School.

      A further medical examination will be arranged in due
course.

             Yours faithfully,
      for SHORT BROTHERS & HARLAND LIMITED

                (O. CARLILE)
          ASST. APPRENTICE SUPERVISOR

LONDON OFFICE: 17 GROSVENOR STREET, W.1   TELEPHONE: MAYFAIR 9541

Shorts

Mr Archer and Mr Black were an excellent team. Mr Archer had been at sea during the war as an engineer officer and was still a relatively young man. Mr Black was younger still - a former Shorts apprentice, until recently on the staff of the Drawing Office. They certainly didn't overload me with work.

I might say that Billy Kirk, a well known racing cyclist also was recovering from a broken knee - or knee injury - in some accident relating to a railway wagon. I'm unsure if that was the reason for him being in the training centre, as a senior apprentice. He was a marvellous illustrationist - drawing was his forte, and eventually he would move into the technical illustrations department of Shorts. But probably the apprentice I remember best was John Gill. I have the most pleasant memories of this most pleasant of young men and our paths crossed from time to time in the course of our apprenticeship. Then I lost contact with him for quite a few years but happily regained that when we were both in the world of teaching - he was then a Lecturer on Fabrication. But not for long. John became ill and passed away a very young man. Deep then was the intensity of my own personal disappointment and the grief of all who knew him.

So three months or so passed, and since everything seemed to be holding together, I received instructions to report to the main factory and be launched once again into my apprenticeship proper, in a centre there. It was to Centre 20, the toolroom, and to work under a Foreman to whose characteristics I was not a stranger. It was to be a difficult re-entry for me and a testing time. So I bade goodbye to my new friends of the training centre and my old friends out in Centre 24 - Billy Knowles, Mandy, Norman McGowan, Harry Keys and a host of others, and prepared to report once again to the main factory, after an absence of nearly two and a half years.

Centre 20 - The Balcony

Accordingly on a Monday morning, I presented myself at the office of Mr Sammy Gibson, Foreman of the balcony small tools squad, Centre 20, where one advantage was that the bonus was guaranteed. Sammy Gibson was not the easiest of men to work for, but I think in retrospect his bark was worse than his bite. He always appeared on the move, going to and fro. I can't remember if I ever enlightened him as to my recent experiences - years of lying in hospital beds, pain, operations and crutches. I probably didn't - to the world you are either fit for the job or not and until recently, disabled people in industry were unheard of. This was still the era when, in a family if one wasn't quite normal - and that covered a wide field of abnormality, they could end up being confined to some attic or upstairs room - locked in of course - something like the lady in "Jane Eyre".

Mr Gibson of course knew I was attending further education, and one day he stopped and informed me that during his younger days a scholarship to (if I remember correctly), Harvard, U.S.A., became available. He was short-listed with the late Mr David Alexander, Principal of the College of Technology, Belfast. "Alexander got it", he said - perhaps with some disappointment. On another day he presented me with a maths text book and upon opening it, I discovered that it contained very advanced mathematics indeed, and I often wondered just how academic he had been - I never found out if he had any formal qualifications. He was a white haired man and not destined to live to an old age.

My immediate boss was a charge hand called Lemon and he it was who gave me my first job in the tool room. Now, I recall how I reacted to this demanding place, to where I was to recommence my apprenticeship in earnest. Again, I worked on my own - I was responsible for the "job" and I hadn't a clue about much of it - but I did before I left, and the dexterity I acquired in the use of a file stood me in good stead in many a place in Shorts and outside it.

However, I was very weak physically, tired, and before long I started having a lot of pain in my stomach. Down to the First Aid at "Medical" I would go - where I had been passed fit for work by the Resident Doctor. After a few visits and some stomach mix I was recognised as "having been there before", and I was asked to see my doctor - "don't come back until you see your doctor". So I arranged to see Dr Weir, who after considering the matter gave me a "line" to be off work owing to "suspect Peptic Ulcer". Although I really felt unfit for work, the recent nightmares of being unable to go to work reared up before me. Somehow I resolved simply to take the medicine Dr Weir prescribed, dispose of the sick line and stay at work. I think I mentioned this to my father who was much concerned about the possibility of me not being able to go on and he suggested that I say to my boss that I "wasn't getting away with things too well - could I get a little help with the job" - these were my father's words. I used these words to Gibson and I think it was he who said he would have a word with the charge hand. Whatever happened, I persevered, and eventually my six months on the balcony came to an end - without being off on the sick. The stomach problem, caused by the sheer stress of the sudden return to real work and study, passed away. But I was to regard others so affected whom I met along the way of life with something more than casual sympathy. I have leap frogged much of what took place there - of substantial interest indeed - but surviving that six months is something I'm keen to record. It's important to realise, that in recording my experiences in the transition from immobilisation to activity again, I do so on behalf of all those in various walks of life who make that painful journey. If you want to feel "normal again", you have to be normal again and anonymous, in that you cannot "canvas" your passage - you don't carry a green flag in front of you. From time to time over the years I meet people who have been laid aside through illness and when I enquire "what's it like being back at work?", it is with anticipation that I listen to their response to what is a casual question from some. I have always considered this area to have been the most stressful in my whole apprenticeship - on top of the fact that it was my first taste of work for nearly two and a half years.

When a tool was completed, a sample component had to be made using the tool and then both would be presented for inspection. One also had to book the time taken on each tool completed. Gibson used to come down, put his glasses on and look at the time taken. Then he would comment "Too much time being booked against - such and such a job". I was not spared his comments either - even though I was just a second year apprentice. But I survived didn't I?

Note: Tools as made in the toolroom of a firm, might be defined as devices in which, or around, production components are formed, precisely and interchangeable.

I.Mar.E. elections to Council 1978

As a result of the annual ballot the following have been elected, to Council for the 1978/79 session.

President

D. H. Alexander, OBE, FCGI,
M.Sc.(Cantab), Wh.Sch.

Mr Alexander first joined the Institute as a Graduate in November 1922 while an Engineering Student at Imperial College, London. He was a Lloyd's Register Scholar from 1922/25 and obtained B.Sc. (1st class Honours) at London University. In 1925/27 he obtained Senior Whitworth Scholarship and in 1927 M.Sc.(Cantab). He was a Robert Blair Fellow at Harvard University USA where in 1928 he obtained an M.Sc.

In 1929 Mr Alexander was elected a Member of the Institute and was Assistant Engine Works Manager at Harland & Wolff Limited. He was Head of the Department of Civil and Mechanical Engineering at Sunderland Technical College in 1934-35 and later became Principal of the College of Technology in Belfast, a position he held until retirement in July 1967. He was awarded the OBE (Civil) in 1947. In 1955 he was a member of the Northern Ireland Panel to which he was elected Chairman in 1963. In April 1961 he was elected an Institute Local Vice-President for Belfast.

Mr Alexander was the first Chairman of the Northern Ireland Branch of the Institute and served on the Institute's Education and Training Committee in 1966, becoming Chairman in 1969. He was elected to the Institute's Council as a Vice-President in 1970 and has served on Council as such since.

Mr Alexander was the Institute's representative on the CEI Education and Training Committee for 1968, to 1973 and on Standing Committee "A", Qualifications and Registration (Chartered Engineer Section of ERB) from 1974 onwards. He was also Chairman of the Northern Ireland CEI Local Committee in 1969 and 1970.

This, in fact was the man Mr Sam Gibson spoke to me about - and with whom he was in contention for the scholarship to Harvard University, U.S.A. - David H. Alexander.

One day, at the College of technology, shortly after I resumed studies - post Musgrave Park Hospital days, I literally lost myself in the College and I made enquiries of someone as to the way. I found out later that the man inquired of was Mr D H Alexander. Some time later circumstances brought us together again, and I was privileged to enjoy many occasions of fellowship with him. Long after normal retirement, I would hear him say that next week he would be off to London, or Singapore or elsewhere - on business relating to matters and transactions of the Institute of Marine Engineers. The extract above, is from the June 1978 issue of the M.E.R. (Marine Engineers' Review) magazine. I meant to ask him, what he did in his spare time, but somehow I never got around to it. I wonder what he would have said?

Finally back to work and study

I was now back to work, it was September and in September the Further Education day release classes (and evening classes) also recommenced. My enforced idleness from education meant that my contemporaries had now moved years in advance of me. I decided to make a fresh start, so I enrolled in a class at the College of Technology, Belfast. It was the shaky start to what would turn out a happy and successful association. But it would be shaky for a time as I tried to adjust to a new routine of work and study - and some very long days. Leaving Shorts at 5.05 p.m. left a couple of hours to be passed before an evening class commenced.

On the evening of the first evening class, I was passing some time around the City Hall, when I met a fellow apprentice from Shorts who would also be joining my class. (A "class" would consist of one evening class and three others held during a one day release from work). My new companion was Raymond Miller who came from Randalstown and he has been a lifelong friend since. However on this evening we had business to do - find where such and such a place was. Such and such was additional classroom space, accommodated on the first floor of a disused mill on North Howard Street, off the Falls Road. The Central College - the College of Technology in College Square, could not accommodate all the students wanting to attend classes in various disciplines, and primary and secondary schools around the city were used for evening classes of all descriptions. Now a new concept in provision would be tried - redundant mill floor space and the one in question was known as Forth River Mill. I believe it had formerly been known as Greeve's Mill. But now the first floor had been cleared, spaces the size of an average classroom were provided by "corralling" the area by (about) eight foot high sheets of board or lamina of some description. Since there were no ceilings as such over these classrooms, if one sat at the back of the Maths class and English was being taught "over the hoarding behind you", you stood a good chance of learning more English than Mathematics!

But what about the other out centre schools? Well, over the next few years, I was to become very familiar with names like, Porter Memorial, Kelvin, St. Mary Magdaline, Park Parade, Botanic and others. Now for this important year of transition for me, I was to attend Forth River Mill for the evening class and the day release classes. I was having to repeat a year and together with the two years plus I had spent "on the sick", it meant that I was now three years behind the original group I had started off with. This was going to take some catching up.

I was at a night class at Forth River Mill when a great divide settled upon civilisation - I heard someone singing "Rock around the clock". Bill Haley had appeared on the scene and with him the demise of traditional music as I knew it. Being interested in traditional music, for me as for many, it was a watershed. I can never overlook this man because he was the influence - even perhaps more than the Beatles, to change a complete way of life, a style and discipline of life - not to mention the wholesale destruction of graceful dancing. Jimmy Shand would never again make it into the charts!

Some years ago, when travelling by car, I switched on the radio to hear a recording of the late Betty Staff (of teaching ballroom dancing fame) being interviewed. She was asked what was the most single entity that brought about the demise of the traditionally high quality music associated with dancing. She answered in two words: "The Beatles".

* * * * * * * * * *

Will he ever walk again?

It is no secret, that many people meet with accidents, or become afflicted with illness, or disease, in various degrees of severity.

For some, healing comes quickly, and any injury etc is rapidly forgotten as that person gets back to their normal routine of recreation and vocation. A full recovery is effected. For others, sadly, recovery does not take place, and lives pass away.

Others survive - perhaps narrowly and painstakingly so - but are unable to return to their normal routine of work and leisure. Some might be even confined to a bed or to a wheelchair, to using walking aids, or other restrictions, as society attempts to side line their careers and prospects as irretrievable. They will probably never make another contribution to the Health and Social Services Scheme.

But there is another category, and in it are those who successfully cross the line, that separates the latter from the former; perhaps crawl over the line would be a more accurate description of this transition. However, they eventually arrive on the job market again, and will hold down a job when far from physically fit - that headache, a reminder of the plate inserted beneath the scalp, or that dull constant ache in the knee - a reminder of better days.

A Raison D'etre

As a result of injuries or a debilitating disease, a person may manifest what he or she has been left with, even though every effort will be made to disguise such outward indicators, as much as possible. It is among these written lines, that the reason for wanting to publish a book like this will be found. All the rest of what is written might be anybody's way of life, except in so far that in my case, a near irretrievable disruption and injury would give concern, real enough for significant people to question the possibility that recovery would be sufficient to allow a new start on my apprenticeship - and on a hefty educational mountain as well. At one time, such things disappeared from my "screen" - I couldn't see the way ahead for such contemplations. But I would eventually scramble over the line (albeit at the second attempt) and regard myself in category four. For those who suffer damage to a leg or legs there is no "let out" of the unfortunate fact that people have to walk on legs - one cannot put them in a pocket if they don't work well - as one might do a damaged arm. Legs are weight bearing components, and in normal life affect the way one performs in walking, running, jumping, lifting heavy loads etc. Now if one of these legs gets damaged badly enough, then none of the above operations might ever be performed properly again. If the owner of such a leg is entrusted with a job, then all these things may have to be attempted. Certain diseases will bring about the same conditions of abnormality.

However, if appointed to what is considered a normal position, normally done by fit men or women, then the person concerned has to appear as normal as possible and go the full fifteen rounds.

On coming back to work after such illnesses a person may not be able to put the feet down properly when walking - a light step and a heavy step may draw mirth from unfeeling observers. Some people are base enough to imitate such steps; or there may be a limp, stiff neck or stiff knee. I have seen all such manifestations of disability and usually the people who have them "pull out the stops" and get on with the job. There were a number of apprentices to my knowledge who had suffered attacks from tuberculosis, and one who was completely white haired.

Ill people who successfully make a comeback, often do so at the extremity of their will power and physical recourse - they are "running" to keep up with the others, who are walking. Surely one of the most distressing and poignant documentaries to appear on the screens of our televisions recently, has been that made about the lives of the brave young men who flew the Spitfires especially during the Battle of Britain. Although often able to bail out of their damaged aircraft when shot down, they suffered appalling facial burns from blazing petrol tanks just in front of them. The wonderful work of the New Zealand surgeon, McIndoe, enabled these brave men to face life again sometimes with rebuilt faces. But it was never easy to disguise the fact that they had extensive surgery - maybe fifty operations or more - skin grafts, bone grafts to rebuild noses or chins. I often wonder how Britain compensated such men - men who faced the might of Hitler on behalf of so many others - and got a life sentence for it. But these were special men - it was this speciality that put them in the Spitfires in the first case. In spite of such adverse circumstances, many reached executive positions in industry, afterwards.

An interview with one man summed up a big problem. He was asked what had been the worst moments of his continuing ordeal. His answer was, "The children. When I am travelling, say, by public transport, and a mother gets into the carriage with a child or young children, I am soon aware that they have spotted my face - I am at once an object of curiosity, even mirth, and then the inevitable tugging at the mother's arm - drawing her attention to me - seeking an explanation or comment about such a strange face".

When I got home from the Waveney Hospital, Dr Weir, my panel doctor, visited me from time to time, during which time opportunity was taken to write the odd "doctor's line". He usually made these lines out for a lengthy period - probably a month at a time. One day he was standing talking to my father on the pros and cons of my recovery as things were moving very slowly, recovery wise. Dr Weir was and happily still is, a man who comes to the point very quickly. "The important thing", he said, "is whether he gets any useful use, out of that leg".

That was precisely the crux of the matter - you need two legs to bear your weight and more, and my shattered leg didn't seem to want to know, at this stage. Shorts would be literally hundreds - almost thousands of miles on crutches away. The months passed slowly.

My corner window in Ward 3,
Waveney Hospital, Ballymena.

The Waveney, February 1996, all boarded up and deserted.
"My" window - top left at the Waveney Hospital.

With my father and niece Margaret
(left leg is still in plaster).
Car is Bill's Austin Seven.

"My Ward" and my first bed - the "top corner bed in Ward 3" inside the door.
This view is from my final corner in Ward 3, Waveney Hospital, Ballymena.
This is where the "rounds" took place - led by Miss Hamilton, the Matron.
Now deserted, Ward 3 awaits its fate.

Musgrave Park Hospital Ward 2B, in beautiful decorative condition, on another pilgrimage, 1996. Now unused, it was finally in use as an occupational therapy centre. My bed was beside the first window, and it was there that my surgeon told me that the bone graft was looking promising. A place full of hope and memories that I am thankful for today.

The Massereene Hospital, Antrim - also about to be closed - according to speculations, Christmas 1996. The former surgical ward, Ward 13, was first floor to the left of entrance door. The private wards, (4 off) were first floor to immediate right of entrance door. I spent a strange yet interesting week there - post S.A.4 days.

Ward 2B (foreground) and other wards, with the original "Model School" in background - Musgrave Park Hospital

Aldergrove: The S.A.4. Sperrin bomber, the modifications completed with two De Havilland "Gyrons" in the lower positions and the original "Avons" in upper positions. The Shorts hangar is behind the S.A.4. (Courtesy: Short Bros. & Harland Ltd.)

Milkbar - thought to be an early I.T.L. (Irish Temperance League) cafe. Note the wooden chairs etc. On offer: "Why not try our special three course lunch 1/- (one shilling).

Three other companions in Antrim of those days - from left: Johnny Kinnen (ex Derry City right back), Matt Quigley, drummer in Antrim Pipe Band, and Scott M'Elrea, fellow apprentice in Shorts.

B C, Matt Quigley and Johnny Kinnen

Chapter 4 - The struggle back begins in earnest

Some Asides and Push Halfpenny

For many apprentices, diverse opportunities arose from time to time that transcended the business of building aircraft. A couple of examples would not be out of place.

There lived in those days a certain joiner - in the joiners' shop. Here it was possible, for the princely sum of five old shillings (25 new pence, referred to by some as a dollar), to obtain the complete cuttings of wood and plywood (even nails and glue - to build a modest tool box complete with two drawers. Remember that I was working in Centre 20 - the tool room balcony under the beady eye of, as already mentioned, one Sammy Gibson. May I just say that Sammy Gibson was a man, not economical with words in the field of verbal communication and used numerous adjectives - many not found in a Sunday School teacher's preparation. However the work of assembling tool boxes usually was carried out during lunch time and the box was eventually finished complete with a beautiful set of stainless steel wings, through which one entered the key to lock and unlock the work of art. In addition to the aforesaid bits and pieces, Aladdin the joiner also supplied the lacquer to paint the box. Alas, one morning I arrived to find that someone during the night shift, had stolen the wings, and I made another pair of duralium. They are still on the box, which I have to this day.

Transcending simple things like work and even important things like making tool boxes, was push halfpenny. I seem to associate Castlereagh again as being the centre for the most devout and maniacal push halfpenny players - although the cult spread to many other regions. But at one time in the main factory we had a beautiful formica pitch, complete with nails for goal posts.

Once the horn for the break sounded (or before) contestant apprentices would rush from all the compass points and soon the shouts of "shot" sounded - indicating a goal of some merit being scored. Even in a game of push halfpenny it's amazing how fouls might be accomplished. There were corners of course. The correct way, consensus ruled, was to strike one's penny (old penny, of course) with say, a six inch rule. It should then strike the halfpenny in the desired direction of the goal mouth, but sliding actions were sometimes resorted to where rule, penny, and halfpenny were mutually propelled to goal, inviting loud cries of protest and outrage from the opposite side. But there were certainly games at the airport as well, as the skills moved around when apprentices moved from centre to centre. Sadly my memory fails when it comes to placing names to the contestants of the day - except for one area - I cannot be sure perhaps Castlereagh again where two of the apprentices came from Carrickfergus. One was an apprentice of a fairly serious nature and to distinguish him from the other apprentice he was called "Old Carrick" (or sometimes "Brown Carrick" on account of his overalls). This was because the other Carrick apprentice known as "Young Carrick" was the very opposite in character - always on the move, involved in various activities of one sort or another, being sought by his journey man fitter and never found save - when the bell went, none was more punctual to enter the push halfpenny fray. Thus "Young Carrick" and "Old Carrick" became landmarks of the game. I can't recall "Old Carrick" ever laughing - I think he wore glasses - and always his brown overalls. He was, I think a serious F.E. student - he has probably a good job now.

Ned Moore - what he was saying

Shortly after I went to Centre 20 and the balcony, I was aware of someone working close by - a small man, who wore spectacles and as I recall, a brown shop coat - not overalls. (Foremen and above wore white shop coats with title embossed - charge hands wore brown coats - title embossed - on left hand of chest - possibly on the collar as well). Anyway, I was soon to be glad of this person's proximity. Having been always fairly slow on the uptake of things, I likewise found tool room work mysterious in parts - quite incomprehensible in others.

Strangely, throughout my apprenticeship, I estimate that I only spent ten months working as a fitter's apprentice - all the rest I worked alone - largely because I was an apprentice fitter/turner and of course when on turning work I had a machine of my own.

However, I learned my trade by degrees. Ned Moore on hearing that I came all the way from Antrim began telling me of how years ago a fitter had worked with him on the tools - during the war. He apparently had a high regard for this man whom he understood was now living somewhere about Antrim. I inquired his name. "He was called Harry Glenn", said Ned. "He was a good fitter and I think he married a woman who owned a farm of land". Around this time Ned gave me a little booklet - a two page, of card material and known as an "Istantus". This was the only "Istantus" I was ever to see. It contained all the information that one needed to drill the correct diameter of hole for tapping all sorts of threads etc and other important information. I recall how he looked at it with some affection - it seemed as an icon to him, but he parted with it and I have it to this day. The things that one remembers.

However I digress. Shortly after hearing of this lucky man who married the farmer's daughter, I was travelling home in my normal bus from Smithfield, where I usually tried to get a window seat because I did a lot of studying on the bus journeys. On this occasion, after acquiring the desired seat, I was joined by a man of fairly stocky build carrying a raincoat over his arm. After a while, he passed some comment on what I was studying.

This eventually led to my disclosure that I was a Short's apprentice.
    "I used to work in Shorts myself during the war", said the stranger. "Where are you working , exactly, in Shorts?" he followed. I said I was in the tool room.
    "Funny - I worked in the tool room myself", he said.
    "Did you happen to know a man called Ned Moore, by any chance?", I asked him.
    "I knew wee Ned Moore well", he replied, "I actually worked beside him - a very decent wee man he was".
    "Funny you should say that", I came back unwarily. "Just the other day Ned was recalling how during the war he worked with a man who, he believes, is now living in Antrim or thereabouts - a very good fitter - apparently he married a woman with a wad of land - took himself off to the farm".
    "Did he now", rejoined my companion, "You don't recall his name?"   "Indeed I do - I remember it distinctly - it was Harry Glenn - you must have known him if you worked with Ned - did you?"
    "Oh yes I knew him" said he laughing - "I'm Harry Glenn".

Little did I know it at the time, but that meeting - even meeting Ned Moore who provided the introduction, was of significance and had a considerable hand, I believe, in shaping my later destiny. Eventually I was to work with Harry Glenn.

More on Centre 20 - The Tool Room

Apart from Ned Moore, there were others who worked in the tool room, Centre 20, and with whom I became very friendly. There was a fourth year apprentice, Owen Donnan (a Presbyterian, who taught me "Kevin Barry"), Ken Parvin, who, I believe later went to Canada, and one Alan Smylie, who lived on the Deerpark Road, Belfast. He was friendly with Owen, and used to come round to our bench to have his tea. Alan and I became close friends, and I recall that he always wore a pair of heavy boots. He was quite tall, and I remember how, when he came around for the tea breaks, he was not very particular as to what job or drawing was sent flying as he ascended a bench top, boots and all, and made himself comfortable. He was a good companion, and very supportive of me, as I was still quite weak in places. Alan had a certain disdain for authority, and against it each day, did those boots carry him. There was another apprentice called Richardson. Someone else I was to get to know better later, but whom I met about this time, was one William Stevenson (Steve). An interesting memory I carried away from the Balcony, Centre 20, was that of a "marker off"- a fitter who had "graduated" from the file to the scriber. He was one of several, whose job it was to mark off work to appropriate dimensions, to which others would work to. Now I recall this man as pleasant, and somewhat laid back - he seemed to find the going fine and not an excitable type. I understood his name was Taylor and it was said that he had served in submarines. As this account will show, I later became interested in tracing the history of certain submariners and certain submarines, and many were the books etc that I perused in search of information. Among these, was the book, H.M.S. "Storm", the S-class submarine of the Second World War, and written by her commander, Edward Young, the first R.N.V.R. officer to command a submarine. Upon looking at some photographs in this book, was one showing the gunlayer of "Storm" - a man by the name of Taylor. The face was identical to what I remembered sitting at the marking off table. I have not, so far, been able to verify, if the gunlayer and the marker off were the same man.

After six months, I, like others, was due a transfer, which I expected would be on to an aircraft production line. But upon my transfer I was off to the airport to work on the jigs in which the nacelles of the Britannia aircraft were to be built. Jack Donnelly was the Foreman, and the squad was known as the "foreign legion" as it was so far from the main tool room base, at the main factory. The building was known as the "Comet" hanger, as it was intended to build the Comet II's there - or at least final assembly, and flight and service. This was for me, a nostalgic blast from the past - the ill fated "Comet I".

The nacelle is the outer covering of an aircraft engine, and each of the four nacelles of the Britannia, was about the size of the fuselage of the "Swift" fighter, on which I had worked with Austin Carson.

The jig is simply a large (in this case) square frame, of suitable length, so that the component parts of the nacelle - frames, stringers, skin perhaps, other bits and pieces, can be located at tooling points and completely built. Then the nacelle is removed and another nacelle is built - to exactly the same specifications as the one before.

The jig has to be built first, and I was to work with a fitter, whose first name was Victor.

Now, at that time in the "Comet" hanger, production work was already advanced on certain Britannia components, and there were quite a number of my former colleagues from various places in the main factory now working around the "Comet" hanger, either on tool room work, or on the production lines. Among these were Alan Smylie, Ken Parvin, and William Stevenson (Steve) and a host of others, whose names escape me. Now, about a dozen of us gathered at a long narrow bench - I cannot imagine what its use was - for the "breaks", and sat along this narrow creation, not unlike the manner of migrating birds in Autumn, prior to departure for warmer climes. And indeed there was much chirping about the journeys of life that lay ahead - especially when inevitably these apprentices left the nest at Mother Shorts. Just at this time (about eight months or so after my return to Queen's Island) the predominant conversation was about going to sea, as soon as they were "out of their time". I remember Ken Parvin talking about a fitter he was working with who regaled Ken with tales about "going up the old Bos" - the Bosphoros Straits, between the Sea of Marmora in Turkey, and the Black Sea. Another apprentice spoke how his mate (the fitter he worked with) told him about coming across the Bay of Biscay in a ship which, after losing a plate on its box (or hollow) rudder, couldn't move the rudder, owing to the weight of water which filled it up. And Alan Smylie topped it, with the story of how his father had helped change a propeller at sea - flooding the ship forward and pumping out aft, in order to lift the propeller out of the water. But meanwhile "Steve" - pronounced Steve-e, had stolen a march on them all. It was as if "Steve" had been on a war patrol, while the rest of us had not, because, in one of his move arounds, he had been sent to the maintenance department - and to work on the boilers, the huge Lancashire fire tube boilers, that supplied the heating elements with energy, and any other requirement, for steam or hot water. (Incidentally, the same boilers that I had used to acquire boiling water, for the tea cans of the men working on the "Swift", during the last few weeks before my accident).

Steve was definitely bound for sea, and was much revered by his fellows, for his knowledge put him miles ahead the others in "hands on" experience in an area significant for would be marine engineers. I must record that my memory of Billy Stevenson is of a person of fairly serious but very even temperament, very nice to know, and one who was never heard to speak ill of anyone.

But as I sat on the periphery of this group - at the end of the long bench, my left leg cringing protectively beneath my right one, I was almost ill with homesickness at the mere thought. How could they think of leaving home and comfort, to launch forth in a narrow tube of steel, further and further across the deep? No doubt, the chat continued, but so did the push halfpenny - the brand imported from Castlereagh and many were the accusations about foul play regarding the use of whatever was employed for dealing the blows on the coins. But like the departing birds in a watery autumn sun, the "birds" of that narrow bench were dispersed in due season, I believe our paths did not ever cross again, and I never knew if any of them ever went to sea.

"Fast to its close ebbs out each little day".

It is interesting to recall, that during this very nice period of work in this area, I cannot remember meeting one obnoxious character. Two new apprentice friends were made, one William Quigley, and one Ernie Loudon. Now about this time, an advert appeared in the local press, inviting applications from engineering students who hoped to study for the Ordinary National Certificate in Engineering Disciplines during the next session, for places on full-time off the job courses - leading to the Certificate examinations. I had the temerity to make an application.

This nice time coincided with an interesting journey I was to make on the Friday before we started our summer holidays. It was an anniversary I was unlikely to forget - the last such occasion when, after collecting (some) of my tea money, I locked my toolbox near the "Swift" assembly lines, and started my inexorable journey out of Queen's Island towards my date with destiny, on the Cushendall Road outside Ballymena.

I was to fly to England from Nutts Corner, and visit London and the South of England - Surrey especially, as I would be staying at the home of my sister, May, at West Weybridge, whose husband John Yoxall was then a senior draughtsman with the Hawker Aircraft Company at nearby Kingston-upon-Thames.

Now time marches on, and shortly after I returned from the July holidays, another shift took me out of the squad but still in jigs - this time for building the fuselage of the Photo Connaissance Canberra bomber, an aircraft that is possibly still flying, as it was highly successful in that role. These jigs were constructed fairly central in the main factory, and convenient enough for me to drop around and see Len Palmer, Billy Taggart, Billy Riddles and others of my early acquaintance. I was now considered mature enough for Billy Riddles to confide in me what his opinion was of the current squad of young de burrers - not like the good de burrers of heretofore! A current song at the time was "To see someone's picture, where my picture hung!"

So I duly presented myself to Mr Billy Neil, the Foreman, and soon found myself working with a fitter called John Parkes. It was there that I also met a fitter called Tommy Bryson (an old steam man, from his days as an engineer officer with Shell Tankers). Tommy, I'm pleased to say now lives in Antrim, and is a close friend of mine. Our paths crossed shortly after he came to live in Antrim, by which time I was teaching in the local Further Education College. I was doing some work, in the field of Adult Education, including an evening engineering class, where a great variety of work was undertaken and interesting things produced. A number of people worked on models of various things, and Tommy Bryson excelled, in producing steam engines of the utmost magnificence.

It's of some interest historically, to recall methods used in working out calculations at this period in time. Generations of students had relied on logarithms to help solve problems - in multiplication, division, roots, powers etc. Another aid was the use of the slide rule which, while being less accurate than logs, was adequate for most calculations. Having mastered logs with some difficulty, I tended to shy away from this newer innovation like a horse before a stone wall. (Eventually to survive, I had to knuckle down and use it - I couldn't have lived without it). Close to me, worked one of my day release class mates, one Bobby Madine (of swimming fame), so the odd homework was sorted out to our mutual benefit. There was "life during work".

Now another Shorts apprentice I made acquaintance with at this time, was Kevin Doyle, originally from Ballyclare but now living in Antrim. He was also a student at the College of Technology and was completing his Higher National Certificate in electrical engineering - at the senior trade scholarship. I would frequently travel home on the same bus with him and on one occasion, I must have mentioned to him my reluctance to involve myself in the new technology of the slide rule. He was of course completely conversant with it himself, but he pointed out to me something I hadn't dwelt upon. "You know", he said, "some of our class started using their rules the other day to multiply (something) by twenty-five - I simply multiplied the thing by one hundred and divided by four conventionally - I had it done before them". Kevin later became a teacher of mathematics, and eventually head of Academic Studies at Magherafelt Further Education College. Another Shorts apprentice, an old friend from Ballymena Technical days, and a fellow traveller from Antrim, was Scott McElrea.

He later joined the Civil Service. When the cancellation of the "Comet" contract caused widespread dispersal of many "Comet" apprentices, I was transferred to the "Swift" contract. Imagine how green with envy I was when Scott got a transfer - to Aldergrove, to work on Canberras!

Such is the luck of the draw!

But, time came for another shift. This time I was to leave the tool room and not return. I had acquired a lot of skill there, but shortly before Christmas, I was transferred back to production - to the Britannia Freight Door.

Just before that happened I was to witness another wave of redundancies - four hundred - the same number which followed the collapse of the "Comet" contract. The squad of tool fitters on the now almost completed jigs for the P.R. Canberra, were thought to be in the front line for the "chop", and the mood was sombre. Nobody knew exactly where the Dead Hand would strike, but the Friday arrived when notices were due - along with the pay packets. I imagine a number of my colleagues had lumps in their throats that day! Speculation and rumour was rife, and even John Parkes, one of the most carefree men I have ever known, was not his usual laughing self. I remember the situations of some of the men being discussed. One such young man (whose name I remember well) and not long out of his apprenticeship, was the owner of a beautiful new car, the then state of the art Hillman "Californian". It was being talked of as being on the "never, never" - hire purchase, and shaking heads indicated that "it would have to go". When the pay packets duly arrived at the usual table, fitters were reluctant to go down to collect, preferring to wait and count the number who had, by going down to the table and collecting their pay, received their dismissal notice or otherwise. The young man with the Hillman asked me to go down several times to find out who had got word to "go". Eventually, he collected his pay and found that he was one of the four hundred. Losing a job on which a family's fortune depends, is indeed a sombre business, which doesn't require expanding.

So I left Centre 20 and moved back to - the "Comet" hanger, at the airport - this time to work on the freight door of the Britannia. As well, I had managed to enrol in third year level studies for the Ordinary National Certificate in Mechanical Engineering. I had just managed enough in the examinations sat earlier, to progress. It would be one day and two nights of study - but I had applied for the Junior Trade Scholarship. If successful, I would be granted full-time study, February until June, to complete studies for this examination.

Before the Evening Classes at the College of Technology, Belfast

There was always something of a problem concerning passing time between work and evening classes. A couple of hours or so had to be 'punched' in, but where? One can understand that cafe owners would not be over the moon, if someone occupied a seat in their nice warm cafe and only bought a cup of tea during a two hour occupation. There were times when one couldn't afford much more, and produced a couple of sandwiches to go with the tea. The "welcome" might be extended through the purchase of another cup of tea - or a bun. In fairness to those cafe owners whose premises I graced from time to time, there was never any concerted effort to expel the sandwich eaters, although occasionally notices might appear saying things like, "Only food purchased here may be eaten on these premises", and so forth. It is of great interest to me now, to find out just how many young people were then caught up in such circumstances - especially those from country areas. So we kept a roof over our heads with questionable methods. I sometimes imagined myself as of another era, with a Dickensian innkeeper casting a suspicious eye as the piece was furtively withdrawn from beneath the table and munching carried on much longer than that required to scoff his bun. As time passed, so did an apprentice's standard of living improve and meals of the order, "Egg and chips, tea bread and butter", would, from time to time become possible. But for a while there was nothing for it but the trenches.

Eventually many of us discovered certain "cafes", tailor-made for our requirements, namely to provide accommodation and no questions asked, a very large cup of tea - a mug in fact - and a large Paris bun for a very reasonable charge. I don't know how I discovered these cafes - I shared the good news with certain of my friends. Soon, I started looking around at all my "new companions", as I sorted out the mug and Paris bun. Now these "companions" were a mixed bunch, characterised in the main by the long coats and caps they wore, shaggy beards and shaking hands. Some got fried soda bread and egg as their fare and all partook the mug. For these cafes, were the I.T.L. (Irish Temperance League) cafes, and

I believe their portals were always painted red and yellow. The seats and tables were of plain wood, but must have been a haven indeed for these men who, for one reason or another had dropped out of society as it is commonly known. I imagine most had problems of one sort or another but had I been much different? I had a problem, that had kept me from what I considered normality, for two and a half years. There were at least two of these I.T.L. (Irish Temperance League) cafes or milk bars, that I was glad to have a mug in - one was in Victoria Square and the other, I imagine somewhere near the Queen's Bridge - I cannot be sure. I am amazed, as, from time to time I discover many men - now "well on their feet" as we say - who had found their way to these very places, and like myself, was glad of a bit of anonymous shelter.

I must say I never felt any threat from the men I shared such shelters with, and it's likely that I have had worse company in church, with some dressed in fine clothes.

But eventually as I said, things improved with time, and I "graduated" to other establishments, most of which are no longer in existence. There was the "Continental", in Castle Street, which would have been convenient, when going to the Forth River Mill, in North Howard Street. I was also intrigued to find, that when approaching the Forth River Mill, I was close to Northumberland Street, where, I believe, my father and mother had set up house briefly after they got married.

But even here, hard times forbade the fish and chips at times, and crafty means had to be resorted to. Mervyn Kidd, the Harland's man, discovered with me, that rather than buy one miserly cup of tea, the "Continental" offered a pot of tea for two - with extra hot water, milk and sugar - and no problem with eating lunches. We usually scoffed the lot! Another place where I frequented, was the "Connoisseur" in Great Victoria Street. This was indeed, "Egg, Sausage & Chips, with tea, bread and butter country", two shillings and sixpence (about twelve and a half new pence). But often one would choose something less - at two shillings and three pence - three pence cheaper - and that was obviously an important reduction for an apprentice. Of great interest to me were the people I met at the "Connoisseur", none of whom I have seen since. There was Bill, a soldier of the 1939-45 War, English and sporting a moustache. There was a young fellow from Antrim, called Baxter - was it Ivan? Also a fellow apprentice from Shorts who came from Lurgan. His name was Raymond and he had ginger hair.

At the upper limit of extravagance, would be the "Country Tea House" in Donegall Place, opposite where Marks and Spencer's now stand. Now this was up market for me, but I really felt I knew how "the other half lived", when I treated myself in that exquisite place - I always remember the dark stained wooden chairs, tables etc. One of the inhibiting factors to rubbing shoulders with the great of the time when, on the odd occasion, I strayed into their favourite eating and watering holes, was the fact that one wore the trappings of one's calling. Mine included a pair of heavy boots - not polished by any means, an overcoat of sorts - no tie of course, and an ex-army stock haversack (in which one might have carried gloves, cap - and the daily lunch). In fairness, no one ever remarked upon it - I was probably more aware of someone's nice suit, polished shoes and bow tie, than they were of me in my "hammer and file" brigade rags. I used to make my way to the "Cotters Kitchen" - a very nice place to dine below street level I believe, and - was it in Howard Street or somewhere at the rear of the City Hall? Anyway, it was there that the former B.B.C. producer, Sam Hanna Bell and his party had the pleasure of my company from time to time - they chose to sit near me! Although I probably eavesdropped, I didn't intrude upon their company further!

As already mentioned one young apprentice I was glad to have as my friend was one Robert Madine - Bobby as he was known. While I worked on the jigs for the P.R. Canberra, he was working on production aircraft not far away. We were in the same year of study and frequently got together to try and sort out some ghastly problem whether in maths, applied mechanics or other nightmare which had reared its head from some homework or other.

I recall him as modest and mannerly and a very pleasant companion. Not all the people around me could be so described - I think it was there that I heard certain apprentices described as "gulpins" - "and it was there that - they were first called gulpins". Anyway, I was still standing back carefully from the scrum, and I appreciated the company of people like Bobby Madine, and I shared his modesty as he viewed the prospects of academic success. Occasionally we would share a meal at the "Connoisseur" before our evening classes started - and it was only recently, that I discovered that he too on occasions, had been a visitor to the I.T.L. cafe in King Street - for that large mug of tea and the Paris bun. He believes this only cost him two pence. In those days, he was a champion swimmer, and was to distinguish himself later as the Irish Olympic Swimming Coach. After finishing his studies in Mechanical Engineering, he worked in the Drawing Office at Shorts, before leaving industry to become a teacher, in Physical Education. Later, he obtained a Masters Degree in the U.S.A., returning again to his present teaching post in Belfast.

I had lost contact with him for all those years - then my attention was drawn to the progress of a young lady swimmer by the name of Madine. When I eventually ran him down, I discovered that the young lady, at present distinguishing herself in the swimming world, is his daughter. It's always nice to hear of someone achieving their goal. There are many along life's way who do not - for a variety of reasons, and not ones that they themselves would choose, given the choice. For some, the difference between success, and something less, is owed to some narrow margin of circumstances, that, as we say, "meant all the difference" - something encountered or missed at a crossroads somewhere. As a result of my own humbling experiences, whether in a wheelchair, crutches or falling on my face, I tend to observe people who are struggling along the way, with heightened awareness. There are many who need help from time to time, over the stiles of life. And I often ponder upon the losses to society, that occur when potential Miltons or Grays, Tennysons, Watts, Telfords, Brunels, and so on, never, for one reason or another, leave the starting pads of life.

Full many a gem of purest ray serene
*   The dark unfathom'd caves of ocean bear:*
Full many a flower is born to blush unseen,
*   And waste its sweetness on the desert air.*

(Lines from: "Elegy written in a churchyard", by Thomas Gray.)

Chapter 5 - Getting to grips with reality

The Britannia Freight Door

When I left Centre 20 before Christmas to go to work on the Britannia, it would be the first time back on production since working on the S.A.4 Sperrin bomber at Aldergrove when disappointment was to be my lot.

When I joined the squad building freight doors for Britannia aircraft, I was sent to work with a young fitter by the name of Jackie Duff. Jackie was not long out of his own apprenticeship, which he had served in a mill - I believe somewhere in Co. Down. Now a mill apprenticeship was a very good one, as there most likely would be opportunities to gain experience on boilers, and also in making parts of machinery, whose original manufacturers were no longer in business. Thus a mill would have a fair range of workshop equipment and a wide variety of work would be available for such an apprentice to "cut his teeth on".

The freight door of the Britannia was quite a beast. There are certain things I definitely remember about it - its number on drawings was 22512 - twenty-two, five, twelve. I'm fairly sure it was being built upside down, and although we mostly worked on the inside of the door, fitting the various frames, stringers and other supports, I seem to recall that the drawing was looking at it from the outside - all these details being in what is known as "hidden" detail and indicated on the drawing using dotted or broken lines. I can remember something of this configuration and that Eric, our charge hand who came from Portadown, often would be in on consultation over some detail or other. When drilling rivet holes through frame flanges and the outer skin panel, we used a small hand held drill, driven by compressed air and called an "Atom". This type was used throughout the firm - I don't recall ever seeing an electric hand drill being used. One morning, when using an extremely long drill (bit) in an "Atom", I was guiding the point of this extension drill past protruding flange edges and other obstacles to progress, with my thumb. Suddenly, the protesting drill broke, and the piece still in the "Atom" buried itself, in the thumb joint. But thumb joints are made to stand up to such things and after an x-ray showed nothing broken, the broken drill was replaced and the drilling continued.

It was while I was working in this centre, that my attention was drawn to the activities of one - perhaps two men who moved among us, dressed in suits. They moved unobtrusively, occasionally with what appeared casual interest in say a panel or some line of rivets - or some repair on a concession from the firm's inspectorate. These men were Government employees from the Air Inspection Department (A.I.D.). They had a particular interest in deep scratches on large panels - occasionally I would see such scratches being "honed" out by some fitter using a piece of silver steel round bar. The bar would be slightly bent and the outside of the bend rubbed against the offending scratch until it was no longer. Many years later when attending a dinner in Belfast one evening, I recognised one of these men who, that evening, was Chief Guest at this function. When I later spoke to him, and inquired, if he had once been in such employment, he said that was so, and that he remembered the freight door well.

When I was working on the Britannia Freight door, I was in daily contact with another old friend of Centre 20 (Balcony) days - Ivan Campbell (from the Clogher Valley). Ivan was working on what I believe, was the last of the Solent flying boats, being refurbished at Queen's Island. And here something was taking place that I beheld with some degree of envy. Ivan was invited to take part in the test flights of this aircraft - something very unique indeed. I think Ivan was working in the centre known to us as flight and service. Apart from the Solents and Sealands, all aircraft produced until recently, were of the non-passenger type - Canberra bombers or the Seamew - an anti-submarine attack aircraft destined to be discontinued - mainly I think, because of the fatal accident involving such an aircraft at a flying display. It was known as the S.B.6. Others included experimental types such as the research S.B.4 Sherpa and the swept back wing S.B.5. Now the first Shorts Britannia had recently flown on the 1st June 1957 and the V.T.O.L. S.C.1 flew conventional in February 1957. The opportunities for a trip, had been therefore few and far between. The Solent was a passenger version of the Coastal Command Sunderland.

However Ivan took off in the Solent on a test flight which took him over the Isle of Man and the Welsh coast. These massive flying boats were of course without landing wheels - they landed on water on their hulls, supported by their floats. When they had to come out of the water for maintenance, they had first to approach the ramp on the seaward side of the hard standing area outside the main factory. This ramp of gentle slope, led out of the water and the huge flying boats were floated onto cradles which had wheels. Once secured, the cradles with the flying boat on board, would be hauled out of the water and into the main factory. And of course, crews had to board the aircraft from a motor boat, while the aircraft floated in deep water - anchored until it would roar down Belfast Lough and take off. It would take a more worthy work than this, to describe the crucial contribution the Sunderlands made to the anti-submarine effort during the Second World War. Many flew from Castle Archdale in company with the Catalena. If one visits the site now, little will be seen - everything is flattened and a caravan site now occupies the area, which previously had been an operational station. If one looks around, they could see a few rings in the ground - these would have been used for securing purposes. But still intact is the "Pembroke Dock" - a dry dock which accommodated the flying boats for maintenance.

But since I was not often on final assembly - strictly speaking only once during my entire apprenticeship, I was not on course for a trip like the one Ivan got.

Had the beloved "Comet II" survived, things might have been different. Later had the "ball run straight" for me - who knows that I may not have sneaked a trip on the S.A.4! So I had to content myself with the freight door of the Britannia.

I worked with Jackie Duff on that freight door all winter, and there were problems arising which meant I never saw one completely finished, during my short period of work there. The freight door arrangement was a large one - I cannot remember what its dimensions were - it might have been eight feet long and eight or more feet high - this dimension curved in accordance with the circular section of the fuselage. A large U shaped alloy channel fitted around the fuselage aperture, thus reinforcing the aircraft's stressed skin at that point. As things turned out for me, I was to be at close quarters with this channel in due course.

Returning to my fortunes educationally, I had borrowed Ernie Loudan's racing bicycle to attend an interview when I offered myself for a scholarship to complete my Ordinary National Certificate in Mechanical Engineering. I hadn't much going for me - not much academically anyway, as when those results of current examinations came out, I had just scraped over the line. It was on the basis of these results that one was assessed for the scholarship - the Junior Trade. My results wouldn't have got me far, but the panel, taking into account other things, actually awarded me the full-time scholarship to run from early February until June. Needless to say, I was greatly heartened - this would make life easier

- no more night classes and full time study during the day. I looked forward to this event as a child does towards Santa at Christmas.

I was to be with Jackie Duff therefore until February, but I would eventually leave him with some misgivings. I was quite happy working there - even the day release and evening classes now at third year level and working toward the Ordinary National, were progressing well.

So, one Friday, I locked my toolbox and took my leave of Jackie and others, to report to the College of Technology the following Monday morning.

Matters of Education and Finances

At the Junior Trade I was to meet up with some other faces from Forth River Mill association and some new ones. Among the latter was a Harland's apprentice, one William (Billy) Grills, from Kilkeel. He was to become and remain a very close friend. Another student in this class - now I imagine he was also a Harland's apprentice - was Michael Barry. I only met him briefly - but I recall two things about this young man. He had a very pleasant manner - and was interested in swimming. Someone told me just lately that Michael later became a Manager with Shell overseas, and then had a similar position, with Shell UK.

These classes were held mostly at Forth River Mill and the weather was extremely cold. But that was not the only misfortune - which goes in threes. Red tape wrapped its tentacles around me when I discovered that the travel allowance payable to students on the course would not be payable to me on the grounds that I already paid to travel to Belfast anyway, myself - so that was the logic on which my exclusion rested. Since the scholarship, which amounted to three pounds per week, was about what I would normally have given to my mother towards housekeeping, things looked thin. My father had recently taken ill and wasn't working.

After a few weeks on the "scholarship", I had to make a decision which was earth shattering indeed. While my father was adamant that financial considerations should not be a factor in the debate, I was unhappy living on such a shoe string. I felt it would adversely affect my ability to concentrate on the work at the College, into which all my colleagues there, seemed to enter with light hearted abandon.

So I set in motion the mechanisms that would (hopefully) restore me to work again and to resume in my former classes in day release and evening study. Col. Thompson was now the apprentice supervisor and was very understanding when I told him I wished to leave full-time study and return to work. So I was told to report to a new centre in the extension factory. It was called the Press Shop - its number escapes my memory. But it was a good move.

The older members of my family being married, there were now four of us at home, my father and mother, myself and my youngest sister, who was still at primary school.

While these circumstances held some degree of disappointment for me I had no regret, as the old maxim - "If in doubt, don't", is a good one. I never cease to be amazed at the imponderables along our respective ways, that shape the lives of men. This or that happens, chance meetings due to someone having missed a bus or some connection - a broken leg, failed interview or successful interview, war - the list is endless. If one little slot in the jigsaw of our lives is replaced, it can, probably will, alter the whole output and destiny thereafter.

I had now hit another little aberration of sorts, and I was, (and still am), grateful to those who helped a lame dog over another stile, to slide back into a comfortable routine again. Some of those acquaintances at the Junior Trade and who are now my close friends, often regale me with how long after I departed, my name continued to be read out at roll call - few could put a face to that name.

About this time I was making the acquaintance of teachers at the College of Technology who would play a major role in my educational rehabilitation over the next few years - George McBratney, Denis Ogborn and others of whom I will say something again. But one person to whom I owe a great deal of gratitude was someone I never met again after I left his class.

He took my O.N.C. Engineering Drawing class - at Forth River Mill in an evening session and was extremely helpful in every way. He was Mr Thompson, I believe a draughtsman in Shorts (I could be wrong). But he especially was very supportive to me when I returned to his evening class after the Junior Trade reversal, but become a ship that passed in the night. It's nice to remember the good things about life.

The Press Shop

When I left the Junior Trade scholarship I was allocated work as an apprentice in the Press Shop, where various spars (mostly of the aircraft wing structure) were, after suitable heat treatment, shaped under hydraulic presses to meet the various contours as required. I was allocated to a team of two fitters working on spars which were the main backbone of the "Britannia" freight door.

These two fitters were quite remarkable in different ways - and very pleasant companions as well.

One, whose name I know but I don't need to write to down, was remarkable in that, coming as a member of the Church of Ireland, he was a most ardent supporter of a United Ireland, and although I cannot recall details of the conversations, he certainly talked a lot to me of his longing for Britain to go and Ireland to be united. I can also remember the name of the street (off the Lisburn Road) where he lived.

The other fitter was the shop steward — we will call him Archie. Apart from numerous absences from the freight door spar - if I recall aright, it was a U shaped channel, he fought many battles with the rate fixer, and since I shared in the "bonus" which both men earned, it was a good thing for me that he always won. Other personal details which I recall about him were that he wore glasses and according to the other fitter was "very bad with his stomach" (and I think that it was here that I first heard the explanation for the bad stomach - "it's the auld drink").

Now technically the spars were curved and then the contour was checked against a wooden "master" pattern. I remember one such spar. In spite of much pressing and hammering it wouldn't simply match the pattern. "I'll soon fix it", said Archie, and immediately, and with some gusto, laid into the curve of the master and eventually succeeded in making it match the vagabond spar. Even I couldn't believe my eyes - they were watering with laughter anyway. "That will sort that out" said Archie. His mate just laughed. I made a mental note, that if I ever had to travel on one of Short's Britannias, I would prepare my morning devotions with additional care!

Well, it was in the press shop that I prepared for my O.N.C. certificate. I had some feeling of dismay when failure was contemplated and I really put my mind to it. I had very good teachers and soon I knew I had the thing back on the rails.

I knew that if I succeeded in gaining the certificate and, at the same time remaining on the pay roll that was giving me a very good wage considering I was only a fourth year apprentice - having only just completed three years of my "time", then, I would have lost nothing, in spite of choosing to drop the Junior Trade Scholarship. On the contrary, I would have gained, financially, as well as academically.

One man I remember well from the few months I spent in the press shop was a very old maintenance fitter. I had the impression that a concession existed, enabling him to work on after normal retirement age. For some reason, he got talking to me one day and upon learning that I came from Antrim, enquired if Rea's Saw Mills were still there - "Sammy Rea - up at the station". I confirmed to him the mill was still in business. "Any steam about it?" he asked. Yes, one saw steam escaping (in fact there was a water pond in which there were gold fish reputedly kept warm by the steam). I can well imagine that this was true - presumably some condensate from a steam engine, would find its way into the pond.

My old acquaintance then went on to tell me that he remembered when working with Craigs Engineering, Belfast (Gt. Georges Street), he was part of a working party sent down to Rea's of Antrim to re-bore the cylinder of the steam engine - and before the First World War! I was amazed at such an endeavour and asked what sort of set-up existed - what drove the boring bar. "We had our own portable boring machine - complete with its own steam engine and boiler". So what do you make of that? (Recently, I saw such a set-up in the Imperial Science Museum, South Kensington, London).

My father meanwhile continued to have difficulties with his general health. He had increased trouble with arthritis in his hands and back. This was the only thing that I was aware he was suffering from, but medical opinion called up more and more tests.

Spring came - I was now away from Musgrave Park one year and six months and all was well. I had just turned twenty-two years old.

The Britannia Final Assembly

So the exams came along - I thought I did OK and shortly after a visit to Mr Ossie Carlisle to discuss what direction I should go, I was transferred to final assembly of the Britannia. I went to work on the wings of the beast and I worked with a fitter I had known in earlier days. The Foreman was a man called Brennan and I seem to recall having an uneasy relationship with him. Eventually, I seemed to fit in alright, but I was only there a month or so when I had another interview with Mr Ossie Carlisle. Apparently, in the Guided Weapon Machine shop at Castlereagh, local management had made a request for a couple of apprentices who would be interested in special work of a highly precise nature. Would I be interested in precision turning - this would mean coming out of my apprenticeship as a precision turner vis a vis the position of union thought - not fitter and not fitter/turner - in which I had actually served my time to date. I would be interviewed by the guys at Castlereagh as well. I would think about it - it would mean giving up any thought about specialising in purely aircraft production - what was projected was of a much more general nature.

I considered the prospects and what skill I was lacking in and realised that the precision skill which might be acquired at this factory would give me a very balanced training, in which I had set out to achieve - an apprenticeship in fitting and turning.

So I had an interview (complete with a special pass) with Matt Smyth the Senior Foreman, and Fred Lowens, the Manager. They must have liked what they saw - I got word next day they wanted me up and I was to be joined by another chap called Harry Matchett, (later a Director of Engineering Supplies, Crossgar). So I left the Britannia and the main factory. (I often wondered if any apprentices got flights in those Britannias).

Back to Castlereagh, Centre 31

When I made my way up to Montgomery Road, it was to be the third time that I had gone to Castlereagh to work - once when the Capstans were moved, in the pre-Musgrave Park days; then, the second time I'll call it post SA4 days, at the apprentice training school. In those days we talked in terms of precision of so many thousandths of an inch. But now that party was over, because here the talk was in tenths of one thousandth of an inch (0.00254mm)! Harry Matchett and I worked together for a week or so on the centre lathe allocated to us. It was an old, fairly large Harrison - top RPM 400! This beast had three buttons - one for forward, one for reverse and one to stop. It also incorporated an electro mechanical brake which gave a lot of trouble to the machine tool maintenance fitters. It was not a machine to become very excited about - I have a better lathe in my own workshop now, but dimensions were adhered to. A good workman doesn't blame the tools - any tool in the hands of the right man will do the job. Nor does it mean that there were not some very modern machines there, and new ones arriving from time to time. But I think some lathes were old enough to have made parts for Stirling bombers in the Second World War!

Harry had recently completed a spell in the apprentice training school - as senior apprentice (just like that "other" chap) and was fairly conversant with machines so I think he "got the ball rolling" with our first job. At the end of the week one of us had to go on the night shift and Harry elected to do the first three weeks on that shift. Because of the nature of the quality of work required - tight limits and tolerances to be maintained etc, all workers there were guaranteed 80% of bonus. As well, the night shift paid an extra one third of our wages so it was possible to have a very good wage indeed. I often relied on the fall back 80% bonus as in finding my way in difficult "terrain", the work was often too difficult to do accurately enough to please inspection and fast enough to make full bonus.

I had recently sat the examinations for the Ordinary National Certificate in Mechanical Engineering and was awaiting the results. All my life I was aware of the sense of urgency that accompanied my father's exhortation to me (and the rest of the family) to press on with education - something denied most of his generation. The acquisition of the Ordinary National Certificate would be a significant step in the right direction. But now, I was also to pass through another phase in life, which most of us pass, sooner or later in our lives - the terminal illness of a parent. There was nothing I suppose spectacular in this visitation except for my unswerving disbelief that it could happen to someone not very old. But my father was admitted to Whiteabbey Hospital and while nothing was spelled out, the older members of my family were unable to disguise concern.

One day after an operation, I visited him and thought his speech was like that of someone who had taken drink. Whiteabbey Hospital was not a pub - he had suffered a slight stroke. But eventually he made something of a recovery from that and was allowed home. In a ward close by, was a schoolboy - I understood his name was Moore. He was Billy Moore, later to become one of my closest teaching colleagues at Antrim Technical College.

Shortly afterwards I received word that I had passed all four subjects in the O.N.C. examinations and had been awarded the certificate. I was greatly relieved - I was over half way there. I probably lost no time in telling my father. But by then he was having to contend with other serious issues in life and I remembered his somewhat muted response, "Oh that will probably stand by you". And that was all.

Meanwhile work went on at Castlereagh and I was getting to know my "neighbours".

I might just mention here, that it was in the autumn of that year during a spell on the night shift, that around the "lunch" break the workers at Castlereagh saw the Russian Sputnik passing over. Such things no longer make the news. I sometimes wonder with what amazement the first demonstration of the wheel was beheld. It wasn't yesterday - anyone visiting Cairo museum will see perfect six spoke wheels, on the chariots the Pharaohs imagined would somehow assist them in their after life - even that was three thousand years ago.

Turning back to the first demonstration of the wheel, the relative excitement of the wheel and the Sputnik would have been about the same because one reads how a well known Greek philosopher walking in Athens was struck by the numerous gadgets and inventions to be seen. "How many things there are", he exclaimed, "of which I have no need!". I sometimes ask the same question when I am rushing through a supermarket looking for salt or pepper and in spite of good intentions, I always seem to come out, like a weight lifter in training. When will I ever learn?

* * * * * * * * *

Harvest time came, and with it the customary Harvest Thanksgiving Services. For someone like myself, reared in the country, surrounded by crops - cows gazing into one's living room from a field outside, assailed constantly with the sounds of nature - the corncrake and the curlew - the ripening crops in fields, Harvest was as natural to me as the sound of riveting guns to someone brought up in Dee Street in Belfast. The Presbyterian way of giving thanks each year for the harvest and in remembrance of God's promise, "While the Earth remaineth, seed time and harvest shall not fail" - is a deeply engrained one, with special music, anthems and hymns and psalms, relating to God's promise of food - and also health, and other blessings, which enables our Ship of Life to steam across the waters. I have, since the occasion when my attention was drawn to it, always marvelled how in the Lord's Prayer, one is taught simply to pray for "our daily bread" - we would never dare ask for promotion in our work, a rise in pay, more bonus or a new car ("how many things there are of which I have no need") - but we do need our daily bread and the health, in body and mind, that enables us to earn that bread.

> *"I have set My rainbow in the clouds, and it will be the sign of the covenant between Me and the earth."*
>
> *Genesis 9: 13 (NIV)*

But work had to go on and as I got off the bus at Montgomery Road the Monday morning after our Harvest Services, my spirits were not high, but who should join me but Billy Taggart, transferred from the main factory. Never underestimate how much you might mean to someone, in their time of discomfort. This was the same Billy Taggart who had been a good friend in my early months at work. Now he was to be the same, again.

Inevitably the recent events were turned over, Billy on the main silent. Then I remembered that at the Harvest Services the previous night I had heard a lovely praise for the first time. "I must find out which hymn it is", I said, "I know part of it goes like "The rolling seasons as they move, proclaim Thy constant care".

"Ah", Billy said, "You see, the key word in that verse - it is the word *constant*".

Coincidentally, I had been given an interesting little job in Shorts factory "across the way" from my own factory. This work involved the manufacture of hydraulic seals made from flat material of some rubber composition.

This work had been pioneered by Tommy McClean, a turner in Centre 31. Tommy now handed down to me, the secrets and mysteries belonging to the "art" of producing hydraulic seals where accuracy, parallelism, and finish, all came under the inspector's beady eye. He had also negotiated an amazing rate for each seal based not on the time required to make a seal (a very short period indeed if all was going well), but on the problematical time taking into account the trial and error procedures sometimes encountered. I would now see such endeavours as adhering to empirical rather than scientific laws!. But by inheriting this work my financial worries were finished for a long time - I was able to "make it" as they used to chant in Centre 24. (Tommy McClean and "Nobby" Clark our Manager, were holders of the Burmah Star, both having served together in the Far East during the war: they have now passed on).

I have no apology as seeing such a move as providential at this difficult period.)The difficulties I faced now, were those that everyone faces when called upon to nurse a sick relative at home.) It was a nice clean quiet place and apart from clocking in and out at my usual place in Centre 31 each day, I spent the next few months in virtual isolation with a relatively stress free job of work, although I had now much on my mind.

November became December and I wondered what sort of Christmas we would have. Soon I was to know. My father became very distressed - then lapsed unconscious one Wednesday evening. I took a couple of days off work to provide extra help about the house only going in to collect my pay on Friday. I remember telling Ken Jones the latest situation - as always Ken was a very courteous and understanding man.

My father passed away on the following Sunday. I had not known, or wanted to know, that he was terminally ill.

The funeral, as usually is the case, was a gathering of the clans - older relatives one only sees at funerals and weddings. My grandfather Talbot - my mother's father was there - in his seventies and still doing a bit of work. I remember him talking to me that day about his early years at sea - he had been a fireman there.

The funeral having passed, I resolved to go back to work the next day even though I couldn't bear the thought. That night, like after the manner of other people facing a similar morrow, I was laid to pray to the Lord for strength to pick up the loose ends once again. Another chapter in my life closed. I had a wonderful mother who would surpass herself, in supporting me as long as I needed it. I wasn't exactly out of the pit. But she survived my father for thirty-four years.

I earlier mentioned some things I remember my parents saying. During the difficult days following my return to work and life was a tiring place, my father gave an additional piece of advice on meeting the coming day: "If you are getting it tight and approaching your wit's end, then in the morning, think of the worst thing that might and could happen during the day. Then at the end of the day - and it hasn't happened - tell yourself that you had survived and were still up and running" (or words to that effect).

As a life long trade unionist and inclined in Socialist thinking, my father tended to treat with suspicion and perhaps disapproval some of the social orders people belong to. He understood with dismay the hypocrisy that attends even our places of worship. But in his latter philosophies on different matters I inferred that on balance he now advocated that some intrusion into the social chapters of society may not be such a bad thing. He probably thought along the lines that if you want companions, you have to move in their direction - they may not necessarily come your way. Maybe loneliness increases with age. I was surprised to have heard him say - albeitly in an offhand manner, "You should join this or that".

There was something else he mentioned - that if and when I completed that apprenticeship I should go to sea to gain experience in engineering and life. This was about the time when I was having my tea breaks on that narrow long bench when my fellow apprentices led by Steve-e, talked about nothing else and I responded by "drawing my left leg protectively in behind my right one".

When I arrived back to Castlereagh the day following my father's funeral, I went to see the Foreman, Mr Ken Jones, to get some work. Upon seeing me he asked me how my father was. I simply held out the black tie I was wearing - none of them knew of the bereavement as I never thought of ringing any of them up - one reason being I didn't know anybody well enough to have their number. But everyone was very helpful and soon I was in the little private area - on my own and back to production. Although it was a nice clean quiet place I had a number of visitors who would drop in. Some were from the research or mechanical laboratory - perhaps with special orders to help some individual tests or experiments to do with hydraulic equipment. I'm sure many of the seals perfected in design and method of manufacture eventually found their way onto the Seacat missile. As well, a rocket research programme was underway, the rockets themselves being known as the G.P.V., or general purpose vehicle. In Shorts at that time there were two men by the name of Roberts - one being a test pilot. The other Mr Roberts had an involvement in some helicopter interest programme. Occasionally I did some work for him and one day I was invited into the "Dome", inside which was a simulator on which I "flew" a helicopter - crashing it several times if my memory is correct. It was a unique experience.

But things they say, happen in threes. A week after we buried my father, my brother's sister-in-law was tragically killed when knocked off her bicycle by a car. Two weeks after my father was buried, we buried my Grandfather Talbot, who had died from a heart attack. Between the latter deaths, we had our Christmas. In the spring of the following year, one of the lads who used to ride up homeward in the trail of Whisseker Wright with me and others, got himself a motorcycle. He was James McMahon a close friend and cheery companion. He took me somewhere on the back of this motorcycle one Friday night. Imagine my dismay when I learned on Sunday, that he was fatally in collision with a bread van, at Lough Road, Antrim, on Saturday. So I attended the funerals of four close relations and friends inside three months.

*   *   *   *   *   *   *   *   *   *

I have mentioned "Forth River Mill" on North Howard Street, and as I had walked up Divis Street, and thence the Falls, I would pass Northumberland Street. It was where my father and mother had set up house after they were married in Sinclair Seaman's Presbyterian Church. As I progressed up the educational ladder in the unlikely setting of that mill, that progress was hollow in ways as my father was then terminally ill. There was some nostalgia in passing Northumberland Street in those days. Both my parents had worked all their working lives in the linen mills - except for a period when my father worked in Shorts at Aldergrove during the war. As linen workers, neither became weight lifters as a result of efforts to lift their wages. My mother was, like those of her generation a "half timer" - half the week in work and half in school. I imagine this only applied to twelve year olds and over, but I think bare feet were fairly common. My mother worked in Jennymount - occasionally I stare at mill photographs of workers at Jennymount, and wonder if she is among the ladies there. She also spoke of working in a mill on the site of the Smithfield Bus Station of my generation, and of how sad the workers were when it was burned down - apparently it was a happy mill to work in. I think it must have been unique in that respect! Later she was to join the army during the Great War.

Now her father - my grandfather James Talbot came from Tullyhogue, Cookstown. He had been a sea-faring man, a fireman, and I shudder to think of the conditions firemen of that era worked in. Often, I heard my mother recall of hearing him speak of seamen "praying that 'she' would go down" - I'm unsure of what conditions brought about this response! I also heard her speak of a Christmas homecoming when, expecting something of a conventional present, my grandfather presented her with three black elephants he had picked up somewhere. (I wish I could get my hands on them now!)

I'm unsure where the family was living then - people tended to follow work in those days and the family lived in Scotland - on the Clyde at one time.

However, later my grandfather came to work in the shipyard at Harlands, Belfast. They were living in Cultra Street, off North Queen's Street. He was a Foreman - presumably of unskilled trades, and as such, he had a workman's hut. Now there hangs a tale. (I also used to hear my mother speak of a time, when he won some appreciation for "getting a ship off the rocks at Islandmagee". I wonder what his job actually was?

Now in those days, there was a gentleman living not far away - on the docks side of the Shore Road. His name was "Buck" Alec. At one time later, he was to keep a lion or two. Throughout her entire life afterwards my mother would recall an incident. I suppose we might think of it along the lines of "the luck of the draw", but in this case, it was the draw of a gun.

One evening as my mother was making her way along a street in the early 1920's, she was startled by a voice ringing out, "Don't shoot Alec - you have the wrong person". Some unknown person - possibly she knew who it was, had saved her. "Buck" Alec was also known to her, as they were all part of the same community, but apparently he had stalked her in the belief that she was someone else, and was intending settling something. These were days when tramway passengers often had to lie flat on the floor during exchanges of gun fire, tram drivers were victims, and apparently there was a serious problem in carrying out funerals, burials etc, with bodies having to remain on the premises where death had taken place, for lengthy periods. There were other family connections living nearby - all from Co Tyrone, and the names included Warnocks (especially a Matt Warnock), Gilmores and Taggarts. Recently, I had the good fortune to walk through this area of Belfast (virtually all rebuilt some time ago), and accompanied by Mr Billy Reilly who was brought up close by. Billy is well known as an official of the Northern Ireland Cycling Federation and he gave me a story: he had sailed from Belfast docks in 1928 upon joining the Merchant Navy. A number of stowaways were discovered on the ship, and were duly removed some distance down Belfast Lough. Buck Alec was among them. Notwithstanding, when Billy's ship arrived in New York - Buck Alec was there before them! He was to outlive my mother by three years.

Now one day, at the height of the troubles which had spilled over into the shipyard, three elderly Catholic men sought my grandfather's help in their search for safety, and he hid them in the hut referred to earlier. These elderly men and their families managed to convey their grateful thanks to Cultra Street eventually. Shortly afterwards, however, someone else arrived at that door in Cultra Street. My Aunt Jean heard some one say: "Jimmy, that was a wrong thing you did". Grandfather Talbot got the message.

So my grandfather, Orangeman and all that he was, was soon back in Co. Tyrone near Tullyhogue, where I believe the initial accommodation was less than palatial. He fired boilers in Coalisland Brick Works, and he was still doing so at seventy three years of age when one day, he passed away, after a heart attack - as recalled.

Now his son John Talbot, who was my mother's youngest brother, joined the R.A.F. on the outbreak of war in 1939, and became an operational airgunner. He survived a serious aircraft crash and was fortunate to escape from Singapore just before the Japanese captured that stronghold. During the war, he married May Phoenix a local girl from the village of Granville, near Dungannon. They would later settle down at Donaghmore, Dungannon. Sadly, he was to die in 1979 - aged fifty-nine years. During the preceding illness which led to his death, I visited him in the Royal Victoria Hospital, Belfast, with May, when, on one occasion he talked about the war, something which he seldom did. This was to tell me about the time British (or Dutch) aircraft had bombed some Japanese ships at Singapore. Unfortunately, they had on board British prisoners of war. Among those lost was a Cookstown pal of John's - I believe his name was Lawson.

May had a nephew from Granville who was to serve in the Parachute Regiment. He later joined the R.U.C. to become a Chief Superintendent. One day, a Chinook helicopter carrying twenty-four senior R.U.C. and army personnel crashed on the Mull of Kintyre, Scotland, killing all on board. May's nephew was among them. His name was Ian Phoenix.

But time marches on relentlessly, people build or re-build their lives, pay the rent and (mostly) get on with it. My apprenticeship moved into final year - as well I was still heavily committed to study. In those studies I had made the acquaintance of another Short's apprentice, a very nice lad by the name of Billy Watson. He was an extremely clever and serious worker. I think I tried to sit fairly close to him on every occasion possible. I wonder what senior position he is in now - I'm sure it is a good one. But our paths didn't cross again after that session. About this time I was fortunate to have as one of my teachers, Mr George McBratney, later to succeed Mr David Alexander as Principal of the College of Technology, Belfast. In later years I was to get to know both these men on a more personal level, but now I was "hanging in there", holding on course. Another teacher who had a significant part in shaping my future and perhaps personality was Mr Denis Ogburn. Both George McBratney and Denis Ogburn had certain mannerisms that I found I copied when in the process of time I found myself in the teaching profession.

Two such mannerisms inherited from Denis Ogburn related to anyone coming into his class late. He always stopped the lecture, looking at the interloper. This, I expect, had the effect of drawing the attention of the rest of the class to the aforesaid. It was thus almost incumbent for the late comer to offer an apology or explanation. I think Mr Ogburn also lifted his head slightly and sometimes would pose a question "Yes?" The other was, that if, in the process of explaining something, a hand went up in a questioning way, he always stopped the lecture and said "Sorry". If it was said thus, I always inferred that he was almost apologising for not having made something clear. On the other hand he may have said, "Sorry?" which would have meant, "Sorry - I didn't hear your question". But either way, one was never discouraged from asking a question - even questions from myself which many a time may have caused him to wonder whether I had been sleeping soundly throughout the lecture!

We had a maths teacher - who was I believe involved in Primary School work, but who was a very good maths teacher. He was Mr Hetherington - now passed on - and together with the above two mentioned gentlemen, I had a lot of mannerly examples to follow, and I think perhaps something did rub off and has made a little contribution in the lives of many boys and girls, I was later to teach, and not born at this time.

Someone who had been my close friend since those days, Billy Grills (a Harland's apprentice), was also in most of the classes I attended throughout my time in Belfast College of Technology, as was Clive Hughes, known to me since early days at Forth River Mill.

But at work, time rang out more changes as my "mate" Harry Matchett decided he had had enough of the old Harrison and left Centre 31 - I cannot remember which part of the factory he went to work in. Many years later, at evening service in Greystone Road Presbyterian Church, Antrim, a quartet from Belfast took part in the service - and one of that quartet was the former apprentice precision turner late of Centre 31 - Harry Matchett.

Eventually the day arrived that I, when lying in that corner bed in Ward 3, Waveney Hospital, Ballymena, thought might never come. I completed my apprenticeship. It was, with a feeling of something accomplished, that "the day" designated as the end of apprenticeship, approached. For my peer group including the Ballymena boys who started with me, the "end" was something just taken for granted - and two and a half years before my "day". But for me the route was studded with many memories of places - in hospitals, of pain, regret, disappointment, many pleasant memories as well, of people I would never have met had I not been in such environments.

And what about that apprenticeship in Shorts? Well I can only speak of my own and looking at it objectively, I had a good apprenticeship and when I eventually left Mother Shorts I was well equipped to make my way in life. One could say I wish I had spent time on "Steve's" boilers or on the jig-borer or whatever. But what you lose on the hobby horses you gain in the swings, and there were times I was glad of the skills imparted to me at the de-burring bench, with Jimmy McDowell on the 3A Wards, the jig and tool fitting - working with alloys of different sorts, heat treatment of materials, the various aircraft I worked on - and the very considerable expertise gained on precision turning - skills on the lathe handed down by "Hendy", Horace Love and Hugh Campbell, Tommy McClean, George, Tim Sullivan, Harry Curry, Ernie Stitt, Joe McCullough, Tim Butler - all these guys and others who never saw me stuck. Nothing in learning is lost as long as it is passed on - I think that in some shape or form, that Shorts apprenticeship has (and still is) been passed on to - I think literally hundreds, at least, of others - many of whom went to work in Shorts themselves - and who had come under my influence in a teaching capacity. But a lot of water (some of it salt) had to flow below the bridges, and Shorts and Musgrave Park would continue to be part of those bridges.

One young man I was friendly with at Castlereagh was Terry Ballance who came from Bangor. I never saw him after I left Shorts. Of two other apprentices with whom I developed close relations was one Derek Shannon from Bangor. He was an extremely nice fellow, a good conversationalist, and I think he studied at Bangor Technical. Now the other was Raymond Gregg*. He came from out the Ballynahinch Road, Hillsborough. I believe the house was called "Laura Vale" or "Popular Vale". He had a graduate brother also employed on the staff of Shorts. The "staff" of Shorts comprised the technical design and managerial side of the firm. (They also started an hour later in the mornings). Now these brothers were a most interesting pair. Raymond like myself played an accordion, and his musical tastes were close to my own. His brother also played the accordion. To cap it, their father was a piper. Raymond and he came to visit me at Antrim, and I recall the father saying that he was approaching retirement and had now a bit of time to try and perfect certain tunes, that had been on the long finger for a time. I must try and find these people - they are also in the ranks of those whose paths have not crossed mine since those days. I feel sadness in this - ships that passed in the night.

The thirty-seven and a half hour week

When I started my apprenticeship, my hours were from 7.45 a.m. until 5.05 p.m. - with break during morning, lunchtime and afternoon, a working week of then forty-two and a half hours. Eventually it went down to forty hours, and then hooray - the workers got the thirty-seven and a half hour week.

(* - I recently met the Gregg Brothers at a meeting of the Premier Fiddle and Accordion Club of N. Ireland).

I have good cause to remember that first week of the new hours - and in particular the first Monday. I was at this time preparing for the end of term examinations - especially a subject dropped during my father's illness. I would now hopefully enter the final area of study - the end of a trail that I had started so long ago - along which progressed many of "those who passed my bench - the de-burring bench" during my early days in Shorts. These had already passed the end of that trail, or should have done so. I was intent on starting the final year of the Higher National Certificate in the autumn. That would catch them up. This was now April and the examinations presently being studied for, were in May.

It was nice getting out of work so early - it was probably 4.35 p.m. and I had been travelling to work by motorcycle for some time. So that first Monday - it was nice and clear when I headed through the "town", over the mountain, round the Horseshoe bend, and on towards the Seven Mile Straight to Antrim. Just where the road starts to dip down towards Clady Corner of the old Ulster Grand Prix days, my attention was drawn to a short avenue, leading to a bungalow or low dwelling on the left hand side of the road. A dog - collie type, was making his way down that avenue. The next thing I knew I was lying on the road, in some considerable pain around my stomach - and a dog also in some distress trying its best to worry and eat me as much as its condition allowed it. I was trying to repel the beast - which was very persistent in its efforts, when a vehicle stopped, and the occupants, who were pilots and air crew of a Shackelton aircraft stationed at Aldergrove drove off the dog (no one admitted to owning it) and summoned an ambulance. I was soon on my way to Ward 10 R.V.H. The aircraft crew had at least one Scot - for a long time I remembered his name but have now forgotten it. They were very kind to me - alas ships that pass in the night.

Well, I was admitted to Ward 10 R.V.H. I suffered internal bruising - the solar plexus area of the stomach and other superficial injuries including the left knee. In view of what was to come later, I often wonder just how much damage was done to the knee. I was there a short time - a week or two and then allowed home. But it brought home to me then just how much trouble an accident prone victim gives to parents and friends - visiting - filling the empty place - worry on the person's behalf.

But during that short space of time, the R.V.H. threw up its characters i.e. people of interest and one in the form of James Carson from around the Greenisland area. He told me how his father was a former sea Captain - in fact I think at one time, Commodore of the Head Line, Belfast and his brother was a Captain at sea - he also lectured in Marine matters at the Marine College, College of Technology, Belfast (now at Jordanstown). But James had no interest in the sea - I gathered this was something of a disappointment to his father. At that time, James (or Jim as he was known by) had some illness which made him fear the worst i.e. that he could be suffering from an incurable illness. After we were both discharged from hospital, he visited me in Antrim on a number of occasions. Then some time passed and I lost touch - until I got a letter from the "Mozambique" - from Jim Carson, 5th Engineer the MV "Crystal Bell". He told me he had gone to sea with the Sugar Line, a subsidiary of the Athel Steamship Company. Also did I know 'a Jim Allen', the "Bells" second engineer, who seemed to come from the Randalstown area? Well, I had to say no to that one, but I eventually located Jim Allen - he now lives outside Randalstown. My next card from Jim Carson was from Dairen, Red China. But I lost touch with him after that.

But once again, I had been at a crossing of roads - mine and a dog's, and had put paid to those examinations. However I recovered ere long and lived to fight another day.

But before that, another example of what this world throws up came my way. There was in my class at Belfast Tech, a more mature student (I do recall his real name and he worked at R.A.F. Aldergrove). Upon learning that my injuries were mainly to my stomach, he said that "did I know this was very serious indeed?" "You know", he went on in his helpful way, "that could cause you to have cancer there, later on". I cannot, but admit, feeling a little dismayed by such a prospect - my father had recently died of this. Actually I had eventually little trouble from that part of my anatomy. I think the injury was caused when I landed on the road - on top of my "piece" box, which, carried in a haversack, could have swung around in front of my body as it descended earthwards and provided a pressure point. But don't you get them everywhere?

* * * * * * * * *

Many years went by, when I again found myself passing that spot where I hit the dog. I was doing some work for the Local Education Board as a home tutor for sick school children, and I was teaching three such people. My typical route was from Antrim, Seven Mile Straight, Ballyutoag Road, Ballysillan Park, North Circular, Antrim Road, O'Neill Road, the Shore Road and Rathcoole! So along the Ballyutoag Road, I approached the spot - sometimes going one way and then another and I must confess that I couldn't be sure, within one hundred yards, where "it" happened. Even the house or bungalow with the short avenue along which I saw the dog - I found difficult to say for certain "That's it".

The Final Years with Short Bros. and Harland Ltd.

I was to be in overalls for my complete apprenticeship, although around the time of my father's terminal illness, I was offered a job on the staff of Short Bros. I respectfully asked the Apprentice Supervision Department to be allowed to decline at that moment, as I would appreciate no disturbance to my routine in view of preoccupations at home. This was agreed - I never regretted that decision - my career was to go in a different direction.

I was to be with Shorts for eighteen months post apprenticeship, when I would part company with them - as an employer, but my association and close contact was to be maintained over many years. Probably my most prominent abiding memory is that of a long line of apprentices, under the benign patronage of Steve-e (the apprentice with boiler experience) and sitting on that long bench in the "Comet" hanger, all talking wistfully of the day they would come out of their apprenticeship, and go 'to sea'. Being just out of Musgrave Park, I think I positively shivered at the thought!

I was however constantly aware that a great many of the fitters (and turners) and electricians I worked with had in fact done just that, and conversations were often reminiscence along those lines.

At Castlereagh I had now another Steve-e, a maintenance fitter (or was he an electrician?) Well, he especially spread the Gospel of the sea to me - talking of his first company - The Thistle Steamship Co - probably from North Shields, and of his last ship, the SS "Roonagh Head" out of Belfast. He talked about things called "steam recips" and "up and downers" - mysteries all.

Then Jack Cunningham my fellow turner had been with Esso Tankers. "I remember", he would say, "being on a tanker lying in Bangor Bay - just before D-Day. We could see the train to Belfast - so near and yet so far".

Then Jimmy Blair who was a fitter - later to become trade union factory convenor, had been at sea on the old "Innishown Head". Another fitter had been with Henry Carson, the now Commodore Engineer of that line. Henry Carson had been at school with my father, and I knew him slightly, as he lived at Carnaghts, Kells, beside my cousin. I was to meet him again. He had a habit of saying "You boy you," when addressing other engineers.

During a time when travelling through a monsoon, this fitter recalled Henry Carson almost going over board when a stauncheon he was holding onto - they must have been doing a job on the deck - pulled away in his hand. I cannot remember this fitter's name but I believe that the incident took place on the aforementioned "Inishowen Head" - possibly when known by the original name of "Empire Glade".

Short Bros. & Harland - apart from building aircraft and employing up to 10,000 people when I started work there, has made a tremendous contribution to education in Northern Ireland, and were in the forefront of day release, for apprentices to attend a technical college one day per week as well as starting apprentice training - off the job training - in the training school at Castlereagh - and later in the apprentice training school in the extension factory, Queen's Island. I used to think that they didn't get a good return for their outlay as figures I got at one time suggested that only 20% of its apprentices eventually stayed with the company in one form or another. I suppose they in turn benefited with a similar migration from other engineering firms - people moving around to gain experience. There was one striking feature which characterised that era: that was, a strange pecking order that existed in men's minds, setting out in order of merit, what firm produced good fitters with "hands galore", and other firms considered weak in producing such specimens. I received plenty of advice from many of the fitters I rubbed shoulders with who assured me that I would be lucky ever to be employed outside Shorts - "Who would want someone lacking in heavy engineering experience", they would say, "This stuff is too light to give you any skill". Anyway, that's what they said, and I truly believed that if I left Shorts, I would end up driving a herring cart, of which a few still existed. But nevertheless, by the time I was starting final studies for the Higher National Certificate in Mechanical Engineering - subject to broken legs and dogs etc - I had gained a fair bit of knowledge - in theory anyway of boilers, steam, and compression ignition constant pressure (Diesel) engines - and in truth, I was curious to get some hands on experience on such like plant. I usually got a whiff of steam from Billy Grills - later to take his "Chiefs" steam ticket on the old SS "Camito", of the Elder & Fyffe Line. (He even went further - with a "double" - taking his motor certificate while with British Railways). I was usually in Billy's classes at the "Tech" as was Clive Hughes - later as already mentioned, to hold a senior position in the College of Technology, Belfast. He was also from Harlands (nobody ever talked about Harland & Wolff - it was always Harlands or the "Yard"), and later took his tickets, with the Blue Funnel Line. In a recent conversation with me, Clive recalled one trip of twenty-one months duration, which included four circumnavigations of the globe! He speedily got his sea time clocked up for his "tickets", and was at this time, the second youngest Second Engineer, in the history of Blue Funnel. There were other notable apprentices from Harlands as already mentioned - Mervyn Kidd from the Cregagh and Richard (Dickie) Mulholland - both eventually to come and live in Antrim following employment in very good positions in the firm of British Enkalon. And I mustn't forget Raymond Auld - also from Harlands.

That motorcycle accident with the dog (which nobody owned, would you believe it?) meant the H.N.C. was put back once more, and I decided I would have a break from studies - and perhaps fulfil a little obligation.

My father, shortly before he passed on, had, in a matter of course remark, suggested that if and when I ever got out of this apprenticeship, I should try and gain some experience at sea. Now he had little contact or knowledge of the sea, but amazingly someone who served an apprenticeship as a linen tenter - one Roy McCormack from Antrim, under his guidance, somehow obtained Amalgamated Engineering Union recognition and sailed as an engineer at sea, during the War. I resolved I would take a break for a year and made my way to see Mr Ted Goligher, Head of Engineering at the

College of Technology, Belfast. I told him the situation and asked could I resit the examination the following year, without registering attendance and homeworks etc - that I had decided to try the sea for a short period and get a bit of heavy engineering experience. "Good idea" he said, "You'll appreciate your 'Strength of materials' after that".

I now had to consider how I should proceed as to the other little matter-finding someone who might take me on - for I had not forgotten what people had said (quite erroneously) about the merits of light engineering. Actually, the particular apprenticeship I received stood me in good stead. I was a fitter and turner and benefited from my precision machining experience. The tool room taught me how to use a file and many other skills. I will not forget to mention what I was taught at the de-burring bench - I remember what Billy Riddles said, that I would never forget how to finish a job properly - always by removing sharp edges - it would become second nature to me. He was right.

I visit the Custom House

Well, eventually after having much advice from all the old salts, I decided I would go and get "graded" at the Ministry of Transport, Custom House, Belfast. This was the process whereby all prospective sea-going engineers had their credentials examined - proof of apprenticeship, examination attainments, etc (in person and in writing no less) and before a Captain (whether R.N. or M.N. I didn't know). I remember those days as a scenario similar to that which occurs in Kenneth Grahame's "Wind in the Willows", where the migrating birds - swallows and so forth, tried to encourage those who had never done so. The Rat was especially encouraged to do so - much to his annoyance - until he met a seafaring rat and for Ratty, it was a case of "almost I am persuaded". In my case, all the old seafaring rats at work - now too old to go to sea, encouraged a young Rat like me, and I particularly remember the advice and good wishes of the aforementioned Steve (not the apprentice Steve of boiler and maintenance reference in the main factory). This was Steve the maintenance fitter at Castlereagh who had sailed with the small "Thistle" Company of North Shields and he had been third engineer in the S.S. "Roonagh Head" of the local "Head Line", also known as the "Heyn Steamship Company", the "Ulster Steamship Company" and I believe also the "Holland and Mountain Steamship Company". Maurice Mann had again surfaced - at Castlereagh, and made a contribution to "migration" and one or two old grizzled maintenance fitters made encouraging sounds. In comparison with earlier days, when I heard all my fellow apprentices talk enthusiastically about "getting away to sea", there was no such talk at Castlereagh - I cannot remember any of my contemporaries having the slightest notion of going away to sea. I think to be realistic, the earlier aspirations of apprentices was due to a desire to escape from the status quo - yes, the thought of going to sea was a kind of option - an escapism. I remember going for a walk one day with my friend and mentor Horace Love and speculating on what sort of experience it would be, how strange - whether it would be better on a small ship or a large ship. We both agreed that life would never seem the same again after getting away - even for one trip.

Anyway I felt pretty naked when I went down and got graded. It would be possible to get a low grade or even to be graded unclassified.

The higher the grade, the greater exemption from certain parts of the Board of Trade Certificate examinations, which one would have to sit in order to become a Second Engineer (Seconds ticket) or Chief (a First Class Certificate). I was much surprised and relieved to receive a grade 2B which pleased me very much and it was a respectable weapon with which to approach a firm or the Shipping Federation. I still had the less encouraging views of the doubters - "nobody from a light engineering background could ever go to sea - they wouldn't take you", and I decided to visit the Shipping Federation who would know which companies were looking hands. So round I went to Albert Square and there beside the "Lifeboat Bar", I found the Federation - sometimes called the "pool" because apparently seamen could register there for work and (I understood) would be entitled to a percentage wage during the time they were waiting for a ship. There were two sections - Officers i.e. Engineers, Navigating Officers, possibly Radio Officers as well (although "sparks" would be more likely to work for Marconi, who would allocate them to ships as required) and seamen, deck hands (E.D.H. - efficient deck hands), AB's (able body seamen) engine room ratings - greasers, donkeymen, firemen, storemen - stewards, cooks - probably "chippie" - the carpenter, as well. I went to the officers side - I hope my memory is correct on this one - there was some demarcation or other. I met Mr Telford and enquired naively if any chance existed for someone like myself, coming from light engineering, getting an appointment as a junior engineer. "Have you a grading certificate?" he asked, and upon receiving this, took some time before informing me that there was just a chance that the "Head Line" of Belfast might be looking such a person. Eventually it was proposed that I make my way over to Victoria Street, to the Ulster Steamship and Head Line building, and ask for the Superintendent Engineer. I cannot recall if I was armed with an introduction or not, but off I went. Well not quite - it was late in the afternoon and I decided that I would go the next day.

Next day, before I eventually went down to the Head Line offices, I decided to go down to the docks - I cannot remember where exactly - I was curious now to have a look at a ship, especially a cargo ship (the only ship I had ever been on was the Isle of Man steamer - the SS "Tynwald"). Now I saw a number of vessels mostly lying alongside various quays - each with at least one hold open to the atmosphere - cargo being lifted - I didn't see any ship loading up. Eventually, one small cargo ship started swinging away from the quayside - the front or what I took as the front doing the swinging, while the rear part of the ship seemed to be held fast - the ship appeared to be pivoting at one end, and, as the side of the ship swung into view, I saw the legend - in very large white letters "HEAD LINE" painted on the side. I also noticed a large Red Hand painted on the funnel, and eventually I was aware that there was a name painted across the back of the ship. It read "Ballygally Head", and underneath was the word, Belfast. By this time, the front of the ship was fairly swinging - still tied to the quayside at the rear, when I heard someone shout "Cast off aft" and the motion of the ship now fell away and the rope attaching the ship to the quay appeared to slacken. At this point, someone lifted the end of the rope - which seemed to be about 3 inches (or 75mm) thick, off the top of a steel pillar of sorts embedded in the quayside and threw it into the water. It was rapidly pulled aboard the MV "Ballygally Head", and soon the ship was in motion again, and made off out of the immediate dockland area, bound for where I knew not. But I knew - as everyone who read the Belfast Telegraph knew, where generally these locally registered ships traded to - it was printed every Tuesday or Wednesday pm, under "Belfast Shipping". Typical information would be,

M.V. Ballygally Head, sailed Belfast, Monday 5 December for Helsinki
or S.S. "Ramore Head", sailed Montreal, Thursday 8 December for
Liverpool and Belfast.

Eventually, I went around to the Head Line Building, and as I paused at the entrance, wondering if I was right in the head - I noticed something that struck me forcibly. The door step was worn down at left and right to a most noticeable degree. Anyway, I was directed up a flight of stairs or perhaps steps, and knocked on the door "Superintendent Engineer". When I was waiting, a young man joined me, and while sitting outside the Superintendent Engineer's Office, I was surprised to learn that he was the Second Engineer Officer of the M.V. "Inishown Head", the "old Inishown", that Henry Carson was almost lost off, during the monsoon. This Second Engineer was the late Gin Beggs from Larne, destined to die early in life. Later, I was also to get to know his father and brother, Billy. A man came out and on hearing of my interest in wanting a position as an engineer, he asked a few questions - then excused himself and went back into the office. Returning shortly he produced a company application form and proceeded to ask a few questions which appeared in writing on the form - answered as follows:

Experience in Water Tubular Boilers - None

Experience in Fire Tubular Boilers - None.

(I thought of telling him that we had an old stove at home which I thought had a boiler but said nothing.) Experience of welding, machining, soldering - I had a bit of experience here and there and I got the impression that I was being given generous credit - yes, I could use a file, but had never used a scraper - did I understand the use of a tensile gauge in conjunction with a flogging hammer? - I had to sit out on that one, as well.

Eventually, I signed this form - in the meantime my interrogator revealed himself as Mr Duke - Mr Percy Duke, Assistant Superintendent Engineer. He was not unfriendly - in the course of our conversation he told me that he was a former manager with Harlands at their Birkenhead works. About a vacancy? "Yes", he gravely inclined, "there might be a vacancy coming up - when was I available?" A short time later - a couple of days, I received word to go for a medical. Now in those days, the Federation doctor was the well known Dr Caldwell. He happened to be away on holiday at the time and I met instead, a young doctor who was standing in for Dr Caldwell. He wasn't taking any prisoners that day - he wasn't too sure about me. He had noticed a lot of injured limbs etc - and the marks of many stitches. The result of this encounter was that he asked me to get an appointment at the R.V.H. - a second opinion was required about certain structures - I cannot now recall if an x-ray was called up, but I now faced serious delay. First my GP had to ask for an appointment. Then the waiting - the Head Line became urgent in their inquiries - ships came and went - I had to wait. Eventually an appointment was obtained and I came away with a clean sheet. I was then told by the Head Line that I was offered an appointment as soon as I was free. I worked a week's notice at Shorts and with hearty good wishes ringing in my ears, I took my leave of all my friends - those who had helped me through difficult personal times (and difficult jobs). I suppose I had mixed feelings but I knew a change would help to reinvigorate the body and mind, and away I went.

The following week I reported to the Head Line Building and was instructed to go and stand by the SS "Rathlin Head", presently at the Alexander Dry Dock. I proceeded accordingly. When I got to the dock, I was told that the "Rathlin" was being towed round to the dock at that moment. Presently, amid the sirens of tugs etc, what seemed to be quite a large ship came into sight. "She" didn't enter the dock but tied up a short distance away. There was a number of people waiting to board and one like myself was a prospective seagoing engineer. I cannot remember his name, but he did sail on the SS "Torr Head" - to the States. (I also met him some years later). Anyway, I made my way up the gangway to seek out the Chief Engineer. He was a tall man with a bald head and horn rimmed glasses. After a few questions, he directed me to someone who would show me where to hang my gear and would take me to the engine room.

That someone turned out to be one George Stewart, who had been sailing as 4th Engineer on the "Rathlin Head". He was leaving. He then introduced me to the Fifth Engineer Officer of the "Rathlin Head" a fellow called Kennedy - he was leaving. He then introduced me to the Sixth Engineer Officer - a chap called Houston - I forget his first name. He came from Lough Road, Lurgan, and he was staying aboard. Houston was one of the most decent and helpful persons I ever met in spite of him not being without his own problems, on the Rathlin Head. I also met Davy McCullough the Third Engineer - he had been with the company for some time having sailed on a number of their ships. I cannot say how I discovered it - perhaps George Stewart had said, that the chap before him in the Fourth's berth was a guy called Wilbur Campbell. It turned out that it was none other than my old school pal of Ballymena Technical High School, and he came from Hillmount, near Cullybackey. But it was many years before I met him again - and he confirmed that he was an earlier "foro" on the boat. Wilbur was a manager with the DOE, Driver and Vehicle Testing Agency Department (Now retired).

Anyway it was proposed I would go on the MV "Fair Head" or the "Rathlin Head" depending on which was ready to leave first. The "Rathlin" was a turbine cargo vessel with accommodation for twelve passengers. "She" had Babcox and Wilcox Water Tube Boilers, impulse reaction turbines, and a service speed of fifteen knots, with one propeller. The ship was moved into the dry dock, resting on blocks placed beneath the flat keel plate and supported port and starboard by timber props extending to the "steps" of the dry dock. I had my first experience of being able to walk around the ship on the dock floor seeing the large four blade propeller and the rudder - I noticed some damage to the tip of one blade where a small piece was missing. There was something else I was to learn here. The propeller, being made of phosphor bronze, rotating within a steel sternframe and immersed in a electrolyte of sea water, creates the conditions for galvanic action; that is, where two dissimilar metals, e.g. bronze and steel, form a closed circuit (in sea water). The steel will corrode as it is the more electropositive metal. To stop this corrosion, zinc plates are attached to the sternframe and being more electric positive than steel, will be corroded instead. These zinc plates are commonly seen - even on fishing boats where they are sometimes fitted to the hull and are referred to as "sacrificial anodes".

During the "layup" in dry dock, various people were coming and going - Harlands' men, (including Billy Grills, my old friend from the College of Technology), and various Head Line people - engineers dropping along from other Head Line ships in port. Sometimes I heard serious conversations or arguments about procedure, among this lot. One day a visiting chief engineer came aboard to see what was going on and I could see that this man took a light hearted view of what was being considered serious by others - he was probably the only chief there I saw laughing at the time - very heartily. He was none other than my old friend of yesteryear, John Kerr*, late Chief Engineer of the SS "Fanad Head". John enjoyed many a laugh - and other things, round at Whitehead. He started his seagoing career with Kelly's Coal boats but joined the Head Line in 1927. He was torpedoed in the SS "Bengore Head", North Atlantic, in 1941 , the transfer to the lifeboat being so smooth, that he barely got his feet wet. He was a mine of information on the rapidly vanishing world of steam at sea.

During the first few days I was aboard, I met Mr Garrett - a company chief engineer who was working on board during this layup. It was he who taught me how to open a steam valve. "Open a steam valve", you might say, "nothing to it - get a wheel key on it and yank it open - don't stop turning until it's fully open".

But there is more to it than that - if you did that always, some day you might not live to open another.

In opening steam from a boiler to a system of pipework, all water condensate must be drained from that system - drain cocks are fitted for this purpose. I was taught to "crack" the steam inlet valve open, using a wheel key - then progressively, open until the spindle was back against the stop. Finally, turn the valve spindle in - perhaps half a turn. In this way the valve could not be jammed fully open. It is important for time to be given to allow all water to clear pipework prior to a steam inlet valve being opened up. If say, some water is left in a pipe adjacent to a steam inlet, and the steam cracked on, steam may pass over this water, and some of the steam will be condensed by the colder water. This leads of a vacuum being formed, and a difference of pressure in different parts of the pipe. Roughly speaking, the water is given energy (kinetic), causing rapid movement of the water, resulting in the giving up of this energy in the form of blows or impact - surgings which could cause severe stress in pipe or valve chest, and could cause an explosion and fracture of the pipework. This has caused loss of life in the past as in the famous case of the SS "Araguaya", Royal Mail Steam

(* - John Kerr died in April 1999, aged one hundred years)

Packet Company of before the Second World War. A technical account of this is given in a paper published by H.M. Stationary office - which was priced at two shillings and three pence. So when, Mr Garrett, one of the Chiefs, spent some time showing me how to open a steam inlet, it was an important lesson. It has happened that a valve be opened so completely and tight against the stop, that it has proved difficult to close it. To my sure knowledge, this happened on a steamer where the throttle valve being opened in full ahead, jammed in that position, when being manoeuvred by a junior engineer. Company policy was altered, so that only certified engineers were permitted to manoeuvre - that's how serious the matter was regarded. This ship had triple expansion steam engines. (See "Jammed throttle valves").

I was alerted to the fact that ships entering ports abroad and in the U.K. when coming from foreign parts are subject to scrutiny of the ship's manifest - a declaration of what crew members might declare as their property - watches, cameras, musical instruments and anything being brought into port by way of souvenirs, cigarettes, wines etc.

I was indeed to see the Custom men at work, when later, coming in from Canada, I had a few souvenirs - cushion covers, models of Red Indian canoes and hatchets and similar trash. Excise duty of four shillings and sixpence (about 23 pence) was enacted! I also saw how some people hid things like watches and bracelets - for example by unscrewing light fittings and filling up cavities with contraband. I had a fear that someone might stash something in my cabin - cuckoo fashion and secretly remove it - if the customs man had not got there before him. It runs in my head that a quantity of cigarettes and whiskey was discovered by customs in below the Diesel generator, (nobody knew anything about it of course). I believe the ship was fined seventeen pounds and ten shillings (£17.50) - moving up on a fireman's salary for a month.

THE WATER TUBE BOILER - BABCOX & WILCOX DESIGN

as installed in the S.S. "RATHLIN HEAD".

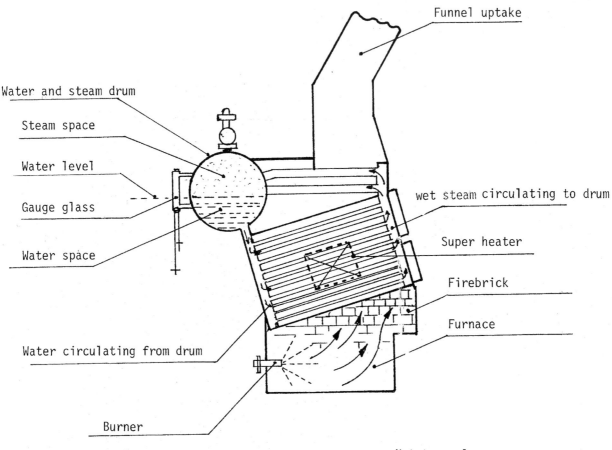

Funnel uptake

Water and steam drum

Steam space

Water level

Gauge glass

Water space

wet steam circulating to drum

Super heater

Firebrick

Furnace

Water circulating from drum

Burner

Not to scale

The sketch above shows the general principle for steam generation in a water tube boiler. Here, water from a relatively small water and steam drum circulates upward through a bank of tubes, which are subject to heat from the furnace products of combustion. Water tube boilers, contemporary of the period being recalled, generated pressures of between 300 - 600 lb/in². In modern water tube boilers, pressures of 1000 lb/in² would not be uncommon.

14.7 lbs /sq in = 1 Bar

THE SCOTCH BOILER - as installed in the S.S. "GRECIAN".

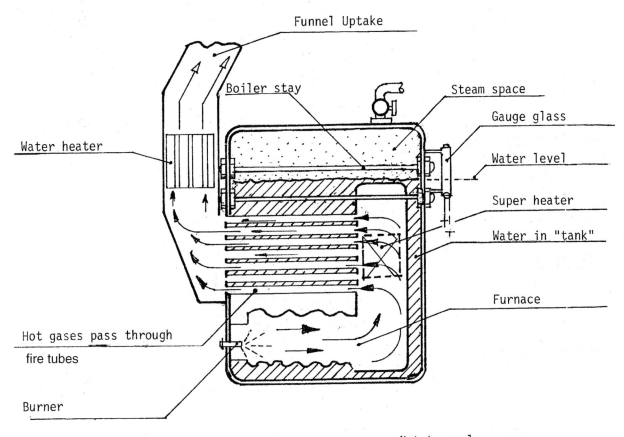

Funnel Uptake

Boiler stay

Steam space

Gauge glass

Water heater

Water level

Super heater

Water in "tank"

Furnace

Hot gases pass through
fire tubes

Burner

Not to scale

Sketch above of typical arrangements for steam generation in a Scotch Boiler, where the hot gases of combustion pass through tubes (fire tubes) which are surrounded by the large mass of water in the rest of the boiler. The Scotch Boiler is also known as a Firetube Boiler or Tank Boiler–because of the large surface area subject to boiler pressure, the pressure would be relatively low, - of the order of 220/250/lb/in².

14.7 lbs /sq in = 1 Bar

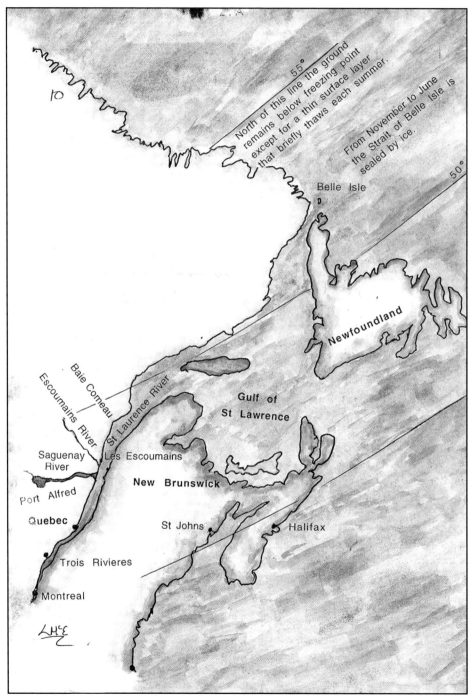

The North Atlantic approaches to the St. Lawrence River

Jammed throttle valves

The inexplicable jamming of both throttle valves at sea was dealt with by the brute force of the engine room crane. But how did the rust get on the valve spindles to cause the jamming?

A most peculiar incident took place on a ship, of which I was the Chief Engineer, when both the ahead and astern throttle valves of the main propulsion turbines got jammed. This happened while the vessel was at sea! The ship was a single-screw 18 000, ton bulk carrier and steam was provided by a single medium-pressure water-tube boiler. Due to some problems with the condenser vacuum the main engine had been slowed down. On restoration of full vacuum the engineer on watch tried to open the ahead throttle but he could not move the wheel. He then tried to close the valve and tried to open it again, but the wheel stayed stuck. Out of curiosity, the astern throttle valve was tried out next. While the valve opened easily enough, on trying to close it, the astern wheel could not be moved either. Fortunately, the astern guard valve did not get jammed, so we were able to keep it shut. There we were in the middle of the sea, with the ahead throttle jammed closed and the astern throttle jammed open!

The driving linkages of both the valves were checked and found completely free. However, the valve spindles on the turbine casing were jammed. The valves had hard metallic packings which were impossible to extract. By using the engine room crane, the ahead throttle spindle was finally forced open with great difficulty but it proved impossible to close it again. The astern valve spindle stayed in the same condition.

Since there was a storm coming up and we were only 200 miles from our port of destination, it was decided to proceed there rather than open up the main throttle valves at sea.

Ahead movement at full speed was no problem, although astern movement was, of course, out of the question. While entering the harbour, speed reductions were effected by the main boiler stop valve, an oiler being posted there and a suitable system of signals arranged. With the assistance of a tug, the vessel anchored safely.

Both throttle valves were now dismantled. In the process the ahead spindle got bent and had to be renewed. Large amounts of rust-like deposits were found on both spindles. The turbo-alternators' steam was supplied through a separate line, which drew its steam before the supply to the main propulsion turbines. On checking, their throttle-valve spindles were, curiously enough, found to be absolutely free and clean. Both the main throttle valves were now boxed back and to the best of my own knowledge, the trouble never occurred again.

Though several probable causes have been advanced, the exact cause has never been clear. The deposits on the spindles were checked by the representatives of the boiler-chemical suppliers, but their findings remained inconclusive. Steam, at the point of entry to turbines was collected and tested, but no unusual solid concentration was found.

The vessel was provided with a Bailey control system and neither the engineers' testimony nor the Bailey charts showed any evidence of boiler priming or abnormal rise in temperature of steam causing thermal distortion of spindles. Chemical companies claim that feed-water additives cannot be carried over with superheated steam.

Readers' comments on the above incidence will be welcome.
A. Muker - Dartmouth, N.S., Canada. JUNE 1979
(Courtesy Inst. Marine Engineer's Bulletin)

Chapter 6 - A world of steamships and men

Some people I met on the SS "Rathlin Head"

The Second Engineer was a guy called Reeves and I am pleased to say that I got on very well with him. I sometimes had meals with him in Harland's canteen which was nearby. In fact George Stewart, who had done several trips with him, remarked that the Second "was sociable", in that he had not a problem being in the company of those junior to him, off duty.

I had a lot to learn, especially as I was asked to go as fourth engineer, watch-keeping on my first trip. In fact, when the second engineer heard this he couldn't believe it - "You'll never do it", he said, "The engine room log is a yard long - and filled on both sides".

During the weeks the "Rathlin" was laid up, all systems were shut down. Boiler furnaces had brickwork maintenance to be done, and various bearings, pumps, etc had to be replaced or refurbished. But although I can't say that I saw or even knew of their existence, undoubtedly the sea water inlet valves were overhauled. These are the valves that admit sea water into the ship-for ballast, engine and auxiliary system cooling and for fire fighting, water for washing the deck etc. The only time these valves can be opened up for maintenance, is during a dry docking. So, for a while the ship was "cold" - and dependent upon power from a shore supply. About this time, another junior engineer joined us - he was Desmond Thompson who had just completed an apprenticeship in heavy automobile (Diesel) trucks etc.

The "dead" ship was eventually floated, and towed out of the dry dock and berthed. The boilers were "flashed" - in those days some waste and paraffin oil were set alight in the furnace and initially the boiler was run on diesel oil. It was necessary to get steam up before the heavy boiler fuel- Esso Green Grade C, could be heated to the required temperature, and the fuel pump brought into action. Most of the pumps were "up and down" jobs (compressed air could be used to operate such a pump until sufficient steam would become available). The superheater tubes - arranged in the hottest area of combustion, could be damaged if steam didn't circulate quickly through them and to prevent damage, the superheater tubes would be flooded or vented. The generators were also steam driven "up and downers" with a diesel stand by generator - a Ruscon Hornsby, I believe. By running the diesel, power could be supplied (as in any emergency) until the steam generators were on the "Board". The electrical system was D.C. and if I remember alright, the average load was about 135A - virtually everything - pumps, engines, generators, deck winches were all steam driven. The hatch timbers were manually put in place covered by tarpaulins, and secured by wedges (I hope my memory is correct here!)

* * * * * * * * *

A change had been made in the engineering guys - the Second Engineer was having a trip off and his place was taken by a relieving Second - one Jimmy Spiers, a Comber man, a Harlands man and ex Blue Funnel. (Many years later our paths crossed again, and we have been close friends since).

The "Fair Head" didn't arrive before we came out of the dock and I was confirmed and signed on as 4th Engineer on the "Rathlin". One Saturday afternoon we went on standby. Engineers assembled in the engine room - all six of us - each with some place of responsibility. My station was controlling the fuel oil pressure on the burner jets and also maintaining the fuel oil at the correct temperature. So I heard the telegraph and engine movements for the first time in my life and eventually the ship passed down Belfast Lough.

The compass was "swung" off Bangor Bay (checked against well known landmarks) and the late Captain Andy Fee set course for North America and Montreal. Montreal was thirty-six hours steaming time up the St. Lawrence river.

The engine room log - which I knew was ahead of me "a yard long and on both sides" was headed "Belfast to Escoumains", Escoumains being where the pilot was picked up at the mouth of the St. Lawrence. Leaving Bangor and heading for the Atlantic, we met the MV "Fair Head" homeward - I very nearly got her.

Later, however, I did meet up with her in Montreal as she docked on her way down the St. Lawrence seaway. I went on board on that occasion and met the Fair's fourth engineer - Joe McRandall from Ballymena.

I also met Nat Savage who was sailing 2nd Mate. Nat came from Randalstown, but I heard of his death, some years ago. (I also met them again in King's Dock, Liverpool).

But now I had a lot on my plate - let's see what an Engine Room watch-keeper should be about. Let me say, that it must be the finest training that anyone in engineering could have. The watch-keeping engineer must use all his senses. Entering the Engine Room on the top platform, he stands observing. Tanks which have sighting glasses to indicate the level inside such tanks can be quickly monitored. Then down to boiler level, checking water levels and boiler pressure. The vacuum in the condenser would be checked one level down. One might observe if sounds are normal -no unusual noises so, move on. One has to grow quickly accustomed to the characteristic smells of a steam engine room - steam, heavy fuel (perhaps the odd leak here and there) hot pipe lagging, new paintwork - paraffin oil perhaps on the tubular work recently cleaned (if this has happened to the rails of engine room steps - careful, there is not much of a grip for your hands). The universal joke of a steamship goes like this :- Some guy is up for his "seconds" ticket and he is asked what steps he would take if, upon entering the engine room, he noticed that the gauge glass was showing no water in the boilers. Classic answer through the ages:- "The engine room steps, Sir, two at a time".

Descending still further, on the manoeuvring platform, oil pressures on bearings, pinions or turbine etc can be checked - have a look at the propeller RPM. The "gennie" (generator) is ok as well. Check feed pump and fuel oil pump - is that scream from the double reduction gearing normal? - move on down the tunnel (you have nodded to the fireman and greaser - they know the job well). Down the tunnel, relative quietness reigns - you touch each huge bearing taking the load of the tons of propeller shaft perhaps 15-18 ins diameter, in sections, bolted at huge flanges. You will know if overheating is taking place - check bearing keep nuts for signs of slackening. Finally, where the tail end shaft goes through the hull (through the stern tube and a bearing of lignum vitae) - check if enough sea water is trickling through to attend to cooling and lubrication needs. Everything seems ok, so back to the bright lights around the front of the boilers - everything ok to sight, touch and smell.

An important precaution that prudent engineers on that type of machinery will observe is to have all stand by pumps and engines opened up ready to start instantly should a lubricating oil pump or a feed pump etc stop - and refuse to start. This usually meant leaving drains open as well as the exhaust. Then to start, all one had to do was to open the steam inlet and hopefully "all systems go." Now such a pump had a way of taking one to the brink. You would see, say a lub oil pump stop. Now a fall in oil pressure would mean that unless pressure was restored in say 2-4 minutes - (depending on design of plan) a steam valve would automatically close -nasty situation - no power on main engines when the ship might be going across the mouth of a river, coming out of a loch, or other situation when control is absolutely vital. One would rush over to the pump (wondering how long it had stopped) and waiting to hear the ear shattering blast of the alarm system if too late. But just as the inlet on the standby pump is about to be opened why the beastly "up and downer" lub oil pump would move, as if there was no tomorrow. Sometimes a tap on the auxiliary spindle, in a "lost motion" period, would coax the beast to start. All light is artificial, dependent on the "Gennies" - ships have standby "Gennies" as well - some, in that era, emergency battery lighting. An EMERGENCY capacity gennie could be mounted on the main deck or even the Boat deck. (In case of flooding below, this "gennie" might be automatic in getting under way, if a major power failure occurs). The Diesel standby in the "Rathlin" was, as far as I can remember, started by turning a starting handle - similar to that used in starting cars at one time. This was the only diesel "gennie" that I ever saw that didn't use a compressed air start. Perhaps it was, relatively speaking, a small one.

The Atlantic crossings at that time of year were fairly stormy - force 10 gales from time to time. My first watch took me past the Donegall coast and well out into the Atlantic breakers. Something before eight p.m., I dropped down into the engine room for the 8-12 watch where I relieved the second engineer Jimmy Spiers (now living in Antrim.) Just as he was taking leave of me, a gauge glass in one of the boilers burst, cascading a torrent of steam and water with a roar like a lion. Above this racket, Jimmy shouted that he would stay behind and give me a hand, as he suspected I had never changed a gauge glass before. He was right - I'd never seen one before. So, with water and steam shut off, we changed the gauge glass. Later, I was to remember this help and tutorial with gratitude when, with a different ship and company I found myself in the same situation - by then I knew how to change a gauge glass. I might say that the first four hours any engineer spends in an engine room is the longest four hours of one's life - and nobody coming off watch, wants to be there any longer than necessary.

The fireman and the greaser were old hands. Around ten o'clock, one of them went 'up' and returned later with coffee and toast. We used condensed milk. But already I was feeling distinctly groggy as the "Rathlin" gently answered the pattern of the Atlantic waves. I remember distinctly that the ship was pitching fore and aft with little roll. After a while, she was really beginning to drop into the Atlantic swell and at eleven o'clock, I was lying draped over a piece of machinery, quite oblivious to all mankind - nay, completely unconcerned had the ship been sinking. Sick as a dog - I was certainly "bringing it up green". The fireman and greaser were well used with such pantomimes and the greaser urged me to drink something - "always keep something down", he said. It was not to be the last time that I saw firemen and greasers and sailors show compassion to their brothers in distress. I simply don't remember how the first log was completed - I think the fifth engineer Houston had a hand in it - I seem to recall that, as he had several trips under his belt, he knew his way around very well. That night, the Chief Engineer gave me a draft of punch and I slept the sleep of the just.

Next morning was a Sunday. Before tackling the job again, I was out on deck after breakfast. Travelling along the great circle route, we would pass over the graves of countless ships lost in the Atlantic especially in World War II and of countless U-boats.

Jimmy Spiers was passing at the time and I suppose I gasped "How did men fight a war here?" "Ah, you don't want to think about that, 4th", he said. He always called me "fourth" or "foro". But sea sickness passes.

Some examples of the set rituals of watch keeping involved for example, ringing the bridge every watch, just before noon and midnight, and saying "Sea water temperature - such and such". As far as I remember, the difference between "normal" Atlantic temperature and that crossing the Gulf Stream at that time of year and latitude was about 4 degs. F. Another involved "blowing tubes" i.e. using a steam "knife" to de soot the outside of the water tubes which, subject to the products of combustion in the boiler, would have a deposit of sooty carbon on the outside surfaces, reducing the conductivity ability of the tubes to pass heat to the water in the inside of the said tubes. So the bridge would be rung up and you would say "Blowing tubes in 5 minutes or 10 minutes". If not safe or convenient they would advise you so.

If it was safe and convenient to do so, the ship would turn, so that it would steam for a short time with the wind blowing across the ship and not in line, bow to stern. This allowed the soot which gushed from the funnel to be blown "over the side" and not down to the aft end where it might descend on some nice fresh paintwork down around the "poop", that little raised platform, right aft. If that happened, news would get around that the Bosun (boss of the deck hands and AB's) was in an angry mood!) After that, the bridge would be rung "Finished blowing tubes". Carried out on the second's watch, I wasn't normally involved in this on the "Rathlin" but I was to get plenty of practice elsewhere later!

As I said four hours on a watch is a long time to pass. You are not normally making anything or repairing something that has packed up - you are constantly on preventative maintenance - lub oil purification, give that filter a couple of turns every hour - keep the air/fuel ratio correct - by checking through a coloured glass you could see the nature of the flame in the boiler furnace - give more air or less - by altering the speed of the fans. Black smoke usually calls for more fan and white smoke might indicate too much fan. This all leads to efficient combustion and keeps burners clean. Of course, things happen that need attention - as above, a gauge glass could blow, condenser tubes and even boiler tubes could develop leaks and would have to be blanked off or even replaced. On one watch I found a propeller shaft bearing overheating and on another occasion one of these bearing housings was coming adrift. The usual drill was, although constantly looking for obvious trouble, you'd walk around the complete job every hour. As well, bunker fuel had to be heated, otherwise it would be difficult to pump. Another ritual was "blowing through" the water and steam inlets to the boiler gauge glasses - first open the drain; open water cock and close; open steam cock; then both cocks and drain open. Water or steam or both would rush into the Engine Room. If satisfactory, these inputs to the gauge glass would then be closed. This was indeed an important job done routinely - a blocked gauge glass could mislead everyone into thinking there was normal water level in the boilers - while this may not be the case! But the watch went past slowly. Then a surprise! Since the sun is travelling west, if we wanted to have the same time as the Canadians, we would have to put the clock back! So on my watch I had to put the clock back 20 minutes - and this has been the longest 20 minutes each watch going west, that ever passed for me.

But soon I was to see a sight which you don't see around the Coast Road in County Antrim - icebergs. These monsters, had presumably been slowly drifting all summer, a fifth above, four-fifth below, and always appeared blue from a distance. I always thought that the air was colder when they were around.

The fourth engineer has a visitor from time to time - the Chief Engineer, who is nominally on watch during the 8-12. Unless something is giving trouble, the Chief would not stay too long, although on the "Rathlin Head" I'm sure the Chief did always stay long enough to feel that all was well - especially when he had a "fourth" with a lot to learn.

So day after day the ship ploughed into the Atlantic - in fact the weather became very rough and progress was slow, but eventually after about 9 days - possibly a couple more than normal, we had passed north of Newfoundland and soon were under the lee of the wide mouth of the St. Lawrence river. (Later as ice crept in on the area, the route would be south of Newfoundland, then later the St. Lawrence would freeze over until the spring). The uncomfortable motion ceased and a steady platform was beneath one's feet. My first sight of a whale was an impressive one - a huge beast, blowing and displaying the huge tail - then land - Belle Isle in the Belle Isle Straits.

The Atlantic transit was over at Escoumains, where a pilot was picked up for Quebec; at Quebec, and the Heights of Abraham which General Wolff's men scaled, and defeated the French under Montcalm, another pilot took us to Three Rivers (Trois Rivieres) where logs were piled in huge mountains everywhere you looked - then the final twelve hours to under the Jacque Cartier Bridge and Montreal. By the way, Escoumains is close to the river of that name, a small place on the St. Lawrence River. During the river passage, "dog watches" were called for - two engineers were required on watch together. A busy river is a dangerous place - if for example you lose power or experience some technical difficulty. So I had to do a "dog" or two, a two hour extra stint along with the Second, Jimmy Spiers. As the crew were mostly from Northern Ireland, chat would tend to centre on local things.

Eventually just before we reached Montreal, we came alongside a refuelling jetty where bunkers were taken on board. This was to be the first time I was to hear "foreign" voices, Canadians working for the oil company. The weather was apparently much warmer than in Belfast.

While in this vast city with a population of two and three quarter million people, we got caught in a dockers' strike.

I took the opportunity one evening to set off and try and find two elderly Canadian sisters - Jan and Sadie Fleming, whose father had lived at the Rough Lane, a short distance from Ladyhill School, Antrim, where I had attended. They lived in the Sherbrook area - Bus 32! It was while trying to get directions etc etc that I experienced being snubbed by French Canadians - I think by bus drivers, who declined to speak English. But I managed it, and I find it hard to describe the obvious pleasure that these first generation Canadians of Antrim descent exuberated. They showered upon me every kindness; I in turn was amazed at the persistence and diligence with which they pursued finding out as much as they could about Antrim. In fact, they had briefly visited Antrim some years earlier and showed me a photo of the pew in First Antrim Presbyterian Church where their father had worshipped (this was in the days when there were family pews). I think I am right in saying that no paternal Flemings of this family circle are living in the Antrim area today, although other descendants still most certainly are - the Bell family and some Gowdy family members. I was to visit Jan Fleming and her sister on several occasions and kept up a correspondence for several years. They've since long passed away.

Montreal seemed to me to have inhabitants who all had sallow - somewhat yellow complexions. I had a reassuring experience however when, along with the Sixth Engineer, Des Thompson, I went to St. James United Church. This was a most interesting experience. Apart from the form of service - something like a Presbyterian - I believe the Presbyterians had united with the Congregationalists and Methodists to form the United Church - there were two Ministers and we were asked to sign the visitors book - they told us they would send a little memento - and were as good as their word. But the most striking thing I noticed was the colour of the faces of the people gathered - they all had white/ruddy complexions just like what you would see in any Irish or British town. So I concluded that there was some ethnic difference between the descendants of the Gauls and those of the Saxons.

A word about nights on board in port: Normal working in port, as far as the engineers were concerned involved doing all sorts of maintenance. This included opening up the turbine double reduction gearing - for inspection. After tea, two engineers remained on board - in case something needed attention, as the dockers worked far into the evening using cluster lamps. These two would be from the third or fourth or fifth or sixth engineers. When not on duty, one was free. I always went up to St. Catherine's Boulevard - a street fifteen miles long. In those days, neon lights were hardly used in the UK but they gave a dazzling display as far as the eye could see, in Montreal. Apart from buying a few souvenirs, walking through Chinatown, or just generally nosing about - I never saw or heard anything spectacular. There were a lot of beggars around, usually outside the taverns - pubs, but avoiding these guys, I never had any tales to tell the next morning. By contrast, every time the others went off duty, the next morning in the saloon (where I must say the food was very good indeed) the talk went along the lines "Did you see the guy getting shot last night?" or somebody was robbed or somebody was imposed upon by a beautiful lady (who just happened to be passing) and such like things. Maybe I wasn't in the right places.

Well, the strike was eventually settled and the day arrived to sail away. I had not had the wit to leave a forwarding address at home - I hadn't even thought about it, but when I saw everyone else receive mail from home - especially as we were there twice or three times as long as normal owing to the strike, I wished I had. I wrote home and gave a forwarding address in Liverpool - then bought a large hamper of Canadian "Macintoshes" and soon found myself standing at my place - the oil heaters and fuel oil pressure pump, as the ship was manoeuvred out into the St. Lawrence and headed East. This time my watch was 20 minutes short each watch - I looked forward to shoving that engine room clock forward that 20 minutes, the way I used to look forward to leaving school!

*   *   *   *   *   *   *   *   *   *

One of the features of travelling up the St. Lawrence is the sight of the maple trees covering the slopes on either side of the river. When Autumn comes, the leaves on these trees turn a most beautiful colour. It is a golden spectacular hue and it's something I would like to experience again - a trip up the St. Lawrence or its tributaries. The "Head Line" ships went to many ports in North America, from Wilmington and New York in the South to St. Johns and Montreal in the North. As well, ships travelled up the St. Lawrence Seaway and into the complex of locks leading to the Great Lakes where they went to the great American and Canadian cities - Detroit, Chicago, Windsor, Toronto and so forth. I didn't, regretfully, manage such a trip.

I think twelve passengers enjoyed these trips - and inevitably on each crossing, there came the ritual of a visit to the engine room, each passenger being kitted out with nice clean white gloves. Down they would come, usually about eleven o'clock in the morning and accompanied by the Chief Engineer. Afterwards they would join the officers of the ship for lunch in the Saloon as usual. I remember I shared a small table with the 3rd, 5th and 6th engineers, at another table close by, sat the Chief Engineer, Captain Andy Fee, Second Engineer, Mr Harris the Mate, and a few passengers. At other tables would be the remaining passengers and the other officers of the ship including "Sparks" the radio operator.

When in Canadian ports, one would often see the Lakers - those long, very long ships with an engine at the back pushing the cargo of grain or whatever. They would have come from the Great Lakes and down to the Atlantic ports where this grain would find its way into the holds of ships travelling to many places in the world. There were other ships of similar size as the Head Line, trading in grain and apples - even copper Ingots - from memory these were about one metre (one yard) long and possibly six or eight inches square (150-200mm). (Time however distorts things - they would have been too heavy I think for the average man to lift). One such other prominent company, was Manchester Liners which came up the Manchester Ship Canal before the Atlantic transit. I remember the "Manchester Mariner" and "Manchester Merchant", also the "Canadian Pacific Liners", and many others that passed in the night.

The North Atlantic was constantly moving, and on one occasion the prevailing motion caused violent rolling sending one skating from beam to beam on the engine deck across the front of the boilers. This motion could be constant for days. After nothing but fresh sea air for a week or more, when approaching the North of Ireland at Inishtrahull off Donegal, one could smell the faint smell of smoke - probably turf. When off Liverpool in the Irish Sea, one could also smell smoke, but of coal this time. A Light ship was on station there in those days and was known as the "Bar Light". There, manoeuvring would begin, and could take four hours before a ship tied up and F.W.E. (finished with engines) would be rung on the Engine Room Telegraph. A pilot might be picked up there or perhaps at Lyness on the Welsh Coast. There were several pilot stations for the Mersey transit - one, at times off the Isle of Man.

On occasion, the "Rathlin" was docked in the Alexander dock, and there I remember seeing the "City of Poona" an Ellerman City freighter - she towered about us - a monster by comparison and I remember another ship passing us in the dock - going very fast as I thought. I looked at the name of the ship - it was "Flaminian" an Ellerman Papayanni Lines boat. I was to meet her again many years hence.

When I was on the "Rathlin" the ship always docked in Liverpool where five days or more might be spent discharging. Then to Belfast - up the "Lough". I remember on one occasion arriving off Belfast one late evening and lying in Carrick roads all night before docking in the "Pollock".

During this time I was trying to do a bit of revision - I had that date with the College of Technology - I wasn't to forget about it. Whatever I was doing or where - my maths book wasn't too far away - I thought of doing a "ticket" (Engineer's certificate of competency) as well. I think socially speaking, I had much rapport with a lot of different people. Apart from the maths book, I had also brought on board a bagpipe practice chanter (much to the Chief Steward's chagrin) and a five row Italian chromatic accordion - something I had bought as a compensation to myself for suffering being brought down to Mother Earth from my motorcycle by the dog, (which nobody owned). This instrument was to prove of interest to some and a great encouragement to others to step up their consumption of beer!

One of the first people I got to know, and who was very helpful to me was a man by the name of Bill Martin, the 3rd Mate. Bill Martin was fond of a beer. But he had other sides to his character. A former gunnery officer in the Royal Navy, he had turned from his former profession and taken up an entirely new one. By what route he was sailing as a navigating officer I cannot recall - to be on the bridge one has either to become a cadet and serve an apprenticeship, or progress through study from the ranks of the sailor - the AB's. I can recall someone - I think Mr Harris the Mate, explaining to me just how difficult such a transition from a professional armament officer (R.N.), to a navigating officer (M.N.), would have been, and consequently there was some respect for Bill Martin's endeavours.

I remember one afternoon Bill visiting me in my cabin where he was telling me with the aid of a can of beer that he had just "got his divorce papers". Just at that time, an A.B. came to the door asking to see Bill. "Come in" I said, but Bill said "Wait, it would be better to go round to my cabin". So we went to the Mates' accommodation on the other beam during which time Bill said to me "I've been here a bit longer than you - it would be less risky if he came to my cabin". What on earth could he be meaning? Simply this, demarcation existed - generally speaking non-officers were not supposed to be on the officers' accommodation deck - presumably he would be able to explain the A.B's presence in his cabin more easily than I could explain his presence in mine. I was learning! Anyway, the A.B. and Bill got talking - the A.B. was up to show Bill his divorce papers! So it was a matter of "Have a look at this", or "Look what it says here" and other more unprintable things, the details lost in the mists of time.

THE APPROACHES TO LIVERPOOL

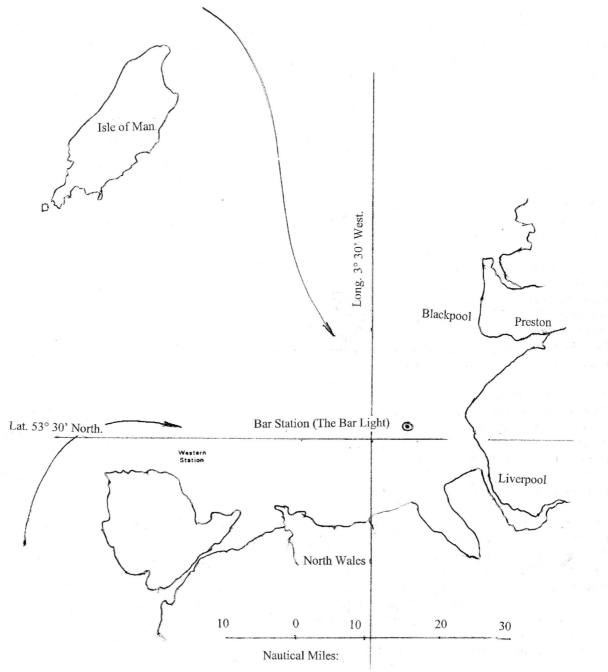

Isle of Man

Long. 3° 30' West.

Blackpool

Preston

Lat. 53° 30' North.

Bar Station (The Bar Light)

Western
Station

Liverpool

North Wales

10   0   10   20   30

Nautical Miles:

The status of sea-going engineers

by H. Campbell McMurray, B.A., M.Sc.(Econ), National Maritime Museum.

With the introduction of steam navigation in the early 19th century, a new class of seafarer emerged: the marine engineer. In the strong, capable, if often dirty hands of this new breed lay the responsibility for the efficiency of the ship's propelling and other machinery. It cannot be said, however, that these pioneers were indispensable to maritime commerce until, in Prof. Graham's words: " . . . the really portentous event in the history of ocean transport came not with the paddle-wheel, the iron hull or the screw propeller but with the final mastery of high pressures in the marine engine."

"A new class of seafarer emerged . . ."

However, the early ships' engineers did encounter a certain amount of resistance from the sailors. It must be remembered that the first ocean steamers were dirty, noisy, smoky little craft whose wheezing, croaking, groaning machinery contributed only a modest, unpredictable share of power. For many years, steamships were built heavily masted, fully rigged, and thus independent of their wretched engines.

"Independent of their wretched engines".

Clearly, the influx of the "rude mechanicals" posed a complex threat to the orthodox sailor and to the traditional stability of the shipboard organization. In a sailing ship most of the crew was needed to manipulate a vast array of canvas. To deprive seamen of this role, as the marine engine, even in its earliest form, threatened to do, was to take away the largest part of their raison d'être.

Later, the deck officers seem to have become the focus of engineers' aggrieved feelings of status deprivation.

While the engineer had full charge of the engine room, the limited nature of his responsibility, in comparison with the all-embracing ones of, for example, the first mate, must have restrained his demands for more influence on board.

With this burgeoning professional consciousness, then, the status of the engineer on shipboard appears to have gained somewhat and in 1893 a paper "The Status of Engineers of the Mercantile Marine" with the discussions takes up over 100 pages of the Transactions.

The author complained that the engineer had no legal authority whatever, and was unable to deal with any fractious hand serving under him. "If he be desirous of punishing any such offender, he must approach the master or mate . . . state his case and beg of him to fine and officially log the delinquent." It was remarked from the floor that, not uncommonly, when the engineer took a man before the captain, the master argued the matter as though it was a difference between equals. The men would take the greatest liberties with the engineer because they knew what would happen when he took them before the captain. However, many another contributor emphasized the excellent relations they had with the master and with the deck department generally.

"—The Master argued the matter as though it was a difference between equals" (see next page)

During evenings in port, I was oversubscribed by visitors to my cabin to urge me to greater heights of musical dexterity. I had bought a "tutor" from which to learn how to play this beast of an accordion (the chief merit of which was that it didn't matter what key you wished to play in, the scale used the same fingering - over three rows). But the men of the "Rathlin Head" had not time to wait for me learning such - so I played the instrument by ear, and have not departed therefrom until this day! Bill Martin was usually first over after dinner and last to be helped to his cabin when my fingers stopped working for the night. Later, Bill went ashore to study for another "ticket" and I never saw him again. But I was to hear about him - in surprising ways. Incidentally, Jimmy Spier's favourite tune was "The Northern Lights of Old Aberdeen" - it still is!

Another chap I was friendly with was Ron - the Second Mate. I used to visit him on the Bridge and he arranged for me to steer the ship from time to time. There was a "traditional" wheel on the bridge, while the "joystick" was just beginning to be used by other ships. As most people will understand, a man no longer manually causes the heavy rudder to turn. When the wheel is turned, it activates either an electric motor (through gearing), which turns the rudder, or a steam engine which drives a pinion in mesh with a quadrant - part of a large gear wheel, the centre of the quadrant turning the rudder post; or, as in the case of the "Rathlin", a steam engine generated hydraulic pressure to service rams which turned the rudder stock. One of the most interesting pieces of technology that someone had to think up was that device which returns the rudder to the neutral fore and aft position after a course change. This is accomplished by the Hunting Gear, a simple but ingenious device. Many years later when working for the Ministry of Defence, I saw that the same problem existed when the wing of a guided weapon is turned through an angle. What returns the wing to the original position? Well, an electrical equivalent to the Hunting gear!

The Chief Engineer was doing his best all along to initiate me into the mysteries of the engine room - e.g. the condenser, de-superheater, auxiliary steam lines, how to put generators "on the board" - all D.C. of course. There was as well, a lot of maintenance to be done in port. Valves had an insatiable appetite for requiring grinding - steam reducing valves especially needed careful grinding. "Stick around, young fellow", the Chief would say - "if you can stick me you'll learn an awful lot". No doubt he was right and that log (a yard long and on both sides), well, I was able to "hack it". It was always interesting at the end of each watch to take the tachometer reading - the number of revolutions the propeller would turn in four hours. At noon every day the total for 24 hours was added up and when multiplied by a constant gave the miles travelled per day. A propeller is like a nut being turned along a threaded bolt, each revolution will move the nut along the thread a distance equal to the "pitch" of the thread i.e. from say the top of one thread to the top of the adjacent thread. Now the pitch of a propeller is the amount it advances in one revolution of the propeller shaft if there were no slip, that is if you assume the propeller threads itself into a solid resistance. There is a method in finding the slip. First find the engine knots (6080 ft =one knot or sea mile). So engine knots is equal to the propeller pitch (feet) multiplied by the revolutions per minute multiplied by sixty minutes - all divided by 6080, and this gives engine knots/hour. With a large propeller pitch, one might be talking of the pitch equal to twenty feet - a fair distance for one turn of the screw.

Now the ship's knots would be less - because although it behaves closely as a solid resistance, the sea allows some slip. This is always referred to as the apparent slip because there is a further complication - the wake tends to be dragged after the ship and one would need to know the speed of the wake before the real slip could be found! The apparent slip is rarely greater than 4%. Now, up top, the device used to try to determine distance travelled is the patent log. When a ship clears harbour and starts the passage proper (down in the engine room it's known as "full away") the "log", a small cylinder with a propeller at one end is thrown over the after end of the ship on the end of a special "logline" possibly sixty yards long, or more. The propeller turns the "logline" which in turn connects to a "clock" mechanism and gives a read out of the knots travelled. At the end of passage i.e. before manoeuvring into the port commences, the log is read and taken on board - if left hanging about during periods when ship is stopped - why it could wrap itself around the propeller or rudder etc! The difference between engine room knots and the ships knots is then expressed as a percentage of engine room knots - the % slip.

I cannot remember where everyone worked during manoeuvring - certainly the sixth engineer recorded the engine movements and the Second was on the manoeuvring platform to manipulate the large chrome hand wheels which opened and closed the valves allowing steam on the ahead and astern turbine blades. The turbine speed - speaking of turbines in general, may be 3500 R.P.M., but since a propeller shaft speed may be as low as 100 R.P.M., double reduction gearing is usually required. A separate part of the turbine is used to give astern motion. This astern turbine is usually mounted on the same shaft at the after end of the rotor, and has blades angled the opposite way vis a vis the ahead turbine, to give opposite motion. The astern hand wheels have usually a second handwheel which acts as a lock - it's very very important that both astern and ahead valves are not open at the same time! If someone attempted it (occasionally they did) a very loud alarm sounded indeed.

One night I visited the Flemings and upon my return I discovered to my astonishment the notice at the bottom of the gangway reading "Shore leave expires at so and so hours".

Hurrying aboard, I discovered that it was true - a hive of activity was around me "everyone to the engine room, we're sailing". Yes, for some reason a decision was made to sail as soon as cargo loading was finished and to this day I don't know by what good fortune everyone got back on board in time - I suppose the decision was to sail as soon as everyone was back on board. Anyway we got away.

On another occasion we were leaving Montreal at eight o'clock - on my watch - this was good. Mr Reeves was sailing Second on this occasion. Passing under the main Boiler stop valves, I looked up and thought I heard steam leaking from a flange joint of this valve. I asked the Second what it was and upon considering it he said this "doesn't look good - I don't think the Chief will risk taking her to the River". Sure enough, when the Chief came down he looked at the flange joint and said it would have to be replaced. I remember the disappointment at having to shut down the job - then the job of dismantling the joints - removing the old and replacing it - everything was scalding. I wondered why we had to go to this bother just for a whiff of steam but I had still to learn that a small leak can suddenly "blow" and become a very large leak indeed. Such a thing could leave you with a ship dead in the water - better be sure than sorry. I marvel today that things like this stick in my memory. I was impressed by this caution!

It now seems amazing how in those days personnel in the noisy engine rooms of ships wore no protective ear muffs or plugs. They just persisted in shouting till their faces were purple, and when the message still failed to get through, red and purple faces gave way to all sorts of rage and frustration - probably ending with "I'll do it myself, you so and so" - so and so never even heard that! Imagine making telephone calls to up top! Later ships had small cubicles which shut out the din - later on came the palatial consoles of today and of press button generators. No poking round heavy generator's or alternator's flywheels with a crowbar till they were on "the marks" - then a blast of starting air and go. No, you now press a button and a "gennie" starts for you on its own - if you need extra power.

Steam in my experience was quieter than motor but I do seem to recall that the double reduction gearing on the "Rathlin" was very noisy. Anyway, nowadays if an engineer should venture out to look around the job he arms himself with muffs or throwaway plugs and is relatively oblivious to the racket. I must point out that muffs tend to reduce one of the senses - hearing, considered very important indeed in watchkeeping folklore. (But now we have flashing lights as well as alarm sirens - for the hard of hearing!)

One trip we went to Montreal and then upon coming down the St. Lawrence, we turned into the Saguenay river, a tributary of the St. Lawrence on the North Bank, and down stream from Quebec. This remarkable river flows really through a gorge, the sides thickly wooded with maples - now on this trip richly golden in their winter coat. High on the port side we came to a large statue of the Virgin Mary. The story goes that some fishermen were caught in a severe storm and all were lost except this one man who found himself swept and deposited on the side of the gorge. In gratitude, he had the statue built on the spot where he was washed up and it is now known as Virginity Point. I remember playing my accordion on the boat deck that afternoon, and somewhere, somebody has photographs of myself and others. I regret that I have no photos of myself or any other crew members of that period and ship.

The terminus for us was Port Alfred, away up the Saguenay. It was on this river, that the film, "River of no return," was made. I believe I'm correct in saying that cargoes from Port Alfred consisted largely of paper - mostly for the printing business. The wood pulp was readily available in the mountains of timber that littered the place.

One night, during my watch, I had a visit from the Captain, Andy Fee (who lived at Islandmagee incidentally). I had rarely seen him in the engine room, but now his interest centred on one of the ship's plates just abreast of the boilers. (The engine room and boiler room were all one in the "Rathlin").

This plate, I had noticed earlier, was cracked with a little water trickling down and since at that point we were below sea level possibly twenty or thirty feet, the pressure would have been quite substantial. However, he didn't seem to think the earth was coming to an end, and eventually departed for his kingdom above the water line. Upon arrival at Liverpool (or maybe it was Belfast) the plate was removed and a new one put in its place. The "Rathlin Head" was a riveted ship and the plate was subjected to a 4" hose pipe blast of sea water by way of testing, and all was well. I never heard the cause of the crack - I must say I watched it very carefully as I did my rounds until we reached dry land!

A most exciting event occurred one afternoon when I was having a read, lying on top of my bunk. The turbine and reduction gearing were quite noisy - especially the latter, and as such, one could certainly hear them even up in the accommodation. Suddenly, all was still - had I heard the telegraph ring?

Then the ship's telegraph certainly did ring (it was faint but I heard it) and knew the ship was manoeuvring. Then it started turning - by that time I and most others who were off duty were out lining the ship's rail and there, in the centre of our turning circle, was a huge yellow buoy and the buzzing went around - "Submarine down - it must have released a marker". So "Sparks" got on the job. Eventually the engines went "full ahead" and we resumed our journey - there had been NATO exercises in the area the week before - no subs. were missing - back to the book.

Once, on leaving the mouth of the St. Lawrence we were accompanied by a huge bird of enormous wing span. There was nothing too unusual about that - often birds circled around. But this guy had been with us three days and eventually flopped down on to the deck exhausted. It was thought he hitched a lift at night, but had to take to the air once deck activity started each day. Some of the sailors put him in the after mast house, where he survived and was, I understand, released into the Welsh mountains after docking at Liverpool. I understood that the bird was a buzzard of some kind.

Sparks was another fellow I used to visit in his radio room and during an especially awful bout of rolling and pitching and icebergs, he said to me, "Would you not be better down the Med weather like this?" I had not thought about it, but the idea appealed to me - if one could choose. "What companies go down there?" I asked, 'Oh, Ellermans, Moss Hutchinson, Prince Line - the lot" he said. The rolling of a ship perhaps appears worse or feels worse than what it really is. For example one day the rolling appeared so bad that I thought we were on our beam ends. But when I looked at the roll indicator, I found she had rolled only 26 degs from the vertical. On such occasions, chairs and tables were "anchored" to the floor by chains and wet tablecloths were used to help prevent plates etc sliding all over the place.

When next in Liverpool, I dropped in to Ellerman Papayanni Lines, Water Street, Liverpool, and there I met Mr Davy - I think he described himself as the Assistant to the Superintendent Engineer, Mr Fergie Brand. Shortly afterwards I received a letter from Ellermans offering me a Fourth Engineer's position and I left the Head Line with minimum ceremony.

It was now December and I arranged to join Ellermans when required after Christmas. But I happened to visit my sister at that time down in Surrey where she and her husband, an executive with the Hawker Aircraft Company, lived at West Weybridge. An unexpected escapade awaited me, as I travelled around.

One day I was passing through Surbiton railway station - the same Surbiton where I had been a few years before in search of an accordion. My eye caught a hand written advertisement for a temporary porter, to assist parcel sorting - 10 days - please apply if you can help. Apply Station Master, Kingston-Upon-Thames.

Always having a slightly romantic approach to things involving travel, unusual experiences and meeting different people, I considered this "appeal" and then went on my way. But the seed was sown - I had a couple of weeks on hand before Christmas and since money is always useful in filling a pocket or (stocking at Christmas) I decided that I would do some work. Amazingly a contact suggested I do a temporary spell at Vicker's who were looking people and in fact I went over to the Vickers Aircraft factory at nearby Weybridge and was offered an immediate start - in a machine shop. Scenes of C24, C31 etc rushed across my eyes as I came away. Incidentally I got a first class view of the curving slopes of the famous old Brooklands racing circuit of the 1920's and 1930's now cut in two, by the Vickers airfield.

But I decided I would be uncomfortable - taking men in, who, acting in good faith would be dismayed when I would jack it in after say 10 days (at the time, it was not unusual for skilled people in the South of England to move after just a short period - such was the abundance of work). I decided against. What now? Well, what about trying a real temporary job - to find out how the other people live. So, I offered myself to the Station Master at Kingston-Upon-Thames, and he seemed very glad to welcome me on board. The job was simply sorting out parcels which arrived in the sorting area - parcels would be put into different address boxes - nothing to it.

Railway Assignment

I must say it was one of the most carefree and interesting ten days, I ever spent. There were students there - university students mostly - all putting their shoulder to the wheel - (with my maths book below my arm, I was also a sort of student). Tea was brewed every hour. I would say to Bill, the Chief Clerk "Will I put the kettle on, Bill?' and invariably he would reply "Jolly good idea, old boy". Most of the men working there - in this large catchment area, were ex-service - Bill had been a

Wing Commander in the Royal Flying Corps - later the RAF, in the First World War - and maybe over the age of retirement! But the chat was good. I met some very interesting people as I was asked to go the odd errand here and there - and I worked every bit of overtime available. But time waits on no man and soon I had to leave these dear friends of only ten days and the dignified and courteous Station Master of Kingston-Upon-Thames Railway Station. Many years later, when having to change stations - I think I was on some careers business or other on behalf of my school, I found myself in familiar surroundings. With some companions on the same business, I had to wait at Kingston-Upon- Thames Railway Station. But I had no one to share the thoughts that were passing through my head during those moments.

All this while I hadn't forgotten Musgrave Park - the left leg reminding me from time to time what I was walking on. But like the ancient watchmen who would cry "Twelve o'clock and all is well", so from time to time I would look at it with a mixture of gratitude and ruefulness and tell myself "all is well". It wouldn't always be so. But until then, much water, fresh and salt, would continue to flow under the bridges of life.

Before I left Shorts, Horace Love had speculated with me how one's awareness of life might alter after some experience at sea. I had now seen how two other sets of people earned their living - and was richer for this.

Ellerman Papayanni Lines

I received a telegram from Ellerman Papayanni Lines the day after Boxing Day 1961. It read,
   "Join Castillion immediately, 4th Engineer Officer. Brand, Liverpool".

So I packed my belongings and the accordion and booked a flight from Nutts Corner to Liverpool. These flights always touched down in the Isle of Man. It was on this occasion, that (apart from myself) there was one other important traveller at Nutts Corner - the great American Negro singer, Paul Robson. I asked him for his autograph which he very graciously inscribed upon my brother's driving licence, the licence being unfortunately lost some time later.

I arrived at the office of Ellerman Papayanni Lines, Tower Building, 2 Water Street, Liverpool, after lunch time, and presented myself at the office of Mr Fergie Brand, the superintendent engineer. I knew the office - I had previously met Mr Davy, the assistant superintendent engineer there just before Christmas. "I wasn't expecting you so soon", Mr. Brand began, "but it says a lot for you that you came so promptly. The "Castillion" is held up at Hull and has still to call at London. I want you to stand by the "Sicilian" until the "Castillion" comes round - probably the middle of next week. You'll find the "Sicilian" at the Alexander. Good luck". So off I went down to the docks - by bus, and eventually found myself aboard the S.S. "Sicilian". By that time it was near time for dinner , during which I met a couple of stand-by chief engineers one by the name of Brand - no relation of the superintendent. It was next morning when I was formally introduced to the engine room - I was in for a surprise. The "Sicilian" had a huge triple expansion steam engine with exhaust turbine, something I hadn't seen before. In my studies in thermodynamics I had come across all sorts of steam engines, etc from the theoretical viewpoint and was familiar with the triple expansion design. Briefly, superheated steam leaves the boiler and enters the high pressure cylinder - the H.P. As it expands, the H.P. piston is driven down, the steam exhausting into a second or intermediate cylinder at a reduced pressure. In doing work on the intermediate piston - the I.P., there is a further reduction in pressure - (the intermediate cylinder is much larger in diameter than the H.P., as lower pressure steam has a greater volume). The exhaust steam from the I.P. then enters the low pressure cylinder - the L.P., drives that piston down and exhausts into a low pressure turbine - the exhaust turbine, at about 7 pounds per square inch and emerges from the turbine at about 0.5 pounds per square inch, entering the main condenser.

In the "Sicilian" and (later) in the "Grecian", the respective diameters of the cylinders would have been approximately 2 feet (600 mm.) for the high pressure cylinder (the H.P.), 3 feet (900 mm) for the Intermediate cylinder (the I.P.) and an enormous five feet - possibly less for the low pressure cylinder (the L.P.). This reciprocating engine as fitted in these ships gave an indicated Horse Power of about 2500 (I.H.P.) with the turbine adding another 25% power when "full away". (I note in my discharge book that the "Grecian" was rated at 3000 Shaft Horse Power which allowing for frictional losses seems about correct. This was enough, to give the old "Grecian" a service speed of thirteen and a half knots, when using three boilers - which now seems fair for the size of the ship. The ship was surprisingly responsive to the opening of the throttle - as a little incident recalled later will show. Note: 14.7 lb/sq inch = 1 bar.

The idea of steam "doing work" below atmospheric pressure was a concept I had some difficulty accepting in the classroom, but by the time I left Ellerman's, I had no more difficulty in understanding its working.

Here, it might be said, I was seeing the last of a "legend', the steam reciprocating engine that had powered the ships of seagoing nations for over a century. Today in the 1990's, it would be virtually impossible to find an ocean-going vessel fitted with such an engine - although tucked away here and there in nations still emerging, one might see such a thing, doing work. For example, the S.S. "Grecian", a sister ship to the S.S. "Sicilian" was sold at the end of her useful life at Ellerman's to the government of the Maldives, a group of islands in the Indian Ocean.

However I got a shock and surprise when I saw the vertical space required to accommodate the triple expansion engine in the "Sicilian". It consisted of the cylinders, the tops of which reached within a few feet of main deck level; the pistons in those cylinders, connected to piston roads, each 6 to 8 inches in diameter and possibly 8 feet long, being constrained to move vertically as the piston rod terminated in a junction known as the crosshead, which was designed to slide in a kind of dovetail groove; the connecting rods joining the piston rods at the crosshead bearing (and being about the same size as the piston rods) and terminating in the bottom end bearing on the crankshaft - as in a car engine. This was a very tall engine indeed. Alongside the massive cranks (and counterweights) were the eccentric sheaves - in effect cams, which operated valve rods which in turn were connected to the slide valves. These valves were always referred to as the A.C. valves, the A.C. standing for "Andrew and Cameron".

This monster was docile in slumber as I descended the almost vertical engine room steps for the first time. A steam generator was running as were gentle hisses of steam from various leaks here and there, and I heard the familiar "clink" of a Weir steam pump somewhere. Although I cannot remember much of the folk working on the "Sicilian", there was a lot of activity - in particular boiler tubes required replacing here and there. For the first time I was at close quarters with boiler tubes and superheater elements - a few words for the lay person may not be out of place just here - not a briefing for some going "up for their tickets" - just a few details.

As mentioned earlier, water in a boiler is heated either by passing through tubes, the outside of the tubes being heated by the products of combustion in the boiler furnace i.e. flame and hot gases - a water tube boiler; or by the said products of combustion passing through tubes and heating water surrounding such tubes - a fire tube boiler. Now as water is heated, steam is formed and occupies that part of a boiler known as the steam space - roughly the top half of the water/steam drum. Some boilers have a special drum (or tank) for steam only, e,g. the high pressure water tube Yarrow boiler. Now steam thus formed is what is known as "wet" or saturated steam, and is led from the boiler to the superheater element - a number of tubes into which "wet" steam now passes. The superheater element is usually placed in the hottest part of the boiler products of combustion, and the steam inside the element tubes first becomes "dry" , and then suffers a rise in temperature, this rise in temperature known as so many degrees of superheat. This gives the steam a great deal more energy and the boiler more efficiency. Some of the boiler tubes in the "Sicilian" boilers had to be replaced - as I said there was a lot going on. The "Sicilian" had three boilers - fire tube or as they were known, Scotch boilers. Fire tube boilers were generally low pressure boilers compared to water tube boilers. The "Sicilian" had a boiler pressure i.e. the pressure maintained while steaming (producing steam) of about 230 pounds per square inch, (about 16 bar). Compare this to the pre Second World War SS "Queen Mary" having Yarrow water tube boilers which were "on the blood" (the red mark on boiler pressure gauge, indicating maximum allowable working pressure) at a pressure of 400 pounds per square inch (27 bar) and a superheater temperature of 700°F.

After a few days I happened to be up at the office and I must have asked Mr Brand if anything in the line of a ship would be sailing soon. Because he asked me if I would go as a "junior" i.e. a fifth engineering officer or below - and not having a "watch" of my own. He also asked had I a preference for steam or diesel to which questions I replied that I didn't mind going as a junior and preferred steam. But I wasn't finished with the "Sicilian" - not for a day or two. Since I wasn't going home at night I had the privilege of being "engineer officer on board". This means one stays on board and is (hopefully) able to deal with any emergency that may arise. The same thing had happened on the 'Rathlin Head' although the Head Line required two engineers to stay on board in the evenings. An allowance was made for this work, of course.

I had been allocated the 5th Engineer's cabin, that incumbent being on a few days leave. I had to push a lot of his rubbish out of the way to make myself comfortable. In so doing I learned a great deal about his habits, both in his cabin and when he was ashore in foreign lands! The "Sicilian" was an "Israeli" ship. At that time, ships that traded with Israel would not be permitted to enter an Arab port but could only go to "neutral" ports in say Malta, Cyprus, Turkey etc. Ellermans had about thirty ships trading at the time, mostly in the Mediterranean, but four ran out to Borneo and one or two made down the West Coast of Africa - as far as Walvis Bay in what is now Namibia. They were either motor ships or steam - steam turbine or steam recip. As well as an engineer on board at night when a ship was in port, there would also be a navigating officer - and a duty fireman. An early problem concerned a list which the "Sicilian" insisted on having, and it concerned the resident navigating officer very much. In fact the ship was almost lying against the dock side, something which I hoped the chief and second engineers would sort out before they went home for the evening. But they didn't bother to do so. Now a ship has tanks for holding fresh water, fuel oil, and ballast (sea water). Fresh water is often in the "double bottoms", tanks below the level of the engine room plates. There would be as well tanks to port and starboard. The same applies to fuel oil, being stored in double bottoms or special bunker tanks which extend upward, port and starboard.

It is usual to burn fuel alternatively from port and starboard - often from small tanks known in steamers as settling tanks - where fuel pumped up from the bunkers can settle and allow water in the fuel to gravitate to the bottom few inches when, by opening a valve, this water can be drained away. These settling tanks are above engine room plate level. I managed to get hold of a donkeyman* who knew the pumping system, and got a few tons transferred from one side to the other, which happily had the effect of straightening up the ship to some extent.

Now it so happened that it was New Year's Eve, and an incident was about to take place while not of a life threatening nature by any means, has found a place in my memory while many other more important things have not.

New Year's Eve in dockland - for any one confined to a ship, is a lonely place. Most people will be somewhere else. On the "Sicilian" there was only the "mate" - the navigating officer up in the bridge accommodation, a duty fireman, a night-

(* - An engine room rating - greaser or senior greaser)

watchman on the gangway, and myself. On such a night the local pubs - the "Nelson" and the "Abercorn" would be doing big business, no ships were "working" (as sometimes happened in the evenings) - nothing moved in dockland. After chatting to the "mate", making tea etc I decided to "turn in" for the night, it being about eleven o'clock. The cabin was well stocked with books, including one about the life of Roger Casement, and I was thus engaged with the "library" when the stillness of the night was broken by some ear shattering siren or other close by. At first I thought it must have a shore origin, but an urgent communication from the "mate" changed my mind, so down I rushed to the engine room where a crescendo confirmed my fears - the duty boiler relief valve had lifted due to excess boiler pressure and was letting everyone know about it. It didn't take long to shut down the boiler, but where was that ghastly fireman? To make a long story short, the call of the "Nelson" proved too strong so he absconded. During that time he had been challenged by the night watchman (usually an elderly retired man) whom he assaulted on his way ashore. The watchman had by now been discovered by the "Mate" in none too good condition - he had not been fit enough to warn us that we had an absentee fireman. So we packed him off home. (The fireman staggered back - well into the morning, and was sacked the following day.)

It was midnight before things were back to normal - well not quite for I was now to experience the nostalgia that anyone who has spent New Year's Eve in Liverpool will understand. At midnight every ship in the Port of Liverpool blew their whistles. Far and wide up and down the Mersey, Everton and Bromboro - came the sound of ships welcoming in the New Year. I can't remember if the "mate" asked for steam - I don't think he did - we had already signalled! That feeling of nostalgia of all those years ago I can still raise up in my memory with little trouble and what happened next even more so. I found myself rummaging amongst the books again, and was probably not in the highest of spirits when upon casting my eye on the flyleaf of one book, I chanced to see a hand written note - the work of an unknown scribe. This is what was written - I've never forgotten these lines:

"The great moments in our lives are not the so called moments of achievement. Rather, they are those moments when, after all seems lost, there arises a spirit which says get up, and fight, and have another go".

I don't know who originated these lines, or who had decided they were worth writing down on the flyleaf of that book - who knows that book may still be somewhere in someone's possession - and anywhere in the world as people who sail in ships get around and sometimes stay there.

But for me it was a piece of philosophy worth a second look - and I have looked at it many times since.

It is a great recovery indeed, when mankind can pull itself up, as we say, by "one's boot strings" (or laces). Sadly for some it often appears impossible to do so. So, if someone should choose to confide that "they are getting things tight" (as has happened more than once in my presence) perhaps we should tarry and help a lame dog over his stile. An extra straw sometimes breaks the camel's back.

Anyway, I think I felt better after reading what the scribe had written and following a descent into the boiler-room to check that all was calm I left the boiler just "ticking over" - without its fireman, and retired for the night.

James McMahon, one of my companions in the days following my recovery from the accident.

Someone with whom I shared much music: Wilcil McDowell, later to become famous as a member of the "Irish Rovers" folk music group.

The SS "Rathlin Head"

"I saw the legend - in very large white letters "Head Line" painted on the side. I also noticed a large Red Hand painted on the funnel, and eventually I was aware that there was a name painted across the back of the ship. It read "Ballygally Head", and underneath was the word, Belfast." (Source: Collection of the late Denis McDowell, Navigator).

Jimmy Spiers, Second Engineer Officer on the SS "Rathlin Head" on my first trip. This photograph actually shows him on the manoeuvring platform of the SS "Carrigan Head".

The "wheels" are effectively the "throttle" for forward and astern motion, the spindles controlling steam pressure on respective turbine rings. Jimmy liked to sing "The Northern Lights of Old Aberdeen". (Courtesy: J. Spiers).

"Leaving Bangor and heading for the Atlantic, we met the MV "Fair Head" homeward - I very nearly got her. (Source: Collection of the late Denis McDowell, Navigator).

The SS Rathlin Head on the Saguenay River

The Jacques Cartier Bridge

Quebec

Jean and BC

Heights of Abraham, Quebec, which Wolff and his soldiers scaled to capture Quebec from the French.

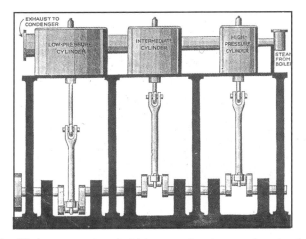

Simplified representation of a triple-expansion steam engine, showing how the high, intermediate, and low-pressure cylinders are related to each other.

The "Grecian" flies the flag at half mast. Earlier our sister ship, the SS "Florian" was sunk off Gibraltar, when in collision with a tanker. The Second Engineer and one other crew member were lost.

Stan Pacer and BC on the SS "Grecian"

On the SS "Grecian". A good day for hanging out the washing. I am wearing that watch, borrowed by the fellow wanting to impress a girlfriend!

Grand Harbour, Malta, with Dghaisas in attendance

HMS Defiance Training Establishment, Devonport, Plymouth, September 1940. Trainees are shown cleaning the mechanism of a torpedo. This shows the engine. (By kind permission of the Imperial War Museum, Lambeth, London).

At the Naval Torpedo Depot, Rosyth, 1940 or 1941. Working on the tails - known as the after bodies of torpedoes. This would be a sight familiar to former employees at R.N.A.D. Antrim! (By kind permission of the Imperial War Museum, Lambeth, London).

The Mark VIII Torpedo - The "engine room" of the torpedo. This sectioned exhibit shows a piston halfway down a cylinder. Note the white trigger, that is released when the torpedo is forced out of its tube by compressed air. The glasses give an idea of size. What a clever piece of engineering, to overcome all the problems that were encountered when first thought about - before the turn of the century! (By kind permission of the Imperial War Museum, Lambeth, London).

Steam Recips - The "Grecian"

The next day I got word to report to the S.S. "Grecian", a sister ship of the "Sicilian". They were both general cargo vessels of about 5,000 tons nett and a crew of upwards of forty. Nowadays, ships like the "Grecian" would be sailing with much less. Anyway, upon approaching the West Bromley Moore dock, I found myself in company with a blue gabardined man - complete with peak cap, and discovered that he was the second Mate of the S.S. "Grecian". His first name was George and we made our way on board the "Grecian".

One of the first I met was Stanaslaus Pacer - Stan to all and a naturalised Pole. He would turn out one of the most interesting men I ever met - and a very good companion. Stan took me to the Chief Engineer, Mr Goldie, a Scot, and soon I was sorting out my cabin. I was in for an interesting time, of places, men and things - and a winter in some sun. The things included working with technology which had its origins at the turn of the previous century - the world of the reciprocating steam engine. A word about these origins would not be without merit - the history of the steam boat.

The early attempts to harness the power of steam to do work were largely those designs which were of the condensing type i.e. where steam was condensed on the underside of a piston in a cylinder thus causing a vacuum, the greater atmospheric pressure on the top of piston pushing the piston down. These were known as condensing beam engines, the best known probably made by Newcomen in 1712 and used for pumping water out of mines. To use the direct power of live steam to do work i.e. in an expanding role, one thinks of James Watt. It is not without significance that he was a technician in the institute where Dr Black, the discoverer of latent heat, also worked. The first technical success in installing steam for marine propulsion was probably the "Charlotte Dundas", built in 1801 at Grangemouth as a tug for the Forth and Clyde canal. Unfortunately it was considered that her wash was eroding the canal banks and she was withdrawn from that role. Fulton's "Chermont" built in New York in 1807 was an immediate commercial success. At Port Glasgow in 1812 was built the "Comet", a ferry on the Glasgow Helensborough route. Later the "Savannah", a sailing vessel with a steam engine (and paddles), crossed the Atlantic in 1819, but it was not until 1838, that the S.S. "Sirius" crossed the Atlantic under steam alone. Until 1850, the boiler pressures were probably of the order of 20 pounds per square inch, (less than 2 bar).

With steam, a new class of seafarer emerged - the engineer. These were pioneers and probably in short supply in the early days of steam. As well, many were very inexperienced - probably many of the "engineers" and firemen came from the ranks of the sailors - a home spun race. Accidents - mostly involving boiler explosions became common and at an inquiry into a steam boat accident in 1839, a witness said that "steam navigation had advanced more rapidly than men of experience and knowledge could be found. Especially in the realms of river boats, men were advanced to the post of engineer who were mere automatons, ignorant of the first principles of the machinery over which they presided, creating, rather than averting danger and accident". It is amazing to read now of accounts of the safety valves on boilers being tied down or jammed shut with a lump of coal or even by an engineer standing on them in an effort to increase boiler pressure. Probably the most famous ship of that era was the S.S. "Great Britain" launched in 1843 and the first of the all metal ships, and the first to be screw driven. Designed by Brunel, she was initially on the North Atlantic run, but after running aground at Dundrum Bay in Co Down on her fifth voyage, she was on the Australian run, later serving as a troopship in the Crimean War and Indian Mutiny. She came to rest in 1886 in the Falkland Islands, first serving as a hulk for storing wool and coal. Fifty years later, she was left to rot until the early 1970's when she was brought "home" to Bristol where she was restored - largely by volunteer workers, in the very dock in which she was built. The relative status of crew members, relative to where they slept changed somewhat with the advent of steam. In the days of sail, the hierarchy was set out horizontally, from the Master's spacious cabin right aft, to the cramped, dark and crowded forecastle right up in the bows. In a steamer it would be set out vertically, from the increasingly gold braided Olympus of the bridge to the hot and sweaty opposite of the engine room and stokehold below. Here engineers apart, there were many whose lives were miserable indeed - trimmers and firemen, greasers, storekeepers, donkeymen - these endured harsh working conditions.

Of course, even in the engineer officers accommodation there was a "horizontal" division of labour in all ships, with the Chief Engineer's cabin the one most forward and next to the saloon, where most meals were consumed. Thereafter the cabins were in descending order of rank i.e. 2nd Engineer, 3rd Engineer, and so forth, aft.

Now I return to the "Grecian"

The following day I met Peter Bridges, the second engineer, and George Hollis, the third engineer from Liverpool, accent and all. George had spent some time on the South American run, working with the South American Saint Company (I would hear about the M.V. "St. Thomas", and the M.V. "St. Peter"). He was also with Houlder Bros. and I would likewise hear tales of when he was aboard the "Langton Grange", a ship which, if my memory is correct, caught fire some years later, and became a total wreck.

But now the S.S. "Grecian" was preparing for sea - there were tanks to "dip" a bearing to tighten down the tunnel - that long passage where the massive propeller shaft rotates in isolation, save for the routine ramble down that way by the duty watchkeeping engineer. Then spare parts to sort out etc. and eventually all was "ship shape and Bristol fashion" - we were ready for departure the next day. But one little duty had to be performed first - I had to "sign on", that ritual that precedes a voyage to sea. George Hollis and the Chief Engineer, Mr Goldie also had to sign on, so in their company, I arrived at the Cornhill Shipping Federation Offices to sign articles. One would produce his discharge book, occasionally one's attention would be drawn to some condition e.g. "A" articles or "B" articles and sign a register relating to the voyage - a round trip.

The next day the "Grecian" was on "standby" sometime in late morning. As "fiver" I had no watch of my own - I would assist the Second Engineer on watch - the "4-8", morning and evening. Later I would be on day work as presently described.

But now we were ready to leave and the engine room personnel composed the Second, Peter Bridges, myself, a greaser and one fireman. By tradition, ships are usually manoeuvred in and out of port on the second's watch - depending of course on local weather and tide conditions. But generally it means that a ship is in port in good time for an early start by the dockers, either unloading or loading.

With the Second mostly doing the manoeuvring, my job would be to log all engine movements to the nearest quarter of a minute and keep an eye on the "job". We arrived in Cardiff a few hours after leaving Liverpool and while there I had time to look at some interesting deck cargo we were carrying. There was an ancient thresher complete with slender iron spoked wheels and bound for Alexandria in Egypt. Alongside over the tops of the hatches were a number of huge elm tree trunks bound for Baillie's Dockyard in Malta. Each was a metre in diameter (over three feet) and was perhaps twenty metres long - enormous beasts. Lashed down with ropes and wedges they looked uncomfortable and unsafe bed fellows. The other cargo - mostly in the holds was largely for the Services in either Gibraltar, Malta or Cyprus.

We sailed for Gibraltar on Sunday evening. I joined Peter Bridges the Second Engineer on the 4-8 watch and would assist him until we cleared the Bay of Biscay, when I would commence work preparing the winches and other pieces of equipment that would be ill used (or well used) by the dockers of many nations over the next few months. Strictly speaking, I judge that on a journey from England to Gibraltar, one is really on the fringe of the Bay of Biscay, and to cross it properly as I was to do later, one has to make for some place on the northern Spanish Coast like Bilbao. But near enough, if rough weather is the criteria - and I would get plenty, during which period, an oil leak developed below the boiler room deck plates. Such a thing can be serious - leaking or fractured oil pipes are some of the causes of fire at sea. I was given the job of sorting it out. It was hot - virtually below the boilers - it was very smelly - boiler fuel oil everywhere - the ship was rolling like a football and as I tightened the last leaking flange bolt - I felt so sick I wanted to die.

However, sickness passes, and before long, Brown our greaser, appeared with tea and toast. Eventually, I would be out of the "wood" again - but not yet. The following morning, as the storm showed no sign of slackening, and I was having a breather on deck, I realised that whereas we should be heading for the sun, it was now far on the port bow. We were heading for America! At this time I noticed a lot of activity on the deck - the hatch covers and the tree trunks. Eventually the bosun explained to me that during the heavy rolling of the ship, the tree trunks had broken loose and the skipper had decided to "hove to" into the prevailing wind until the logs were secured, and the weather improved. By the afternoon, we had resumed our course for Gibraltar.

The engine room of the "Grecian" differed enormously from that of the S.S. "Rathlin Head". The boiler room with its three Scotch (or fire tube boilers) was separate from the engine room and of course the triple expansion engine bore no comparison to the turbine machinery of the "Rathlin". Of immense height due to the crosshead type of design, the engine required a different approach from the watch keeper. The cranks were "open", and I had to acquire the "knack" of judging the movement as each bottom end bearing came to the top of its stroke - then deftly place the edge of my hand on the bearing and - follow it round for a few degrees of crank movement. The cranks rotated, when full away, at about one hundred revolutions per minute, so one did not have too much time to decide if a bearing was running hot or not. But I surprised myself at how adept I became in this precarious occupation. (Thirty years later I was working at Belfast Docks in a voluntary capacity on the refit of the M.V. "Logas II" one of two ships operated by Operation Mobilisation in the world wide distribution of literature, the Bible and the Gospel. During a break for tea, where I was in the company of engineers from many nations working voluntarily, I, in a contribution to reminiscence, recalled "palming the bottom end bearings" and asked if "any of you ever had to do this kind of thing". Bill Mason, from near Newcastle upon Tyne - a Lloyds surveyor no less, held up three fingers of one hand. "How do you think I lost that finger", he laughed. He was an old steam man, and happily he had been hiding the other finger behind the others.)

Eventually the heavy weather gave way to tranquillity and sun as we steamed off the coast of Portugal and I was taken off watches to commence day work. Happily this was to be mostly on the deck machinery, overhauling the bearings of the steam winches - a chore well known to generations of junior engineers. The winches really took a hammering as the dockers from many nations drove them like dervishes as loads would be swung out and into the ship's holds. The plain, brass bearings of piston rods ends and connecting rod ends sometimes were "gold" as the brass literally "ran" out of bearings being flogged to death. Although it was winter, from then on I frequently wore shorts as I set about my tasks. Just before I broke off watches on the 4-8 watch, I became aware of a little ritual enacted each morning about six o'clock - just as Brown arrived with the tea and toast. I thought I heard a loud click somewhere above my head on one such tea break - then at the same time next morning, there it was again. I decided to investigate. It came to pass that I discovered the origin of the click to come from a heavy steel door of the cold store or refrigerator - visited each morning by the old sea cook. His ritual was such that he unlocked the door and carried a load of provisions up to his lair - leaving the door open, because he needed two loads of meat, vegetables etc. I must say I listened for that click each morning with boyish glee - we were never short of apples and oranges from that time forth!

A brief word about the navigating officers of the ship - the skipper and the three "mates". The navigating officers comprised the skipper, Captain Whipp (yes, that was his name), Mr Gardner the Chief Mate or First Mate, George the Second - and I cannot remember the name of the Third Mate. The Skipper and Mr Gardner (who walked with a limp) each wore their Second World War ribbons - Stan could have worn his but I never saw him do so. There were also a couple of navigating apprentices - cadets.

These apprentices approached me one night and asked me if I had heard the new song written about me. It was "I want to be Bobby's girl". Another new song at this time was "Sailor", sung by Petula Clark.

The Grecian was a comfortable ship, with good cabins and a large saloon. I dined in the saloon, seated at the same table as Stan and George Hollis, the Third Engineer. I had seen everyone - that is all the officers, except Captain Whipp - he had not appeared. Upon inquiring as to why this was, I was told that the Skipper was a very poor sailor and frequently stayed in his cabin - had meals there etc until he had crossed the bay. Eventually I made my way to the bridge - paying a visit to George, and I noticed on my way up a number of framed passages of Scripture here and there on bulk heads at different levels. One I remember - "And He bringeth them to a safe Haven where they would be". (This was also the caption to a painting in the Flying Angel, Mission to Seamen, Liverpool). I thought the skipper might be a Sunday School teacher, but later, when I heard him shouting at a stevedore in some foreign part - I think Cyprus, I revised that thought! Actually any dealings I had with him were always very cordial - he kept to himself - except during Captain's round, when accompanied by the Mate, or the Chief Engineer, he did his weekly inspection of our cabins.

Gibraltar was a wonderful sight to be seeing for the first time - a massive grey rock rising almost vertically to over one thousand feet. We tied up beside a couple of destroyers, having on the approaches to Gibraltar counted over sixty ships (including an aircraft carrier) passing through the area to and from the Mediterranean or the West Coast of Africa - perhaps some on a South Atlantic route. Being in Gibraltar for three or four days was an opportunity for some relaxation - I had an accordion with me and naturally it was a source of some diversion. I was now with people not from Ireland but from the Outer Hebrides, England, Scotland and Poland, but the social habits and rapport was much the same. They all knew "Westering Home" and Goldie the Chief was a good singer, and often sang "Donald where's your trousers". One man from Stornaway was a great lilter of piping tunes, and when I produced the practice chanter, I discovered him to be a very good performer on it. From him I was introduced to the march 'Dovecote Park' - one of my favourites still today. Murdo the bosun was another good singer - he came from the Isle of Skye. But I was still learning - in particular on board etiquette, as the following will enlighten. One day, following a sing song - possibly in the Second's cabin which accommodated a larger throng, I was to be accosted by Mr Goldie. "I saw the bosun in your cabin the other night - he should not have been there you know". I didn't know exactly - I had some vague notion about it. Goldie went on "Make no mistake about it - there's demarcation on this ship - that's why we are up here and they are down there". I was learning we were a class apart, but I have a feeling, that Murdo always managed to be at all the parties. Apart from being a nice fellow crew member, he really knew his job. I was especially impressed on the occasion when, at Latticia in Syria, we broke our anchor chain and lost the anchor in the harbour (recovered on another trip). Murdo in a very professional manner organised the spare anchor in place in a very short time. But demarcation - well, when I think that those "down there" included the cook and the stewards - they literally had your life and health in their hands. Years later, when working on the M.V. "Irish Coast" during term holidays (I was teaching then) I was to see, at close quarters, what happens to someone's food, if they try to rub a steward's nose in it! I recall this later.

Gibraltar had been my first taste of where West meets East - traders of different ethnic origins merging in Western society - then over to Africa into Spanish Morocco, to Ceuta for bunkers - oil for the hungry boilers. Then Malta and the Grand Harbour, following the route of those epic convoys that managed to keep Malta supplied during the World War II. I thought of the S.S. "Ohio", the tanker that settled on the bottom (as I understand) as soon as she limped into the harbour, supported on either side by two other vessels. Her 16,000 tons of fuel is said to have saved Malta.

On watch Peter Bridges was continually organising jobs to be done and making adjustments to this or that. On one occasion he closed the throttle somewhat - I cannot remember what adjustment was being made - it was somewhere he had to bend down among pipes and all sorts of projecting objects. He arranged with me that upon a given signal I would wind the throttle (steam to H.P. cylinder) wide open - he was probably tinkering with the governor. Well, I opened the throttle and was very surprised to feel the instant response. Peter felt it too, being thrown off his balance as he knocked his head (sharply) against some hard object. Well, that day I heard words and adjectives in forms new and varied that I hadn't heard before (or since) and all ending in "ing! It's funny how things stick in one's memory - while others fade as in the case of me not remembering who the Third Mate was.

Another very interesting thing for me to partake in was taking an indicator "Card" of one of the cylinders. This "Card" gave an accurate indication of the expansion performance of the steam during the passage of the piston up and down (the engine was double acting, steam on top of piston and on bottom) and an even more interesting piece of engineering knowledge was in taking "leads" of main bearings. A thin strip of lead was placed on the journal, then the bearing put in position and tightened. When the bearing was dismantled again, the now flattened lead would be measured, this dimension being the clearance. This was engineering! Adjustments, which may have included removal of shims if clearance was too large, or by scraping the bearing, if the clearance was too small, might then be made.

At Malta, a berth was unavailable so we anchored stern to the dockside and off loaded into barges alongside. To get ashore however, Dghaisas* were used, those queer high stemmed row boats, peculiar to the Grand Harbour. They plied their trade between the gangway and a set of steps on the dockside that looked as if they could have been used by Richard the Lion Heart when on his way to the Crusades.

Other trips I was to make to sea were either as 4th Engineer or 3rd Engineer, responsible for a watch. Here as "fiver" I had different duties, and Ellermans had peculiar arrangements that gave variety. As recalled I assisted the second - mostly upon approaching a port or leaving, and on day work as required, but when in a foreign port, I was assigned to the night shift - partly to keep an eye on the engine room and also to carry out emergency repairs etc like a bearing to replace, valves to recondition or some pump to sort out. This meant that during the day I was left to my own devices. To sustain the "fiver" during the wee small hours, the old sea cook left a liberal supply of bacon and eggs (usually four) to fry up in one of his massive pans. I think I learned a lot about looking after myself, food wise in this period. The cook also left a goodly supply of bread, butter, tomatoes and black puddings (these latter I declined). As well, those nights in the Mediterranean were very beautiful and often I would spend time gazing at the stars which appeared large and low in the sky.

(* - Gaily painted Maltese Gondolas and pronounced Dy-so)

133

One night just as I commenced the work that had been left out for me, I heard a commotion of sorts coming from the gangway side of the ship. I found a man and his boat, (dghaisas), at the foot of the gangway. He spoke an unintelligible language but beckoned with his finger to the boat. There, resembling something between a scarecrow and a bag of potatoes, was one of our firemen. He was seemingly unconscious. So I descended the ladder of the gangway and the dghaisas man and myself literally carried this beastly drunk fireman to the top of the gangway and dumped him on the ship. Then I returned from whence I came. A few minutes later, I again heard the dghaisas man calling, and upon investigation discovered that our drunk and "unconscious" man had quickly recovered, and disappeared, "forgetting" to pay his fare on the dghaisas. Another example of craft and experience - I couldn't believe it as he had acted completely limp and it wasn't without some effort that the beast was hauled up that gangway. I was learning.

My uncomfortable travelling companions, the elm logs were also left at Malta. While there, I visited St. John's Cathedral - and saw the Island's George Cross which was on exhibition there.

I suppose the ambition of sea going engineers is to obtain their Certificates of Competency i.e. those certificates known as First Class, required by those appointed as Chief Engineers, and the Second Class - the "Seconds" ticket. Sometimes, dispensations might be applied for to enable someone with experience to be advanced temporarily to a senior position for a period. The possibility of obtaining a 'Seconds' ticket was real enough as I had an exemption for part "A" of the ticket, in view of my existing level of technical study. So getting in the sea time - especially as a watch keeper in charge of a watch was the goal I had to aim for. I had a priority however - that of finishing the studies presently being pursued, and my date with the College of Technology, Belfast, was ever drawing near for my resit. Mr Ted Goligher's prediction about me appreciating "Strength of Materials" was proving very true indeed. Even acquiring simple skills like using pulley blocks was newly acquired. The first occasion I had to use them was to enable me to replace a blown boiler gauge glass. (I then remembered Jimmy Spiers giving me assistance on that very duty on my first watch on the "Rathlin Head"). Here on the "Grecian" some person had fitted the safety rails of a catwalk (across the boiler front), right on top of the gauge glass, preventing replacement of the glass front. The rails were sprung clear using a block and tackle.

One of the essential areas that required frequent supervision was checking the temperature of the large bottom end bearings which rotated in the open. Another place of concern was the eccentric straps (or sheaths) as they were sometimes known. (This strap was a kind of hoop surrounding the eccentric and transmitted the "life" to the guadrant bars and thence the A and C valves). These sheaths splashed into the coolant and normally were kept cool, but when revolving slowly as when manoeuvring, they didn't "splash" so much, and occasionally got hot - when some additional coolant and lubricant would be applied. Another thing I kept my eye to, was the level of salt in the feed water. The boilers in the "Grecian" were fire tube or Scotch boilers. One was out of action, requiring some tube replacement - we steamed on two giving an outward speed of eleven and a half knots. Now it was thought that we had a leaking condenser. There was a common water tap on the side of the Scotch boiler and one simply took a sample of the water in a tall copper vessel into which was placed a salinometer, an instrument made of (in this case) glass which consisted of a stem with a hollow bulb, about one third the distance from the bottom, the latter weighted down with lead shot.

The salinometer therefore floated high or low, dependent upon the specific gravity, and in turn indicated the amount of salt in the water. It was marked in 32nds. This was because 5 ounces of salt per gallon of water = 1/32nds since one gallon of water weighs 10 lbs, and 16 ozs = 1 lb.

i.e. $\dfrac{5}{10 \times 16} = \dfrac{1}{32nd}$

I suppose one should have got worried if it read 3 or 4 ie 3/32 or 4/32, but the "Grecian" was shipping more salt than that. There was only one thing to do - open the main condenser and try and find the leaking tube.

We were arriving at Alexandria in Egypt where I had hoped to set off in search of the Pyramids of Giza. But it was not to be - all hands had to turn out to carry out vital maintenance, especially the leaking condenser. This was an interesting repair - the steam space being flooded and the leaking tubes identified and plugged. The condenser had no less than five element doors front and back. (I know, because I had to put them all back and secure them that night). I did however stand on the soil of Egypt, as I managed a quick run ashore and bought a few things from an Egyptian trader. Earlier in the day an Egyptian photographer had come on board looking for some business including the development of film. I indeed had a black and white film waiting to be developed, and I did business with him satisfactorily.

During the course of the day, Egyptians of all descriptions came on board. Some were dockers of course, but others wore that long striped dress with a kind of fez for headgear. These latter would be barefoot and intent on selling a kind of liquorice and other less typical drinks. Then other types came down into the engine room looking for scrap material - even the light strapping securing boxes of spare parts wasn't proof against their "acquisitional" skills. Later we were not able to find various buckets, oil cans etc., used by the greaser in the lubrication of the hundred and one links, bearings, and moving parts, that required attention by the hour. There was worse to come for me - early that morning I had washed my spare underwear and hung it up to dry on a line above the engine room. At sea, owing to the heat endured - it might be 80°F or 90°F on the control platform - but 140°F in the fidley at the base of funnel, we wore little under our overalls and such required changing often. However the locusts carried all before them - nobody had warned me about them - it was well known that you had to have everything under lock and key in Alexandria!

During that time, Egypt was in unison with Syria - part of the U.A.R. (United Arab Republic) and photography was forbidden, but I managed to take a long distance shot of the former yacht of ex-King Farouk. My lasting impression of Alexandria was the harbour and the long approach - miles of channel. Anyway, we sailed away, wiser and poorer, the work on the condenser proving a success, but I would have liked to have seen the Pyramids. (I was to wait a long time before eventually seeing them - in 1993.)

Of the strange places the "Grecian" took me to, Mersin, on the southern coast of Turkey was an eye opener, second only to Beirut for strange goings on. On the coast, about thirty miles south of Tarsus, the birthplace of St. Paul, it was the poorest place I had ever been to. I had been on the watch that brought in the ship, the morning we arrived, and therefore I was free most of the day - it was a Saturday. I went ashore myself that morning about eleven o'clock and I had such a cultural shock that I was back by one o'clock. The place was cobblestoned i.e. the main street, and had a high population of animal drawn vehicles, horses, donkeys etc. What passed as butchers shops were open fronted - the only meat that I remember consisted of complete goat's heads - with horns. The flies were having a field day, and there were dilapidated people of all ages everywhere and mostly begging. I had no Turkish money, the only "currency" I had was (pretty standard practice) some duty free cigarettes which I was pursuant of exchanging for a souvenir. I was sorry I had not some money, because shortly I was accosted by a little boy on crutches - my own favourite method of personal transport only five years before. But this little fellow had lost a leg - obviously recently as the blood was still seeping through the white bandage over the stump. I turned away sorrowfully. Actually had I considered the matter, had I given him some duty free, he probably could have exchanged them for currency to his benefit.

That afternoon, Stan asked me to go up again and we went into the back streets. There I saw a sight which I couldn't believe existed on the shores of the Mediterranean - houses that consisted of four poles driven into the ground and a thatched roof. Just before we left Mersin, visitors arrived on board - Americans from the air base at Adana close by. One of the "Americans" interested me very much - because he spoke "fluent" Belfast. His name was McCann and his parents lived in Jubilee Street off the Antrim Road. We had a great chat - he had immigrated into the States earlier and was serving in the U.S.A.A.F. I promised to call and see his parents - but I regret I neglected to do so. There was one incident which happened that stuck in my memory. Stan and I, walking in the "suburbs", came across a barn where oranges were being stored - just the way potatoes were stored in the British Isles - a metre deep. We indicated to the man - maybe the owner, that we wouldn't say no to an orange but he apparently found great difficulty in understanding our sign language. Just as we were coming away empty handed, a beautiful Turkish child - possibly twelve or thirteen appeared, and in her beaming way, interpreted without difficulty our desire for an orange and immediately gave us a handful each and beckoned us on our way. Stan said "What an ambassador for her country", and was so taken on by the incident that he talked about it throughout the rest of the trip.

The next day we arrived at Iskenderun, a Turkish Naval base and port. The only thing of note at this place is the huge Crescent cut into the snow capped mountainside. I don't know the history of how it came to be there but I have seen photos of it in holiday brochures and magazines.

Not all memories are as pleasant as that of the little "ambassador". We had arrived off Syria to anchor and discharge into barges off the port of Latticia, when a gale blew up and even though it was quite warm, the seas become as high as what I had seen in the Atlantic. So the ship very quickly lifted the anchor and stood off the shore a few miles, there to parade up and down. The skipper was nervous because in that very place, the "Anglican", one of Papayanni's ships, had run aground some months earlier. She was salved and towed back to the U.K. The bad weather lasted six days and we paraded up and down - I remember the bridge rang down for eighty eighty revolutions - this must have been the speed to enable a regular pattern, say, each hour or half hour of steaming from point A to point B, and back.

Eventually, we came to anchor again and unloading commenced. One day, while having lunch in the saloon an "incident" took place. I was dining with Stan and George Hollis the Third Engineer, when suddenly the Mate jumped up and gesticulating aggressively, started shouting "Out, out, out!" The Skipper also joined in the affray and even George was on his feet. I turned round to try and see the object of their displeasure, and there, standing in the doorway of the saloon, stood an Arab docker. He was trying to communicate - he had something urgent he wished them to know about. But they would not countenance such an intrusion into the saloon. The fellow withdrew in a crestfallen, if not a sullen manner and peace was restored, all feathers unruffled and in place. But for Stan the incident jarred badly. "That guy is the stevedore - a very important man - he controls the dockers and has a lot to do with good loading procedure. For you and I", he went on, "that's a reason why you and I can't walk safely about a country like this, without being afraid of getting a knife in our backs!". He referred to what might be known as negative ambassadorial skills - (the Arabs didn't know that an Englishman's home, is his castle!) Anyway, who would have thought that someone from that de-burring bench in Shorts, would come to acquire such insight into the way men's minds work? I was learning - more.

Another incident illustrates how frequently people take chances. As will be understood, swinging a ship on an anchor while discharging cargo overboard into barges, is fraught with danger e.g. should a sudden gale drag the anchor. In order to bring the ship under control should anything happen, boiler pressure was up and the engine room telegraph was on "Standby". This meant the engineer of the watch was standing by at the controls, ready to move at an instant's notice. It was a nice day and I was sitting on the deck, when the Third Engineer, George Hollis, who was on watch, appeared on deck "for a breather". "I think things are pretty steady", he said, "I wouldn't mind a dip". He disappeared and reappeared shortly afterwards in his swimming trunks. "Let me know if anything happens" and with that he dived overboard. I couldn't believe it - but these things happen when somebody wants to "take a chance". I ambled down to the engine room - just in case! Anyway, the anchor held and nobody knew he had left his position. But it's something I wouldn't have felt comfortable doing.

It was then off to Tripoli, Lebanon, then Beirut, where I saw the real cedars of Lebanon. Beirut at that time was, I suppose, a beautiful city by Arab standards. There was a lot of French influence - it was formerly under French mandate and street names were in Arabic and French. The place that I remember was the large square in the city centre known as the "Square of Martyrs" - I never knew - still don't know, why it was so called. I suppose the Square of Martyrs was a central part of the City and was probably a showpiece in architecture of a culture that, while Arab, was certainly penetrated by something Western. The square was something after the area of a large football pitch, but punctuated at regular intervals by stone pedestals - about three yards (or metres) long, by one yard wide and about two yards high. On top of these - which were set out in line up each side, at regular intervals, were either floral arrangements or the statue of some person or other on a horse. The next time I saw the Square of Martyrs, it was shown on television at the height of the civil war many years later, with a lot of rubble lying around. I was unable to figure out which part of Beirut it was in - East or West etc or who controlled it.

I was having a prowl around with Stan - we had a most persistent "guide" who simply wouldn't depart, and I remember Stan saying as we were trying to cross a busy street, "Bob, this is a very old place - if you got knocked down, nobody would want to know who you were". We went into a cafe where pure orange juice was being served - squeezed out by hand press and a jute box was playing - what? No less than "Three coins in a fountain". I had last heard it in the Waveney Hospital in Ballymena, lying in that corner bed next to the Cushendall Road.

But to get back to what was happening on the "Grecian". For one thing I remember writing to the registrar in the College of Technology, Belfast, asking him to enrol me for the examination I was preparing to resit. We were also headed to Cyprus again - where we had unloaded cargo in Famagusta - in the Turkish sector. Now, we were coming back again to load potatoes and oranges. There was the difference of night and day, between the old Turkish part of Famagusta, and the Greek sector. The Turkish sector was very primitive, but after walking half a mile one came to the Greek sector, and you might as well have been in Ballymena or Lisburn, the contrast was so great - at least that's what my memory says. Cyprus was very green - I remember walking around Othello's Tower and gathering some sponges in the old Turkish Harbour.

But Spring had arrived in Britain and we were heading that way. We now had the boiler tubes replaced in the third boiler and would be going home on three boilers - giving a speed of thirteen knots. One thing I remember was buying monster size oranges on the quayside of Famagusta at the rate of twenty-four (2 dozen) for one old shilling - one halfpenny each, old money. This of course approximates in value to the halfpenny saved by us Short's apprentices who got off the trolleybus at Bell's Bridge on the Cregagh Road - rather than go on to Montgomery Road - and then to run across the former Rugby pitch where Castlereagh Further Education College now stands. Another funny little incident I recall, concerned parting gifts of potatoes and oranges from the Cypriot exporters.

Some cases of oranges and bags of potatoes were presented, but there was a pecking order to acknowledge in the manner of distribution. Some like the Chief and the Old Man, would probably have got a case and bag of everything going, then lesser mortals half a case and half a bag - when it got down to Stan and myself it was "Here are some oranges and potatoes - divide them". Stan would have none of it - let them keep them - "Bob you take them".

Gathering up his oranges, he insisted on putting his share in my cabin. There they lay and the word got around he wasn't pleased at the discrimination thereof.

Some time afterwards, upon returning to my cabin after the watch, I noticed they were gone. Stan had had second thoughts!

It took us fourteen days from Famagusta to Glasgow. We had a leisurely life, boat drill off Malta, and bunkered again in Ceuta. One little duty I had to perform was greasing all extended spindles to the fuel valves every Saturday morning. These spindles extend from the settling tanks to the boat deck, the idea being that in the case of evacuation of the engine room with the engine full ahead, fuel can be cut off to the boilers eventually bringing the ship to a halt. It was the universal joints that were pressure greased, as were extended spindle joints controlling the draught fans. The boat deck would be the highest deck from which to conduct emergency action like this. Again mention might be made to the settling tanks in a steamer. It is there, in port and starboard settling tanks, that oil is pumped from the bunkers. Sediment but especially water can "settle", and water being heavier than oil, settles to the bottom, where it can be drained off. Each tank would contain enough oil for about twelve hours steaming. In a motorship, the equivalent would be the daily service tanks, into which diesel oil is pumped, after purification, from the diesel bunkers.

Looking across the Mediterranean from Ceuta, Gibraltar lies about thirteen miles away, standing like a great inscrutable Sphinx of the Western World. In passing the Straits of Gibraltar, one goes briefly south before rounding Tarifa. Next, one passes Cape Trafalgar (don't tell the French), across the Gulf of Cadiz, Faro in Portugal, and finally at Cape St. Vincent one goes north for the haul up the Spanish and Portuguese coasts past Cape Finisterre. Now comes the passage of the Bay of Biscay, then sighting the land in the form of the French Island of Ushant. Finally, crossing the English Channel, one passes Land's End and the Scillies to enter the Irish Sea.

I was visiting the bridge when passing Belfast Lough and was surprised at the quality in definition, on the ships radar, of the outline of the Lough. Soon we passed Ailsa Craig (Paddy's Milestone), and sailed up the Clyde to Prince's Pier, Glasgow.

There was to be a change in the engineering compliment. Peter Bridges was going ashore to take his Chief's ticket - George was moving somewhere and I was promoted to 4th Engineer, so this was good news - not the least financially. Actually I was getting more money per month as a "fifth" than I had got as a "fourth" with the previous company. Additionally, I was getting a bonus in respect of having an exemption from Part A of the Seconds "ticket".

Upon returning to Liverpool after a week in Glasgow, we found that a new Second had arrived - I think his name was Wilkinson - a Scot. The next trip was scheduled to go up the Dardanelles to Istanbul, Pireas in Greece, and Lisbon, in addition to some of the previous ports. It would be interesting.

I returned home for a few days during which time I got the timetable for the College of Technology examinations, and discovered that it was going to cut things fine, if I did the next trip. I had no alternative but to return and tell Fergie Brand that I would have to prepare for the examination.

So I returned to the "Grecian" and "worked by", as the expression goes, until she sailed. She had a new fifth engineer as well - he came from the South of Ireland. There was also a new fourth - a South African, Stan took George's place as Third, and I watched as the "Grecian" manoeuvred out of the West Bromley Moore and into the Mersey, smoking badly. But I would meet her again.

*   *   *   *   *   *   *   *   *

Moving back into study mode, I joined Mr Boyd's maths class a couple or three weeks before the examination and successfully passed the beastly obstacle to progress.

The MV "Hibernian Coast"

Now the next thing was to contact Fergie Brand again to see if he had anything for me to do, but before I got around to doing that, out of the blue I was asked if I was interested in a temporary spell on a coaster. Now I had heard mixed stories, not only about the quality of living on a coaster but also that the weather around the coasts could be unpredictable and wicked at times. But since it was for only a few weeks, I said that I was interested.

I got a telegram which simply said "Join "Hibernian Coast", Bromboro, Saturday, Third Engineer, Cantlay, Coast Lines." I never met the person called Cantlay, but I believe he worked for the Superintendent Engineer, Coast Lines. This was not to be the last time I would do business with him.

I again flew from Nutts Corner on a B.E.A. flight to Liverpool via the Isle of Man, and I would be cutting it fine. I hadn't a clue where Bromboro was, but I had a tongue in my head and I used it. I had the utmost good fortune to fall in with a likely guy, who was wearing a traditional navy blue gabardine, favoured by seafaring officers. I think he was on the bus from Speke airport when I posed my questions - I discovered that he was skipper of a sister ship, the "Colebrook Coast". He knew the "Hibernian Coast" well - "a fine twin screw sixteen knot vessel", he said. And Bromboro lay the other side of the Mersey - I would need to take the ferry and a bus as well.

It was four o'clock before I reached Bromboro using the Mersey ferry and a bus to Bromboro dock. There was only one ship lying alongside, black hull and white upper works with a distinctive X on her funnel. She looked smart enough with bridge forward and engine room aft - the M.V. "Hibernian Coast" of 1000 tons, G.R.T. I was to sail as third engineer.

When I got on board I was received by the Chief, an elderly Dutch man called Van Den Ent. The "Hibernian Coast" had twin British Polar Diesel engines, two sets of eight cylinders, and three very noisy diesel generators. Central heating in the engineers' accommodation was by an ancient coal fire stove which was supposed to supply heat via radiators in the cabins. It didn't. The galley was in the forward accommodation under the bridge, and food had to be conveyed by a steward along the open deck sometimes staggering and sometimes swimming! I can't remember having anything to eat that went down easily!

However, there was little time to think about anything but getting underway. This was set for 6 p.m. and I found myself standing with the Second - an elderly man, in the engine room at 5 p.m. The second showed me how the engines were started, one lever for the compressed air start, another one for the fuel - the R.P.M. control. He went up for his tea and at 5.30 the bridge rang down for 'Stand By'. I was very much on my own, although there was a very experienced donkeyman.

However the old second had returned by the time we got the first engine movement and he took over.

Amazingly, the telegraph in the engine room was operated by a chain - something like a bicycle chain. It passed over various gear idlers and guides around corners, all the way to the bridge and in answering the movement, one always swung the telegraph arm past the position of the indicator and back to the required position.

The "Hibernian Coast" carried all sorts of general cargo. One item only I remember - cartons and cartons of TIDE! The ports visited were Plymouth - all rebuilt after the war, Southampton, Portsmouth, London (West India docks) then Dublin and back to Liverpool.

The weather was very poor, and leaving London for Dublin the weather really opened up and a gale estimated at force 10 blew up. I turned in at the end of my watch picking up a sports coat and hanging it up. I got over to sleep only to be awakened by the ship's whistle - it was an emergency. Then the mate, a chap from Bangor, North Wales, put his head round the door and asked me to turn to - we had lost our steering engine. I looked down at the floor and discovered four inches of water - lying there also was the sports coat.

A hand for yourself and one for the ship.

The "Hibernian Coast" had, as already referred to, split accommodation i.e. the Bridge personnel, galley etc was up forward, while the engineering folk were right aft. The sailors, greasers etc were in accommodation below that of the engineers. Now, the entrance to the seaman's accommodation and the steering gear was by way of a stairway, the entrance of which faced right aft. This meant that any following sea, overtaking the ship, could well come over the after side of the ship and flood down the stairs. This is what happened at about five o'clock in the morning, while passing the Isle of Wight - a following sea really came over, flooding the seaman's accommodation and the steering gear - which was electrically driven.

The ship, being of a very old design - built about 1946, had an emergency steering, incorporating a wheel mounted on a pedestal above the rudder on the after deck. By some system of chain and leverage, the rudder could be turned, and so the "Hibernian Coast" crawled under the lee of the Isle of Wight. We cleaned up as best we could. Some of the wave that did the damage carried on over the engineers' accommodation deck filling everywhere with filthy sea water. All the scuppers appeared to be blocked - what a job getting that water out. Eventually, new fuses were fitted and the steering motors dried out - but we didn't venture out for some hours. Between ships waiting to dock in Southampton or Portsmouth and those sheltering, I counted over fifty ships at anchor. Under way again that afternoon, we arrived in Dublin the following day, before lunchtime. Between poor food, terrible accommodation, a very, very, noisy engine room - and worst of all a Chief Engineer who spoke imperfect English, I felt I was earning my money in a way I had not done before.

It's amazing looking back, that someone with little experience of diesel (only that of a generator), was given a chance to take a watch - as third engineer, on a motor vessel. But the reality is, that main engines at sea are usually the least of an engineer's concern. Give them clean fuel, clean lubricating oil (and water, if, in a steamer), keep temperatures and pressures correct, and the main engines will hammer away. The other things are common to both motor and steam. Bilges, water on deck, generators on the board, transfer of fuel to settling tanks (steam) or to daily service tanks (motor), purification of fuel oil and lubrication oil, filters, pumping systems and other auxiliaries etc - by sorting this lot out one gets by (at least I managed to scrape along - to plough new ground, one has to enter the field - sometime). After we arrived in Dublin I noticed among the people who came aboard for one reason or another, a fairly youngish woman with long black hair. The seamen seemed to know her well, and she was known as the "Gypsy". Since gypsies traditionally sell things, everything seemed in order, although later, when I considered the matter, I was puzzled somewhat since she didn't carry the wicker basket which I imagined was traditionally carried by travelling people. I was to see her again.

When I boarded the "Hibernian Coast", there were only two engineers aboard - the other two had disappeared. Just that week, conscription ended, and men, who had chosen to spend time on the Merchant Service instead of the Armed Services, had no longer a reason to stay at sea. As far as I became aware, they were walking off ships in droves. So we were a man short.

However, at London we had got help in the form of another Dutchman - I cannot recall his name and he was now settling in. He seemed to me a guy who moved around - and was virtually alcoholic. I might just mention that although I had my faithful accordion with me it was never out of the box.

We were in Dublin a few days - it was an interesting experience for me - arriving at the North Wall - and seeing Dublin for the first time. I visited O'Connell Street, saw the Post Office and other places now of interest to any traveller to Dublin.

It's of some historical interest to me now to recall things like cartons of washing powder etc being transported from Liverpool (Bromboro) to Plymouth, Southampton or London. Who would dream of sending such a thing by sea, when the articulated lorry is now so available? Thus, the changing face of commerce.

One day around lunchtime and no work being in progress - loading or unloading, a few of us noticed a bit of a commotion aboard the old M.V. "Leinster" a cross channel passenger and cattle motor ship lying on the other side at the North Wall. Cattle were being loaded up quite a narrow ramp - a lot of cattle could be seen compressed in a very small area. One bullock, had had enough, and jumping over the side fence of the ramp, made it into the Liffey. He actually swam directly across the river and upon seeing this, the few crew members or dockers present, set about a rescue mission. The beast pressed on, and was soon rounding the bows of the "Hibernian Coast". Round the bow he came, between the ship and the North Wall, but it was a cold day, no doubt the water was very cold, and there was not a lot of him above water. Soon however a winch whirred into life, and a hook appeared above the sinking swimmer. Some intrepid sailor or docker produced a sling with eyelet at each end, and standing on or leaning outboard on something - he may have been actually standing on a tyre barrier up the side of the ship, attempted to pass the rope of the sling below the beast. Eventually and none too soon, the rope was prodded in below the beast where what would be armpits in a human being, and the two ends brought together - a most remarkable and persistent effort of salvage. The winch hook was then passed through the eyelets, and winding away, the animal was winched from the water. It couldn't have been comfortable for him - half a ton or more of animal suspended by a thin rope around his middle, aft of his front legs. The jib of the crane on which the hook was operating then swung inland, with its erstwhile swimmer of the Liffey suspended below. Being rather unceremoniously dumped on the quayside, the beast, which only minutes before was drowning, gave itself a shake, did unspeakable things on the quayside and set off like the clappers in the direction of O'Connell Street. Whether he was recaptured in time to join the "Leinster" that night I cannot say. I don't know about pigs flying, but bullocks are good swimmers!

That evening, I took the opportunity of going ashore, as we were due to sail later that night. After buying a few odds and ends, I was returning in good time to the old "Hibernian Coast" when I met the new Dutch Engineer who had joined us at Southampton. He had been drinking and asked me if I would have a coffee with him in a cafe close by. In we went, and when he was ordering the coffee, I saw no less a lady than the "gypsy" who had "boarded" us as we docked a couple of days previous. No recognition flares were sent up until, when returning with the coffee, my Dutch friend also spotted her and immediately made a remark which while I couldn't decipher it at all she had no difficulty in understanding because her attitude became at once hostile and threatening. The Dutchman, proceeded to jeer and presumably made some fun at her expense. What happened next I cannot be sure - at any rate a most horrendous row broke out - chairs and abuse alternatively flying through the air. I think the fact that the Dutchman was drunk and just kept laughing made the "gypsy" more angry and I decided for a host of reasons that it would be better to have clear water between me and the fracas. I can remember distinctly feeling very uncomfortable because I simply didn't want to share the blame for the consequences of the racket.

I made my way out and left him and a number of onlookers - and the gypsy. Some time later I was aware he had returned to his cabin. He passed the thing off as nothing. I wonder who drank my coffee? Soon it was time to leave Dublin - I can't recall the details now except we arrived in the Mersey the next morning at about 7 am and had a long wait outside the Prince's Dock before we entered. The ship was not at anchor but way was maintained against the tide by giving the engines a "kick" now and again.

I had decided in a chat with the skipper that I would sign off some time after we tied up. So around 10 a.m. I collected my discharge book and my pay and walked off complete with my accordion and case, thinking I wouldn't see this old coaster again. But I was wrong!

Epitaph to a Third Engineer

When the last crank and crosshead's been tightened,
And the Third Engineer laid to rest,
And his tools are all rusted and broken,
Divide what you think are the best.

No red hot cranks, no Second's pranks,
Will there the Third annoy,
But in robes of white, a shining light,
Somebody's fair haired boy.

No rods to swing, no gear to sling,
No bottom ends to tighten,
No glands to pack, no nuts to slack,
No firemen to frighten.

But on the bright and happy shore,
Beyond the turbines and gears,
Where Seconds cease from troubling,
And there are no Chief Engineers.

So leave him alone in God's acre
He died in his own belief,
That Heaven's reserved for Juniors,
And Hell's set apart for the Chief.

I am indebted for this poem, to my old comrade in the Naval Ordnance Inspectorate (N.I.) Sam McCarton,
late of the Bank Line and many watches on the four to eight. I am unsure, however, of its origin.

I had now decisions to make and quickly. I decided I had better button up my studies, started so long ago - it would mean getting a position where I could settle down for a hard year's work and study. Then up came an interesting one for which I was short listed - Assistant Engineer, Royal Victoria Group of Hospitals. I was fortunate in knowing Mr Archie Barr, Engineer at Holywell Hospital, Antrim. Archie very kindly agreed to show me round the engineering end of the hospital. That he did - I was enthralled at the sight of the up and down steam generator - and my old friend the Weir feed pump. I told Archie the name of the man whom I might be working for. "I know him - a very awkward customer". Coming from Archie, a man himself never to use two words if one would do, this was straight from the horse's mouth.

At the interview, before I presume, the hospital management plus Mr X (the awkward) I felt I had done quite well. But I had a rival, Tom McCormack - again one of my old day release comrades - and a Forth River Miller. Tom was ex-Harlands and by now ex-British India Steam Navigation (George of the Grecian's old company). He got the job. He was a most polite fellow and I believe he may have been related to Mr D Ogburn, my former teacher. He left the job after six months. Speaking to him years later when we were working for the same employer, I found that Mr Archie Barr had given me good information!

I was then interviewed - a good interview, with the Naval Air Station Sydenham. At the same time a similar interview took place at the Royal Naval Armament Depot, Antrim. Just before the latter took place, I was asked by a friend if I would visit his uncle who wanted to hear the pipes. This uncle was Alec Gribbon, a fitter in the R.N.A.D. at Antrim. When I discovered this, I mentioned that I was going for an interview for a fitter's job myself. "That's interesting - I must mention that to Harry Glenn", said Alec. "Harry Glenn", I said slowly, "Would he be a Belfast man who came down and married a woman with a farm of land?" "Yes - that sounds like him - he's the shop steward". He was talking about Ned Moore's friend - Ned who worked with me in Centre 20 - the Balcony! He was man I had told Ned's version of events to - on the bus. I got the job.

Just about this time I got another offer from Fergie Brand at Ellermans. I was offered a Fourth's job on the SS "Venetian". I toyed with the idea, then reluctantly rang him up and thanked him and explained that I was going to pursue the H.N.C. He was a good man, and had circumstances been different I would have liked to work for him and I still had some aspirations as well, to get a "ticket"!

Now I started with "the Admiralty". I wasn't to be disappointed as, looking back, I think they were very good to me.

Chapter 7 - Towards A New Career

The Mark VIII Torpedo and the Royal Naval Armament Depot, Antrim (R.N.A.D)

The Royal Naval Armament Depot was originally established by Messrs Stone Platts to manufacture and maintenance torpedoes for the Royal Navy. The factory was built off the Randalstown Road, a short distance from the town and on the banks of the Sixmilewater River. Thus, convenient to the wide expanse of Lough Neagh, access to open water was easy from the Firing Head, which was established in shallow water, close to the mouth of the Sixmilewater. A firing range was established from the Firing Head over which torpedoes could be tested.

(The factory, still largely intact, is now the home of the Army as the Massereene Barracks. The remains of the Firing Head can still be seen - it is now a declared bird sanctuary and as such has become a feature of the shores of Lough Neagh at Antrim.)

As well, there were also facilities for the maintenance of naval guns, and paravanes used by mine sweepers to stream the devices used to cut the mooring wires of mines which, coming to the surface might be disposed of by gunfire.

I found a number of things to my agreement. I discovered that the Admiralty, would allow workers who wished to study approved subjects, day release, to do so. Now this was indeed something - I was no longer an apprentice and here I was being allowed to take a day off each week. There was, working at R.N.A.D. at that time a man, one of whose responsibilities included looking after time cards, leave and such like things. One day I remarked to him that this was "a bit of alright", considering that I might leave this employment after obtaining such qualifications being studied for. "That's not as important as it seems", he said, "your education is in the national interest". I have often thought about the wisdom of his views - his name was Sam McCracken, and I was to teach with his nephew, Billy McCracken, in Lisburn Technical College some time later.

Most of the employees at R.N.A.D. had been there a long time, some transferred from other Ministry of Defence establishments being closed down. As well, many were "tied" through establishment, an arrangement whereby they were guaranteed employment (with the M.O.D. somewhere). As well, these jobs were pensionable. All employees had sickness benefit to the tune of thirteen weeks sick leave. I knew some of the employees, but I was to make many friends. One of the first to welcome me was Harry Glenn. A Harland's man, he had been to sea for a period before the Second World War - on, I believe, the South American run. As such he qualified under Horace Love's philosophy that after a trip to sea, life somehow would never be the same again. I was to benefit greatly from the things that "rubbed off" people like Harry, Alec Gribbon - and quite a number of others.

The Foreman of the factory (F of F in Admiralty jargon) was Mr Abel - he told me that he had a brother who was a Chief Engineer with the Athel Steamship Co. The Personnel Manager - I forget the Admiralty term for it, was Mr Deadman - quite a nice chap in spite of the name, and the Manager was a Mr Jeans, who rejoiced in the title of S.A.S.O. - Senior Armament Supply Officer.

The engine of the Mark VIII torpedo was a most remarkable and complex piece of technology.

In service since about 1927 - various modifications being added over the years, it survived as a dependable front line weapon into the 1980's and two Mark VIII's sank the Argentinian cruiser, "Belgrano", as mentioned elsewhere.

Being of a classified nature, the explanation of the engine was dealt with in fairly vague terms in any books on torpedoes I had read, and I was very glad indeed to receive the information and the exploded view of the engine shown opposite. This was through the good offices of the Naval Museum, Gosport, and eventually Ministry of Defence permission was given to use this material. Now to examine the drawing, information etc.

The engine is described as a semi-diesel. (A diesel engine uses what is known as a constant pressure cycle). The part diesel element in the engine design relates to the fact that fuel is injected into the cylinder head, and so the designation of constant pressure cycle is technically correct. But - this engine has no compression! Where does ignition come from? External to the engine is a component known as the generator where fuel and air are combined in a gas (at 600° C) by the firing of three cartridges, triggered as torpedo is fired out of torpedo tube. This generator feeds the hot gas through a pipe (induction ring), passing each cylinder in turn, and an inlet valve allows gas to enter the cylinder head just after fuel has started to enter, causing immediate combustion. Exhaust is by way of ports in the cylinder walls and the top of piston, eventually escaping via crankcase and propeller tail shaft tube. Its brake horse power was of the order of 350.

I went to work on mechanisms that had to do with controlling the direction and depth keeping qualities of the torpedo. I must say it was most impressive, seeing rows of torpedoes awaiting a complete overhaul in every detail. I have never ceased to marvel at the design of that weapon - and that similar weapons existed before the turn of the century. In World War I, torpedoes were used with devastating success by the warring navies in submarines, destroyers and in a primitive way by early sea planes, and German torpedoes were feared at 4000 yards; in World War II HMS Devonshire was torpedoed at 5000 yards. (Recently I looked at the sectioned Mark VIII on display at the Imperial War Museum and the specifications on it credit this weapon with speeds of forty knots over 7,500 yards and forty-five knots over 5,000 yards, and up to depths of forty-five feet). I never cease to marvel at the technology of this weapon, at the wonderful yet compact four cylinder (axial) engine, with the connecting rods using one common crank pin, and that of 5,121 fired by British submarines in World War II, 1,040 hits were obtained - 22.6%. The Mark VIIII version, as used by surface ships (see the one on display on HMS "Belfast", Tower Bridge, London) apparently had an even greater range - 11,000 yards at forty knots, and 15,000 yards at thirty-five knots! A number of workers especially in the various management areas of the complex, came from England and Scotland. Jack Frobisher, my Chargeman (Admiralty term for Chargehand) was a Scot, as were two assistant Foremen Andy Brown and Andy Drysdale. But local men were up there too - Eddie Brown from Dunadry was in charge of the machine shop. I was later to work for him in the machine shop, and a word to his credit would not be out of place. I have mentioned the main road side of Dunadry village and how opposite Foxes Pub (now called Ellie Mays), there was a sign relating to cycle repair. I understand that Eddie had at one time carried on a cycle repair business there. He was a gentleman indeed, who carried out his supervisory duties in a most unobtrusive manner - the work in the machine shop progressed in a very relaxed atmosphere. I was to remain good friends with him the rest of his life.

The engine cycle (*Fig.* 17)

43. The engine is a four cylinder radial engine working on the semi-diesel cycle.

44. The gas in the induction ring, which is connected direct to the generator outlet, is at a temperature of approximately 600 degrees C. and contains sufficient uncombined oxygen to promote combustion of the injection fuel in the engine cylinders. The gas is admitted to each cylinder head in turn through its poppet valve just before top dead centre. At this moment the cylinder head contains atomised fuel which has been admitted from the injection fuel system through the fuel timing valve just before the inlet valve opens. Combustion of the uncombined oxygen and the injection fuel takes place, with a consequent rise in pressure, forcing the piston on its downward stroke.

45. Exhaust ports in the cylinder wall are uncovered by the piston near the end of the stroke. After the exhaust ports are closed on the upward stroke of the piston, the cylinder is cleared of exhaust gases by gudgeon exhaust ports cut in the piston head. These gudgeon exhaust ports are opened and closed by the small end of the connecting rod rocking about the axes of the gudgeon pins. The exhaust gases pass through the cylinder skirt and piston head to the crank chamber and finally out through the tail through the hollow propeller shaft.

46. A pressure stroke occurs in each cylinder on every revolution of the engine.

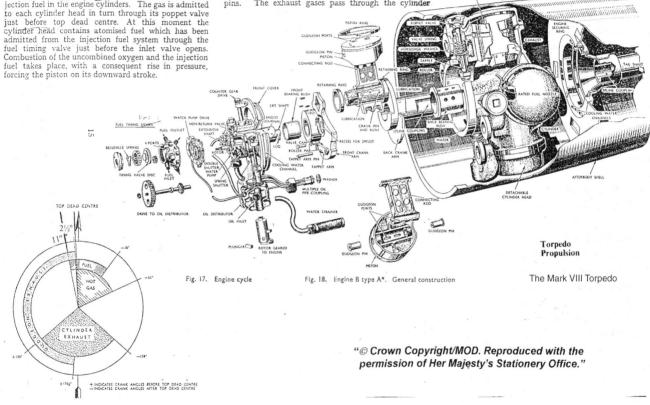

Fig. 17. Engine cycle

Fig. 18. Engine B type A*. General construction

Torpedo Propulsion

The Mark VIII Torpedo

I couldn't mention the Admiralty at Antrim without remembering my old friend Archie Lennie. A Scot living in Belfast, he started the same day as I did. He was something between a brother and a father to me, a wonderful workmate full of wisdom flowing from his apprenticeship on the Clyde. He was a passionate bowler, a member of - was it Bloomfield Methodist Bowling Club? - and I got my fill of bowls. Later a personal friend of mine, Reg Strutt came to work as a joiner at R.N.A.D. Reg as all who knew him, was one of this world's gentlemen. He was a Welshman who had married a local girl when stationed at Aldergrove during the war (1939-1945). He was gifted with musical talents - he sang in High Street Choir and also in the Linenhall Choir, Ballymena, and earlier in life was a violinist in a Welsh orchestra. I am now the proud possessor of his violin, passed on to me by his widow.

Reg joined Archie and I at the tea and lunch breaks and shared in the contents of a bright red enamel teapot. It's good to remember the simple things of life - the complicated things are such a weariness of the flesh.

About the time I started, another recruit appeared - George McFadden, an old friend from my early days in the Junior Boys' Brigade. George had originally served an engineering apprenticeship, but had left it to become a male nurse. Now it was second harvest for him in engineering. He was to return to a successful career in nursing, but in the meantime shared with me the ups and downs of life among the torpedoes.

There were many men with whom I worked who in turn passed on to me much needed specialised skills. Jimmy Brownlees, Antrim, explained the mystery of servo motors, while Bobby Wallace, from the Grange, Randalstown, imparted secrets as to how to deal with recalcitrant depth gear - very often with a mallet, while someone else explained the workings of the complicated engine. The R.N.A.D. was the only place I was ever to see Brake Horse Power tests carried out on engines - under the direction of Harry Lyttle, from Kellswater. Harry told me that when a boy, he remembered my uncle setting off for Canada in a horse drawn trap from Kellswater Station.

Another chap I worked with was called Bertie. He came from Armagh - but had served in the RAF during the war and had serviced the infamous Fairy Battles as they were annihilated by the Luftwaffe over the skies of Dunkirk. I think it was around this time - that the Blood Transfusion Service started visiting factories, as I see in my blood donation "discharge" book two entries "R.N.A.D. Antrim".

Around this time also, I first rattled a collecting box for the Musgrave Park Ex-Patients' Association, and I recall at this time, that we purchased radio headphones for some of the wards - possibly my own Ward 2B - what a place forever sacred in my memory. I started to walk there, and that salvage miracle had carried me a fair bit into life's battles so far. Also, I became the proud possessor of a black A30 Austin car which carried me up to the College of Technology on my day release forays - and also to evening class, parked in College Square North. There was no column lock fitted in cars of that era and nobody even thought of a chain around the steering wheel, for the simple reason nobody stole cars as a rule, in those days. Isn't it ironic, that, as a result of the evil of thieving cars, a huge multi-million business in security has grown up, providing numerous jobs making and selling devices to counter the thief. They are not very successful. Why do we not simply switch off the petrol?

I mustn't forget to mention the "homers" that were made in the beautiful copper and brass pieces of scrap. Horses' heads - now Joe Smith was very good at drawing you a horse's head, and making canaries was the stock in trade of the specialists. In over all "charge" of canary production was one Hamilton (Hammy) Kennedy, a product of the Rainey Endowed Grammar School in Magherafelt, and a former R.N.A.D. apprentice.

Hammy later became a teaching colleague of mine, and assures me, that he "exported" canaries all over the world! I'm inclined to believe this. He is now Mr Hamilton Kennedy MSc, Lecturer in Electronic Engineering, and the Author of the text book "112 Electronic Circuits", soon to be in schools throughout the U.K. and Ireland.

The Inspectorate of Naval Ordnance

But time waits on no man and another stage loomed up for me. Opportunities existed for several places in the Inspectorate of Naval Ordnance. These guys went round inspecting the work on refurbishing armaments or in the case of new work, at the manufacturing stage. Among the existing I.N.O. men was someone who proved a good friend to me - Bob Ramsey. An ex-RAF man, I had known Bob in my days at Castlereagh where he carried out Naval Ordnance Inspection duties on guided weapons, destined for the Navy. I applied for an interview - first by George Dunn, a Foreman of inspectors and another Scot. I went over everything I had done in life and he didn't seem impressed until I mentioned the tool room. Then he sat up. "You've been on tools - now ah know a hae got a good mechanic". (The inspectors rejoiced in the Admiralty grade, mechanic examiner). After George Dunn, I had another interview, this time with Lieut. Cmdr McMullan. Finally I had a more critical interview with Cmdr Poole. I don't recall answering many of the questions he asked, correctly, or identifying faults in samples he presented to me for my opinion. Anyway, they gave me a job but I was in for a big surprise! The vacancy for me was not at Antrim, but at Short Bros. & Harland, Belfast. Had I ever heard of it? Sometime previous to this, Hammy Kennedy and Jimmy Higgins were also recruited to the I.N.O. - both to have quite exciting careers and much travel. Jimmy took part in gunnery trials as far away as the Persian Gulf (he also served at Simonstown, South Africa) while Hamilton Kennedy's duties involved the Polaris submarine project, during which he dived in atomic as well as conventional submarines. So, after about one year and a half in the R.N.A.D., I hung up my overalls for the last time, bid farewell to the red teapot, to Reg and Archie, Harry Glenn, and Alec Gribbon - all my new found friends to whom I owe a great deal, and eventually I presented myself to the I.N.O. at Shorts. The work involved inspection of the Seacat guided weapon components - after they had passed through Shorts own inspection. A kind of police action, it still was not foolproof as will be seen. I was up at Castlereagh where I met all my old friends in C31 and also in C24. Nothing had changed much here. Then I was shifted to the guided weapon complex established in the extension factory, at Queen's Island. The guided weapon enterprise had thrown together some very interesting people. In the I.N.O. "bond", as we called the room where we examined components for size and quality of finish, there was John Deeney, an ex-chief E.R.A. - a man of wide experience. There was Sammy Valely who had sailed on the battleship "Royal Sovereign" and Ken Powell who had been an E.R.A. on HMS "Bulwark", the aircraft carrier. He had also been on HMS "Vanguard", the last battleship to be built and not to see service in World War II.

Missile work demanded a high degree of cleanliness and the assembly and gyro areas had to be entered through an air lock. To work in the gyro room extra special gowns and overshoes were essential. As well, many of the employees in this "clean area" were female, sorting out and soldering etc the electronic package of the weapon. There were again some new and interesting characters - who will forget Fergie Fowler or Eddie Kidd. Fergie was a mechanical fitter while close to him was an electrician by the name of Montgomery with whom I was very friendly. I was glad he was there - he helped me out with some electrical problems I had - by this time I was studying electrical engineering as well, because my work involved dealing with electromechanical devices, and I would be expected to go to England on courses relating to such. One Shorts Inspector I worked opposite was Gordon Hedley - I seem to remember that his wife was related to the late Rafton Pounder, MP - but congeniality went further as Gordon had sailed on tankers on the Mississippi/New Orleans route, and had much to tell me. Among new acquaintances in the Shorts workers I was to become well acquainted with was Bobby Barry, an electrician working in the missile division. He was a leading piper, Pipe Major of Ballykeel

Black Watch (Co Down) Pipe Band and a most agreeable companion. Near him worked Wesley Wallace from the Woodburn Pipe Band near Carrick. Ballykeel, under Bobby's guidance was playing in Grade II, and Bobby was a frequent entrant in the solo playing stakes. Our friendship has continued throughout the years.

All materials and components bought into a firm from outside providers, usually has at least a visual examination, done on some sort of sample test and examination. For example, a component made of stainless steel will not be affected by a simple nitric acid test, but if perchance it has been made from mild steel, nitric acid will soon show up the fraudster. I was working on such components in what we called the Inwards Bay, when I got to know a man, who cut materials on a large modern revolving saw. I discovered he was a World War II submariner. This was before my interest heightened in such matters as later will show, and I regret I don't seem to recall a name. He was in Japanese controlled water when during a depth charging, the skipper was forced down to 600 feet. The skipper called the crew, "and told us to pray". I wonder who this man was?

Other items on the inspection agenda, were welded components. I had never welded myself, so in order that I might approach this end of the business with more confidence I organised short courses in gas and arc welding - it was to be useful - later on.

I mentioned earlier that while working for the Ministry of Defence, I enjoyed the privilege of day release to continue my studies at the College of Technology, Belfast. Opposite the College was a cafe - where business was conducted by the stern Mrs Morton (actually the heart of gold). Cups of coffee too numerous to calculate were consumed by students and staff alike. One day, I found, sitting right beside me, no less a person than George Stewart, whose place, as fourth engineer I had taken on the SS "Rathlin Head". He was now at the Marine Engineering School, where he successfully studied for his "tickets" and later became a Chief Engineer with Caltax Tankers. As well, one day I had a glimpse of Mr Reeves, one of the "seconds" I had worked with on the "Rathlin Head" and shortly afterwards I literally bumped into one of the donkeymen (greasers) with whom I had worked alongside, in that ship.

By this time, I had met yet another teacher from the College of Technology, Belfast, to whom I would owe a great deal, and who in no small way, enabled me through his teaching skills and mannerisms, to feel comfortable in confronting the examinations leading to the Higher National Certificate in Mechanical Engineering. In those days, this qualification was of a standard high enough to extend most of us students, required a significant amount of laboratory evidence, and which even today, I am still very very proud to possess.

The teacher referred to was Mr G Moag, a former Shorts apprentice and destined to become Chief Executive, Belfast Education and Library Board. In the process of time, circumstances led to a renewal of our early association and for many years I have been privileged to share some occasions with this most unassuming of men. Naturally it came as a pleasant and most interesting surprise when I learned from him, one day, that he had worked on the SA4 Sperrin bomber, in his early days in Shorts. So, in 1963 I finally passed the Higher National Certificate in Mechanical Engineering. Some of my earlier colleagues had already achieved it four years before. But I was amazed to find out how many others had fallen by the wayside, and in a sense I had now caught up and passed these. But you can never recover the years, eaten by the locusts. My eternal thanks is to those people in Shorts, like Col. Thompson and Ossie Carlisle, Mr Kirkpatrick, Mr Pickering, Mr Archer, Mr Black and Mr Adams from Short's Apprentice Training Department and to Mr Denis Ogburn, Mr George McBratney and Mr Gerry Moag and other teachers in the College of Technology who dragged me - kicking and squealing "over the line". Subsequent to the work of the Waveney Hospital, Ballymena, and the essential work of my surgeon and the nurses of Musgrave Park Hospital, my rehabilitation was as near complete as it would be. What had been destroyed in seconds that day down the Cushendall Road, Ballymena, had been put together again, in a manner of speaking.

In the guided weapon assembly area at Queen's Island, there was a strong representation of "Caroline" men - men who were serving in the Royal Naval Volunteer Reserve, centred on HMS "Caroline", the veteran light cruiser - the sole surviving ship of the dozens that had taken part in the Battle of Jutland, and I think, the only surviving warship of the First World War. Among these were Jimmy Ryan (Shorts) and John Deeney (I.N.O.). The I.N.O. staff consisted of a dozen or more, and during my time there, some departed and new faces arrived - most of whom were ex-Royal navy - Brian Watterson was one I remember who came straight from the R.N. My boss was a man called Harry How, who was a very pleasant and approachable fellow and supportive in the little controversies that arose between Shorts inspection and I.N.O. over whether a job was OK or not. Of course, I knew most of Shorts inspectors - some of them had "reared" me, and I had very good relations with them. One in fact was Hugh Campbell, my mentor from Castlereagh. But there was a lot of work being rejected - one week it reached 40% and it couldn't go on. Not all of this would be scrap - most could be accepted on concessions where it would be assessed on a kind of "will it do the job with enough margin of safety?" approach.

Shorts called a meeting of employees and to which we were invited to observe. It was addressed by Mr Hugh Conway, Chief Engineer. Mr Conway referred to the scrap and said it couldn't continue. I remember his words. "The more we look at this missile (the Seacat) the more we realise how (bleep) clever it is. Let's make it work!" The Seacat did work. It played its part in the Falklands War eighteen years later. Around this time the U.S.S. nuclear submarine "Thresher" was lost. The causes were speculated on. Hereafter, when some job came along which was a borderline case as to whether it was scrap or not, we would say "Remember the Thresher".

I must not forge to mention two Indian colleagues in the I.N.O. One was David Ghosh - he was at I.N.O. Castlereagh. Mani Khrishna was at Queens Island, someone I have pleasant memories of . Both were artificers on board the Indian Aircraft Carrier "Vigrant" building at Harlands, when they married local girls. I believe they had to leave the Indian Navy, after their marriages.

* * * * * * * * * *

A gyro is used for guidance purposes in weapons and has many components, including a stabilising device to hold, temporarily, the moving gimbals stationary until the rotor has reached full revolutions. During a period of work in the Gyro room, I was sent on a course to England. Someone would stand in for me. When I returned, a number of gyros were sitting, completed and boxed up, and ready for service. The final inspection was an outside "visual" - and a final stamp. All the various components as assembled would (hopefully) have been inspected. They were certainly all stamped up on paper. I duly added my stamp on the outside of these gyros and off they went.

* * * * * * * * * *

One day, some time later, my boss, a three ring commander came to speak to me. It was the kind of meeting which commences with "Mr Cameron, may I have a word with you!" My commander had some bad news - a Seacat, selected for a quality control firing had gone berserk before ending up in the sea. It was duly retrieved, and upon examination, it was found that the stabilising device in the gyro had not been properly fitted and this had been missed even with a double inspection procedure. Worse, the gyro bore my number on its outside casing! I consulted my records, and sure enough, it was one of the gyros completely assembled when I was in England. Sadly, that commander, who was an extremely pleasant and approachable man, passed away suddenly - he was in his forties. But life went on for others.

An opportunity came along for anyone interested in going to work for the Air Inspection Department, that government body of inspectors who were responsible for safe building practice and maintenance of aircraft. Anyone interested, would be interviewed in England. I put my hand up, and was flown to Manchester - Newton Street precisely, where I had the toughest technical interview, I have ever had in my life. I had tough and experienced opposition - some from ex-RAF people. I didn't get the job.

But soon through internal promotions I was sent to Ensleigh, Bath (Ministry of Defence, Admiralty Division) and after interview, I was offered work in the Drawing office, tool and design, Ensleigh.

A date was duly set for my leaving the I.N.O. and eventually air tickets and travel vouchers came through in the usual way. But I wasn't to use them. An important matter of concern at this time centred on my forthcoming marriage - the uncertainty of my future career, was complicating the search for accommodation! About this time, I had been considering teaching vacancies and I had applied for a number of vacancies. Two posts were offered me at the one time. One was as a lecturer in Strabane Technical College. I often wonder how my career might have gone in teaching had I taken that job, because the Principal, Mr Rainey, was a distinguished man. He had flown as one of the Pathfinders, and I would have been proud to have served under such a man who was a holder of the D.F.C. But another job became available nearer home. It was a Ministry of Health and Social Service appointment as an engineering instructor in a new workshop built at the rear of Antrim Technical College. Here were trained the first year apprentices from the new company in Antrim, British Enkalon. Also there were a similar number of unemployed boys sponsored by the Ministry of Health and Social Services. I decided to decline the Strabane job in favour of the latter, and I now had the delicate job of going into work the next day to receive a farewell gift and good wishes from my companions in the I.N.O. (my tickets were still in my pocket). I now wish to recall and record one of those character building exercises in respect of which I owed so much to the better types that I was so fortunate to meet.

I had a choice of procedure. I was tempted to say nothing, take my leave and go over to Bath for a couple of weeks and leave - or tell Lieut Cmdr McMullan that I had something to tell him before he made a presentation to me.

I decided to take the presentation, as, in the event, the Commander was unable to come down from Castlereagh due to some emergency. Harry How deputised and I received a beautiful present - a canteen of cutlery with book vouchers and best wishes. I was leaving, but not all knew where to.

I talked the matter over with my old friend Joe Miller of 3A Ward days. Joe gave me advice, which enshrined the principle of being straight about things - especially when dealing with the people we work with. "Ring Cmdr McMullan up and tell him you have something to say to him. Tell him you have got a job, you're not going to Bath and that you wish to work your notice". I say again that I have been fortunate indeed to have had such markers in life to guide my path and thinking. I saw Cmdr McMullan later, explained my position showing him the offer.

He wished me well, and inside a fortnight, I had found accommodation on the Cliftonville Road, Belfast, had become married on 7th September, 1965 and started my new work in Antrim. Jean, my wife, was working in Belfast at this time.

A change of direction - apprentice training, Antrim

So I took up a new job - I became a member of the Northern Ireland Civil Service (the I.N.O. was Imperial Civil Service). The two years I spent with those young men were among the most satisfying in what was the start of a teaching career, Not only were they exceptionally nice fellows but the quality of the work they turned out for me, was never again surpassed, progress wise, by any other of my students in other places in subsequent years. Quite a few of these boys are currently holding very responsible positions in either teaching or industry today. It's difficult to visualise such a thing nowadays, but these 16/17 year olds, these first year apprentices, became capable, during that one year off the job training, of fitting to an accuracy of one and a half thousandth of an inch (0.038mm) - using feeler gauges. Time brings changes and on modest promotion, I moved to Felden House Training Centre, Belfast. My being at the workshop at Antrim, was by way of secondment, and I was now to work under Mr Eric Duke, the Manager - my nominal boss, even when at Antrim. Again, as everywhere I worked in industry, I very soon picked out the interesting men - there were quite a few. My brother John was also instructing there and we shared transport. My responsibility related to the training and retraining of adults - men in engineering skills. Some had held responsible positions in industry or the Services- becoming redundant and taking the opportunity to retrain - perhaps in turning or milling or welding. Now, they all had one thing in common - they were looking for new work and preparation for that work. I found it sad that some of these mannerly and dignified men were having to start - all over again - losing employment is not a joke. Included also in my responsibility was a tool room, and the very capable Jack Bowman was looking after that - a most pleasant colleague, later to go on to higher management in G.T.C.'s - I was to meet up with him in later years. As well I had a unit giving instruction on Vehicle Maintenance and overhaul and here Billy McBride and Archie Gordon were the instructors looking after things. Sadly Archie was to pass away suddenly in the not too distant future. But as is recalled later I had also met one Arthur Mulholland, who instructed blind men to operate Capstan Lathes and - one Bob Cooper. Both were old seafarers.

* * * * * * * * * *

The welding instructors were very experienced men indeed - mostly ex-Harlands and some from the oil fields of foreign lands. They were expert pipe welders - and in my spare time I picked up some highly useful techniques from them. I have to guess, but I believe three of them were called Messrs Adamson, McClean and Rush.

Some of the instructors for whom I had responsibility (believe me they kept me right) I had met before. One such and most agreeable colleague, had worked at Castlereagh. His name was Montgomery. I remember him saying to me that his selection for instructor was the first promotion of any kind he ever had.

Another was George Robinson, an ex-RAF man, a milling instructor.

One thing, will surely not pass unnoticed in this reminiscence by anyone reading it, and that is the striking number of people I worked with who passed away suddenly. Of the two first and excellent classes of apprentices I taught, one from each group was dead within a short space of time - one through an industrial accident. The same would be true of the last named instructors.

Reflections - and a sample of seafaring again

During the years I spent with the Royal Naval Armament Depot, the Naval Ordinance Inspectorate, and the Civil Service, I became acquainted with large numbers of people of widely diverse backgrounds, abilities, and experience, and was led to reflect just how much knowledge there is in that part of our industrial might called engineering. In particular, I had been deeply impressed by what I had seen in marine engineering, and what I had heard discussed since - it seemed everywhere I had been in recent years, there was someone with marine experience. One of these encounters held deep interest for me, for it brought me news of Bob Martin, the Third Mate of the SS "Rathlin Head" and someone who, I must say, was very well disposed towards me and steered me round a few awkward corners on that first trip - I recalled him earlier. But I had lost contact with him when he went ashore on ticket leave. I will never forget his account of how during the war, a torpedo warhead was detonated accidentally close to where he and a friend had their bunks. That friend was in his bunk - I believe it was in a destroyer, when the tragedy occurred. Bob had helped hose the remains from the bulkhead. In the intervening years, I had been shocked to learn that Bob had gone missing - presumed overboard, from one of the Port Line ships - five miles off the Australian coast. Now when I joined the Northern Ireland Civil Service to instruct apprentices in Antrim, new machines were being installed and aligned in the workshop. I got talking to one of the fitters doing this work and sure enough, I discovered that he had been "on the boats" - I believe he was an ex-second engineer. When I mentioned that I had a friend lost or missing from a Port Line ship some time back, he revealed that he had been sailing with Bob on that very ship. He further disclosed that Bob's cabin was found locked, and there were some items missing from Bob's belongings. So there had been some speculation that perhaps Bob may have made it ashore. It would have been five miles in shark infested waters.

Meeting the aforementioned people not only caused me to reflect - it constantly drew my attention to how much I didn't know about engineering in all its vastness, and would never know. But knowledge can only be acquired by "hands on experience" in the right environment. I had decided upon a working holiday that summer, to renew acquaintance with real live tools again. I wrote to a couple of shipping companies offering to take a watch of limited duration i.e. coastal duties, and a couple of days before I was due to commence my holidays I received a telegram which said "Join Irish Coast Dublin Saturday Cantlay, Coast Lines". That telegram ushered in an era, spread over a decade or more when I was to acquire knowledge of developments in the field of marine engineering - some of it light years away from the friendly old SS "Grecian" with its Scotch boilers and triple expansion Bauer-Wach combination engine. I would use part of my long summer vacations to accomplish such gainful experience at sea.

So I joined the MV "Irish Coast" at the North Wall, Dublin, and Mr McClelland, a Scot, the Chief Engineer. He was somewhat crestfallen at the mention of steam - "I've got two sets of ten below", he said, "Dirty big oil engines". But he brightened when I mentioned having been on the MV "Hibernian Coast". "Van Den Ent', he exclaimed, "You must have known Van Den Ent!" I certainly remembered the old Dutch Chief. "Well, he's long gone now", said my new Chief, "But you'll likely do".

*   *   *   *   *   *   *   *   *   *

Just before I returned to my "normal" way of life, an incident took place that gave me and some of my companions much amusement and to me especially further encouragement to contemplate the ways of mice and men. I would later recall this to Bob Cooper and Arthur Mulholland when I returned to Felden after my "holiday", and I would remember what Mr Goldie, Chief of the "Grecian" had to say to me about demarcation!

Now it was like this: The engineers on the 'Irish Coast' could take their meals in the saloon (which meant dressing up) or they could take their meals in a little mess not far from the top entrance to the engine room. So I had my meals in this little mess - it was handy. Now it also happened, that this mess was close to a little pantry where food, destined for the first class dining saloon (and our mess), was given the final touch up by the stewards employed thereto, before presentation to the recipients, thereof.

In these days of self service cafeteria in cross channel ferries, it is perhaps difficult to imagine the service, where someone is waited upon by another.

One day, I had just taken my place in the mess, when I became aware of ruffled feathers among the stewards who serviced the first class dining saloon, as well as the engineers' mess. I overheard one steward enquire, "Which one are you talking about?" To which the steward being enquired of replied, "That table by the pillar -it's the old witch in the fur coat who is doing all the complaining about the sirloin. We'll see how she likes this!" So, a steward had been well and truly lectured upon the type of service someone expected. As well, a sirloin was undercooked, and milk jugs were short of milk.

What happened next was a salutary reminder of how vulnerable one becomes, if dependent upon another to prepare that most personable commodity - food. When one considers that you wholly depend upon the other fellow to wash and select the food properly - in particular to wash hands, and keep everything hygienic - my, do you get the message? The offended steward meanwhile had lifted one sirloin off a plate, a plate which he had just borne in ignominious retreat from the saloon, with uncomplimentary remarks following in his wake, from a lady wearing a fur coat.

I will not dwell upon the gory details of how that sirloin was seized by a "leg and an arm" subjected to appalling treatment in unspeakable places on the steward's person, before being placed below a small grill (used for such adjustments). His fellow steward also warmed to the affray. "So she needs more milk", he said, lifting a large enamel jug which, from memory, I estimated held a gallon and a half of the liquid. This second steward then proceeded to raise the jug to his lips, drank deeply and then filled the lady's small jug to overflowing. "Maybe that will please her", he said to his mate, who by now, having given the sirloin some "heat treatment", proceeded with jug and sirloin, and disappeared in the direction of the first class saloon. The engineers present, having had a grandstand view of proceedings enjoyed the scenario with great glee but I don't think we missed the message. I recalled the cook and the stewards "down below" in the "Grecian". I now hoped that I had never annoyed them.

Chapter 8 - The World of a Teacher

Lisburn Technical College

Shortly after I "returned to earth" again - to regale Arthur Mulholland and Bob Cooper with stories of salt water and stewards, I was offered a job in Lisburn Technical College as Lecturer in Mechanical Engineering. Now the exact title may have been Assistant Lecturer, but my job was to teach, in that "tech". An ex-Harlands man was Principal - the late Mr David Wright, and he told me he had eighty full-time staff and one hundred and forty part-timers -and "I'm the boss". He also told me that I would have visitations from the Northern Ireland Inspectorate of Education. "Don't let them annoy you", he said, "They are only there to advise". But I was to be long enough in education to see, that some of these visitations would result in certain teachers losing the positions to which they had been appointed. One of these was an acquaintance of mine. But education's loss was another's gain - in the space of a few years, my acquaintance was Chief Engineer of a super tanker - and earning a lot more than he had been - as an Assistant Lecturer! Perhaps he didn't get the good wholesome advice and instruction that was passed down to me at Lisburn Technical: "When your inspector is known to be on the premises, don't complete the afternoon register. Let him find something wrong like that and he will be in good form for the rest of the afternoon!" I was to be exactly twenty-five years in Further Education if one counts the two years working as an engineering instructor for apprentices when under the administration of the Principal of Antrim Technical College. In spite of Mr Wright's comment about 'advising', I cannot ever remember getting any advice from the inspectorate. During the final seventeen years in further education, I had taken on board that most unquantifiable of side shows - that of careers adviser. I believe it was an important job and worthy of support, but I never had a visit or a word of help or advice during that period - except when some one dropped in during a general inspection. The Careers Department in many institutes of learning is, I fear, the Cinderella of the system. It should not be - by any means.

It seemed that the team I had joined, at Lisburn, had an average age similar to my own. These men of the engineering and building departments were, without exception, a very fine bunch of colleagues, capable and helpful. Not everything that happened there pleased us all - all of the time. But considering everything, with the benefit of hindsight, I believe I was reared in a well run college. David Wright was a great advocate of punctuality, and often would appear near the front entrance consulting his watch as the hands approached 9 o'clock. The registers for the day were located nearby, whence I repaired each morning - but from the rear of the college, where I earlier had joined the scrimmage for a car parking space. When twenty-three years later, I found myself fighting for the same parking spaces as I returned on a temporary half term assignment - my former colleagues just looked the same. We had grown old together! When I first arrived, there was an elderly lady in the office - I imagine she was in charge of it. Her name was Miss Bowden and I was invited one day to join with others at her retirement presentation and cup of tea etc. If my facts are correct, her association with the college had lasted fifty years.

I was to meet many interesting students at Lisburn - especially adults who attended evening classes, like welding etc. There were humorous incidents as well.

One of the first I met was Jimmy Shirlow - "Flash Shirlow", the wrestler - a very nice fellow indeed - in the welding shop! He was a Belfast Harbour Policeman, and some years later, after I had left Lisburn, and when taking a bus load of students to visit Shorts (or maybe it was Harlands), I had a pleasant reunion with Jimmy, who was on duty at the Queen's Road, Harbour Gate. Now, I was not as wealthy then, as I might be now (bit of a joke, but it will do). I was driving an old Ford 105E - and it had little by way of an exhaust pipe. So, one evening before the night class started I whipped part of it off with a view to affecting some repair - it was a total emergency, and was a mess of holes everywhere. I had managed to get a few holes filled up when an early arrival positioned himself at my elbow. As I worked away, he watched silently. After a few moments I felt I had to say something which wouldn't give too much away: "It's terrible the jobs some people give you to do", I said. "It definitely is", he agreed, and by that, the class assembled - so I laid the exhaust pipe aside and got everybody going on their welding tasks. After things settled down - "full away" like, I recovered my exhaust pipe - I literally had to cast brass rod over it to fill the holes. (I always paid for such materials, of course!) Almost immediately, my early arrived friend was over watching. But eventually he could contain himself no longer. "Do you know what I'm going to tell you", he began. "You see the man who gave you that to repair - he is a nutcase, and no harm to you, you're not much better!" I agreed!.

One day shortly after I took up teaching duties at Lisburn, I had a visit from the technician who looked after the heating arrangements in the college - one Cecil Downey, and afterwards I visited his place in the college - the boiler-room. There what did I see but my old friend the Weir feed pump clicking away getting its feed water back to the boiler. Cecil was to be a lifelong friend. There was also a whiff of steam about the staffroom, because Robert Tweedie the teacher of technical drawing was an ex-Third Engineer Officer of Royal Mail Lines. A couple of years later I moved back to Antrim Technical, but I would, as already mentioned briefly work with these colleagues, many years later.

I believe a tribute should be paid to the men and women from industrial or commercial disciplines who were the traditional backbone of the Technical Colleges. I have already paid the highest tribute I can to those who taught and helped me at the College of Technology, Belfast, and it was about this time that I became friendly with Mr David Alexander, the Principal there, during my struggling years. He was an amazing man, actually engaged in the affairs of the Institute of Marine Engineers, long after normal retirement.

None of my teachers (as far as I knew), and none of my contemporaries at this time, had undergone formal teacher training. Some of us had taken what was known as the Workshop and Technology "Manual", a Northern Ireland Ministry of Education assessment of workshop skills and teaching approach.

However, eventually a number of technical teachers including myself were awarded a sabbatical year to take a formal teacher training qualification at a large educational establishment outside Belfast.

I will limit my comments about this course to merely saying that my discomfort with it grew as the year progressed, and it left much to be desired in organisation, course content, and delivery.

At that time, my employers, the County Antrim Education Committee (later part of the N.E.E.L.B.), did not approve of any work outside teaching duties, but I took the view that an annual foray to sea during some part of the long vacation in summer was fundamentally sound in that it was the way a teacher of engineering subjects could enhance his or her capability - by getting hands on experience. In the end, wiser counsels prevailed, and in a letter from the late George Tombs (an ex Spitfire Pilot) and a senior education officer for the North-Eastern Education and Library Board, it was indicated that he considered such experience a desirable thing and approval was granted. Further, my satisfaction was total when the Board introduced the "teacher return to industry" scheme, and my last such trip to sea was made in 1981 when I sailed on the ill-fated MV "European Gateway" on the Larne Cairnryan run for a period - and was given leave during term time to do so. The "European Gateway" was lost through a collision in the North Sea afterwards. (All this was in the future.)

Six die as ferries collide off Felixstowe

"The European Gateway ferry disaster illustrated the breadth and importance of the work of the Felixstowe Sea-farers' Centre. On the day before the fatal collision, Rev Malcolm Pears had held a service on board "European Gateway". They sang hymns, read verses of Scripture and said prayers. A few hours later tragedy claimed the lives of six seafarers and the same Chaplain spent many hours comforting bereaved relatives."

('From the Chart and Compass International' - British Sailors Society, Summer 1983).

*   *   *   *   *   *   *   *   *   *

In the year I started teaching 1967, an event was taking place at the submarine museum at HMS "Dolphin", Gosport, near Portsmouth. In the Gallipoli campaign of 1915 in the First World War, British submarines dived through the mines in the Dardanelles to enter the Sea of Marmora. The third successful submarine to do so was the E11, earning for her commander, Lieut Cmdr Martin Nasmith the V.C., and every member of the crew was decorated. During this patrol, the E11 penetrated the harbour at Constantinople where Nasmith torpedoed a Turkish transport, becoming the first enemy to visit the City for five hundred years. During this time, the submarine grounded off Leander Tower - apparently amidships, and the compass indicated that the E11 was swinging about the midship point, due to the cauldron of currents acting at that point in the Bosphorus.

Eventually, Nasmith reckoned in which direction safety lay, blew the tanks (which had been flooded to prevent the submarine breaking surface) and soon they were on their way to safety. The E11 was to see the war out and was eventually scrapped. But her bell found its way to Canada. In 1967, it was returned to the Submarine Museum, where it now is, and three veterans of the crew, George Plowman, Bill Wheeler and Bert Cornish attended the ceremony. Many books, and references in many other publications tell of the exploits of these submarines, making truth more interesting than fiction. It was another seven years before I found myself researching those very events. By that time, only George Plowman, the Leading Signalman, was surviving, (as was the wife of Bert Cornish, the E.R.A). But George was a first class prime source of information and I was to visit him many times at Wellingborough where he lived. *His model of the E11 made on board that vessel over a period, occupied an honoured place in his home. At this time I was studying European mainstream history from 1854 to 1972 and much of it dwelt on the events and politics surrounding the Crimean War, and the two World Wars. I was extremely interested in the events that took place (sadly with such losses), at the Dardanelles and sought means of gaining first hand information.

*   *   *   *   *   *   *   *   *   *

(* - Now in Antrim - see photograph).

By now, another summer had arrived and with it the long summer vacation. During August I had been offered a Fourth Engineer's job with McAndrews & Co, Royal Liver Buildings Liverpool, and thence I repaired to the dock known as Canada 3. There was always a demand for relief engineers to cover summer holidays, etc.

There lay the MV "Velarde", a cargo ship that looked like a yacht. McAndrews traded in the Western Mediterranean - especially Spain. So I sailed as Fourth (relief) engineer - there were five engineers on board and we would go first to Bilbao in Northern Spain, then enter the Western Mediterranean. Shortly after I returned I wrote an account of it for someone. I would like to have given that account here, but space is pressing and hopefully the "Velarde" trip can be recalled in another setting. But there is a small incident I must recall as the "Velarde" returned to the Mersey.

* * * * * * * * * *

The Bay was misty, although the crossing was in calm weather and in daylight, but it thickened around the Scillies with the engine room on "Stand by" and proceeding at reduced revolutions. However time and distance lay behind us and we arrived off the "Bar" light at 2400 hours on Thursday 22 August 1968. The Pilot came aboard and the "Velarde" started the river transit at 0230 hours. I was turned in by this time but the "Velarde" didn't tie up until eight o'clock the next morning - there had been delays in the river and some problems in the locks. By this time I was on the deck watching proceedings and on passing the end of a dock I saw something that called for a second look. A black coaster. A black coaster with a large X on the funnel - with engine room aft - I couldn't believe it, it was the MV "Hibernian Coast". Later, when having a break from whatever I was doing, I made my way - with camera to her. No mistake - it was the "Hibernian Coast", but she was deserted - no one on board. I went on board, walked into the engineers alleyway, went to the engine room door - but alas, it was locked - the "Hibernian Coast" was in moth balls. I then looked at the quaint old emergency steering wheel over the rudder which we were glad to use on one occasion, thought of Van Den Ent and the other Dutch engineer who created the racket in Dublin - memories only. The "Hibernian Coast" looked as if she was going to the knackers yard.

Recently, I attended a wedding in Sinclair Seamen's Presbyterian Church in Belfast - the bride was the youngest daughter of a sea Captain. Later at the reception, I was sitting close to Captain Campbell Kerr, Belfast, who was recalling his early days on a coaster called the "Hibernian Coast"

"Did the mate, by any chance come from Bangor in North Wales?" I asked.
"Yes, he certainly did - how on earth did you know?"

Antrim Technical College

I was to teach at Lisburn Technical College for only two years. A teaching post became vacant at Antrim Technical College - in my home town, for which I applied successfully in 1969 and remained there until, as recorded later, I severed my connection with Further Education in 1990.

Antrim Technical College, in Railway Street, by tradition always had a good reputation as a commercial college, quite a number of students there gaining Royal Society of Arts medals. Indeed Mr David Alexander, the former Principal of Belfast College of Technology, speaking to me about these successes on one occasion, recalled how he had often remarked upon this to Mr John McCoubrey, a former Principal of Antrim Technical, and asking him "how he did it?" Both men knew each other well, as both had worked for Harland & Wolff Ltd. at one time. The College later moved to Fountain Street in Antrim. It became known as a Further Education College.

Shortly after I joined the staff there as a teacher, a photograph taken in the year 1970-71, reveals that there was a total of nineteen teachers plus two office staff employed. Lisburn Technical was bursting at the seams with engineering work of every kind when I left - I had hopes that engineering would expand at Antrim Technical, in my home town. Later I refer to the type of work traditionally carried out in technical colleges, before the onslaught of the "New F.E.".

By this time, I had other preoccupations - I had a son, Ian, and a daughter, Moyna.

During the first ten years I was at Antrim Technical College, I cannot remember teaching any students who would sit for external examinations i.e. City & Guilds, 'O' level or whatever. It was at this stage that I had a sabbatical to partake in a year's formal teaching training course - referred to earlier. In the ten year period referred to, I had fellow staff members who had been there for many years before me. During the following ten years their places were gradually taken by new teachers, and by the time I left, only one teacher remained who had been on the staff when I first arrived to care for the British Enkalon apprentices and other apprentices, whom I have described as the best engineering students I ever taught. There was little expansion for most of the remaining time I was there, although during my final year I was to see some recovery. Some worthwhile work which perhaps I did, was in the varied work in careers advice, and a surprising number of Pre-apprentice students - who sat end of the year internal examinations - joined the services, in some engineering capacity or other, and so I was to get postcards from far off places.

Interesting accounts were given to me eventually, by certain who served in the Falklands - one by a signaller, another by a crew member of H.M.S. "Arrow" which went alongside the "Sheffield" and helped affect the rescue work after the "Sheffield" was mortally wounded by an Exocet missile. (A brother of the "Arrow" crew member later was serving on the cruiser which had Biggs, the train robber aboard as a visitor, during that cruiser's visit to South America). This brother had also attended Antrim Technical College. Another former student eventually served on board the submarine "Conqueror" on a trip to the Falklands - but that was after the conflict.

Turning again to the home front, I earlier recalled that Jean and I were married on 7th September 1965, and how only a couple of weeks before, we were uncertain as to whether I would be working in Bath, Strabane or Antrim! But Antrim it was, and there our children were born, Ian in 1966, and Moyna in 1968. Attending local schools, I cannot recall either of them ever being absent from lessons for any reason, Ian being credited for one ten year period of unbroken attendance. With both now grown up, it's difficult to imagine some of the things that would have been important then - Jean taking them on their first day to the local primary school, Christmas Parties, or, eventually the school sports. Early family holidays took the form of visiting my sister in England, and borrowing their caravan at the "Witterings", near Bogner Regis on the south coast of England, or camping in Scotland or Guernsey. A couple of holidays in Bulgaria - then Ian and Moyna were off themselves through the annual camps of the church organisations and later, school trips abroad. Jean has enjoyed walking holidays and I the odd cycling foray in Scotland or France. The pictures tell the story, and as one grows older the startling realisations is just how quickly life goes by. But I would never have believed it myself, when going up past the Belgium soldiers on my way to Ladyhill School all those years ago! How I looked forward to leaving that school - and as recalled, the only other thing that compared to that anticipation, was waiting to put the engine room clock forward twenty minutes, when crossing West to East on the North Atlantic!

But now I embarked upon a course of study at the Open University and became greatly engrossed in a new area of study - the Arts. There were also still opportunities to get a little sea time in towards that "ticket". A few weeks at a time. One that was very beneficial to me in a number of ways, I have chosen to recall.

AWAY FROM THE HERD AGAIN -
THE MV "VILLEGAS"

At the beginning of July 1975 I received a call from MacAndrews - was I available to take a watch on a ship leaving Liverpool shortly? I decided I was available and sailed for Liverpool on a Sunday evening. I presented myself at Canada 3 dock around 11 o'clock on Monday, and having my first sighting of the "Villegas", experienced some qualms upon seeing the engine room, and accommodation aft - this would be some seesaw in the 'Bay'.

I made my way to the Chief Engineer's cabin to meet one Mr Tom Birch. Now Mr Birch was a big man, a Cockney and seemed to have a slight misalignment of one eye - whether through an accident or other I wasn't to know. He took me to meet the second engineer, a Welshman, who was very preoccupied in the engine room with the transmission of power to the propeller shaft. "If that lot packs up" he said without looking up, "we'll need a tow. What a box of tricks!"

"That lot" was indeed a unique box of tricks - for the "Villegas" had pneumatic transmission - the drive from the engines to the tail-end shaft and propeller was by means of a pneumatic clutch. This in essence, was something like a large tyre - when inflated it connected the driver to the driven, and I was to discover that the air pressure had to be maintained at 400 lb per sq inch (27 Bar). However, I was experiencing some apprehensions and as usual, was not unaware of the possibility that something could happen which would make it difficult to be in attendance at the beginning of the term staff meeting - that pneumatic clutch for example packing up. In the event, the pneumatic drive performed perfectly, and it was something else that threatened to delay my home coming. Now I was anxious to be underway, but for some reason we didn't leave Liverpool until late the following Thursday. I had ample time to look over our neighbours in the neighbouring berth. In particular, I recall those great all black ships of the Nigerian Shipping Company - the "The River Niger" was tied up close by. As later recorded I was to meet one Alec Clark - the greaser on my watch.

The reason for finding space to describe this trip on the "Villegas" is to illustrate how one can be wrong in first impressions, The trip was, in the end, a straight run there and back, but there were interesting technical features to be acquainted with, and unusual things happened, but every misgiving that I might have entertained was proved without foundation. Like other MacAndrew ships, the "Villegas" had a deck cargo of I.C.I. petroleum additive, in large steel containers. These were always beheld with some concern - lest a leak should occur.

The "Villegas", a small ship of about 1,500 tons register, was powered by unusual engines - two diesel sets of eight cylinders - port and starboard - and they were M.W.M. U-boat engines, made in Augsburg, Germany! They were four stroke, trunk engines, the controls for each set mounted together so that one person could operate both engines, the control to the one furthest away, connected by a long chain. When manoeuvring, one engine ran ahead, the other astern, and each could be connected to the propeller shaft by simply turning a lever through 90 degrees - and blowing up the "tyre".

Mr Birch, who would nominally share my watch proved a tonic to work for. He encouraged me to acquaint myself with everything I would need to handle - changing generators etc. and in particular, he made a point of instructing the second to make sure I knew how to start and manoeuvre the engines to my satisfaction. Importantly, I was extremely fortunate in having a very reliable greaser with me on watch, one Alec Clark.

Now, there was something else of deck cargo besides the petroleum additive - six greyhounds were accommodated in a large pen, placed on top of the hatches. These creatures were on their way from Dublin to Barcelona, and had two or three men acting as handlers.

One day shortly after we crossed the "Bay", a greyhound escaped from such custody, and raced from one end of the deck to the other, defying all efforts to apprehend him. During one such excursion he decided to run through the engineer's accommodation, ending up in the Chief's cabin where the door had been open as the Chief went to sort out something in the engineer's office close by. Meanwhile the hound committed an act of unspeakable indiscretion in the cabin while being finally cornered. I was to experience what a Cockney sounds like when swearing, after he, Mr Birch, returned to his cabin!

Our first port was Cartagena - we were going in on the Second's watch shortly after lunch and I was casually observing the approach from the deck up forward.

The "Villegas" was approaching the dock at an angle of about 30 degrees where a large crane was positioned. She was travelling quite fast and I was waiting for "stop" and "astern" movements which would pull the way off the ship. Eventually I realised that for some reason the ship was not slowing and before I knew it, had ploughed into the dockside at the base of the crane which swayed dangerously before it stabilised. It was simply unbelievable to my eye - but it had happened and we were holed on the waterline!

Questions as to who was to blame were accompanied by relief that we had not toppled the large crane - had it split some of the containers on the deck, consensus was that everyone in the docks would have been poisoned by leaking gas. Anyway the "grapevine" blamed the skipper - and the bows were packed with water resistant cement. It was to have some significance for me before we finally docked in Liverpool, but for now we completed the calls at Tarragona and Barcelona (where the greyhounds disembarked), then departed for Valencia where, during loading up - onions as I recall, we met our old friend Henry Rees* again complete with the tricycle trailer.

We were about to go on standby prior to our departure for Liverpool, when during a casual check on temperatures and pressures, I discovered to my horror that oil pressure on the main engine was reading zero.

The main oil pump was driven by an electric motor and appeared to be working perfectly - but no pressure on the system.

The second and the Chief couldn't come up with an answer so a small electric emergency oil pump was started - it had a separate oil circuit, and pressure was soon on the main bearings again.

The second was concerned - "If that tiddler stops, we've definitely had it," he said.

(* - Henry Rees, a Spaniard of Welsh origin, and who supplied wines etc to visiting ships at Valencia).

I must say I watched it very carefully - it was indeed a small pump, literally screaming with its revolutions and it ran very hot - but it held out and eventually, when we had time in Liverpool to investigate the original failure, the Second discovered a large hole in the side of the delivery pipe from the main oil pump - how it got there remains a mystery.

These things aside, it was probably the most pleasant trip I was to make. One summer previously I had joined another MacAndrew boat, the MV "Palomaris". We had sailed before the cladding could be replaced on the main engine uptakes (exhaust pipes) and I had suffered very badly with gas - through leaks in joints. I was very sick, and at Gibraltar a doctor, called for an opinion, decided to remove me for observation to St. Bernard's hospital.

In the event I was kept there five days and the "Palomaris" sailed for Casablanca without me. On a previous trip, the Fourth engineer had taken sick and had struggled along, but on the return journey his illness was causing concern and the ship had to re-route to Lisbon in Portugal where he had an operation for appendicitis. This time they didn't take any chances. After collecting my discharge book and wages from the local shipping Federation, I eventually had a pleasant evening in the Montarik Hotel, and watched the "Carnival of Flowers" where the procession, floats etc. was led by the band of the Argyll & Sutherland Highlanders - stationed there at the time. I flew home in a Vanguard - from that very unique airstrip which stretches out into the sea.

I was learning that the "best laid plans of mice and men are apt to go astray."

*   *   *   *   *   *   *   *   *   *

But I digress - the "Villegas" again!

This trip was a rewarding one - especially in that I learned a lot technically, and I found Mr Birch a very interesting, caring man, with whom conversation came easily. During one watch toward the end of the trip the phone in the engine room rang - it was the Chief. "I just wanted to know, Mr Cameron (he always called me mister) if you would like a reference?" I, of course, would be pleased to get a reference. Then "are you strictly sober?" I still possess that now faded reference.

But we were not home and dry yet. One morning we arrived just off the "bar" lightship as I came on watch, and I therefore would manoeuvre the "Villegas" up the Mersey. All went well and, as noon approached, the Chief suggested that as we were just outside the locks would I continue to bring her in - it would save the Second from turning to. I was perfectly happy to do so, as I had enjoyed manoeuvring this strange hybrid - submarine engines in a surface ship with the peculiar transmission system of using the pneumatic clutch - all part of the adaptation necessary for such a mix.

We eventually entered the lock and I was surprised when after putting the ship full astern in response to a telegraph command, I got a double ring for "full astern". As the "Villegas" was already set full astern, there was nothing further I could do - apart from answering the ring (I was also writing down the engine movements as well). Then the Chief came running down - followed by the Third Mate, "Is the engine full astern - we've nearly rammed a submarine in the lock!"

Apparently the submarine "Grampus" was ahead of "Villegas" in the lock and although I had put the engine full astern as requested, the R.P.M simply didn't pick up, way did not come off the vessel and there was real concern lest we push the sub through the lock gate. The "Villegas" had behaved again, just as at Cartagena!

One day, before I left the "Villegas', to return to my classroom in Antrim Technical College - I casually placed a crowbar in below the camshaft of the engine which had been running astern as we had come up the Mersey - there was a lift of over one eighth of an inch play - or 3 mm - maybe this had something to do with reluctance to power up!

It was a memorable few weeks I had spent on the "Villegas", and she got me home before the first of September. It was memorable because of the Chief, Mr Birch - a gentleman, and Alec Clark, that decent man whom I shared the watch with. We had our moments with that engine that was "slow on the uptake" - and one particular greyhound!

My first group of students - engineering apprentices receiving off the job training during their first year at Antrim Industrial Training Unit, in a workshop at Antrim Technical College. Most of these boys were apprentices with British Enkalon. Back row from left: Leslie McNeilly, Ronnie McIlhagger, Sinclair Hanlon, Thomas Frew, Eunan McCormick, Joe Carey, Michael Laverty, James McQuillan. Front row from left: Sean Mallon, Norman Houston (technician), B C, Ronnie McNickle, David Herron, Norman Hunter (the late), and Thomas Allen. Brendan Smith is missing. (1965/66).

My second group of students - engineering apprentices - on the same course as the first group. About half were apprentices from the new British Enkalon Company. Back row, from left: Oliver Totten, Mervyn Caulcutt, Stanley Bovill (the late), Vincent Magee, Albert Scott, George Richardson, Robson Tait, Danny McCann, Malcolm Johnston. Front row, kneeling: William Greer, Robert Arrell, David Simpson, B C, James Parkinson. Wallace Service is missing from this photograph (1966/67).

Staff at Antrim Technical College, 1970. Back row from left: J. Ramsey, J. Davidson, W. Moore, A. Hunter, W. J. Brownlees, G. McDowell. Centre row from left: C. Nesbit, B C, Mrs. Blair, J. D. Fransey, Miss J. Caldwell, Mrs. Coulter, J. Gribben. Front row from left: Janet Curry (office admin), Caroline McNaul (office admin), Miss S. Gardner, J. Bell (principal), J. Andrews (vice-principal), Miss J. McKernan, Mrs. J. Fisher, Miss Caroline McDevitt.

One of my teaching colleagues at Antrim Technical College Mr. Samuel McMurray and with whom I later cycled around the Somme battlefields was largely responsible for organising and encouraging students at the college to partake in cycle outings. Here, some fit young men are on a tour around Lough Neagh, in 1983. From left, back row: Russell Laycock, B C, John Neil, Leslie Allen, Martin Kane, William Shields. Front row, from left: Warren Cullen, Simon Scott, Chris Thornton, James Balmer, Steven Thompson.

Manoeuvring platform
of the MV "Villegas", MacAndrews
Line Liverpool.

In search of a tan - passing
Gibraltar in the MV "Villegas".

The Langton Lock, Liverpool - the man on left with uniform cap is
probably the Lockmaster. He may have a microphone or megaphone
in his hand - for shouting instructions, as ships pass through the lock.
The submarine Grampus and the MV "Villegas" lie side by side in the
lock. Happily, the incident in the locks had no lasting implications.
(Courtesy: Liverpool Echo)

B C with Billy Grills on an
excursion to the Isle of
Man, during which we
visited the engine room of
the SS "Lady of Mann*".
This old turbine steamer
had a unique boiler room.
It was pressurised, albeit
a small amount - probably
a few pounds giving some
force draught to the
furnaces. The boiler room
was therefore entered via
an airlock - the only such
I ever saw on a ship.

Billy Grills, (later C. ENG,
AMI. MAR. E.) qualified
as a Chief Engineer with
a combined "ticket", first
class, while on steam with
Elders and Fyffe, and on
motor with British Rail.
"Retired" as a lecturer, he
is now in Voluntary
Christian Service.

The MV "Hibernian Coast" in "mothballs", Liverpool

(* - spelling as on ship)

SHORT BROS' WORKS AT EASTCHURCH, 1910.

SHORT BROS' WORKS AT LEYSDOWN, SHEPPEY, 1909.

*Shorts moved to the Isle of Sheppy from Battersea around 1909, first at Leysdown, and later to Eastchurch.
Eventually, the firm set up at Rochester on the River Medway close to the Estuary of the River Thames. (Courtesy: Short Bros. & Harland Ltd.)*

This well known photograph was taken on the Isle of Sheppey at the house known as "Mussel Manor" on 4th May 1909. This group encompasses the pioneers of aviation - of the U.S.A. and Britain. Back row (standing) from left: J.D.F. Andrews, Oswald Short, Horace Short, Eustace Short, Frank McClean, Griffith Brewer, Frank Hedges Butler, Dr. W. J. S. Lockyer and Warwick Wright, a motor cycling and aviation pioneer. Front row (seated) from left: J.T.C. Moore-Brabazon (later Lord Brabazon), Wilbur Wright, Orville Wright and Charles Rolls. (Courtesy: Short Bros. & Harland Ltd.)

Sunderland EJ164 about to enter the water on its cradles. It was later lost on 3.10.1944 in the South Atlantic. Note the Stirling Bomber close by. This photo was taken sometime between October 1943 and February 1944. Note Anchor Chain on the "Bows".

The Seamew production line. In an adjacent bay, and separated by the large plate heaters etc, are some B.O.A.C. Britannia aircraft. Note the engine nacelles - with no engines. Also the large weight which simulates the action of the weight of an engine on the nacelle structure. These aircraft had been at Shorts for modifications required by their B.O.A.C. owners. (Courtesy: Short Bros. & Harland Ltd.)

Canberra Production Line (Courtesy: Short Bros. & Harland Ltd.)

An early Canberra bomber. Shorts first Canberra flew in late 1952. (Courtesy: Short Bros. & Harland Ltd.)

One of the first hovers of the P1127, the forerunner of the Harrier.
Note the special grid under the aircraft and the telephone cable passing out of the tail. Bill Bedford is the pilot. (Courtesy: BAe Systems).

The SC1 in early test conditions, still tethered to its gantry.
(Courtesy: Short Bros. & Harland Ltd.)

The accident with the SC1
(Courtesy: Short Bros. & Harland Ltd.)

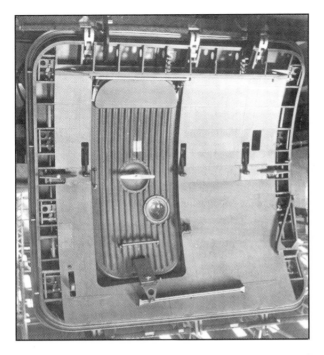

The Britannia freight door. The small door was used by the crew for purposes of entry and exit. (Courtesy: Short Bros. & Harland Ltd.)

The old waterwheel at Moylinney, Muckamore - the rack and pinion mechanism which lifted the sluice gates to regulate the water flow. This pinion (or small gear wheel), had a similar function to the input pinion in the Proteus turbo prop engine of that Britannia airliner, (which ended up on the mud flats of the River Severn). The teeth of such pinions are curved in profile so ideally, they roll on each other as motion is imparted. But they do engage each other by an impulsive force, and failures occur. Note the broken teeth on the technology of the nineteenth century - and the traditional method of using pegs to effect a repair. (In the Britannia they choose to change to a helical gear!)

The Short Brothers became the first commercial aircraft manufacturers in the world when they built six "Flyers" for the Wright Brothers in 1909.

Wing span: 12.49m (41ft)
Overall length: 8.84 (29ft)
Max. level speed: 43 knots (80km/h; 50mph)
(Courtesy: Short Bros. & Harland Ltd.)

Chapter 9 - There is life after school

A Study of History and Politics

The O.U. level of presentation was of the highest in course preparation and quality. I was introduced to an entirely new world, of literature, music, history (and especially the key elements of historical research) poetry, art, philosophy, and, of particular interest, European History (1854 - 1973). This included technical developments that took place during three major wars - the Crimean and the First and Second World wars. Further work included the history of science and technology - here in ways I was studying the history of my own industrial background. In Political Studies, one of the areas majored in, was Politics of the Soviet Union.

My interest in historical research led me to visit the major areas of conflict in the First World War, while interest in Russia found me in one intriguing situation - I relate something of this in due course.

In the pursuance of studies relating to the great conflicts, I organised some travel that would go some way to satisfying my curiosity about three things, one, namely the nature of the Dardanelles - that forty one miles of waterway, linking the Aegean Sea to the Sea of Marmora in Turkey; two, that area of conflict, now distant in time, namely the Crimea, in Russia. Thirdly, associated with the latter, I would try and find the Florence Nightingale connection i.e., her hospital. (Later, I would visit the River Ancre and Thiepval Wood in France.)

At the time of this visit, I was discussing such things with someone I was privileged to know very well in the latter part of his life. He was my late old friend, Charles W Clark, The Hill, Rathmore, Antrim. He was well qualified to speak on the subject. He and his well known family were farmers, but he joined the army when aged twenty-one, in 1915, first I believe in the North Irish Horse, but for some reason we can no longer ask him, was drafted into the 54th Anglican Division - he called it the East Anglicans, and was, after some training at Littlehampton on the South coast of England, on his way to the Gallipoli campaign. Briefly, the action at the Gallipoli peninsula in Turkey, and the Dardanelles, which flows along its eastern flank, was planned to knock Turkey out of the war in which Turkey was aligned with Germany, thus permitting the Russians access to the Dardanelles, their southern exit to the Mediterranean. The Dardanelles Straits were lined with artillery (some of it mobile), lines of mines and a steel mesh net, extending down some eighty feet and eventually it was thought, down to one hundred and forty feet. This was some technological feat in 1915, and undoubtedly was supplied by the Germans. This net was in response to the eventual penetration of the Straits by British submarines. It was thought that the Straits could be forced by the battleships of the Royal Navy and the French Navy. Their failure to do so called for an army landing, first more or less around the tip of the Peninsula, (with the Australians and the New Zealanders on the western coast at "Anzac"). Following the stalemate after that, a new, very large landing took place at Suvla Bay, just north of the Anzac landing beaches. It was there that Charlie Clark landed in August 1915. One of his colleagues was also fairly local, a Mr Copeland from Newtownards (I also had the privilege of speaking to him - he remembered Charlie very well.

Charlie was evacuated two days before Christmas 1915, to Lemnos Island, with severe frostbite in his feet. He and his colleagues were to return via the Mediterranean, through Southern France in time to join the Ulster Division at the

Somme. He was commissioned in the Royal Irish Fusiliers in 1917. I remember one evening going to visit Charlie - it must have been on the 30th June 1979. There were no lights burning, and I found Charlie sitting near the front door, which was unusual, as he always sat at a table in his living room in the evenings. "I have just been sitting here thinking of that night sixty-three years ago, and all the boys I knew, who went over the top the next morning at Thiepval Wood". In remembering the morning of the first of July, 1916, that first day at the Somme, Charlie recalled hearing bird song after the initial bombardment ceased, and before the whistles blew and the bugles sounded for the 36th Ulster Division and many other divisions to go into action on that terrible day.

In planning the places I wanted to see, I found a ship, the "Ithaca", July 1973, chartered by Thompson's Travel, going my way - eventually to Russia, and so, I passed up the Dardanelles. The Straits had only two forts remaining, Seddul Bahr at the entrance (meaning gateway to the sea) and Kilid Bahr, about half-way up. (See page 176)

History had been made here from ancient times. When Xerxes, the King of the Persians tried to invade Greece in 448 B.C., he built a bridge of boats, but the current swept it away; so he punished it with 300 lashes and called it a salt and treacherous stream! Byron the poet swam the Dardanelles - (it was known as the Hellespoint). History was to be made again during 1915 and there were easily identified landmarks where incidents of that time - now well documented in books etc. took place.

It was fairly easy to approximate where the submarine E15 (Lieut-Cmdr Brodie) went aground and was lost in the first attempt at Kephez Point, a short distance up on the Asian side. Then just off Nagara Point, the E7 (Lieut-Cmdr Cochrane - later to become a Conservative MP at Westminster) was caught in the net after a detached wire had fouled the propeller shaft. The E7 was scuttled, and the crew taken prisoners. But the AE2, the Australian E class submarine, commanded by Lieut-Cmdr H G G Stoker became the first to get through safely into the Sea of Marmora on 26th April 1915, sinking a Turkish gun boat by torpedo. Sadly the AE2 was lost a few days later in the Marmora, Stoker and most of the crew surrendering to become prisoners of war. Stoker was a Dublin man, later to have a successful career on the London Stage. One could fill a book on the Dardanelles, and numerous books are available covering the conflict and especially the epic of the submarines. (Sadly also, the AE1, Australian sister to the AE2, disappeared without trace off the Galapagos Islands in the Pacific, when returning from Australia in 1915.

I resolved to try and trace any survivors of the British subs that had successfully passed the Dardanelles into the Marmora upon my return to the U.K. As recalled earlier, I eventually became good friends with George Harry Plowman, D.S.M.

Travels - Florence Nightingale's Hospital at Scutari

During the journey through the Dardanelles and the Sea of Marmora onto Istanbul, I had made the acquaintance of some interesting companions - one in particular being Owen Shepherd, a research scientist from London. Another was known as "Captain" by virtue of a seafaring looking peaked cap which he wore. It was with these two, that I made my first attempt to locate where Florence Nightingale had her main hospital. I only knew that it was in a vague kind of way "over there in Scutari" - across the Bosphorus.

Arriving late in Istanbul (the Constantinople of 1915) we attempted to reconnoitre at least, the Asian side of the Bosphorus, opposite Istanbul. We managed to get on a ferry but were aware that something was afoot - there was something of agitation in the faces of the Turks making that crossing. As well, the ferry (and others like it) was crammed with the largest and most unusual collection of military hardware - mostly the largest earth moving machines, I had ever seen. We got to the other side - I wanted to get as close as possible to Scutari where I believed Florence Nightingale had had her main hospital in Turkey (there were others e.g. at Balaclava). But it quickly became obvious that this was no night to be wandering aimlessly in a strange country at midnight on a hopeless quest. We couldn't understand the atmosphere of belligerency that was evident in the glances one got now and then. We returned to the European side as quickly as we could - no heavy plant going that way! Shortly we heard that Turkey had invaded Northern Cyprus - the earth movers would be needed in that exercise and I didn't get to Scutari that year. But I did the following summer and I will now leave Owen and myself and our journey to Russia and jump a year to describe being somewhere - a place not visited by anyone else that I have talked with - not even members of the nursing profession - Florence Nightingale's Hospital at Scutari.

*   *   *   *   *   *   *   *   *   *

The following year I was in Istanbul again. This time, I chose a morning to launch my quest - I would attempt to find the former hospital at Scutari set up in a Turkish Military Barracks (Turkey of course was the ally of France and Britain at the Crimea). I had a good local map on which the building - again reverted to its former use as a military barracks was clearly marked. But getting directions was another thing - I didn't speak Turkish. I had however an amazing stroke of luck. On my way to the ferry, I was bid "good morning" by a Turkish Army Officer - I may have spoken some question to him first. Anyway, he expressed great interest in me because he was learning English, and wished to practice on someone. Eventually, upon the further explaining of my intention, he declared that he was stationed in those barracks and he would accompany me there. He further explained that part of the barracks was kept in much the same way as Florence Nightingale had left it - a kind of museum. Now I was getting somewhere!

Any traveller passing down the Bosphorus past Istanbul, may see this red roofed stone building on the Asian slopes of the Bosphorus (The Bosphorus is a channel which joins the Sea of Marmora to the Black Sea).

So we walked perhaps a mile or so and came to this large building where my new found acquaintance explained to another officer my desire, and took his leave of me. This other officer asked me to wait in a room close by. The large building was the army barracks built by the Turkish Sultan Selim III (1789-1807). It was called the Seliwiye Barracks and later became the hospital where Florence Nightingale worked during the Crimean War. In 1954, a Turkish nurse sought to create a museum in memory of Florence Nightingale, and what I was about to see was made public in 1955 - the year I entered Ward 2B in Musgrave Park Hospital. (There is of course another Florence Nightingale Museum in St Thomas's Hospital London, close to Waterloo railway station. It is also worth going to see - mostly photographs, letters etc).

The room was sparsely furnished. I sat on a wooden form and took stock of the other occupants seated around. These were rather scruffy looking characters who shifted uneasily on their forms. After about fifteen minutes and when I was beginning to feel uncomfortable, a different person came in and beckoned me to follow. What happened then was worth all the effort in hunting this prize down. First, he took me to a large room which had been kept as the museum ward. It was, from memory, about thirty metres long by a width, say fifteen metres. The area was bare, save for black rectangles painted on the floor to indicate where the wounded soldiers lay on their straw palliasses. There was an oil lamp hanging at one entrance. This was a moment of some historic realisation for me - a great person had once been here. My guide then beckoned again and took me to Florence Nightingale's day room. Apart from a desk complete with nib, pen and a couch and chairs, there stood something like a china cabinet. In this were many letters she had written to different people on a variety of subjects - mostly for medicines, cleaning materials etc. I have since wondered how they all found their way back to her! I remember seeing one addressed to a man called Herbert. He was a member of the British Government. There were also numerous letters received by her in Scutari. The guide had something else to show me - Florence Nightingale's night room. To get there, I ascended an iron spiral set of steps - I hesitate to call them a staircase and found myself in a larger room than the day one. The most striking thing here was a sofa, rather much the worse for wear and I estimated its length to be about two and a half metres and of width one metre, possibly a little less. It was a monster couch indeed - I cannot remember what else was in that night room.

I knew that a British Cemetery was close by - more men died of infection, cholera, etc than died of enemy inflicted wounds. I enquired if I might visit it but was told no. I was well satisfied and longed to photograph the place but I understood that photography was forbidden because it was a military establishment. (Eventually, I took a snap of one wing).

So thanking my guide I made my way down the hill to the ferry. But I have never since met anyone, nurses included, who has visited Scutari.

The Odessa Incident

This is now a convenient point to return to the earlier journey up the Dardanelles to Istanbul when, with Owen, (now a University Lecturer, London University), I took that ferry across the Bosphorus in search of Scutari and found all that heavy earth moving equipment in transit - just prior to the Turkish invasion of Cyprus.

Eventually we passed up the Bosphorus (linking the Sea of Marmora to the Black Sea) and after travelling across the Black Sea arrived in the Russian port of Odessa. The Black Sea is supplied with water from some of the great rivers of Russia and other countries (including the Danube in Romania). Although considered "fresh" water and not so dense as "sea water", it is also considered to be "brackish" and not particularly pleasant to taste.

Russia, (as part of the USSR) was at this time still in the grip of Communism and travellers had certain obligations to undertake in those days prior to setting foot on Russian soil.

A personal detail card had to be filled in six weeks before arrival - this included the answers to questions like: "Where do you work?" "What is your occupation there?" etc. Now for me, that was not to disclose earth shattering revelations or make hearts and minds beat faster in the Kremlin. But as events will reveal, this was not the case for others; the Russians were very interested indeed in the occupations of some visitors!

From "The Odessa Incident"

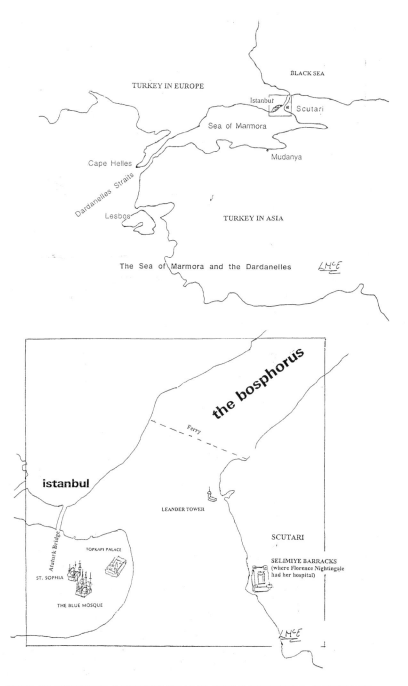

THE FLORENCE NIGHTINGALE CONNECTION, SCUTARI

The port of Odessa is approached by way of a long channel - that's what my daily record of the events of those days tells me - and all passengers were informed that photography of the port facilities was prohibited.

Nonetheless, I couldn't resist the temptation to sketch (or attempt to) an astonishing array of communication, surveillance, or listening devices evident on the upper works of a Soviet warship - something the size of a destroyer, as reproduced. This vessel monitored our appearance and progress - we probably picked up a pilot and custom officers as well. Owen had informed me that an opera show was on offer that evening and we had duly booked our seats accordingly at the Odessa State Opera House. Before that we had dinner, during which I was engaged in conversation by an Englishman whom I had got to know slightly, earlier. It happened to be the eleventh of July 1973 and this gentleman rather surprised me by asking me "if I would be walking tomorrow*?" Upon enquiring of him how he figured out a connection, he informed me that he had been in the Royal Flying Corps in World War I, recruitment officer in Northern Ireland for the RAF in World War II and subsequently had been a Manager with Rowantrees, Ireland. He further enquired if the "Seven Mile Straight was still there - and did I know Gerry Cupples?" (I knew that the late Gerry Cupples had been in the Great War and I was very friendly with his son, Derek). It appeared that a sister of Gerry Cupples, had been this gentleman's housekeeper!

I had met one Norman Batley, whose aversion to conforming to any rule, regulation or simple request - either on board the "Ithaca" or ashore with the Russians, earned (from us) for him the title of "The King".

Owen and I embarked on one of quite a large number of buses leaving the quay that evening for the Odessa State Opera House. This was organised by Intourist - the State Tourist Organisation - and as always in the Russia (USSR) of the Brezhnev era, it was highly regimented in procedure. All passports having been handed to the authorities, we were each issued with a port card - a temporary "identity" card - and each bus allocated a guide.

Our guide, for some reason, made herself known to us on the bus in the short drive from the quay to the Opera House. Her name was Natasha Sokolskaya. I have always understood the pronunciation as Natasha Koriskova.

In a short time Owen and I were seated - right in the middle of the Odessa State Opera House - and in good time for the opening of the performance. We estimated that the audience was of the order of five hundred people - I imagine all from the West.

Eventually, we were aware of someone - a young lady, who appeared not to have a seat - walking along a distant aisle. She retraced her steps, and then started to progress along the row of seats on which we were seated - there happened to be a spare seat beside us - and soon we recognised her as our guide on the bus.

The Odessa State Opera House was the most magnificent such building I had ever been in, my experience of such venues being limited indeed - I had been to the Shakespeare Memorial Theatre at Stratford-on-Avon and our own very worthy Grand Opera House in Belfast. My companion, Owen, on the other hand, living in London, "limited" himself to a visit to the opera once per month!

When I found that I was to share the company of a real live Russian (or Ukrainian) for the entire performance of Aida, that here was someone who would interpret the opera, scene by scene (it was sung in Russian) or answer all the questions one might wish to ask - well I simply thought we were very lucky - this was a bonus.

(* - a reference to the 12th July Parades)

Natasha was a young lady of perhaps thirty years of age and talked freely (with a slight American accent). One of my opening bats was to comment on her coat - "just like ones I would see at home". "Oh yes", Natasha replied, "I get all my clothes made in London" - and then she turned to what we worked at. She then outlined the main plots in Aida and at the end of each scene, suggested we go for a walk - "Shall we visit the Tsar's box?" During these sorties I willed myself to sense some romance between Owen and Natasha - she was telling him that she had a friend in London!

At this stage I remarked to Natasha that in the event of her falling in love with Owen - "how would he get her out of the country?" I was unprepared for her reply: "Oh, there are more ways to skin a cat than one!"

How could a Russian have such an intimate knowledge of our sayings and euphemisms? However at a later date my curiosity about such things led me to discover that most foreign language students learn another country's idioms of speech - euphemisms etc.

Eventually there was further discussion about our occupations - not much though about mine - and Natasha would direct her enquiries rather in Owen's direction. "You must send me a Christmas card - and we must exchange addresses", and she then proceeded to write her address on the inside of my programme. It is reproduced below.

Odessa, U.S.S.R.
Rosa Luxemburg st. 14
Sokolskaya Natasha

We were scheduled to have a full day tour of Odessa the following day, and Natasha told us she would be on duty as a courier on one of the buses - we would meet again.

While this side show was taking place, the magnificence of the performance of Aida could not pass unnoticed. The decor was wonderful, the stage management superb - how did they manage that boat to pass over the water - it was probably - because of several factors, an evening of cultural exchange that I don't think has been equalled in my life since!

Aida came to an end and five hundred people stood to applaud. We would have Natasha's company back to the docks during which time she filled in quite a bit of background of Odessa - we would see it all tomorrow. The only other incident that has remained of that evening in my memory was a delay in returning to the docks: an English lady in our company fell on the steps outside the Opera House and broke her leg. Eventually she was taken to Moscow and flown home.

The next day we were up bright and early - it was a beautiful day and Owen and I looked forward to an interesting day, and hopefully have Natasha for our guide. But it was not to be - we searched each bus - I believe eight were sent to accommodate those wishing to complete the tour of Odessa - but Natasha was not there. "I hope she hasn't got into trouble for talking to us last night", said Owen.

*   *   *   *   *   *   *   *   *   *   *

I had no further contact with our "guide to the Opera" - but someone else had - Owen.

Come Christmas he would have received a Christmas card and a couple of letters. The central question was not, surprisingly, "please come and get me out of here", but "How is the job going?" Then one day the phone at his work rang, and a voice said "This is Natasha's friend".

Owen was a science graduate and was currently employed on related work in a Government department in London. At the time of his travels in Russia, he was not unaware of something in his work that would excite the interest of a foreign power.

*   *   *   *   *   *   *   *   *   *

It was a full year before I could get the full story. I was on a similar holiday - this time accompanied by my wife, and Owen was having the same holiday - a cruise on the Ithaca - but in the Holy Land, Greek Islands, and the Dardanelles areas (this was the occasion when I visited Florence Nightingale's Hospital at Scutari).

I met Owen in the aisle of a Boeing 737 and soon I would know his story. After Natasha's friend made that phone call, Owen had a discussion on these things that had come to pass with his boss. He was then directed on a certain course of procedure which would follow all future contacts - there was indeed a reason why such an interest was shown in Owen's work. I simply couldn't wait to ask Owen, "What could they have been after?"

The answer it seemed was not difficult to pinpoint. Although I was completely unaware of it, the establishment in which he worked was one of four in the UK which had received minute samples of moon rock dust from the Americans - for analysis! Talking to Owen in London in 1997, I discovered that Owen himself had in fact been involved in the analysis of the moon rock dust.

As I said, that night in the Odessa State Opera House was a cultural exchange, but I was also on the outside of the glass, looking in on something, that eventually I would want to tell folk in Antrim about - but who would believe me - a very ordinary person like me being in such a bizarre scenario? It was another of the crossroads that we approach each day in our lives - you collide with the Owens or you miss them!

When I was growing up in Antrim I was acquainted with a young man - then quite academic - who belonged to First Antrim Presbyterian Church Youth Club. He was Billy McMaster, later to be Dr Billy McMaster, a physicist who would marry Miss Ann McKillop, another close acquaintance of mine, whose family lived in Fountain Street, Antrim. Billy and Ann would eventually live in Welwyn Garden City, England.

Around the time of the "Odessa" incident, I had been living on the Greystone Road in Antrim for about four years. Some time after I had heard the revelations about the moon rock dust, I was working in my garden when Billy McMaster and his wife, over on holiday, happened to be walking up the Greystone Road, and stopped with me. Now here was someone I would tell my "story" to.

Billy listened carefully to what I told him and eventually concurred - the establishment mentioned was, he believed, one of those allocated the moon rock dust for analysis.

*   *   *   *   *   *   *   *   *   *

Life as I know it stops again

During the years following my brief working period on the SA4 Sperrin bomber at Aldergrove, and my subsequent successful return to work when that cracked bone had healed, I walked through the turbulent years of apprenticeship, study, then on to ships, armaments and many years of teaching to eventually discover that all was not well. I had been walking on a time bomb. I started feeling pain, in the knee of my previously injured leg, and I requested an appointment at the Musgrave Park Hospital External Clinic held at the Waveney Hospital. The Consultant now, was the then Registrar of all those years ago and the Surgeon who performed the successful bone grafting operation. "I haven't seen you for a long time", he said as he looked at my x-ray. He was fairly non-committal but recommended a course of physiotherapy at my local hospital. For a while things improved - even back to normal, but the pain returned eventually and was causing distress. A friend suggested I take up cycling, his reasoning being that by using toe clips, the push and pull action of pedalling would strengthen and sort out the knee mechanisms. So I got a cycle and started recording the miles. The problem persisted and I was soon back to my Surgeon. He looked at the x-rays again. "Now, where are you getting this pain?" I indicated the place. "That's where I would expect you to be getting pain". He then drew my attention to the x-ray of the knee joint - in particular the width of the joint at one side, compared to that of the other. "One side of the joint is almost closed and you are getting an arthritic effect". "Why is that?", I enquired. "It's because your leg is bowed - turned in - thus transferring more weight to one side than the other and squeezing the joint until the bones are tending to touch". What was to be done? "There is only one thing to do - we will have to start again", he said. "We will have to disconnect the bones". "Do you mean break my leg?" I asked. "Yes - but it's not a big thing - I'll put your name down for a bed, although the waiting list is long - even for an old customer".

*   *   *   *   *   *   *   *   *   *

I left that clinic in a state of shock - as if I had experienced a bereavement. I came down into Ballymena and who did I run into but Jimmy Spiers - who had been Second Engineer on that first trip I made to sea. He had come to work at British Enkalon in Antrim. I told him my story - I was to see a lot of him in the coming years.

The worse nightmare I had was the memory of the nineteen full length plasters that I had suffered having put on - and more especially hacked off with those ghastly shears that inevitably dug deep into the wounds. When a bed did come up, I convinced myself that the leg was on the mend and the pain not so bad. I wrote to my Surgeon and told him that I thought the knee had stabilised and I would wish to defer having the operation.

But six months later I was reduced to using a stick at times - how I managed to bluff my way, teaching around - I'll never know.

So I once more saw my Surgeon, and said that I was very willing now to see if anything could be done as I was about finished. Arrangements were made for me to go on the waiting list for Musgrave Park Hospital. Eventually, I got a letter, say on a Thursday, to report the following Tuesday. I went in to school, said I would be getting my leg broke and reset, and had no idea how long I would be off. I tidied my desk, told my students that I wouldn't see them for some time - and life, as I knew it, came to an end for the second time in my life. Everything stops when you enter hospital and prepare for an operation. It's like all the rushing about we do prior to travel abroad. Once the aircraft has lifted from the runway - there is nothing more that you can do. You are in other people's hands.

As one trained to think, in terms of force, lines of force and the points forces act around, I had little difficulty in understanding what imbalance had brought about the deteriorating knee. Nature simply does not tolerate any misalignment or imbalance of forces, (forces usually meaning our body weight), acting on body members and their joints. If one is injured on one side (as I was) there is a tendency to "take the loads" on the "good side". Even here, nature will protest sometimes, resulting in a "stress" fracture on the "good" side - somewhere. I was to know about that eventually.

But now, I was concerned with pain in the inside of the knee joint. This was caused because my leg was not straight, it bowed inward from the old fracture site downward, and instead of my body weight being evenly distributed across the inside and outside of the knee joint, the inner joint had taken more than its share. Over the years as I rambled around Shorts, Belfast College of Technology, ships, the Admiralty (Antrim), railway stations and dear knows where - as well as countless classrooms, spreading the word, the inner joint was getting thinner and thinner. This approaching doom would have been indicated on succeeding x-rays, but I had come to understand that the professional surgical opinion would have been to delay surgery for as long as possible. Too early and perhaps, perhaps it might have to be done again. "You could live until you're ninety", my Surgeon said to me one day. This was in response to a question of mine relating to the pros and cons of plastic or mechanical joints. These "things" don't last for ever.

Now, I had become very lame - but there are always ways of disguising the real extent of an impediment.

When my leg "cracked" following my first abortive attempt to resume work, the leg otherwise straight, had taken a "bend". It had gone undetected in the local hospital where the leg was simply re-encased in plaster. The seeds of disaster were encased as well - I would have needed Dr Hannigan to "wedge" it again!

Thus it was that I re-entered Musgrave Park Hospital on 16 March 1982 and was admitted to a bed in Withers 4. This was something different to my old Ward 2B, the Nissen Hut. The Withers Block was named after one of the consultants of my youth, Mr Withers, who, as well as Messrs Martin, Baker and Wilson, was often seen in Ward 2B.

Upon being admitted to Withers 4, I found myself in a very modern open plan type of arrangement. Several small wards were arranged to open onto a thoroughfare, accommodating, among other things, the Ward Sister's table or headquarters. On the other side of the thoroughfare or corridor, were a number of conventional single rooms - with doors.

The operation I was to have performed on my leg was known as an osteopathy or angulation operation. I had been curious as to what was going to happen here and I was very fortunate in living close to someone who was now Senior Registrar in Musgrave Park at the time, and shortly to become an orthopaedic consultant himself. He was Mr Joe McClelland. Upon enquiry of him, he very kindly invited me round to his home where he illustrated, by drawing, the nature of this type of operation, typically. I was greatly impressed by how deftly and accurately he drew a knee joint - it looked like illustrations I had seen in books - but then who would know more about it than he?

My own Surgeon planned to disconnect the bones just below the knee and "swing" the leg out. This would relieve the pressure on the inside of the knee joint. If the "swing" was too much, the outer joint would be taking too much load - then it would start "objecting". I had the temerity to enquire of him, how many degrees did he think it would require. Outlining the problems, he thought about fifteen degrees. He came to see me the day before the operation with an enquiry. "I was looking over your old x-rays", he said. "When you left here after the bone graft, your leg was perfectly straight - but it now has a definite bow - did you have another accident?" I started to say "No", but then remembered the "crack in the graft" when the leg was re- encased in plaster. I told him. "That explains it", he said. What a pity I had not found my way to Musgrave at that time - I might have been saved a lot of pain and trouble!

Naturally I was curious to see again my old Ward 2B. The Nissen huts were still there - some of them anyway, so I made my way the evening before the operation to "red square" - a crossroads of two corridors where the intersection was painted a bright red, and down the "tunnel" - the passage leading to the Nissens - I found Ward 2B. It was empty, but I went in - past the sisters office etc and stood where, as a boy of eighteen, I had done so one July morning many moons before. There was nothing in the "ward" - completely cleared of beds etc. But I looked to where I had lain, then where Fred Johnston's bed had been, where George from Tessa in Armagh played his record player - where I had first taken an early step on crutches, after the bone grafting operation, so long ago. Then I returned to Withers 4 - tomorrow would be a long day.

I must say that I paid particular attention to my devotions in the hospital service that Sunday before the operation! I remember the Chaplain - Dr Alfred Martin - a former Moderator of the Presbyterian Church in Ireland. I sometimes reflect on the yobs of this life - the loud mouths, the over confident, those making their way up the ladder of progress while kicking as hard as they can at others trying to follow; all the smart alecs, who devote their lives trying to gain advantage over as many others as possible. Let's face it, there are many in this world who are under resourced, in what they come into this world with i.e. in what's on top of their little shoulders - and what they acquire later on. They are the fodder in the game of who gets what, when and where. I am saying however, that a levelling takes place when the unsavoury yobs are knocked over by a stroke, heart attack - accident, even a good old fashioned broken leg. All has to stop and minds tend to be concentrated by the creature on the Creator.

The operation was completed the next day. I was surprised when becoming awake, that I had no plaster on. The leg had been "disconnected" just below the knee, and swung out. Two Neilson pins were then inserted through the tibia, (shin bone) one immediately above, and one below the break. Large clamps drew the pins together and thus the broken bone ends were constrained to calcify (knit) in the desired position. Two days later, my Surgeon came to see me. "How does it feel?" he enquired. "I want you to lift your leg". I nearly died! "It's ok - it won't fall apart". So I lifted the leg - not too much, but clear off the bed. He appeared satisfied.

It must have taken fine judgement to get the correct amount of offset. Now the Surgeon, in a cautionary comment, indicated that in some cases, the pain did not diminish - in any case, experience was that such operations gave about five years service - and after that problems arose. But happily eighteen years have gone past, and I have little to complain about. But two days after the operation I was far from out of the wood. I was allowed up on crutches - now these crutches were very modern - arm crutches made of aluminium alloy. I was allowed to go to the dining room for lunch and dinner. But as well, I was subjected to rigorous physiotherapy - lifting the leg - pulling it back towards the body - bending the knee. One day, I discovered one of the thumb screws tightening the clamps, was slack. Now there was a problem! How tight should I put them - after all, the clamps were only holding a broken leg together! To ease the pain and enable me to carry on with the exercises, painkillers were made available - I became oblivious to pain - I also got a sleeping draught. My physiotherapist was a student from the School of Physiotherapy at Jordanstown. She was very thorough and demanding - no short cuts. I owe a lot to this student - but in the early days, I hated to see her coming - such was the discomfort. A word about those pins - Neilson pins I believe they were called. They were pins of approximately the size of a six inch nail - complete with a blunt point but no head - quite visible to the naked eye - a testimony to the wonderful progress in modern surgery.

One day my Surgeon came to see me - would I mind appearing at a meeting of Surgeons from the local hospitals where perhaps every week, case and methods were discussed. So I was pushed into this august assembly of surgical bishops, my x-rays were displayed, questions asked of my Surgeon - and one or two of me.

Shortly, I was discharged. But a day or two after discharge I was to experience something which helps me to understand the dreadful curse of drug taking!

I was sitting in a chair in my home, alone. I could see the crows in a nearby rookery sorting out their domestic affairs - when I was overcome by an overwhelming sense of despair and despondency. My "reasoning" ran like this. In a sound frame of mind, I had walked into a hospital and allowed someone to break one of my legs - culminating in my present helpless position. Time seemed to have stopped, the day interminable. I burst into tears - I was having some pain as well and sleep was difficult. In a rare moment of inspiration, I rang my doctor, who had made all the necessary clinical appointments for me vis a vis the Musgrave Park Outpatients. My doctor was not only my doctor - I was even more fortunate, in that Dr Joan Reid was a teaching colleague in the small technical college where I was employed. She brought her considerable prestige to the college, by giving lectures, relating to nursing studies. I described to her my sorrowful conclusions - was it real or a nightmare! I actually heard her laughing over the phone. "What tablets were you on", she asked. "Oh - such and such - but they were all left in Musgrave Park Hospital". This was true. After living a life of oblivion for three weeks, I was discharged without my backup - and there had been no communication so far, with my G.P. Anyway, when my doctor friend stopped laughing, she informed me that I was suffering from drug withdrawal - I would be put back on tablets again - tablets of a lower strength and gradually reduce the dose. And so it was, but I had been on a trip and didn't know!

Four weeks later, I was recalled to Musgrave to have my pins withdrawn. I was suitably apprehensive. How much pain - would they come out easily? Would I be given an anaesthetic?

So back to Withers 4 - but for some reason, I was given a bed in a single ward, and prepared for a general anaesthetic - a special bath - I cannot remember where the leg went - and a new "paper overall" - no loin cloth was on the menu - they had had their day! But I got the usual pre med injection.

When taken to the theatre, I was received by a sister and two nurses. "It will save you some inconvenience", the sister said, "if these pins come out without an anaesthetic - will we try them, then?" I agreed, and what happened next was an example of the professional at work. This sister knew what she was about, and even to my (now) drowsy teacher's mind, it was an excellent lesson. "Now", said the sister, "I am gripping the end of the pin". She actually described the tool being used - it was identical to a chuck type tapping spanner, used in engineering. "I am now going to turn the pin", she went on. "right - there it goes - is everything alright?" I was feeling no pain. "Ok, I am now withdrawing the pin - it's moving well - it's nearly out - there it's out". And the next one the same. I was some relieved. Next, the team put a "walking cylinder" on the leg - a full length plaster, but leaving the foot free to take a shoe. I would be on crutches for another seven weeks.

It was during this time that I was to become aware of that peculiar habit that people have when enquiring about an incapacitated person's condition - the question is not addressed to that person, but is asked of a third party - a relation or other "is he able to use a" - or "will I butter his bread" - or something like that. You see "he" is conceived as less than - different from us.

I had been attending the Musgrave Park External Clinic at Ballymena where "my" Surgeon was usually in attendance. After seven weeks, I was summoned again - and Mr Joe McClelland was in attendance that day. He examined the x-ray and said the plaster could come off. On a previous visit I had discovered that the dreaded shears were no longer in use. I probably said "thanks be rendered", because with the bits and pieces that made up my left leg, my mind was scarred for life by the shear agony when those shears had made a double pass down nineteen full plasters. So I came out of plaster eleven weeks after the scalpel, saw and chisel, had done their work. Just inside three calendar months, I was on my bike - I was without pain. I got back to school for the last week in June, and five months after the operation I was at John O'Groats - on the bike. I sent Mr Joe McClelland a card. All had been worthwhile.

Chapter 10 - In Retrospect

The Price of Progress - At The Frontiers Of Technology

From the earliest correspondence that I had with the firm of Short Bros. & Harland Ltd., I was aware that they were "the first manufacturers of aircraft in the world" - the statement was there in black and white, on the headed paper used by the company. In fact, the earliest headed paper had a balloon, or perhaps two, as a motif, proclaiming the award of a Gold Medal for quality of balloon manufacture, and presented by the Aero Club, at their exhibition at Islington, in 1907.

Later the balloons disappeared from some headed paper, and a new motif appeared - that of the Society of British Aircraft Constructors. The brothers Oswald and Eustace Short entered the aviation industry by producing balloons at Hove in Sussex in 1901 some two years or so before the Wright Bros. in the U.S.A., ushered in the era of powered flight, in 1903. Expanding business took them to larger premises in London in 1905, at different locations, firstly, I believe, to the arches under a railway bridge, at Battersea. In 1908 a third brother joined them - Horace Short, the engineer in the family, and in 1909 they began construction of their first heavier than air, aircraft.

Aircraft of my acquaintance

The Sunderland Prototype K4774 first flew at Rochester on 16th October 1937 and Sunderlands entered service with the R.A.F. in 1938. The Sunderland was fitted with four radial air cooled Bristol Pegasus engines of 950 H.P. each, eventually being changed in later versions e.g. Mark V, to Pratt & Whitney engines. It was these engines that I saw, when I first became acquainted with the Sunderlands at Queen's Island. It seems that, for a new aircraft, it took a remarkably short time for it to be pronounced fit and well for active service and suggests that its ancestry was well proven. The Sunderland was the first flying boat to have power operated gun turrets, had a wing span of 112 ft. 9 ins. (about 34m) overall length 85ft 4 ins. (26m) and a maximum level speed of 185 knots (just over 200 m.p.h.). They were to remain in service for 21 years.

Another important contract underway at Queen's Island at the time was that of the "Canberra" twin jet bomber - fitted with Avon engines. The Canberra was an English Electric design, and I was there to witness the first Shorts' production Canberra fly low over the main factory on October 30th, 1952. I "followed" its path - I knew where it was going. It would land at Aldergrove, where Shorts still had a hanger, and it would do its final acceptance trials there. I would have liked a transfer there - so close to Antrim. It was a good contract - in all 130 were built, and it became a mainstay of employment.

In the now modern jet age, a need arose by the Ministry of Defence for a jet bomber capable of carrying a "modern" bomb i.e. an atomic bomb. Shorts designed a four jet bomber called the S.A.4 Sperrin. This unique aircraft had two jet engines on each wing - one above the other - figure of eight configuration. First flying on 10th August 1951, the S.A.4's (there were two of them) were in "mothballs" when I arrived on the scene, being parked on the hard standing outside the main factory, all openings secured, windows covered etc - deserted. It was an experimental design, the contract for heavy, four jet bombers eventually going the way of the Valiant (Vickers), the Vulcan (Avro), and the Victor (Handley Page). But I was to meet the S.A.4 again, as already recalled.

A military aircraft of some potential was the Seamew, an aircraft designed to answer what was perceived as an urgent need for an anti-submarine aircraft, following the failure of the Fairy Gannet to fulfil that need. The Seamew, regarded as a lightweight ante submarine aircraft to be operated from an aircraft carrier, first flew on the 23rd August 1953, and a production line came into being in the main factory. Now at an air display at Sydenham in 1957, pilots of 502 Auxiliary Air Force Vampires, had started their engines prior to a take off scheduled to follow a Seamew display over the airfield. But the 502 pilots were then told to shut down engines - the Seamew had crashed, killing Shorts test pilot Wally Runciman. The contract was cancelled in 1957.

Another purely research aircraft was the famous SC1, the world's first vertical take-off and land aircraft. This was a Ministry of Supply project. The SC1 programme for the Ministry was basically to investigate vertical lift off and forward motion using four jets to lift the aircraft and one to power forward flight. Such an aircraft needed a sophisticated stabilisation system to control the aircraft in flight. The first SC1 (XG900) first flew conventional on 2nd April 1957, followed by free vertical flights in May 1958. The transition from hover to horizontal flight took place on April 6th, 1960. Sadly one SC1 suffered what I understand was a gyro stabilisation failure and crashed, killing a Shorts test pilot.

The SC1 was a follow on to a Rolls Royce project which had acquired the name "flying bedstead", a reference to the peculiar shape of this project - to investigate vertical take off and land, which appeared as a jet engine on four legs, tethered to a gantry. No orders came Shorts way for any further V.T.O.L aircraft, but the SC1 programme was linked to a feasibility study relating to the use of vertical lift passenger jets in city or inner city airports.

*   *   *   *   *   *   *   *   *   *

Now another project to investigate vertical and forward flight using swivelling engines, was under way at the Hawker Aircraft Co, on premises at Kingston Upon Thames and at Dunsfold Aerodrome, Surrey. This contract was for the P1127. It was flown at Dunsfold Aerodrome, near Godalming in Surrey where my brother-in-law, Mr John Yoxall, was now Works Manager. The P1127 was the ancestor of the Harrier, without which it is unlikely that Britain could have regained the Falkland Islands.

*   *   *   *   *   *   *   *   *   *

Around the time as I prepared to resit examinations after my two and a half year lay-up, the SC1 made its maiden flight on 2nd April 1957, from a conventional take off - at Boscombe Down, in England and a year later, a "tethered" vertical flight was made - on 23rd May 1958. Around this time I had reached the O.N.C, examinations, held in May. Later, the first "free" vertical to forward flight happened on 6th April 1960. (This time coincides approximately with the time when a dog choose to come to close quarters with me and my motor cycle, and land me into the Royal Victoria Hospital). The initial design of the SC1 had begun in 1954.

Now the Hawker P1127 made its initial tethered lift off in 1960, and its first "transitional', in September 1961. So the Short SC1, was the first V/STOL - (Vertical, Short Take Off and Land) aircraft in the world.

We apprentices were well aware that such a development was taking place - at Castlereagh I had machined SC1 components. But as for how the SC1 lifted and was maintained stable - without the usual forces available on the aircraft control surfaces - these things didn't penetrate the mind. I just knew that jet propulsion lifted - four engines, and another engine provided forward thrust. I never heard anyone ask what would happen if one of the vertical jets - say number one, cut out - or what would happen if one, two and three called it a day! Had those questions been addressed, or that of the problem of port and starboard (left and right) stability, there would have been much to exercise our minds. Even now, such problems provide fascinating contemplation in trying to understand how they were overcome.

Although it didn't occupy my mind much - it was already filled with broken limbs and studies etc, I was probably unique among Short's apprentices in one respect. This was because my brother-in-law was closely involved in the development of the P1127 through its Kestrel stage, and eventually the various types of Harrier. His family home was "Primemeads Farm" - inside Dunsfold aerodrome - I think that certain Hawker test pilots - probably Neville Duke or Bill Bedford had lived earlier in this house. I was therefore a frequent visitor to Dunsfold, familiar with Murphy's Cottage (Murphy was another Ex-Dunsfold pilot), the stocks, still in position outside Dunsfold Parish Church, and the "Three Compasses" local, outside the airfield security gate. As I say, had I not been preoccupied with other orders of the day, I was in a unique position to acquire some knowledge indeed about V/STOL projects, especially as the P1127 was using a different approach to lift and propulsion, from that of the SC1. This system, using the Bristol Pegasus engine, incorporated two sets of nozzles per side, such nozzles on each side acting in unison, and capable of rotating, so as to give thrust to provide lift or horizontal motion, or both. These were known as vectoring nozzles. Referring to the problems, that might have exercised an apprentice's mind, the question of control and stability is of central importance. How does one ensure that the lift, for example, lifts the aircraft - on an even keel? Since a jet engine consists substantially of a large air compressor or compressors, air is readily available, and "puffer" jets, as they were called, were fitted to each wing tip, the nose and tail. The SC1 used a gyroscopic, automatic stabilisation system - as indeed had Rolls Royce with their "flying bedstead", but I understand that control of these "puffer jets" in the P1127 and Harrier was through special Reaction Control Valves (R.C.V's) and here the "puffers" responded to the movement of the pilot's control column - something like that of the control column in conventional flight - but a little more sophisticated. Although these puffer jets may have been capable of thrusts of 1000 lbs of force, there were certain other adverse forces - and acting in a destabilising manner, that had to be neutralised, or overcome. Neutralising proved the satisfactory method, because these forces emanated from the gyroscopic reactions due to the high speed rotation of the engine, and a simple understanding of gyroscopic reaction would not be out of place here. The principles of gyroscopic reaction can be readily demonstrated if one takes the front wheel from a bicycle, and holding the wheel by the axle at either side, imparts motion to the wheel. If the axle is now turned while being maintained horizontal i.e. level, the wheel and axle will immediately react by tending to resist and deflect at 90 degrees to axis of axle (axis of disturbance). This movement is called precessing. Imagine the forces which thus act on a ship at sea, where propulsion is by a heavy steam turbine (and associated reduction gear) the turbine rotating at 3000 R.P.M. The spinning turbine represents the rotor of a gyroscope, (or the cycle wheel), the axis of rotation being along the fore to aft axis of ship. Any yaw (movement) to port or starboard will, through precessing, cause the ship to lift or plunge the bows, and any plunging fore and aft, will cause the ship to yaw left or right. Pity the guy on the wheel!

It will now be evident, that such forces will surely exist on whatever structure or platform is holding a gas turbine, rotating at 11,000 R.P.M.! In vertical lifting, there are *none* of the normal forces available at the control surfaces as there is during conventional flight - no air flow over these surfaces to assist in creating stability. Such forces, as available in conventional flight, are sufficient to control gyroscopic reactions created by conventional jet or other engines. These control surfaces, would be those of the rudder and tail unit (elevators and fin), the ailerons, flaps, wing surfaces etc. The answer was found by using contra-rotating engines or in the case of the single Pegasus, as fitted in the Harrier, two halves (or spools) of the compressor are contra-rotating, thus neutralising these gyroscopic forces. Although Shorts had development plans for a follow on to the SC1, no further orders for V/STOL were forthcoming, as already mentioned.

One necessary ingredient for the development of both the SC1 and P1127 was money. My understanding is that American money, through a U.S. organisation set up to organise projects within N.A.T.O., and known as the M.W.D.P. (Mutual Weapons Development Program) initially provided development money for the P1127 successor - the Kestrel, and money subsequently became available from a Tripartite consisting of the U.S., Britain and Federal Germany. Both the SC1 and the P1127 suffered set backs. The SC1 suffered a stabilisation failure and crashed, killing a Shorts test pilot. During the development of the P1127/Kestrel programme, Bill Bedford had to eject when control was lost after a nozzle fell off. It's interesting to note, that the forward pair of nozzles on this aircraft use compressed air for lift and propulsion, and the after pair use the exhaust of the engine, each nozzle giving equal thrust. The forward and aft nozzles act in unison, being originally designed to be connected by a chain - motor cycle chain.

It is interesting now to look at the techniques used by the companies, on this threshold of technology and vertical lift off. The SC1 used four permanently secured lift engines, and initially the aircraft was "tethered" beneath a gantry for the first lift offs, before the first "free" hovers took place. As already mentioned, the SC1 initially flew conventionally about one year before a hover was attempted.

The P1127 made the hover flights first. (Sir Sydney Camm, the Hawker Chief Designer was reputed to have said, "Sure everybody knows it can fly conventionally!") The first hover used tethers attached to the ground, and anchored (beneath the aircraft) to a specially constructed grid designed to direct the engine exhausts away from the intakes. The first hover lasted one minute and forty-five seconds. An unusual aspect of this first P1127 hover, was that Bill Bedford, the Chief test pilot, "flew" the aircraft with a broken ankle sustained in a car accident in Germany where he had been demonstrating a two-seat Hunter, a few days previously.

The first P1127 hovers were conducted with some caution - the aircraft constraints being of the order of four feet (something over one metre) and it was not until twenty one tethered hovers were completed, that the first free hover took place. My brother-in-law, Mr John Yoxall was closely involved in the development of the P1127 being appointed P1127 Co-ordination Engineer in 1967 (the year Sir Sydney Camm died) and Works Manager, Dunsfold in 1972. Later, in 1984 he became Chief Production Centre Manager by which time of course Hawkers was part of British Aerospace (BAe) and he had flights from time to time in both the Harrier, and the Hawk trainer, both then in production.

In 1985 he had a trip in a Harrier TMk60. It lasted twenty-five minutes, and the pilot was Taylor Scott, who had joined the company in 1979 from the Royal Navy. (See photograph page 222)

*   *   *   *   *   *   *   *   *   *

Some time - after John Yoxall retired, and had come to live in Antrim, a GR5 Harrier was observed from an American C5 transport aircraft. It was heading West, and appeared to have no pilot on board. The Harrier was shadowed until it crashed into the sea after running out of fuel. Later video photographs taken of the pilotless Harrier at the time, revealed a hole in the canopy. The body of the pilot, was later recovered on land - it was that of Taylor Scott.

188

It was thought that the drogue gun (which pulls out the parachute) had, in some way been accidentally fired by, perhaps a loose torch, thus putting the pilot through the canopy. The video recording appeared to show that the well seat of the Harrier was intact.

The loss of a Britannia aircraft is presently described - on a chilly parallel with that of the Harrier. Such sad losses remind us with some penetration, the price paid by the brave men who cross unknown barriers, in seeking to make the path safe for others.

*   *   *   *   *   *   *   *   *   *

Without follow on orders, building single aircraft through research programmes, does not provide much work in bulk; but soon, Shorts were involved in an order that did - building the Britannia turbo-prop airliner, designed by the Bristol Aeroplane Company, of Bristol. Shorts would eventually build thirty-five Britannias - for passenger companies, and the R.A.F. The Britannia was considered to be an aircraft with many advanced systems, and such a new aircraft called for a considerable test and proving programme. Some of the customers had different requirements to others e.g. one company - I believe it was North East Airlines of Canada, required additional fresh water capacity. During the proving programme, situations unfolded which must have reminded some people of the ill fated "Comet" contract. Because, during the test and proving programme of flying the Britannia at Bristol, two aircraft were lost - one sadly with the loss of all on board. The Britannia was powered by the Proteus turbo-prop engine, and a Britannia first flew on the Proteus II version, in May 1952. A redesigned version, Proteus III, was flown in a Britannia in August 1953. Now the gas turbine shaft of the Proteus turned at 11,000 R.P.M. The propeller was designed to turn at 1,000 R.P.M., and in principle, the reduction was accomplished by straight toothed spur gearwheels, i.e. a small gearwheel (pinion) rotating at 11,000 R.P.M., and known as the input pinion, in mesh with a large output gearwheel, driving the propeller at the appropriate reduced R. P. M. In practice this was normally affected through a number of such gears - i.e. in a gear box. During the series of proving flights leading to the aircraft being type tested for civil operations, a party of people from K.L.M., (the Dutch airline) potential customers for the aircraft, joined Bill Pegg, the Bristol Chief test pilot, on such a flight, on board G-ALRY. It was February 1954.

The next day, that Britannia hit the headlines in all the national newspapers, its photograph splashed across the front pages, as it lay stranded on the mud flats of the Severn estuary. I remember very well those pictures - a huge silver aircraft being overlapped by the tide. All personnel escaped unhurt, although the Britannia had sank into the mud up to, and over the windows. It was a total loss as an aircraft, although various components were used as practice units for training operational crew e.g. the undercarriage etc to simulate the lowering and retraction of landing wheels, etc.

Investigation showed that the teeth on the input pinion* had stripped. The turbine, free of its load oversped, and broke from its shaft, breaking through the casing and cowling etc. Parts passed through the engine oil tank, setting it alight. During the next nineteen minutes as the aircraft headed back to Filton, Bristol, extinguishers contained the fire but the pilot decided to ditch in case the wing, weakened by the fire, might collapse. Thus, this Britannia made a very good belly landing on the Severn estuary.

A helical reduction arrangement solved the problem, and was soon fitted to the next aircraft in line, since an engineering executive, uncomfortable about the pinion arrangement, had received the go ahead to design an alternative helical reduction, and actually had some sets available - on the shelf.

(* - See page 171 - Old Water Wheel at Moylinney, Muckamore)

A number of other things were happening in aero industrial matters. For one, shortly after the forced landing of that Britannia, some reorganisation of Short Bros. & Harland Ltd. was taking place, with the Bristol Aeroplane Company acquiring a fifteen and a quarter per cent interest in Shorts, thus helping cement the co-operation etc desirable mutually, in the shared production of the Britannia. (As for myself, I was about to leave Castlereagh, Centre 24, for the "Comet" at Queen's Island).

Late in 1956, another problem developed, when a Britannia, on a final tropical clearance flight, had the engines cut out at 20,000 ft (6,000m), while flying over Central Africa. The engines were eventually restarted, and the problem was traced to ice formation. Now, in this area, with sea level temperatures of 40°C and high evaporation levels, ice crystals can be found in the air at 20,000 ft. Ice was thus forming inside the engine cowlings, while growing in volume to break off in large pieces, large enough to cause a compressor stall, or even extinguish the flame in the combustion chambers, if they entered the engine. I understand, that the racket they caused was quite audible to the flight crews. The problem was initially solved by fitting glow plugs, which were heated by the burning gases and fitted in the combustion chambers. These retained enough heat to re-ignite the fuel/air mixture and restore power. To satisfy B.O.A.C., test flying continued, and a series of modifications to the cowling ducts overcame the problem - two years on. These proving flight tests had therefore continued all the time that I had been "getting to know my neighbour" in three different hospitals. Shorts first Britannia flew on 1st June 1957 - just before I made my first passenger journey in the Viscount from Nutts Corner. (Shortly before this, the SC1 made its first conventional flight on 2nd April 1957 at Boscombe Down, in England). A large proving flight programme got underway some of it shared with the Bristol Aeroplane Company, where Sir Matthew Slattery, Shorts Chairman, became Chairman there as well. These proving flights had to do with endurance - fuel consumption etc, systems (including the air conditioning temperature throughout the pressure cabin) and the thousand and one things, that have to be safe and reliable. As mentioned, some of this work was shared with some Shorts personnel on flying duties on Bristol built Britannias, from time to time. Part of this had necessarily to do with acquaintance courses etc, anyway. One of those thus involved, was a former R.A.F., pilot, who had been working in the engineering design side of things in Shorts. He was Richard Spencer, and was now flying as flight engineer / second pilot.

*   *   *   *   *   *   *   *   *   *

It was customarily the case, that a flight engineer, new to an aircraft type being tested, would have some initial acquaintance flying in the company of another flight engineer, familiar with the aircraft. The engineer, new to the aircraft, would then be more adequate for his first flight as flight engineer - preferably a short one. On 6th November 1957, Richard Spencer was scheduled to take off on a relatively short routine proving flight of four hours or so from Filton, Bristol, in Britannia G-ANCA. He was subsequently re-scheduled to fly on another Britannia proving flight - of fourteen hours duration. This was in order to give a young, ginger haired Scot, a short trip as flight engineer. His name was Donald Charles Cameron. That flight of Richard's took the Britannia across the Bay of Biscay, then over the Pyrenees, the Eastern Mediterranean - and back to Bristol. Having adequate fuel, the Britannia then flew up to Shetland and then back to Bristol. When they got back, a solemn mood was evident, and when an enquiry was made, as to what was wrong, they were told that Hugh Statham had "gone in", and the entire flight crew had perished.

The deaths of so many skilled and experienced men is too sacred a thing for speculation or gossip by those who have no business to do so. To pursue questions, the answers to which might prevent such an accident happening again, is another thing. An inquiry was got underway, and eye witnesses asked to recall what they saw. A great variety of accounts, diverse, as from seeing a ball of flame in the sky, to the tail breaking away, or a wing coming off, contrasted greatly with what one witness, a local doctor was able to be very precise about. He said that "just there, above those trees, a wing dropped, then the aircraft nose dived into the ground". The site evidence showed consistence, that it was a nose impact that had taken place. The problem was now how to trace back what control areas would arbitrarily or otherwise cause the manoeuvre, as described by the doctor. He appeared, as a very reliable witness.

Now the people who made the auto pilot were also in on the investigation, and attention focused on two soldered terminals. Had these two been short circuited, it first of all would have had the effect of negating the pilot's option to disengage the auto pilot, i.e. the auto pilot would have "locked on". (Such a short circuit could have been caused by a stray wire, or perhaps conducting mineral dust, or maybe even dampness.)

Richard Spencer : Crash of Britannia G-ANCA

On 6th November 1957 the above aircraft was returning from a test development flight when from 2,000 feet (600 m) it plunged into the ground, suddenly, on the outskirts of Bristol.

Following inspection of the wreckage and the interviewing of many eye witnesses (most of whom were inaccurate as their evidence did not "square" with the crash site) the following sequence was established.

The aircraft had suddenly banked until the wing was vertical (and so not providing lift). It would then fall sideways (side slip) and the fin and rudder effect would cause the nose to drop. The aircraft hit the ground in a near vertical attitude.

The crash was sudden as no distress call was made by the Captain - Hugh Statham - an excellent and very experienced test pilot, with many flying hours on the Britannia.

Weeks of investigation ensued to find the cause. Among the many possibilities was the fact that the instruments were being photographed on the flight. If a flash bulb had exploded it could have blinded the pilots.

However Smiths who made the auto pilot (SP3) eventually discovered the most likely cause after extensive bench testing.

The auto pilot controller was between the two pilots. Selection ON was by pulling a knob up, and OFF by pushing it down.

In addition, on each pilot's control column was a thumb button. If either pilot operated their button the auto pilot was disconnected and they had instant manual control.

Smiths proved that on a printed circuit board, in the control box, two adjacent soldered joints close together could have been shorted. If large deposits of solder had been used in construction, shorting could easily occur by say a metal object (a screw or piece of wire etc) or by liquid, water or even spilt coffee. Loose metal was virtually ruled out by the quality control procedures, and moisture was considered most likely.

The effect of such a short were -

1   Full aileron would be applied.
2   The pilots thumb buttons would be bypassed and so would not operate.
3   The main auto pilot selection OFF button would also be bypassed and so inoperative.
4   The pilots could not overcome the force of the auto pilot.

The only way to disconnect the auto pilot would be to cut the electrical supply to it.

This power was from the inverter at 115v 400 cycles per second - (accurately controlled).

The same power drove the radar, auto throttle controls and other instruments, so four inverters (one per engine) supplied normal needs. A fifth one was available as a stand by in case of a failure.

Controlled from a position behind the flight engineer's seat, the inverter panel consisted of a bank of switches, each of which had three positions. Up for ON, "mid for first transfer" and down for "second transfer".

If an inverter failed, the flight engineer would have to stand up, turn round and select the failed inverter to "first transfer". The stand by unit would then restore power and all systems would be maintained.

If another inverter failed, "second transfer" would have to be selected in which case some of the systems would be lost.

By a somewhat complicated selection of switching, the services "lost" could be determined. For example, one way would cause the radar and two auto throttle controls etc to be lost (emergency switches then controlled those two throttles). Switching the other way the auto pilot and the other two auto throttles would be lost.

This is the only practical way (and quickest) to cut the auto pilot. Electric power circuit breakers were located in banks in cabinets at many places in the aircraft and were not touched by the air crew.

The flight engineer, Donald Cameron, had been checked out after training and this flight was his first "solo".

The aircraft was preparing to land so the engineer would be strapped into his seat between the two pilots where he could operate the throttles, flaps and undercarriage.

If he had realised what was going wrong he would have to unstrap from his seat, stand up, turn round and operate the inverter switching in the correct sequence to cut the auto pilot power. But, by the attitude of the aircraft, he would most likely have been thrown across the cockpit.

Even if he had managed it, there would have been no time for the Captain to recover - there was no height, as they were at 2,000 feet to start with.

This was considered to be the only explanation that fitted the known facts.

The cure: A redesign of the circuit board to move those two soldered junctions apart, and ensure that they could not be shorted. This modification was immediately carried out on all Britannias.

No other Britannia ever suffered with this problem.

* * * * * * * * * *

The Britannia Aircraft had to do with the Shorts concept for a really heavy lift aircraft - something that could carry a tank, and eventually the company started the design of the Shorts 100 ton* "Belfast" freighter of which ten were made, and one is still flying, on heavy lift duties. By the time it had its first flight in 1964, I had left Shorts employment, but was back working under Shorts roof, in a Ministry of Defence role, involved in the inspection of the Seacat missile. The missile programme is also an important part of Shorts history and just as the British Aerospace Harrier from Dunsfold played such a vital role in the Falklands war, so did the Seacat, credited with six "kills", on Argentinian aircraft during the liberation of the islands.

* * * * * * * * * *

Finally, I want to turn to an aircraft that still occupies my thoughts from time to time and what might have been, for the British Aviation industry - the beautiful De Havilland Comet. As mentioned earlier, the Court of Inquiry into the Comet disasters, revealed some stunning information. Its painstaking search was costly in terms of material and time, but we must never forget the other cost - the deaths of the crews and passengers on the very frontiers of the prevailing technology of the day. Perhaps the torture of figures and technical explanations can be lived with, when one remembers again that without such considerations, we wouldn't be flying with the degree of safety we enjoy today.

* * * * * * * * * *

With the benefit of hindsight, it is now possible to look at prevailing attitudes of that period, to the possibility of material failure through stress and in particular the failure that is caused through metal fatigue. Fatigue might be described as a weakening of metals through the intermittent application of a load, a load which is applied and then removed. Materials will fail under such a load even though they can support a much larger static load without distress. De Havillands were not unaware of fatigue in metals - it had been studied generally, over the previous hundred years. But the Comet fuselage would be subjected to a fairly new field of load application, the stress in a cylindrical structure subjected to a pressurisation, then the removal of that stress. It would be shown subsequently, that the safe life of such a structure would be measured in so many pressurisations. An aircraft therefore, subject to such a cycle every, say, three hours (short haul), might expect half the life of an aircraft on, say six hour flights (to use round figures), all other things being equal. Clearly, the testing of such a structure as a fuselage, which is going to be subject, in the main, to fatigue inducing loads, would be of crucial importance, and more pertinently, that such testing would subject the structure to treatment likely to be significantly more severe, than that which would be met with, under normal conditions in flight. An important value in these matters would be the difference between the pressure inside the cabin and that outside, regulated to 8.25lbs/sq inch and referred to as P. A safety valve was set to open at 8.5lbs/sq inch. Note: 14.7 lb/sq inch = 1 Bar.

(* - All Up Weight)

The Bristol Aeroplane Company, Limited.

Order

for

The Memorial Service

at

Bristol Cathedral

on

Tuesday, 19th November, 1957

12.00 noon

To honour the memory of those
who lost their lives in the
Britannia aircraft G-ANCA on
6th November, 1957

Remember before God

John Kenneth Barker
John Edward Burton
Donald Charles Cameron
Albert Edward Ebling
Philip Norman Edward Hewitt
Donald Matthew Hunter
Kenneth Graham Lucas
Dudley Neville Stephen Moynihan
Frederick William Mycroft
John Harold Parry-Jones
Ernest Hugh Statham
Nigel Morris Thorne
William James Todd
Bernard Francis Waite
Frederick Charles Walsh

REDUCTION GEAR Bristol Proteus Engine — Sun and planet compound epicylic.

Reduction gear ratio 0·0862:1 (propeller shaft to propeller turbine).

Outlay based on information, thought to be from the OVERHAUL MANUAL, **Bristol Siddeley Engines, Ltd.**

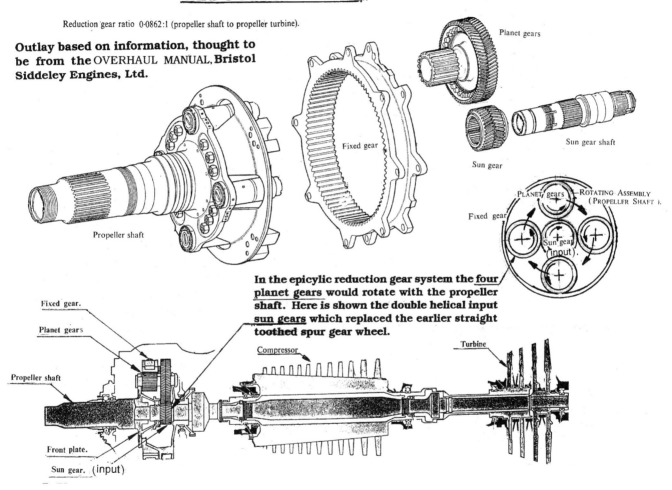

Planet gears

Fixed gear

Sun gear shaft

Sun gear

PLANET gears — ROTATING ASSEMBLY (PROPELLER SHAFT).

Fixed gear

Sun gear (input).

Propeller shaft

In the epicylic reduction gear system the four planet gears would rotate with the propeller shaft. Here is shown the double helical input sun gears which replaced the earlier straight toothed spur gear wheel.

Fixed gear.

Planet gears

Propeller shaft

Front plate.

Sun gear. (input)

Compressor

Turbine

I have been very privileged to have had the opportunity to read through a copy of the report of the Court of Inquiry into the accidents to Comet G-ALYP on 10th January 1954 and Comet G-ALYY on 8th April 1954, (Ministry of Transport and Civil Aviation). The British Civil Airworthiness Requirements, called for a proof of $1^1/_3P$ (under which the cabin must show no signs of permanent deformation) and a design pressure of 2P. This later would seem to have been presented (initially anyway) as a static test requirement. De Havillands were to use a design pressure of 2.5P, and tested the cabin to 2P. The findings of the Accident Report contain some very interesting indicators as to current thinking on the relevance of fatigue in design considerations. De Havillands had opted to adapt higher figures for testing criteria than had even been recommended by the British Civil Airworthiness Requirements, as shown above. The Report's comment is revealing on this area: "Their reasons (De Havillands) for adapting these substantially higher figures were:

1.   They believed (and this opinion was shared by the Air Registration Board and other **expert** opinion) that a cabin which would survive undamaged, a test to double its working pressure 2P, would not fail in service under the **action of fatigue** due to the pressurisation to working pressure, P, on each flight and to other fluctuating loads to which it is subjected in operations.

2.   They (De Havillands) also considered that it would 'ensure a larger margin of safety against the possible failure of doors, windows and hatches'. They also tested window panes to very high pressures. Now to simulate conditions for testing, De Havillands had built two **separate** sections of the pressure cabin, one front part 26 feet long and the centre part 24 feet long. These were subject to pressures of between P and 2P some 30 times to the front part, with a series of 2000 pressurisations to rather over P'."

Significantly the report goes on: 'These tests were **not** intended as a test of the fatigue resisting properties of the structure, but rather as providing an assurance that the cabin would be satisfactory as a **pressure** vessel'.

An observation on fatigue

Another significant relevation of contemporary thinking is contained in the Report: 'Until the middle of 1952 the likelihood that the fatigue resistance properties of a pressure cabin demanded further precautions, either in design or test, than were provided by the current **static** strength requirements, **had not been realised'.** (Comet G-AYLP - Yoke Peter, Captain Alan Gibson D.F.C., had a total of 3681 flying hours at the time of the last fatal flight. There would have been a relatively few pressurisations, compared to the number the fore part of the cabin was subjected in the testing described above, 18,000 applications of pressurisations. However, up to this moment in time, no **complete** pressure cabin had been subjected to such testing.) In October 1952, the Joint Airworthiness Committee of the Ministry of Supply called for a static test of pressure cabins to 2P and a proof test to one and one third P with repeated loading tests of one and one quarter P applied 10,000 times (equivalent to 10,000 pressurised flights). One would assume however, that what is meant here is pressurisation of the **complete** cabin. About the same time, the Air Registration Board (A.R.B.) in reviewing the civil side, called for a static test to 2P, a proof test of one and one third P but raised the number of applications of one and one quarter P to 15,000. This was intended to cover the number of applications of P during the aircraft's lifetime.

De Havillands carried out repeated testing, applying 16,000 applications of the working pressure P, to the **fore** part of cabin. Later, by September 1953, the fore cabin in question had withstood 18,000 applications of P, although as a result of these applications and other severe tests, this part of the fuselage actually was tested to destruction in that a fatigue fracture occurred at the **corner** of a window. It was accepted however, that it was long past a 'normal' lifetime.

The R.A.E. Investigates

On the 8th April 1954 Comet G-ALYY, which was on charter to South African Airways, disappeared from the skies near Naples. The aircraft, known as 'Yoke Yoke', went down in very deep water making salvage impossible. The Comets were grounded and Sir Arnold Hall, Director of the Royal Aircraft Establishment, Farnborough, (under the Ministry of Supply), was asked to investigate. A few pieces of wreckage had been recovered, but much more was needed, and an effort was set in motion to locate the site of where Yoke Peter was lying, in relatively shallow water off Elba. (See appendix 1). Using underwater cameras, Yoke Peter was located, and eventually over 80% was recovered, taken to Farnborough and reassembled. Attention was focused on the nature of the windows and hatches. The windows were square, but with some radius at the corners. A full scale simulation of a pressurised aircraft was called for, a Comet would be placed in a huge water tank, the whole pressure cabin would be essentially surrounded by water and pressurised inside using water. Water was used because it is not compressible to any great degree, and would not hold much compressibility energy. If air (which is highly compressible) were to be used, then the release of such energy in the case of skin failure, would destroy much of the evidence, being sought. In fact, it was later estimated, that the escape of pressurised air following the assumed rupture of the fuselage of the downed Comets, would have been equivalent to the effect of a 500 lb bomb exploding. This method of hydraulic testing was not new, such activity had been common in the testing of high pressure air vessels, cylinders, etc, sometimes using oil which like water does not acquire high compressibility energy.

Such a tank was constructed, and the fuselage of Comet G-ALYU, Yoke Uncle, under hydraulic test pressure, eventually suffered material failure at the forward escape hatch, blowing out the side of the aircraft. Micro structural examination of the aircraft skin, showed fatigue crack growth from a rivet hole, near the rear lower corner of the forward escape hatch. Similar conditions were thought to have been produced in three or four other hatches or windows. (At this time, another Comet G-ANAV, had been sent to the R.A.E., to undergo flight tests on a number of matters that could only be explored in flight). The fuselage of Yoke Uncle was repaired and subjected to similar test conditions with increasing attention being directed towards windows, hatches, etc. Strain gauges were "fitted to the surface of the skin, at various positions near the corners of typical windows, including the one corresponding to that which had failed, but on the other side of the cabin" (extract from Accident Report, Paragraph 68). One test gave an estimated stress of 43,000lbs/sq inch. As a result of the information obtained from such tests, the presenter of the Accident Report commentated at this stage, "It is sufficient to say here, that the highest stress in the skin at the edge near the corner of that window of Yoke Uncle, was probably over 40,000lbs/sq inch (2.72×10^5) KN per square metre) and that the general level of stress was significantly higher than had been previously believed. In the light of the known properties of the aluminium alloy D.T.D. 546 of D.T.D. 746 of which the skin was made . . . I accept the conclusion of the R.A.E., that this is a sufficient explanation of the failure of the cabin skin of Yoke Uncle by fatigue, after a relatively small number, namely 3060 cycles of pressurisation".

But the mystery of Yoke Peter had not been completely solved and efforts were renewed off Elba, using trawling gear in deeper water to try and recover something which might suggest where the failure took place in this aircraft. As a result, a piece of skin was located by an Italian fishing boat, it contained the Automatic Direction Finding (A.D.F.) windows and adjacent pieces, and these parts confirmed that the cabin had burst catastrophically in this neighbourhood, that here the first fracture in Yoke Peter took place.

The Report again: '. . . it took the form of a split along the top centre of the cabin along a line approximately fore and aft, passing through the **corners of the windows**'. The investigation further suggested that the failure started either in the area of a countersunk hole (where experts showed fatigue had existed) or where the fracture passed through a small crack about 0.2 inches long in a reinforcing plate. This small crack is of interest in a general way, because such cracks are traditionally dealt with by drilling small holes one sixteenth inch diameter in their ends. These are known as 'location' holes. De Havillands had dealt with this crack in the traditional manner and presumedly through the normal concession procedure. Although the crack had been 'located', no Concession Note was available for inspection. However, to the inquiry, in relation to this crack, this was accepted as probably a defect in the Concessionary procedure. One other interesting though unrelated feature, concerned the condition of the hubs to which the turbine discs of the engines were bolted. The engines were recovered with the centre selection of the wings. One turbine hub had broken, and the discs were missing, the other hubs were shown to be on the point of fracture. The most probably explanation was a sudden and very rapid rotation of the whole wing while the engines were still running normally. Such a rotation, being about an axis at right angles to the engine shafts, would produce gyroscopic couples tending to bend the shafts in a sideways direction. These conditions were later simulated on a special pivoted framework where the forces mentioned were reproduced.

The conclusions that emerged from the Court of Inquiry were a blend of factuality and a fair bit of understanding of De Havilland's position. The Report contains 163 fairly lengthy points, plus a section on questions and answers etc. Thus point 117 contains ' - confirms the impression I formed that De Havillands were proceeding in accordance with what was then regarded as good engineering practice'. Then ' - De Havillands cannot be blamed for not making greater use of strain gauges than they actually did, or for believing that the static test that they proposed to apply, would, if successful give the necessary assurance against the risk of failure during the working life of aircraft'.

Later, the question of the highly stressed areas at the corner of the windows is dealt with: 'During the design of the Comet, De Havillands **did not** make use of calculations in an attempt to arrive at a close estimate of the stress distribution near the corners of the windows. We have examined such of their calculations as had a bearing on this question'.

Summary

1. Briefly, De Havillands appeared to believe that the stress in this area would be of the order of 28,000 lbs/sq inch (1.9×10^5 KN/sq metre). The ultimate strength of the alloy in question was understood to be 65,000 lbs/sq inch (4.42×10^5 KN/sq metre), and thus, since this was twice the assumed working stress, there was a margin of safety. This was their position.

2. However, the tests earlier referred to being carried out by Yoke Uncle **in flight**, revealed a stress of 70% of the ultimate strength! This was obtained by adding to the 43,000 lbs/sq inch noted earlier, another 2700 lb/sq inch due to other loads, giving a figure of 45,700 lbs/sq inch (3×10^5 KN/sq metre). This was in sharp contrast to the figure of De Havillands own estimate of 28,000 lbs/sq inch.

So it would appear that for our much loved Comet, a sufficiently accurate estimate of the real stress in areas likely to be subject to high loading, was not obtained.

Further, sufficient cognisance was not taken of the nature of failure by fatigue, in that this failure is by way of repeated applications of a load much smaller than that which a structure would happily bear under **static** conditions.

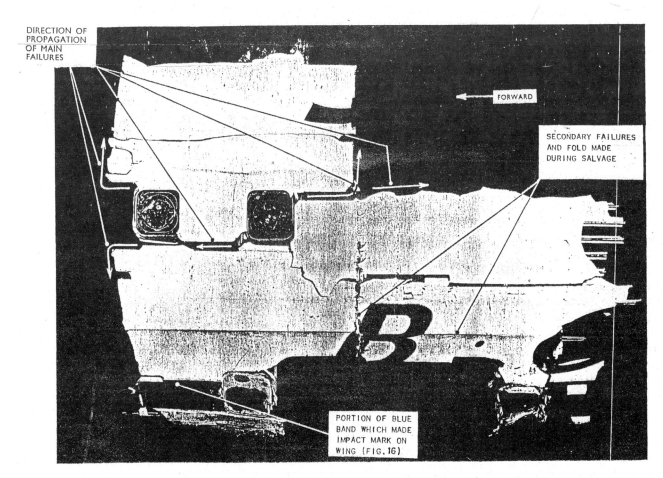

DIRECTION OF
PROPAGATION
OF MAIN
FAILURES

FORWARD

SECONDARY FAILURES
AND FOLD MADE
DURING SALVAGE

PORTION OF BLUE
BAND WHICH MADE
IMPACT MARK ON
WING (FIG. 16)

PHOTOGRAPH OF WRECKAGE AROUND ADF AERIAL WINDOWS—G–ALYP.

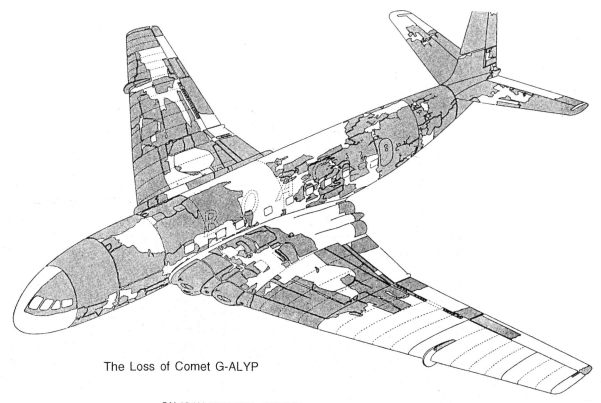

The Loss of Comet G-ALYP

DIAGRAM SHOWING AMOUNT OF WRECKAGE RECOVERED—G-ALYP.

De Havillands did seem to put great faith into static testing. They had not apparently given a complete fuselage repeated pressurisations though, in order to ascertain the effect of fatigue. Maybe the absence of a suitable test rig, as ultimately was required by the R.A.E., discouraged such approaches.

Thus the failure on Yoke Peter occurred in the A.D.F. window, the automatic direction finding window, which was in the top forward section of the passenger cabin. All this pointed to the design of the openings, of a square nature, with a radius at the corners. The stress was increased due to the proximity of rivet and bolt holes etc. De Havilland expected that stress in the area would be of the order of 28,000 lbs per square inch, but in actual fact, the stress was of the order of 45,700 lbs/sq inch (3×10^5 KN/sq metre).

A new association opens with Short Bros. & Harland Ltd

So I had no further personal knowledge of what was going on at Shorts after the Britannia and Seacat contracts, but, I was to have continued association with Shorts until it became Shorts Bombardia. This association was firstly through my lengthy friendship with Bill Archer and Wesley Black, the latter taking charge of the training school when Bill left Shorts to teach in the College of Technology. Wesley Black continued to play a very important part in my journey through life outside Shorts, and I will be ever grateful to him for a lifetime of encouragement, starting with those faltering steps which I took, upon resumption of my apprenticeship with him in the Apprentice Training School at Castlereagh, and later, as I worked in training, eventually to emerge in a career in teaching. Secondly, through my role in further education, and with the increase in works visits by students (and later through work experience programmes), I frequently returned to be met by none other than the late Ossie Carlisle, the assistant Apprentice Supervisor - the very man I had approached the first week I worked in Shorts, to request (like Oliver Twist asking for more porridge) a special pass to leave work early thus enabling me to get to that evening class in Ballymena Technical College. I think I was more than mildly surprised when he now addressed me as "Bobby", but I must admit, I probably felt pleased to be patronised in this manner, and marvelled inwardly at how time rings its changes. But more importantly, every effort was always made to facilitate my students, to let them see what large scale industry was like, and many eventually went to work there and now hold much better positions there than I ever did. Naturally when circumstances permitted, I was able to show some of them at least, where it all started - at the de-burring bench in Centre 30! During one such visit, we were taken to the airport to see the Shorts 360, a 36 seater airliner, at the flight and service stage. The Foreman was none other than John Rankin, an old contemporary acquaintance from my apprenticeship days - especially during my ill-fated sojourn on the S.A.4 at Aldergrove - we called him then, "The Duke of Crumlin".

Sadly, I was to enjoy Ossie Carlisle's patronage for a brief too few years. Time like an ever rolling stream, bears all its sons away, and Ossie, sadly, passed away suddenly. I was to enjoy a continued association through George Barclay, who later handled apprenticeship training matters - but one day I rang him up - and discovered he had retired. Other contacts were renewed most years when I received an invitation through my college to attend the Company Prize Day - and this continued until the company was finally returned to the private sector and I never received any other invites. A new Pharaoh had risen, who knew not Joseph.

The new company - now in the private sector, continues to be on the threshold of aerospace technology. It is, I believe, the largest single employer in Northern Ireland, and work progresses on two fronts - aero structures, (work on aerospace and associated engineering work, for other companies) and missiles.

*   *   *   *   *   *   *   *   *   *   *

Another Brief Visit to Musgrave Park Hospital
For the Fourth Time

Life went on after that operation to realign my leg - on into what is described later as the New Further Education era. Six years went by somehow, and then I started limping again. But to my consternation, the pain causing the limp was in my right foot. An x-ray, read locally, was interpreted as arthritis, and tablets were prescribed. After six months of this, I asked to see my Surgeon in Musgrave Park again, and when I eventually attended the Musgrave Park Hospital orthopaedic clinic - still held at the Waveney Hospital, Ballymena, I was somewhat surprised to learn that my Surgeon, the man in the white coat who stood discussing my case with Mr Baker at the bottom of my bed when I first entered Musgrave Park Hospital as a boy of nineteen, had retired and I wouldn't be seeing him again in this role. Mr Cowie would now look after me, and after the foot was x-rayed again, he held the x-ray up for examination.

"What is that line across the big toe joint?", I asked him.

"That is a fracture", he replied.

"How could such a thing happen - that's my good foot and leg?" I almost cried out.

"It can happen", the Surgeon replied, "when the good limb is perhaps overused - as for example when there is reluctance to use a damaged limb - the good one is called up to take extra load". "And what is that thing sticking up on the joint?" I further enquired.

"That's a piece of bone fragment", he again replied. "I'll have to take you in and remove it. That is what is causing the pain". And so once more, I was on the waiting list for Musgrave Park Hospital.

*   *   *   *   *   *   *   *   *   *

I had, as earlier related, taken up cycling, in the forlorn hope that it would "correct" in some way the pain in my knee which had eventually resulted from the misalignment. My interest in this was maintained and I became a member of East Tyrone Cycling Club, which was centred in Cookstown. My cousins belonged to East Tyrone. Later, in 1989, I became a founder secretary of the reformed Old Bleach Cycling Club, Randalstown, and in June of that year we held our first ten mile time trial on the Portglenone Road, Randalstown. It was on Monday 19th June 1989, and my time for that ten, was a modest 27 mins. 12 secs.

The next morning I entered dear old Musgrave Park Hospital for the operation to remove the offending bone fragment from the toe joint. I was prepared for Musgrave Park Hospital this time, with very little apprehension.

This visit was so different from the previous affair. I got a lift to Belfast, used a bus to get to Balmoral, and walked into Withers again.

The night before the operation, I made a pilgrimage - as I had done in 1982 to visit a Nissen hut, known to me as Ward 2B. I now made my way to that crossroads inside Musgrave Park corridors known as red square, and thence down what many of us used to call the "tunnel", the passage between the rows of Nissen wards. Then, over that characteristic of the route known as the "hump" close to a bend and familiar territory; I had arrived at 2B. It was being used at that time as a physiotherapy room or it may have been occupational therapy that was going on. But it was the same place - but no beds - a lot of seating - chairs etc. That place holds some memories for me, solid in my mind, when many other more recent ones, have failed to gain a foothold there.

Mr Cowie was to do a good job, and I was out in a week or so. I actually reported back to my college for duties just before term time ended for that year. I was now able to reflect upon how much propping up I had needed from Musgrave Park, to have enabled me to have lived such a very full life since that bleak winter when Mr Baker, filling me with hope, had told me, "Yes, you should be able to walk again, but we will have to give that bone some assistance". I was fairly soon mobile after the operation, and moving about on crutches, had got to know my neighbours. Round the corner was someone getting treatment to improve - if my memory is correct - the flexibility of his hand and therefore the ability to operate a clutch lever (or open a twist grip throttle). He was recovering from a recent accident, and his name was Joey Dunlop.

The gratitude that I feel towards Musgrave Park Hospital, and those Surgeons and Nurses who helped a lame dog over those stiles, is one that I hold in almost sacred trust and, it is never far from my waking thoughts. This is because, the small amount of pain that is part of my daily life, is a constant reminder of it being a small price to pay, for being able to live a reasonably normal life; it also reminds me of the pain, restriction, and consequences for life, had the attention and expertise that I received at Musgrave Park Hospital been missing.

With two young members of Ballymena Road Club - Colin Hughes, (Ballyclare High School), left, and Colin Deane, (Cambridge House Grammar School for Boys, Ballymena).

The re-formed Old Bleach Cycling Club, Randalstown (before our first time trial after the Club being re-formed) with Mr. James Graham, Mayor of Antrim. B C looking preoccupied - tomorrow I will be admitted to Musgrave Park Hospital for the fourth time. All will be well however. From right to left: B C, Alan Lee, Tommy Talbot, Martin McCormick, Tony McCusker, Wesley McFetridge, Stan Connolly, Martin Kennedy, John McNeill, Drew Murray. There are visiting cyclists from other supporting clubs in the background.

Cycling in Scotland.
From left: David Millar, B C and Martin McCormick.

Bob Cooper -
3rd Engineer Officer
MV "Lenamill"

The MV "Lenamill" ex "ARNGAST", Deep Sea Tug and one time tender to the German Battlecruiser, Scharnhorst.

A PART OF BALLYMENA DISAPPEARS

This view is from "my" window - now that one nearest the Cushendall Road. I would watch the nurses coming on duty each morning at 8 o'clock, from their accommodation - and through this front entrance to the Waveney.

The corner INSIDE the door to Ward 3, Waveney Hospital, where Mr. Hanna told me "You content yourself - you are going to be here a long time".

The bulldozer approaches - August 1996

Boxing Day 1996 - much of the Waveney has disappeared - only "my" wing remains - but it is apparent that it will be so not much longer. The large black object in foreground is the former hospital's water tank.

THE WAVENEY HOSPITAL BALLYMENA

Going, going,

gone

Aboard the "Fanad Head" - The Chief - John Kerr

Censored War Time Letter Card

John Kerr on his ninety-ninth birthday with friends of seafaring connections, Islandmagee Masonic Hall, August 1998.
Front row from left: BC, John Kerr, Eric Dunwoody, Patrick MacDonnell.
Middle row from left: Robt. Cromie, G. Deany, J. Stanley, B. Kane, J. Henderson, J. Walsh. Back row from left: J. Spiers, A. McDonald, J. Bothwell, J. McAuley, B. Ross, D. Young   Photo: Robin McIlwaine.
(See Page 228)

The forbidden photograph. One corner of the Seliwiye Barracks, Scutari, which is characterised by one such tower on each corner. The barracks became Florence Nightingale's hospital during the Crimean War, after which it reverted to become a military barracks once again except for the museum area as described.
(See Page 176)

My fellow apprentice in Shorts -
Raymond Gregg, B.Sc., C.Eng., M.B.C.S.

Tom Birch, Chief Engineer Officer, M.V. "Villegas"
(Photograph: Courtesy of Jim Bothwell, Master Mariner)

The ceremony at H.M.S. "Dolphin", Gosport, Portsmouth, when the bell of
the E11 returns from Canada. Three surviving crew members from the E11
during the epic journeys up the Dardanelles, are from left: Bill Wheeler, Bert
Cornish (former E.R.A.); fifth from left, George Harry Plowman (former leading
Signalman). (From George Harry Plowman's Collection). (See page 158).

BC and brother John

Mr Birch's reference: I have happy memories of this most agreeable man but I fear the typing was subjected to a few corrections before he handed it to me. Some remain - see Liverpool! These were the days before word processors or Tipp-ex!

Mac Andrew Line

m.s. " Villegas "

Port of Liverpool.

Aug. 18th 1975

To whom it may concern.

This is to certify that Mr. R. Cameron has served aboard the above vessel as 4th. Engineer for the period July 8th. to Aug. 19 th. 1975.

During this period he has been in charge of the main and auxiliary engines on watches of 8 hours in each 24 hour period at sea.

I have found Mr. R. Cameron to be a good mechanic, a conscientious worker and sober in his habits. I wish him well in his future employment.

1st. Class Motor 108100.

C/Eng

Machine shop in the "European Gateway"

*The Engine Room Console of the "European Gateway"
- a far cry from the SS "Grecian!"*

*The model of H.M. Submarine E11, made by George Harry Plowman D.S.M.,
during service as its leading signalman at the Dardanelles, 1915. It is now in Antrim. (Photo: Ronald Moffett) (See page 158).*

Chapter 11 - People of Interest (but for different reasons)

Bob Cooper - The Man who sailed with Miss Victoria Drummond, M.B.E.

Before I could become an engineering instructor with the then Ministry of Health and Social Services, I had to take an oath - it was a Civil Service job. I also had to pass a written test, and a trade test - the latter consisting of standard engineering workshop skills, especially fitting and turning. There were perhaps a dozen or more men being thus tested and the tests were supervised by, amongst others, two men - engineering instructors, both of whom I was to meet a couple of years later, when I was transferred as an engineering instructor - to Felden House Government Training Centre. I distinctly remember these two men, unobtrusively moving amongst us during that test. When I moved to Felden, they happened to be instructing in the workshop for which I was to be responsible and I was now to meet two very interesting gentlemen, distinguished in their own ways - and one was to link me to an epic that I had been unaware of, namely the remarkable life of Miss Victoria Drummond, the first British woman to serve as a Chief engineer at sea. He was Bob Cooper, and the story he told me has waited thirty years before I got around to research it.

The other man referred to, was Arthur Mulholland. Arthur taught blind men how to operate capstan lathes (and read a Braille micrometer). How my thoughts went back to those two blind men, who had been close by me, when I worked the old 3A Wards, during my first year of apprenticeship in Shorts. But there was something else of great interest to me about Arthur - he had sailed on quadruple steam as an engineering officer, on the China run. Reference has already been made to both these men in an earlier passage.

Through these two gentlemen, I was introduced to yet another interesting person, one Maxie Hunter, also an instructor at Felden House. For Maxie had sailed with, I believe, the Harrison Line, whose ships were identified with a large cross on the funnel and had names like the "Philosopher", "Tactician", "Politician" etc. Maxie, a fit and energetic type, sadly died a relatively young man, shortly after.

Bob Cooper had a story to tell. Men whose lives become exceptional, become so, because of the circumstances - often through no choice of theirs - into which they are assigned by fate. Such circumstances could be those occasioned by a life at sea - or by war, etc. Bob had been an engineer officer at sea after the war, and there, he had sailed with a woman as one of his fellow engineers - the remarkable Miss Victoria Drummond. In fact, she was his Second engineer, and they were on at least one motor vessel. Bob spoke of her outstanding knowledge and ability to set away a steamship, but certainly recalled the time when she found herself in difficult circumstances on a motor powered vessel. He told me that he, with previous motor experience had been able to give her a lot of timely help on this job. Bob was sailing as a Third Engineer (as evident now from his discharge book), although I cannot now remember that being discussed. And further to that comment above on Miss Drummond sailing on a motorship, I was later to find in the October of 1994 M.E.R. "Bulletin", that, quote, "In 1946 she passed the (then) Board of Trade's Second Class Motor endorsement examination, making her the first woman to hold a combined Second Class Certificate. She had held the Second's Certificate for steamships since 1926".

I recall how Bob told me - as he understood it, that Miss Drummond was the daughter of a man with substantial financial assets - I had a jumbled version in my head that this man may have been a Superintendent of the Blue Funnel Line, and as such, she may have been encouraged to tackle a life at sea. At any rate she was a Second engineer when Bob Cooper met her.

Shortly after I met this interesting man our ways were to part. Bob, and the machines on which he instructed - the automatics, were transferred to Knockmore Training Centre at Lisburn. Shortly afterwards, I also went to work in Lisburn - at Lisburn Technical College. Our paths unfortunately did not cross again. It had been my intention to get up to see him at Knockmore - I drove close to it every day, and Bob Cooper would be numbered among those "worth knowing". Before I could do so, I was told to my intense dismay, that Bob had become terminally ill, and had passed the Great Divide. How many things in this life, do we leave too late? Actually, this information was prematurely incorrect - as I have just recently found out. Bob died some time later, and naturally I didn't see him again.

Twenty-nine years passed before I got around to finding out who the female engineer really was, who had sailed with Bob Cooper. I was perusing some old numbers of the "Marine Engineering Review", when my attention focused on a brief announcement in their "Bulletin". It was headed "Victoria Drummond Award", and referred to the intention of the Merchant Navy and Air Line Pilots Association, to present an award every four years for an outstanding achievement by a woman member of the Association, to perpetuate Victoria Drummond's memory. It also referred to the notice in a "Bulletin", published a few months earlier, giving her obituary. I am grateful to the Institute of Marine Engineers Publication, the Marine Engineers Review, for permission to reprint this obituary. The traumatic events for which she was awarded the M.B.E. in 1941 took place on board the S.S. "Bonita" when 400 miles from land. Her biography by her niece, Cherry Drummond, the Baroness Strange, has been published by the Institute of Marine Engineers, on the one hundredth anniversary of her birth and is entitled, "The Remarkable Life of Victoria Drummond, Marine Engineer".

Victoria Drummond
Chief Engineer

It was with great regret that the Institute learnt of the death of Miss Victoria Alexandrina Drummond, M.B.E. who died on Christmas Day aged 94 at a Haywards Heath nursing home. Born on 14th October 1894, this grand character, a god-daughter of Queen Victoria, made her name as the only woman ever to serve as ship's engineer in the British Merchant Navy, later rising to Chief engineer on foreign flag ships. During her 40 years at sea Miss Drummond sailed virtually every route and saw action in the last war for which she was awarded her M.B.E.

She began her career with a five-year apprenticeship at the Caledon shipyard, Dundee before taking to the sea in 1922 as a junior engineer on a passenger ship. The sight of a woman in the engine room aroused great consternation at first, but it was not long before Miss Drummond, in the words of a Chief engineer, "had the crew eating out of her hand." More importantly, she had a way with engines. A colleague noted that she could get more speed out of a ship than anyone else. When asked how she managed this she said "Oh, I just talk nicely to them. You can coax or lead engines to do what you want; you must never drive them." It was this skill at her job, together with her bravery that earned her award in 1941. When her ship was attacked by a German bomber in mid-Atlantic she remained at her engine room post and unaided, helped save the ship by pushing the 'maximum speed from 9 to $12\frac{1}{2}$ knots.' Her M.B.E. citation called her devotion to duty "an inspiration to the ship's company". Following her retirement in 1962, Miss Drummond found time to take a great interest in the Institute and it was rare not to see her sitting in the back row of the Lecture Hall for the Tuesday evening meetings.

Miss Drummond joined the Institute on 4th October 1921, became an Associate Member in 1926, Member in 1953 and Fellow in June 1973. (With acknowledgement to Ocean Transport and Trading Ltd. for information.)

I.MAR.E. BULLETIN FEBRUARY 1979.

Upon reading this most interesting book, I was able to more accurately put together what meagre scraps of information were still retained in my memory. It is also interesting to compare what one perceives is the sequence of events - second or third hand and diminishing in accuracy amidst the mists of many years, and the account that appears in the book. For this reason, I have retained the misty account, and it shows the reason why writing history demands the most exacting research. Miss Drummond served a marine engineering apprenticeship in the Caledon Ship Works in Dundee and it would appear that her father had not any shipping interests, and her inclination for a marine career seems not to have originated from encouragement in her home. (She may have been encouraged by what she heard from the Foreman of the garage in which she worked prior to entering the Caledon Ship Works - he had been a Chief Engineer at sea). However, one evening, when awaiting a train at Dundee West Station, she was introduced to a Mr Wirtley, by a manager from her company. Now Mr Wirtley was a Director of the Blue Funnel Shipping Company, for whom, the Caledon built ships. "Come and see me when you have completed your apprenticeship", he said, "and I promise you a ship". Thus the Blue Funnel connection. (Sadly, when she contacted the Blue Funnel she discovered that Mr Wirtley had died, but Blue Funnel said, that they would substantiate the promise earlier given and she sailed on the S.S. "Anchises", as Tenth engineer). There is indeed also reference to a tug. Townsend of Leadenhall Street, offered a job - bringing over a tug from America. But that is the only information about a tug - in the book. The transition from steam to motor appears to have taken place when she got a job as "Assistant Engineer" in April 1944, on the M.V. "Karabagh". This would appear to have been a Fifth (junior) engineering position, as eventually she signed on as Fourth Engineer. References to officers from Northern Ireland mention a Mate called Warner, and a Chief Engineer from Donaghadee (Chief on the M.V. "Lenamill"). One thing is clear. Miss Drummond faced a lot of opposition at sea - it is probably quite true that she faced discrimination at the hands of Chief Engineers, Seconds and Skippers. Thus when Bob Cooper laboured the point, that he stepped in to help her when she found herself on unfamiliar ground in a certain motor ship, it is now clear that situations developed when such help was timely. Of great interest to me is her description of her apprenticeship days, and I was struck by her recalling three experiences which I have already described - as my own!

One, was the journey from her home to the railway station by cycle. Another concerned the construction of her toolbox. Thirdly, what the apprentices of the Caledon Ship Works talked about during their breaks:-

"We apprentices used to sit along the bench before the whistle went, and talk of things we were going to do when our apprenticeship was completed. Most, including me, were going to sea. One or two had already planned the Company they were going with." Thirty-six years later, apprentices in Shorts sat on that "long narrow bench" in the Comet Hanger, and had much the same things to talk about. (See pages 78 & 79).

My interest was now well and truly awakened and I decided I would try and make contact with Bob's relations.

After two weeks, and a chain of five contacts directing my search, I had the privilege of speaking by telephone to Mrs Cooper, Bob's widow, and shortly afterwards I was delighted to meet her.

She was well aware of Miss Drummond, as Bob had often spoken about her. Not only that, but she was able to name ships that her late husband and Miss Drummond had sailed on, together. As the book "Victoria Drummond, Marine Engineer", contains a list of her voyages, ships and dates, it seemed an easy matter now to identify the vessel, or vessels, on which they sailed together.

Now, there was in Belfast, until after the Second World War, a company which owned ships, and whose offices, I believe, were not far from Sinclair Seaman's Presbyterian Church - but these premises are now no longer in existence. The company was called Lenaghans. Shortly before my telephone call to her, Mrs Cooper had been sorting out some paperwork and had had occasion to lift her husband's Merchant Navy discharge book, and to my delight was able to quickly produce this prime source document. I there saw that Bob had sailed on one of Lenaghan's ships - the M.V. "Lenamill" in January 1948, and was still there a year later. His discharge book showed that he had signed up for his third trip (now as Third Engineer Officer) on 22nd February 1949; Victoria Drummond, had signed on as Second Engineer Officer two days previously - the 20th February 1949!

Miss Drummond's account of this trip highlights the type of animosity and resentment which she experienced from time to time.

She "did not like the Chief Engineer, who came from Donaghadee in Northern Ireland". She found the work on this boat hard and "the Chief was almost impossible to get on with". Later she told him to, "Stop it! I have had enough!" According to her account he replied, "I hate having you here, and I would not have done, if the owner had not insisted. So I will take it out on you all I can". This ties in very well with what my misty memory holds of my conversations with Bob - that he had been able to help her with her problems as he had by then been on the ship for over one year, and doubtless was quite familiar with all the engine room "gremlins". Mrs Cooper even recalled how Bob would sometimes find Miss Drummond in tears in the engine room. The problems emanated more from the personal, rather than the practical i.e. difficult people to work with. She had at that time her Motor endorsement to her Second's steam "ticket", and Bob had by all accounts, a high opinion of her engineering knowledge and ability - especially on steam.

The discharge book showed that Bob himself had had quite a varied and distinguished career on a number of ships, with world wide destinations, including some amazing cargoes - both human and general!

He sailed on the M.V. "Dundalk Bay". Miss Drummond also sailed on the same ship - but the dates don't agree - Bob having been on this ship some years before Miss Drummond, according to the book, was there. Yet, as I joined Mrs Cooper in conversation about Miss Drummond, she immediately reeled off the names of two ships which obviously had association with Bob and Miss Drummond - the M.V. "Dundalk Bay" and the M.V. "Lenamill". She too thought that both had served on a tug, although documents are silent regarding the tug, which other evidence suggests, was a vessel on which both worked. It is perfectly possible of course for someone to work on a ship and for a number of reasons an entry and discharge may not appear in a discharge book.

I am left wondering on what machinery both served on for Bob to acquire such a high opinion of her ability to "set away a steamship". I am almost sure, it was on triple expansion machinery, somewhere.

However, they both sailed on the M.V. "Lenamill", although Miss Drummond left the ship after it put into Trieste for lengthy repairs. This was trip number twenty-nine for Miss Drummond, and when she had finished with the sea, it was after voyage forty-nine! What can one say? A lady with immense marine experience, remarkable and unique.

Such contemplations as above leave me in a sense of some bewilderment, as to the value that our society places on things. Our press and media seem to concentrate on meaningless trivia, day by day (especially on Sundays). And wouldn't it be nice, if society adapted as their role models, the real people in our midst, those whose lives are ordinary in demeanour, but outstanding in what they have achieved, often against all odds and strife. I never cease wanting to quote Captain H. G. G. Stoker: "Happiness lies in the striving and not in the winning".

In epilogue

The MV "Lenamill" alias ML "Arngast"

Now around Islandmagee and Whitehead, live many with seafaring traditions. One night, I attended a barn dance in Islandmagee - literally set up in a barn - in order to raise money for a local church. It was, in the main, supported by members of the local Rambling Association. I saw a couple of former senior staff from Shorts there - but the sight that gladdened my heart was that of two burly sea captains, Jim Bothwell and Reg Rendall, taking the floor. The next morning Reg would fly to South Africa, to bring home a 60,000 ton tanker - Jim would likewise soon depart on a similar mission to the Gulf.

*   *   *   *   *   *   *   *   *   *

Some time later, I was telling Jim about Bob Cooper and the "Lenamill" and was "all ears" when Jim enlightened me, that the "Lenamill" had been a former German tug and owned by Lenaghans, the firm he had served his apprenticeship with. Not only that, but his friend Reg Rendall had recently presented Jim with a large framed photograph of the "Lenamill", derived from an advertising poster, which he had purchased somewhere - knowing Jim's interest in the former company. So that was the answer to the "tug" that Bob Cooper had worked on with Miss Drummond as his Second Engineer.

The "Lenamill" according to the information on the photograph, was the former German ice-breaking tug "Arngast", built by Blomn and Voss, the last to be built (in 1940) for the German Navy before the outbreak of war, and was a powerful vessel - of 1548 HP. The legend continued 'Deep sea salvage tug "Arngast", Yard No 737 (Stuicken), delivery 1940.' She was at one time, a tender to the German battle cruiser, Scharnhorst. The "Arngast" survived the war, operated under the new name of "Lenamill", was sold to a new company in 1950 - renamed "Wotan", and finally, after another twenty years service was wrecked in 1970.

You can't win them all!

*   *   *   *   *   *   *   *   *   *

The Man at the R.N.A.D. Antrim

The workshops of the Royal Naval Armament Depot, Antrim, where I was employed working on the Mark VIII Torpedo, lay but a short walk from the disused jetty on a bank of the Sixmilewater River and not far from where that river entered Lough Neagh.

One beautiful Friday morning in June, I forsook my usual companions of the morning break, and proceeded with my "cuppa", down to the jetty. It was indeed a beautiful morning, one might say, one without peer, with birds singing, and bees buzzing among the wild flowers near the water. As the river murmured along, its receding level had begun exposing the banks - something like a scene from Kenneth Grahame's "Wind in the Willows", and in particular the chapter entitled "The River Bank", where the poor Mole eventually fell into the river, and had to be rescued by the Water Rat.

While I was thus occupied enjoying the nature all around me, I was joined by someone, a man who worked in the factory. I regret that I don't seem to have found out who he was - his name or where he worked in the factory. It's such a pity, for he has left posterity with a legacy of mirth.

I noticed that he too was not unaware of the good things around him, and in particular he seemed to pay attention to the sky, finding it entirely clear and blue as he, shading his eyes from the glare of the sun, surveyed the horizon from East to West.

Eventually my companion of that morning spoke. "Do you know what I am going to tell you?" he challenged. I confessed my inability to meet such a challenge but with a reasonable amount of interest and curiosity. "Well", he pronounced, "if that weather sticks it, and I have my health and strength, I'll be on the sick on Monday!"

By the time that solemn and sincere intention had been delivered, it was the end of the breaktime. But I must have identified him to someone, because the following week, I was made aware that such and such a person was off "on the sick" - and apparently remained so, for a goodly time.

One can only conclude therefore, that this man was in very good "health and strength" and that we had a very good summer that year! But I had spent two and a half years - on the sick. Anyway, that's what the man said. The attitude was less unique than you would think, because some time later, while working in another department of the same employer, a dispute arose concerning the level of our wages, compared with those in the private sector. A commander R.N. made a point: "I cannot give you a rise in pay - that is controlled by the Whitley Council. But remember this, you have thirteen weeks extra leave - albeit sick leave - I cannot force you to take it, of course".

And that, is what that man said.

"I'll have a home, even if I have to work for it!".
Charlie Chaplin.

Chapter 12 - The Great Betrayal of the Further Education Lecturer
The traditional place of the technical college.

Technical Education traditionally occupied an honoured place in the structure of industry and commerce. Reference has already been made to the tremendous contribution of one such place - the College of Technology, Belfast. This is the name it was known by to my generation and to many before that. In addition to engineering students - mechanical, electrical, civil, and marine, there have been many others in the fields of commerce and business, textile, home economics, the arts etc. who found adequacy of education in the technical colleges. My generation thought in terms of the Junior or Senior Technical Certificate examinations, which, while featuring heavily on English, Maths and the Sciences, also took in one foreign language - and Art. For many, the practical subjects of technical drawing, engineering workshop practice and woodwork, would provide a life skill that would enhance their ability in general terms for the rest of their lives - even though their vocation may not have been connected to it. For myself, the entrance to this Mecca of possibility was by way of an examination in Arithmetic and English - at thirteen or fourteen years of age. Thirteen year olds had therefore the possibility of obtaining a Senior Certificate (equivalent to the old GCE 'O' level or thereabouts) and still be young enough to commence an apprenticeship in the skilled trades. When I commenced teaching in Lisburn Technical College, in 1967, entrants to this level of study were now eleven plus - they had passed the eleven plus examinations and were currently studying for 'O' levels and beyond. There were other students there, who were fifteen years of age. These students had passed an entrance examination to study for one year - largely along skills orientated lines. These classes were designated "Pre-apprentice Classes", and while some teachers would have preferred such students to have been more academically motivated, in retrospect this kind of course made significant contributions to the national education, and actually many of these former students, encouraged in practical orientation, are now captains of our industries, while others made their way into the professions. One of my acquaintance, eventually studied at Cambridge University.

The decline

Eventually, the option to enrol at a technical college through the eleven plus examination was withdrawn. In the same decade, the opportunity for fifteen year olds to enrol in a one year Further Education Pre-apprentice course was withdrawn as well. These were errors of the greatest magnitude, and our young people were denied the influence of the technical college environment - during their important formative years. Staff levels seemed to keep rising. But what were they to teach?

The "New" FE

Some technical colleges had always taken day release classes from industry - had I not been part of this myself? But, now, these classes, were in short supply, especially in the smaller colleges, and especially those that had failed to attract such day release, or failed to promote such, successfully. About the time under consideration, which I identify as around 1982, other changes had come along. Uniforms had already been done away with, and new people began appearing in the corridors. These were known as Y.T.P. (Youth Training Programme) students. Margaret Thatcher proclaimed that all sixteen year olds would be offered training - and they would not be entitled to their dole, £29/week, if they did not accept such training. I guess that the sociologists of education, now had a field day. To some of us, there was an uncomfortable feeling that the day of first name terms for teachers, and feet up on the desks, would soon be the order of the day. There were many meetings, to discuss what was called the "New F.E." Teachers were invited to all sorts of workshops, to be indoctrinated into new ways of viewing future 'students'. I remember attending one such high powered meeting for those of us about to move up to the front. A person from the Department of Inspection, Northern Ireland Ministry of Education, took the floor, and started a lecture which he entitled "The Philosophy of Y.T.P.". As he warmed to this earth shattering topic, he became overheated, and asked to be excused while he divested himself of some garments. As I sat through this event, my thoughts turned to Stan Pacer of the SS "Grecian", or Leslie Webb, with whom I worked on the "Comet II", Lionel Palmer and Billy Taggart my mentors in Centre 30 - others, and it was then that I realised how fortunate I had been in life, to have worked with so many down to earth, sane, sensible people.

The "New F.E." was a disaster. Other people now arrived as students in Further Education. These were what was known as Link classes - day release students from secondary schools. In the main, these appeared to come from classes not intent upon pursuing much in the line of academic achievement. It was presumed that they would relish practical work, in further education. They didn't.

One of the saddest moments in my experience came one day, when I heard a college principal say (throwing his hands in the air). "We are no longer our own masters - we have to do what the D.E.D. says!" I later understood that the D.E.D. did subscribe towards the wages of lecturers appointed to Y.T.P. positions. By the same token, when the Y.T.P. numbers declined, the D.E.D. funding declined as well. This of course provided redundancies among such teachers. As well, an offer was extended to all teachers (provided that they had been born early enough), to "get out of it", with enhanced early pension, etc. It was an exit, that many were glad to seize and thus depart. There is little doubt in my mind, that the severe stress of being asked to do the impossible, probably led to permanent illness and an end to the careers of some teachers and to many accepting the opportunity to "get out" - many who had prepared well to enter teaching, and who had brought to the classroom maturity in industrial know how - which can be acquired in no other way, than by having been in industry to acquire it. Speaking about the importance of having people with practical experience around, Sir Stanley Hooker (the man who "put the power" into the Rolls Royce Merlin engine) says in his autobiography: "My later experience with Rolls Royce showed me that no university course could possibly compare with the knowledge gained by rubbing shoulders with experienced, practising engineers., actually doing the job in a factory".

I leave FE with no regrets

For myself, I was glad to take up what was offered, and in 1990 I ran like a hare on four wheels for the gate, shaking the dust of my feet thereof. But I was sad, that so much collective technical expertise and experience across Northern Ireland, was now withdrawn in one form or another from the system in the shape of early retirements through created redundancies etc.

"For a day in thy courts is better than a thousand. I had rather be a doorkeeper in the house of my God, than to dwell in the tents of wickedness." Psalm 84 v 10.

* * * * * * * * * *

New opportunities in education

Someone's loss, is often another's gain. Happily for me, it was to be gain. My departure from further education opened-up areas of considerable interest to me.

I worked in a number of Grammar Schools in Co. Antrim and Belfast - in particular, Cambridge House Grammar School For Girls, Ballymena. This excellent school appeared to me to be a good place to be for both pupils, and staff. Many of the latter travelled long distances to be there. I was very happy to work there, and will always remember the kindness with which I was received by both pupils and staff.

But of great personal satisfaction to me has been the other work I became involved in - teaching young people laid off school through illness. This is varied - from good old fashioned broken legs to degrees of illness approaching the terminal. The Ward 2B's of the past, are still as full as ever, today.

Our environment shapes us, and makes us what we are. Would I be so interested in the rehabilitation of students, had I, my studies and my career, not taken such a set back that day on a road outside Ballymena?

Some time ago while engaged in this work of teaching those students absent from school through illness, I found myself passing the Waveney Hospital several times each week. As it was obviously being prepared for demolition, I made a nostalgic visit to my early "residence", (and in the following weeks, a photographic record of its demise.) I found it closed up - virtually in mothballs - just like the S.A.4 when I first saw it sitting at the airport at Shorts. But as well, a high angle iron fence was in the process of being erected to deter vandals etc. The words of the poem came to mind as memories flooded back - the wedging of the plaster, the regimented ward rounds, nurses etc.

> *I feel like one who treads alone some banquet-hall deserted,*
> *Whose lights are fled, whose garlands dead, and all but he departed!*
> *Thus, in the stilly night, ere slumber's chain has bound me,*
> *Sad memory brings the light of other days around me.*

Lines from: "The Light of Other Days" - Thomas Moore

The Waveney had been sold to private developers - I understood that it was being converted into residential or nursing home accommodation for the elderly. I had not been in Ward 3 since that day Mr Hanna said "You can now go home for a while - nothing much is happening". Now I was curious to see inside the former hospital, and eventually I arrived one day when the workmen were there, pulling a lot of it apart. I walked into Ward 3, and immediately looked into the corner behind the door where, all those years ago - over thirty-five - Mr Hanna had told me "You content yourself - you're going to be here a long time". I was able to remember clearly, where this one and that one had lain in bed - the corner nearest the Cushendall Road where I had spent the last three months and where, through the radio headphones, I had heard of the death of Austin Carson. Then into the theatre, where that 'wedging' of the plaster had taken place - without anaesthetic! A final look into Ward 3 - and I was gone - what memories. The Waveney has since been demolished.

* * * * * * * * * *

One morning, I was ascending the marble like stairway of a certain prestigious grammar school in South Belfast, on my way to a class during an assignment there. I was stopped by a greeting from another ex-F.E. lecturer going to his class - someone who had been a Head of Department in Lisburn Technical College. Taking me by the lapel of my coat, he made a profound statement: "Wasn't what took place, an awful betrayal of the lecturer in F.E.? What a dumping ground they made of us."

I couldn't have put it better myself!

We attend a wedding.

With Ian and Moyna, Bulgaria 1979.

Ian, "Jessie" and Moyna.

Ian, Jean and Moyna at the Black Sea.

At the River Jordan: Jean, Owen (of the Odessa incident at the back), and Mark, his cousin hiding.

The "Potemkin Steps" Odessa, 1973.

→

My companion, Owen, took this forbidden view of the "Potemkin Steps" looking toward the sea. At this period during the Brezhnev era, this, if observed by the authorities, would have been enough offence to merit detention and likely arrest. Such a person - especially a Westerner - could then have been exchanged for a U.S.S.R. citizen being held in a Western country for, e.g. spying.

The "Potemkin Steps" Odessa, 1973.

Adult evening classes at Antrim Technical. Tommy Bryson (the Shell tanker man) and in whose squad I worked as an apprentice in the tool room in Shorts. Note his magnificent model steam engines. He seems to be reminding me of some incident in Centre 20 in those long off days. George McFadden, who once shared my work on the Mark VIII torpedoes, at R.N.A.D., is listening carefully.

Piping the French into dinner. The 25th Anniversary Dinner of the Nancy Quest Rotary Club (with guests). Mr. John McKee welcomes his guests as Club President. Founder of the McKee Institute in Nancy where English is taught to French businessmen, John McKee was educated at Rocavan Primary School, Ballymena Academy and Queen's University.

With my sister Mrs. Audrey McClean (now M.B.E.) and my daughter Moyna (now M.A. Hons) at my OU Graduation, 1985.

"I don't know what it's like at the top, Sir Philip, but its rough near the bottom".
(with Sir Philip Foreman)

*An Ancestor of the Harrier, this P1127 is photographed as the gate guard
at Dunsfold Aerodrome, Surrey, but is now at Brooklands Museum.*

*At Dunsfold Aerodrome, Surrey.
Taylor Scott (left) and John Yoxall,
with two seat Harrier in the background.*

An RAF Britannia, showing freight door.

*The SC1 in vertical flight
and independent of the gantry.*

*Richard G. Spencer, former test pilot,
Short Bros. & Harland Ltd., Belfast*

*Back: James McClean, B.C., Mother, May (Mrs. Yoxall)
Front: Audrey (Mrs. McClean), Moyna, Jean, John Yoxall*

With some charming girls at Cambridge House Grammar School for Girls, Ballymena.
From left, back row: Judith Kirkpatrick, Isla Graham, Laura McAuley, Louise Ward, Lynsey Harris, B.C.,
Mr. Alistair Law (Head of Technology Department), Victoria Green, Laura Adair, Joanne McAleese, Rachel Douglas.
From left, front row: Alison Hamilton, Diane Agnew, Laura Adger, Angela Glendenning. Photo: Jim McCaw

Some young students, to whom I gave
home tuition during recent illness.
From left: Ian Harvey (Cambridge House Boys, Ballymena), Heather
Pitts (Ballyclare High School), Lisa McErlean (St. Patrick's Ballymena).
The Buccaneer bomber in the background actually flew into Langford
Lodge - to take its place in the Ulster Aviation Society Museum.
Photo: Ronald Moffett

Robert Arrell (former engineering apprentice, see page 165)
and his daughter Alison, a student at
Cambridge House Grammar School for Girls, Ballymena
(Photo: Mrs. Edna Arrell)

Chapter 13 - Some Recollections and Philosophies for Living

A brief review of events and consequences

I had a serious accident at probably the worst possible time in my life - in the middle of an engineering apprenticeship and planned technical education.

My subsequent recovery, while not without heartbreaking set backs, allowed me to return to these channels of learning after a period of two and a half years.

That recovery, was, within certain parameters, sufficient to surmount many of life's hurdles in order to earn my daily bread, while placing an exclusion order on others - some faculties were gone. I have always seen, in a somewhat humorous way, an analogy with what Pasteur said of the Scriptures: "They are light enough for my path, and obscure enough to keep me humble". People suffering defects after illness or injury, sometimes have to be humble in a physical way - and "cut the suit according to the cloth". Having said that, such deficiencies can be modified by pulling out the stops at times, and "running", while others walk.

My subsequent career in engineering had to do with cold materials and frantically moving pieces of machinery. In teaching technical subjects I was able to pass on to another generation of young men some of the experience gained in a life that had some variety, some danger, some travel - and seen many, many different examples of human nature. Then that was over, and later one morning, the charming girls of Cambridge House Grammar School for Girls in Ballymena, found that a new technology teacher had arrived to take their classes for a time.

It was here I discovered that so much water had "flowed under the bridge", that I was teaching my second generation in a family. One of my students, Miss Alison Arrell, was the daughter of Robert, one of my second group of engineering apprentices undergoing training at Antrim, and who appears in the photograph of this group. (I might say that I observed this thing that had come to pass with mixed feelings!)

It has been mentioned, that necessity brought about my interest in cycling, and this was to open up for me the opportunity to meet a wonderful bunch of guys from various clubs, and a lot of encouragement as well - in fact from all my friends in the Northern Ireland Cycling Federation.

The photographs show some of my young friends with whom I shared much interest in cycling, and others with whom I share traditional music. There is that other more serious aspect of work - teaching those, who like myself all those years ago, are unable through illness, to receive normal education for a time. I currently meet a wide cross section of our young people in my work here - illness is not a respecter of any class.

* * * * * * * * * *

What the man in the I.N.O. said:

Speaking of our throwaway society, I can now complete a reference made earlier to lunch papers. I was working for the Ministry of Defence - as already recalled - on inspection duties, and had been sent to Short Bros. to do some work, where I had perhaps, the upwards of twenty colleagues with me in the Naval Ordnance Inspectorate. One day, as we finished our lunches, and put away the cups, some of us found ourselves addressed by one of our number - a person by the name of Frank Hutley. He was, interestingly enough, the brother of Eric, with whom I had worked on the "Swift", all those years before.

"I have been watching you men", he said, pulling heavily on his cigarette, "and it is easy to see those of you who have been brought up to be careful with what you have - and waste nothing - and those of you who do otherwise". We all looked around at the source of this philosophical pronouncement, this source having seated himself upon a high table, before delivering his edict like utterance. You can imagine a scene where each of us in turn was placing a pointing finger to our breasts and saying "Is it I?" Eventually Frank was asked to explain the nature of his inspiration.

"Well", he said, "I was watching you in turn finishing your lunch, and I simply noted those of you who carefully smoothed your empty lunch papers, folded them and placed them in your pockets - and then, those of you who left them lying behind you, or threw them into the bin. It's as simple as that". I certainly was brought up not to waste anything - in fact I don't recall having had much to waste, my childhood having been spent during wartime restrictions. A prevailing ethos at that time was "Look after the pennies - and the pounds will look after themselves".

What the Chief Engineer had to say

But some credit must go to another source - what the Chief Engineer of the SS "Rathlin Head" had to say about waste. One day in some port or other, I had just finished renewing a joint between two flanges. I was cleaning up and was about to throw the small cuttings of the joint material into the local bin, when I heard someone bellowing from afar. Looking around I perceived the Chief Engineer, no less, making his best rate of knots in my direction. Picking up the small pieces of joint material - I fear some had already made their way into the bin, he said "Never, never, throw pieces like that away - even the small bits. They could save your life some day".

He was perfectly right. Eventually all the large pieces would be used, and in an emergency - the small pieces might do the job - stop a leak somewhere etc. Better stopping that, than a tear - "Waste not, want not", he said. That Chief had something else to enlighten me on, when he and I exchanged views on the suitability or otherwise of a certain officer on board the ship. I had been saying that in the time I had known him, he had been a good sort. The Chief had reservations. "Young man", he said, "It might be a bit ignorant to say it to you, but you never know anybody until you sleep with them!" There was more than a grain of truth in what he said. In fact, he was saying that it takes a very long time to get to know someone. During this time, that person has to be assessed - not only over social niceties or lifting the collection at church - but under pressure - when looking over the shoulder! Perhaps the Chief was reflecting that sometimes you don't know some people until the knife, that they have taken years to work through your back - comes out the front. By that time a lot of damage has been done - behind your back - of course (naturally of course).

There are more ways of robbing a man than by putting your hand in his pocket.
And a truth that's told, with bad intent, beats all the lies, you can invent.

The Chief would, of course, have concerns on his mind about safety, and safe routines, and having sufficient back up in order to deal with emergencies. When lives are at risk, one cannot have the "luxury" of chopping and changing procedures as is often done in - a teacher's world, for example. In ordinary every day life, guide lines have been handed down by earlier generations - indeed from time immemorial, on the consequences of changing for the sake of change - which is the philosophy of the change battalion of the flat earthers. Yet how often have wise people, who having learned a thing or two, told us to "leave well enough alone". Yet dabbling about with things and routines is a fatal attraction for some people. (I suppose the remedy comes with advancing years).

What a fitter said to me

Harry Lyttle was a fitter at the Royal Armament Depot, Antrim. At the time I worked there, he was involved in bench testing the engines of the Mark VIII torpedo. Reference has already been made to this amazing piece of technology, thought to have emerged in its final development in 1927. Two of the Mark VIII's sank the Argentine cruiser "General Belgrano" off the Falklands in 1982 (The "Belgrano", was the ex- U.S.A. Navy cruiser "Phoenix" - a survivor of Pearl Harbour). The remarkable engine of each torpedo overhauled, was given a bench test to check the Brake Horse Power - which was probably equal to four or five Ford Fiestas, a Froud Dynamometer being used. Harry was a cheery sort, he had come from Kellswater, and, as a boy, remembered an uncle of mine, John Cameron, setting off in a horse drawn trap for Kellswater Railway Station - the first of a journey that was to take him across Canada. I have been told that it was common practice for such travellers to stand on the carriage buffers, if they couldn't afford a fare, and I understand that my uncle was not so blessed as to afford a fare. From time to time I consulted Harry on a great many things, and now, I had acquired my first car - that black Austin A30.

For no good reason other than advancing miles, I decided that the A30 required serious maintenance, and mentioned to Harry that I was going to remove the cylinder head and grind the valves. Harry was listening to me as he carried out an odd adjustment here and there on a Mark VIII engine.

"How is she going?" he eventually asked me. "Oh, she is not going too badly", I replied. Harry then stopped what he was doing, and looking at me said, "Would you bother then?"

As far as I know, the valves on that A30 are still waiting to be ground! Leave well enough alone. Change should take place when things are not well.

What the Roadman said to me.

I have spoken of that journey from Antrim to home, which we people of the hills had to make each evening - by bicycle in the early days of my apprenticeship. One night I had the company of Bob Irvine, a neighbour, employed by the local council on roads maintenance. There was ample opportunity for wide ranging chat - during the hour or so that was spent making our way up the three miles of hills. The chat on this occasion related to the daft things some people got up to, and Bob made a statement matched only for its brevity by its deftness in hitting the nail on the head. He said that "the want of an arm or leg, was nothing, compared to the want of common sense!" Bob did not learn that at university - because he hadn't been to university. But he had been in the College of Life, and had taken careful note of what was going on there!

On Encouragement

Often it is the helpful encouragement of others, who make it difficult not to respond. In my early apprenticeship I had Len Palmer, the fitter from Lisburn, who had served in the Great War, Billy Taggart, James McDowell others. But it was help of a different kind I needed at the time when Mr Baker, the orthopaedic Surgeon said "Yes, Cameron old boy, you should be able to walk again - but we will need to give that bone some help". Then the occasion when on my first engine room watch on a steamer, the gauge glass blew up, and the Second engineer said, "I'll just stay behind and help you with it". (A small thing perhaps for him, but it meant a great deal to me).

Many years later, well into my teaching career and on one of my summer forays to sea during vacation time, I had taken a watch on the cargo liner, M.V. "Villegas". (That trip is described elsewhere). My donkeyman/greaser was Alec Clark, who came from Liverpool. The first watch took us into the channel, and during that time Alec, upon hearing that I came from Northern Ireland, informed me that he visited Belfast from time to time. He also told me that he was a Catholic, and that he had friends (I think this meant relations) up the Falls Road, in Belfast.

Generally I always found that Liverpool men - from I was first acquainted with them, tended to identify with their faith, more so than other regions, including Scotland.

Twenty- four hours later, the "Villegas" was ploughing heavily into the Biscay waves as I entered the engine room - and I began to feel "bad". Now the "Villegas" was the first ship I had seen with a telephone cubicle and - a chair - this was certainly a first. After twenty minutes, I was glad of that chair. Alec could see I was "under the weather" and just said "You hang in there - I'll keep my eye on the job". Alec turned out one of the finest men I was ever privileged to work with, and I had a very good time with him, as my greaser, on that trip. Later, in Liverpool, his wife came down to see him and knowing I had a camera, he asked me to take a photograph of them. I had run out of flash bulbs, but coming through the docks, I had noticed the SS "Carrigan Head" lying not far away and whose Chief Engineer I knew to be one Henry Carson from Kellswater. He had been at the local school with my father, and was the same Henry Carson, whom that fitter had spoken about on the old MV "Inishowen Head". I thither repaired and Henry Carson (Big Henry as he was known) upon hearing who I was, said that if there was a flash bulb on board the "Carrigan", I would get it. (Incidentally, Henry Carson would have been at school with Uncle John, at Tullanamullan, Kellswater).

And so it turned out. I took the photo of Alec and his wife and later sent it to Liverpool. Such a good companion when you needed one. Soon I would be back in a classroom, and Alec, sadly, a ship that passed in the night. But his simple act of taking a bit of load off me has found a place in my memory and this record.

Ships that pass in the night,
        And speak each other in passing,
Only a signal shown and a distant voice in the darkness,
        So on the ocean of life,
We pass and speak one another
        Only a look and a voice -
The darkness again and silence.

Henry Wadsworth Longfellow (The Theologian's Tale)

*   *   *   *   *   *   *   *   *

Lest We Forget

The event that had wide reaching consequences. -
The sinking the SS "Bengore Head":

Since this book was written in its original form, one of my close friends, and an acquaintance of many years, passed away a few days after having attained his one hundredth birthday. He was John Kerr, late of Whitehead and Islandmagee, the former Chief Engineer Officer of the SS "Fanad Head" and whose jocular manner caught my attention all those years ago during the lay up of the SS "Rathlin Head". Needless to say, the occasion of his one hundredth birthday had been marked by a great gathering of his friends and many of his former seafaring colleagues, at a venue close to the "Island". But his ninety-ninth birthday had also been celebrated in some style, at a dinner hosted in Islandmagee Masonic Hall when again friends came from far and wide to join in a memorable occasion. As John arrived at the hall to be piped in with due ceremony and wearing his World War II decorations (something he rarely did) he remarked to me that he had received a phone call before he left his home that evening: "I think there is some German connection", he said.

He was referring to a phone call made by someone who had read an account of the evening's proposed activities in the press, and had telephoned John to tell him that he had recently spoken to the radio operator of the German submarine U110 (the submarine which sank John on the SS "Bengore Head" in 1941). This was a phone call from Mr Kenneth Boyd, Portadown.

This radio operator had been, with the rest of the crew, ordered to abandon the U110 after it had been forced to the surface with depth charges. In doing so, however, he left behind something which arguably, set in motion a sequence of events that changed the history of the battle of the Atlantic. John Kerr watched the event from the deck of a trawler which had rescued him - the "St. Appollo".

Upon recalling the events of that day in 1941, opportunity is afforded to reflect once again of the debt we all must surely owe to the men whose duty it was to sail in the dreadful waters of the North Atlantic during the Second World War. John Kerr was to make ninety-one return trips on the North Atlantic.

In the course of my reminiscence I recalled the loss of the "Athenia" (sunk by Lieut Lemp in the German U-30), the badge of the "Athenia", shown to me by Molly Clark (Nee Rainey) and the shipwreck of my old friend John Kerr, from Whitehead, following the sinking of the SS "Bengore Head", on May 9th 1941.

Lieut. Julius Lemp was the commander of the U-Boat which sank both ships, but the sinking of the "Bengore Head" started a chain of events that arguably had far reaching consequences on the outcome of the Battle of the Atlantic - and possibly shortened the War by two years.

The "Bengore Head" was one of about forty ships in a convoy (UB318) heading for North America. The convoy was sailing in ten rows - the "Bengore Head" being the leading ship in the third row from starboard. She was carrying, as John Kerr remembered, a load of rope, from Belfast Rope Works.

Lieut. Julius Lemp was now in command of U110 and was in contact with the convoy during the morning of May 9th 1941, closing and firing three electric torpedoes at 11.37 am.

All torpedoes found a target, one of which was the Ulster Steamship Company's SS "Bengore Head". All members of the crew were rescued, except the galley boy, lost when jumping into a life boat.

The escorts under Commander Baker-Cresswell, were quickly on the scene, and depth charges from HMS "Aubretia" and HMS "Broadway" forced the U110 to the surface, Lemp having given the order to abandon the submarine. The "Broadway" had approached so close, that the U-boat's stern hydroplane damaged her plating, causing an oil leak.

This latter event, ie the ramming of U110, has significance, as it hastened those still below - in the German submarine, including the wireless operator and radio petty officers, to rapidly abandon ship. In so doing, they omitted to carry up with them, the secrets of the German signalling system - the Enigma M-3 and the priceless Signal Logs, ciphers, current tables for use in setting the Enigma keys (the Enigma was, in appearance, like a typewriter - but much more sophisticated and complicated), and various codes.

It is possible, that Lemp may have tried to board the submarine again, as he realised that she could be captured if not scuttled - he was not one of the survivors, eventually picked up by Royal Navy vessels.

Although the U110 eventually sank under tow, the priceless haul of the secrets of the German U-boat code system was captured intact, a result of which was the rapid deciphering of German signals by the British naval cryptanalysts, and thereafter in large measure success in cracking most U-boats signals, resulting in the re-routing of convoys around the U-boat packs and ultimately to the defeat of the U-boats in the Atlantic, their supply tankers, and U tankers.

Germany paid a heavy price for that salvo of torpedoes - one of which sank the "Bengore Head".

Thus Lieut. Lemp provides a connection between Molly Rainey's badge, John Kerr and what King George VI described at a subsequent investiture (the award of the DSO to Sub Lieut Balme, leader of the boarding party on the U110) at Buckingham Palace as "the most important single action of the war at sea".

Sadly Molly has now also passed away.

*   *   *   *   *   *   *   *   *   *

Eternal Father, strong to save,
Whose arm doth bind the restless wave,
Who bidd'st the mighty ocean deep
Its own appointed limits keep;
O hear us when we cry to thee
For those in peril on the sea.

William Whiting 1825 - 1878

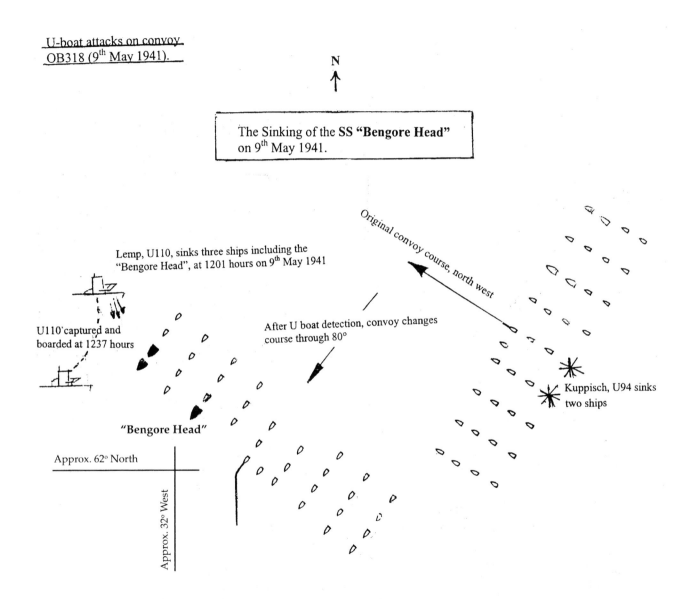

N

The Sinking of the SS "Bengore Head"
on 9th May 1941.

Original convoy course, north west

Lemp, U110, sinks three ships including the
"Bengore Head", at 1201 hours on 9th May 1941

After U boat detection, convoy changes
course through 80°

U110 captured and
boarded at 1237 hours

Kuppisch, U94 sinks
two ships

"Bengore Head"

Approx. 62° North

Approx. 32° West

230

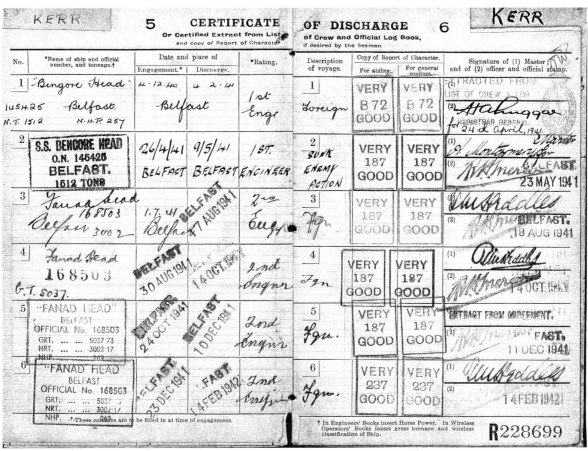

An extract from John Kerr's discharge book. Note the date of discharge from the SS "Bengore Head" - the 9.5.1941, the date of sinking. In general, pay stopped on the day a Merchant Navy ship was sunk.

Georg Högel the Enigma operator who has visited Northern Ireland in recent years - Georg Högel, the former Radio Operator of the German submarine U110 which torpedoed the "Bengore Head". Now living in Bonn, he is pictured at the Battle of the Atlantic, V.E. Day Memorial Service in Lisahally, Londonderry 1995. He has appeared in a television documentary of recent years - recalling events as he abandoned the U110 - and the enigma principles.

Photo: Kenneth Boyd, Portadown.

During my years in Further Education, probably the most worthwhile innovation to the status quo came about in the work's experience programmes, which became available for those in their final year - a one week placement for such students in a working environment. It helped students compare a vision of what they believed was the ideal occupation for them with the reality, as placement was made as closely as possible to what, by and large, they wanted to be involved in - although by the nature of opportunities available, this was not always possible, chapter and verse. Eventually, such opportunities became available for teachers in the "Return to Industry" schemes, where a teacher spent a week in industry during term time.

It is not unusual to see Headmasters and Headmistresses nowadays, spending a full year participating in such schemes. My time for participating in the return to industry weeks, came in the 1980's. I was placed in various environments, and since I was engaged in careers work as part of my teaching timetable, on one occasion I spent some time in Belfast, seeing how Manpower Services organised opportunities for the unemployed, including school leavers. As already mentioned, I spent some time on a cross channel roll-on roll-off ferry, the M.V. "European Gateway" on the Larne Cairnryan run. It was a great opportunity to see how technology had moved on, with modern engine rooms equipped with console, where what was happening could be monitored in relatively sound proof conditions. Ear plugs were the norm, when an engineer went "outside" - into the engine room for some reason. (It puzzles me nowadays, to compare the measures taken in industry to protect one's hearing, yet nothing seems to be done in the world of modern entertainment to give protection from loud music etc).

I remember another "works experience" with a sentimental touch, because I had an opportunity to spend some time with Ellerman Papayanni Lines, Liverpool. But Fergie Brand was gone as was Mr Davy - even Fergie Brand's successor as Superintendent Engineer, Mr Miller, was gone as well - victim of a heart attack. I was sent up to the King George V dry dock in London to work on the M.V. "Sangro" a small but beautiful ship of the Ellerman Wilson Line and as such, was normally on the Scandinavian run. During my time there, the death was announced of Sir John Ellerman, who was Chairman and owner of the Ellerman empire. I met some great characters there, including Mr Pallister, the Chief during the dry docking. A most affable man, I remember that at the time I was there, he was reading a book called "The Mark of the Mason", and usually at lunch time, he would "turn over" what he had read the previous night. One day just after the "Sangro" came out of dry dock and was preparing for the river transit to Millwall Docks, he was showing me some features of the main engine. Now the "Sangro" was at that time a very modern piece of machinery with bridge control of the main engine, and variable pitch propeller etc. (I became familiar with AC switch gear and got a lot of practice putting alternators "on the board", synchronising the phases and cycles etc.) Mr Pallister was showing me things like the "Amot" valves - with automatic thermostat control on cooling systems. He was then showing me the sensors which were essential for the remote bridge control of the main engine. I queried some point, and made to point out the component being queried. As my pointing finger reached out, Mr Pallister, nearly took a heart attack as we say. "Don't touch, -don't touch!" he cried, "She stopped outside Gothenburg a couple of weeks ago, and we couldn't get the engine started for two days". (There had been difficulty in overriding the remote control sensors). This was the interface of new technology, and the engineers were having to learn new techniques.

* * * * * * * * *

So the "Sangro" sailed away and eventually I received a card from Ralph, one of my fellow standby engineers - from Istanbul. I was given accommodation, before returning to class room duties, on an Ellerman ship close by. This ship was none other than the MV "Flaminium", a ship I had last seen "going very fast" as I thought as she passed the SS "Rathlin Head" in the Alexander Dock, Liverpool, when I first docked there in the "Rathlin Head", many years before! Another blast from the past.

Apart from updating technology, experiences like this dry docking provided tremendous opportunities to expand one's social horizons - I was making a small part of my life in terms of time into something substantially large - I seem to remember every detail of what we did and what people said to me, on these escapades. The memory is, as remarked upon elsewhere, very selective. By contrast, much of my teaching experience has vanished from the "screen". I was not the only teacher in Northern Ireland to spend part of vacations on marine engineering activities. I knew several who did - most of whom - perhaps all, had at least one "ticket", and all in Further Education. I have carefully analysed the possible reasons for such activities. I suppose a few extra pounds gave one a comfortable feeling (and I enjoyed the sun - once off the Portugal coast.) But perhaps another reason was summed up by Sir Francis Chichester. Edward Heath, the former Premier, recalled talking to Chichester after the latter had sailed single handed around the world. "I asked Francis Chichester", said Heath, "what makes a man of sixty-seven, already famous as an aviator/explorer - want to do such a thing?" Chichester replied, "Because it increases the intensity of living". Incidentally, I happened to be at Portsmouth the day Sir Alex Rose sailed into the harbour, after he too, had sailed around the world single handed shortly after Chichester. I think what is still incredible about these feats, is the advanced ages of both men. Rose was, I believe, only slightly younger. He had served during the war with the Royal Navy as an E.R.A. (Engine Room Artificer).

*   *   *   *   *   *   *   *   *

Well, I have come to the end of my reminiscence. It started that day when I entered the machine shop of Short Bros. & Harland Ltd., Queen's Island, Belfast, and has been largely about this firm and Musgrave Park Hospital, both places very central to my life. I have tried to set down how life is different for those of us who, for one reason or another, spend long periods in hospital or other places of convalescence - and then rejoin the march of every man sometimes just "hanging in there" and picking up the "revs", eventually. But once badly injured in some part of the body, one is never the same, There are painful restrictions, no matter how careful one is to conceal them, and putting one's "best foot forward", means exactly that - literally.

In World War Two, Peter Cremer was the commander of the German U-Boat, U333. In his autobiographical work, "U333: The story of a U-Boat Ace", he tells of the time when he was severely injured, and his crippled U-boat could barely crawl back to base. Eventually he returned to the war in U333, on a patrol in the North Atlantic. This is what he has to say:

"Strangely, on that long patrol I discovered once and for all what courage is. A fighting man will allow matters to come to the crunch and accept the risks - and is usually buoyed by the feeling: it won't happen to me. But once he has been marked as I had (and possesses wound badges in black and silver) and, barely recovered, returns to the fight, then things look different: he has experienced wounds and pain and knows that he can suffer the experience again at any moment. He knows that imminent death is not merely possible but indeed probable. To carry on regardless requires real courage. I am not applying this particularly to myself. It is assumed as a matter of course that a professional fighting man is ready to sacrifice himself. At any rate that was the case in those days, and especially among officers."

From time to time in the life of a teacher or, in the lives of those in industry, the vexed questions of conditions of service - pay increases, hours worked, promotions etc, exercise many minds. Following a week in which such things were prominent, I had that interesting little experience at church one Sunday morning, referred to earlier. We were repeating the Lord's Prayer, and had got to that part which says "give us each day our daily bread", when my mind riveted on this request, to the exclusion of all the rest. I was simply struck by the simplicity of what was being asked - not a step up the ladder, rises in pay or changed conditions but - bread. Thus at face value, it asked for the reassurance, that the harvest wouldn't fail. Now if such a material interpretation is allowed and considered, this portion means a great deal more. It, de facto, must imply physical and mental health to earn that bread, in this increasingly complicated world - to cope, and earn one's living. Many are unable to do this. I know only too well, that for far too many, these are not problems - because unemployed people don't have the dignity of earning bread. I wish that were otherwise because low self esteem often flows in a structure perpetuated by external factors - and over which an individual has little influence. This simple spiritual experience continues to hold significance for me. In my case as well, perhaps my sub conscious thoughts were reminding me, that the difference between not being able to earn one's bread - through being bedridden, or in a wheelchair, and being able to earn that bread, is sometimes very small indeed. Some injured and ill people just crawl "over the line". I certainly remembered a time when I felt I had done just that.

 Cremer talks about returning to the line "barely recovered". And of course it doesn't take broken limbs and minds only, to empty people's lives of something worth striving for. The author of "Middlemarch" had some remarkable insight into the way emotions play a devastating part in how lives develop or - otherwise. Now the heroine, Dorothea, had views on striving and failure: "Failure after long perseverance, is much grander than never to have had a striving, than never to have a strivance good enough to be called a failure". Someone with other perceptions was Mr Ladislaw and this is what he concluded: "There are certain things that a man can only go through once in his lifetime; and he must know that some time or other, the best is over for him. This experience happened to me while I was very young - that is all". (Happily, Dorothea helped him to "get up and fight and have another go" - and they lived happily ever after!).

 Although I eventually lost contact with Shorts, I will be on the books of Musgrave Park Hospital for the rest of my life. I may need more "running repair!".

 When Musgrave Park Hospital eventually returned me in a serviceable condition to industry, limits had been set which allowed life to continue within those limits of physical capability, and I suppose I have exercised within those limits, "right up to the wall", being constantly inspired by the strivance of others noticeably much more severely handicapped than I ever was. But nevertheless, I was on a lease - a fairly long one, though.

During the preparation of this reminiscence someone remarked upon how little description there was of a lengthy part of my life in Further Education, in response to which I probably asked for another sheet of paper! But in life, we do have short intervals of time that merit long descriptions and long ones that simply have no merit. I have found it thus, and as earlier mentioned, much of my teaching experience has "vanished from the screen".

One day I was asked by someone, what a gulpin was - after I had been heard to describe someone as such, and I discovered to my discomfort that I couldn't readily come up with a satisfactory definition - although most good dictionaries will attempt to do so. Because a gulpin could be the mindless hoodlum who persists in breaking a piece of my cherry tree every time he passes under it - or be a headmaster (or headmistress) lurking behind the large polished table in their study, or a civil servant. Each can be equally destructive of societal values - perhaps the "Head" as a useless manager of resources, or, as in the case of the civil servant, the innovator of new procedures which, at the stroke of a pen, can remove values and standards, that have taken ages and generations to craft, mould and crystallise into something of proven worth and meaning. The change for the sake of change flat earthers have some strange bed fellows. In the time of the U.S.S.R., all the secretaries of the Communist Party of the regime from Lenin onwards, altered or added to, the philosophy of the communist principles. They were expected to do so - it was taken that each exalted one, would be "led" to do so. So they each in turn manufactured some earth shattering pronouncement the last notable one was by Khrushchev that "a full communist state would be in place in the year 1984!"

Sir Stanley Hooker was a brilliant mathematician, who, before the Second World War, had won almost every available scholarship and academic prize available. He joined Rolls Royce in 1938 and within a short time, had, through his work on superchargers, increased the power of the Merlin engine (as used on the Spitfire, Hurricane, Lancaster bomber, Mosquito, the P51 etc) by thirty per cent. He was later to become technical director of Rolls Royce. His wonderful autobiography (which no student of thermodynamics should be without) has interesting and telling comments to make about the behaviour of man, as well as aero engines. In one passage, he speaks of the time he went up to Brasenose College, Oxford. There was a rule which required all students to attend a minimum number of Chapel Services each term - from 7.00 p.m. - 7.30 p.m., and just before dinner. He comments, "These very simple and short services gave me great comfort - this rule was revoked during my time at BNC." He goes on: "Like many others, I seldom went again mainly because time didn't seem to permit. The half hour before dinner was thrown away in idle chatter - the custom of going to chapel before dinner - which had been going on for centuries and gave so much ease to my mind at least - was thrown away, as I know many other customs at BNC have been, all for nothing more than the so called "march of progress". His autobiography is called "NOT MUCH OF AN ENGINEER".

We have to go back to what the roadman said - "that the want of an arm or a leg, was nothing, compared to the want of common sense". I think this roadman knew what a gulpin was!

One of my favourite books - already quoted from - is "Middlemarch", because it concerns what people think of values. This is an extract of a conversation between Dorothea and Celia.

Dorothea: "Many things are true that only the commonest minds observe".

Celia: "Then I think the commonest minds must be rather useful".

The lines from "Middlemarch" - George Eliot

My reminiscence has been about the people of my generation - what they said, and what they did. The environments where these things took place are included - after all these help form our perceptions, which in turn, are programmed into our minds to shape us and make us what we are.

Regrets? Well, circumstances destined me never to sit for my "ticket" at sea as an engineer. I would have liked that. I have respect for those who hold a "ticket".

*   *   *   *   *   *   *   *   *   *

Someone asked me one day how many of the people I was acquainted with were "worth knowing". In what I thought was a suitable light hearted reply I said, "5%". My friend declared that my estimate was much too high - so I compromised and we laughingly agreed to institute the "Worth knowing or 4% Club". (Believe it or not, certificates of membership have been awarded - some to people as far away as France, near to the German Border!)

So what has one learned about people of their own generation? Well, it is true that some people are worth knowing - and others less so. People are worth knowing for what they say, for what they give - unselfishly - of what they have to share, for what they do, all of which could lighten life's burdens for others and so brighten their lives. A funeral took place some time ago of someone who lived in the locality I was brought up in. At the graveside comments were made about how long "he" had lived. Thereupon, a young farmer from the neighbourhood was overheard to pose the question, "and was the world anything the better for "him" ever having been here?"

One's memory is remarkably selective - mine seems to have been "programmed" to carefully store the doings of the "4%", whilst apparently rejecting much of those of the "96%". I suppose when one troubles the mind enough, things originating from obnoxious beings can be uncovered - but then why would one pollute the world with such things if one doesn't have to?

Perhaps there was a lesson for life at that humble de-burring bench where we apprentices were taught to take the sharp edges of machined components. If we would make the conscious effort to take the sharp edges of our lives, it might enable some benighted traveller to pass along the way more easily - or perhaps we might contemplate the words of Stephen Grellet:

I expect to pass through this life but once.
Any good thing therefore that I can do,
Or any kindness that I can show to my
Fellow creature,
Let me do it now.
Let me not defer or neglect it -
For I shall not pass this way again.

Words by Stephen Grellet.

Bibliography

Pioneers Of The Skies,
Michael Donne (GB Publications Ltd)

Shorts Aircraft, The Archive Photographs Series,
compiled by Mike Hooks (Chalford Publishing Company)

Not Much Of An Engineer,
Sir Stanley Hooker (Airlife Publishing Ltd., Shrewsbury)

U333,
Peter Cremar, The Bodley Head Ltd., 1984

Victoria Drummond, Marine Engineer,
Cherry Drummond, published by Institute of Marine Engineers, London

Various publications of the
Marine Engineering Review, Institute of Marine Engineers, London

Captain Victor Campbell MBE

Died peacefully at home with his family on Sunday, 10th September 1995.

Victor Campbell was born on 2nd October 1908 in Ballymoney, Co. Antrim, the son of a Master Mariner. Like his father before him he felt the powerful lure of the sea during his childhood, and at 16 joined the Merchant Navy to embark on a maritime career which was to span nearly half a century.

In 1937, aged 29, he repeated his father's achievement in becoming a Master Mariner, and on the outbreak of World War II was engaged in the Baltic and Continental Trades. In 1940 the German War Machine made further such trade impossible, and his last passage of this nature was to assist in the evacuation of British Expeditionary Forces from Brest.

During the following two years he commanded convoy vessels in the lethal waters of the North Sea and Dover Straits at a time when Hitler boasted that the latter were closed to enemy shipping. In 1942 he transferred to the Royal Navy and was appointed to the Admiralty Marine Salvage Department with the rank of Lt. Commander. He trained with the renowned McKenzie Brothers at Scapa flow in 1943/44, and there acquired the salvage skills which were to serve his country so well in the years to follow.

In June 1944 he sailed with the invasion fleet on board the first salvage vessel to arrive at the Normandy beaches, and had the distinction of entering Port en Bassin, the first French port to be captured. His mission was the removal of wrecks to clear the port for Allied use. His success and courage under fire earned him the MBE - Military Division, although his natural modesty restricted his subsequent account of this period to the telling of a story involving a hair-raising trip to Bayeux on the back of a colleague's motor bike, in search of the Tapestry and some French beer.

In 1948 he accepted an Admiralty invitation to continue his marine salvage career in a civilian capacity, and was appointed Boom Defence and Salvage Officer attached to the Mediterranean fleet based in Malta. During the following seven years his achievements included the supervision of the clearance of the wreck strewn Grand Harbour in Malta, and the recovery of the first Comet jet airliner, which crashed in very deep water off the island of Elba - an operation for which he received a commendation from the Commander in Chief Mediterranean Fleet, Lord Mountbatten.

He returned to the UK in 1955, but was recalled to Malta in 1956 to prepare for the Suez Crisis. He was soon sent to Port Said where he oversaw the removal of the largest blockship in the Canal, the "Paul Solante". This difficult and dangerous operation was to earn him an invitation to accept the OBE, but, typically he declined, preferring instead to retain the military MBE his wartime efforts had earned.

In 1958 a further challenge called for his skill and experience, but this time back in the UK, he was asked to take charge of the Boom Defence and Salvage Depot in Dover. The Western entrance to Dover Harbour had been unusable because of blockships since 1940 and earlier attempts to clear the wrecks had been unsuccessful. He masterminded the complex and often hazardous operation lasting nearly three years. Victor Campbell's team cleared the entrance, to the rejoicing of Dover's citizens. For this work he was, once more, offered an OBE, but again wished to retain his wartime MBE.

He spent the following three years on the staff of the Commander in Chief, Portsmouth, moving to Rosyth in 1964, where he became Command Mooring and Salvage Officer, based on HMS Safeguard. His years since 1961 were spent passing on the skills he had acquired during his remarkable career in marine salvage, and in 1968 he was given the additional responsibility of Superintendent, Marine Service School and Salvage Depot.

He retired in 1971 and together with his wife Mary, spent a long and happy retirement in St. Margaret's Bay, their home overlooking the Dover Straits he had sailed 30 years earlier. He remained very active and greatly enjoyed his family, having spent so much of his career away from home. His was a life inextricably linked with the sea, and he lived it with a quiet modesty which belied his courage, skill and determination.

He is survived by his son, two daughters and four grandchildren.

* * * * * * * * * *

Some years ago, I had the privilege of meeting Captain Campbell's daughter, Myrna, originally from Whitehead, Co. Antrim, but now living in England. During the "Comet" salvage operations, she was living with the family in Malta. I am very indebted to her, for giving to me a copy of her father's obituary reproduced here. Note: The Ballymoney referred to, is a townland in Islandmagee, Co. Antrim - not the town of that name.

B C